THE PRIVATE ROOTS
OF PUBLIC ACTION

THE PRIVATE ROOTS
OF PUBLIC ACTION

Gender, Equality,
and Political Participation

NANCY BURNS

KAY LEHMAN SCHLOZMAN

SIDNEY VERBA

Harvard University Press

Cambridge, Massachusetts

London, England

2001

Library of Congress Cataloging-in-Publication Data

Burns, Nancy, 1964–
The private roots of public action : gender, equality, and political participation /
Nancy Burns, Kay Lehman Schlozman, Sidney Verba.
p. cm.
Includes bibliographical references and index.
ISBN 0-674-00601-1 (cl : alk. paper)—ISBN 0-674-00660-7 (pb : alk. paper)
1. Political participation—United States. 2. Women in politics—United States.
3. Sex role—United States. 4. Social institutions—United States.
I. Schlozman, Kay Lehman, 1946– II. Verba, Sidney. III. Title.

·JK1764 .B87 2001
323′.042′0973—dc21 2001024928

To Scott, Stanley, and Cynthia

who, as we do, hold this truth to be self-evident:
that all men and women are created equal

Contents

Acknowledgments   *xiii*

1. Introduction: Citizenship and Unequal Participation   *1*

2. Studying Gender and Participation: A Brief Discourse on Method   *39*

3. Civic Activity: Political and Non-Political   *61*

4. The Political Worlds of Men and Women   *99*

5. The Legacy of Home and School   *137*

6. Domestic Tranquility: The Beliefs of Wives and Husbands   *152*

7. Domestic Hierarchy: The Household as a Social System   *174*

8. The Workplace Roots of Political Activity   *198*

9. The Realm of Voluntarism: Non-Political Associations and Religious Institutions   *219*

10. Gender, Institutions, and Political Participation   *246*

11. Gender, Race or Ethnicity, and Participation   *274*

12. Family Life and Political Life   *307*

13. What If Politics Weren't a Man's Game?   *334*

14. Conclusion: The Private Roots of Public Action   *357*

Appendixes   *387*
    A. Numbers of Cases   *389*
    B. Ranges of Variables   *392*
    C. Supplementary Tables   *399*
    D. Explanation of Outcomes Analysis   *435*
Index   *439*

Tables and Figures

TABLES

3.1 Voluntary Contributions of Time and Money to Politics   *68*
3.2 Organizational Involvement   *76*
3.3 Organizational Affiliation and Activity   *78*
3.4 Affiliation with Organizations That Take Political Stands   *80*
3.5 Secular Activity outside Politics   *82*
3.6 Religious Activity   *90*
3.7 Voluntary Contributions of Time and Money to Politics   *91*
3.8 Overall Political Activity by Work and Family Circumstances   *96*
3.9 Overall Political Activity of Married and Unmarried Women   *97*
4.1 Measures of Psychological Involvement with Politics   *102*
4.2 Religious Attitudes and Orientations   *106*
4.3 Group Orientations: Experiences of Discrimination and Group Consciousness   *109*
4.4 Gratifications from Political Participation   *116*
4.5 The Issues That Animate Political Participation   *120*
4.6 Socioeconomic Advantage and the Issues That Animate Political Participation   *126*
4.7 Parenthood and the Issues That Animate Political Participation   *128*
4.8 What Women Need to Work on Together—What Men Need to Work on Together   *130*
5.1 Reports of Political Experiences at Age Sixteen   *141*
5.2 Educational Attainment   *146*
5.3 Experiences in High School   *148*
5.4 School Experiences of Those Who Attended College   *149*
5.5 Interests and Commitments during the High School Years   *150*

6.1   Beliefs about Equality in the Household *154*
6.2   Consistency of Beliefs about Equality in the Family   *157*
6.3   Characteristics of Egalitarians and Traditionals on Gender Roles *159*
6.4   Predicting Egalitarian Gender Attitudes for Wives and Husbands *161*
6.5   Predicting Couples' Views on Gender Equality in the Family *162*
6.6   Policy Attitudes of Husbands and Wives *164*
6.7   Agreement between Wives and Husbands on Political Matters *166*
6.8   Dimensions of Attitudes of Husbands and Wives: Factor Analysis *168*
7.1   Earnings of Husbands and Wives   *179*
7.2   Allocations of Time in the Household Economy *182*
7.3   Contributions to Household *183*
7.4   Division of Household Chores *186*
7.5   Control over Money: Responsibility for Bigger Financial Decisions *189*
7.6   Joint Decision Making: What Couples Say *191*
7.7   Family Decision Making *192*
7.8   Division of Household Work and Child Care by Husband's Beliefs in Gender Equality *194*
7.9   Responsibility for Major Financial Decisions and Husband's Beliefs in Gender Equality *195*
7.10   Predicting the Percentage of Housework the Wife Does *196*
8.1   Predicting Working *208*
8.2   Job Level *212*
8.3   Predicting Job Level among Working Women and Men *212*
8.4   The Effect of Job Characteristics on Participatory Factors *215*
8.5   Participatory Factors by Gender and Work Force Participation *217*
9.1   Predicting Organizational Affiliation *223*
9.2   Predicting Participatory Factors from Non-Political Organizations *225*
9.3   Participation Factors Acquired in Most Important Organization *227*
9.4   Gender Composition of Main Non-Political Organization *228*

9.5   Participatory Factors and the Gender Composition of
        Non-Political Organizations   230
9.6   Predicting Church Affiliation   233
9.7   Predicting Participatory Factors from Religious
        Institutions   236
9.8   Participatory Factors Acquired in Church   237
9.9   Approval of Women as Full Members of Clergy in
        Religion   239
9.10   Approval of Denomination's Position on Women Clergy by
        Political and Religious Commitments   241
9.11   The Acquisition of Participatory Factors in Institutions:
        Summary   244
10.1   Participatory Factors Acquired in Family and School   247
10.2   Participatory Factors Acquired in Adult Institutions   248
10.3   Time and Income as Participatory Resources   249
10.4   Experiences of Gender Discrimination   251
10.5   Participation Factors and Political Activity: An Outcomes
        Model   252
10.6   Effect of Obligated Hours and Hours Volunteered for Other
        Purposes on Hours Given to Politics   261
10.7   Participation Factors and Amount of Money to Politics: An
        Outcomes Model   262
10.8   Psychological Orientations to Politics   267
10.9   The Effect of Psychological Orientations to Politics on Political
        Activity   268
10.10   Explaining the Gap in Political Activity   268
10.11   Effect of Gender Consciousness on Women's Issue-Based
        Activity   271
11.1   Political Activity by Gender and Race or Ethnicity   279
11.2   Secular Activity outside Politics   282
11.3   Religious Preferences and Activity   284
11.4   Participatory Factors Acquired in Family and School   287
11.5   Institutionally Based Participatory Factors   288
11.6   Mean Time and Income   290
11.7   Reports of Experiences with Discrimination   292
11.8   Political Engagement   293
11.9   Group-Based Political Orientations by Gender and Race or
        Ethnicity   294
11.10   Level of Participatory Factors   296

11.11 The Source of Group Differences in Political Activity *298*

11.12 Psychological Orientations to Politics and Political Activity *301*

11.13 Effect of Consciousness on Issue-Based Activity *302*

11.14 Race and the Issues That Animate Political Participation *305*

12.1 Political Discussion as a Family Activity *313*

12.2 Voluntary Participation as Joint Activity *315*

12.3 Marital Status by Gender *318*

12.4 The Direct Effects of Marital Status and Children on Overall Political Activity *319*

12.5 Mothers at Work and Mothers at Home *324*

12.6 Family Hierarchy and Citizen Participation *330*

13.1 Women as Candidates and Elected Officials: Impact on Orientations to Politics *344*

13.2 Women as Candidates and Elected Officials: Impact on Orientations to Politics (NES) *347*

13.3 Do Female Senate Candidates Affect the Gender Gap in Involvement? *348*

13.4 Women as Candidates and Elected Officials: Impact on Salience of House Candidate's Sex *352*

14.1 Does Education Predict the Acquisition of Participatory Factors? *367*

FIGURES

3.1 Political Participation by Gender *65*

3.2 Political Activity over Time *70*

3.3 Overall Political Activity by Education *92*

3.4 Overall Political Activity by Race or Ethnicity *93*

3.5 Overall Political Activity by Age *93*

5.1 Percentage of College Graduates, Age 25–34, 1940–1998 *144*

5.2 Percentage of College Graduates, 1940–1998 *145*

7.1 Percentage Active in Work Force, 1948–2000 *176*

7.2 Percentage of Family Income Brought In by Wife, 1974–1998 *180*

11.1 Overall Political Activity by Race or Ethnicity *278*

13.1 Is Politics for Women? *338*

13.2 Where the Women Are *339*

13.3 Percentage Who Can Name One Senator *343*

Acknowledgments

The wonders of modern technology have transformed the process of producing a book based on quantitative information. Nevertheless, it still seems to take as long, cost as much, and require the assistance of as many others. Any project as protracted as this one incurs many debts.

For superb research assistance, we are grateful to Molly O'Rourke, Anna Maria Ortiz, and Melynda Price at the University of Michigan; to Gratia Cobeen, Kyle Dell, Jesse Donahue, Jennifer Erkulwater, Tim Pearse, and Colleen Shogan at Boston College; to David Campbell, Elizabeth Haynes, Limary Carrasquillo, Casey Klofstad, Janet Newcity, and Shauna Shames at Harvard; and to Danny Schlozman and Julie Schlozman at home.

For institutional support of many kinds, we would like to thank the University of Michigan, Boston College, and Harvard University. William Wei kept our computers crunching data. Sandee MacDonald, Doris Powers, Matilda Van Es, and Bernardine Pachta helped in countless ways.

William McCready of the Survey Research Lab at Northern Illinois University and Santa Traugott of the Center for Political Studies at the University of Michigan provided valuable advice and assistance with sampling and with data collection and cleaning.

We received generous support from the Ford Foundation, Hewlett Foundation, National Science Foundation, and Spencer Foundation for the conduct of the Citizen Participation Study. The Kellogg Foundation provided further support that made possible the third-wave and couples surveys. Without this assistance this project could not have come to fruition.

Over the years we have presented pieces of this work on numerous occasions and have benefited greatly from the conversations thus stimulated. We would especially like to mention the lively discussions at the Workshops on Gender and Race and Politics at the Center for Political Studies and the Institute for Research on Women and Gender at the University of Michigan and at the conference on "Political Participation: Building a Research Agenda" at the Center for the Study of Democratic Politics at Princeton University; as well as comments from our friends and colleagues Henry Brady, Barbara Burell, Richard Hall, Don Herzog, Ted Huston, Kent Jennings, Donald Kinder, John Kingdon, Jan Leighley, Ann Lin, Jane Mansbridge, Laura Stoker, and Elizabeth Wingrove.

A colleague once said that "it is better to have your friends criticize you in manuscript than your enemies trash you in print." We are especially fortunate that we have colleagues, students, and even a relative who also are friends and who were willing to give our manuscript extremely careful readings. We appreciate the constructive and tough-minded advice provided by Kristi Andersen, Jeffrey Berry, DeAunderia Bryant, Jesse Donahue, Laura Evans, Mark Hansen, Jane Junn, Corrine McConnaughy, Virginia Sapiro, Danny Schlozman, Colleen Shogan, Theda Skocpol, and Clyde Wilcox.

One of the themes of this book is the way that commitments to family and to work are intertwined. Nobody knows this better than Scott, Stanley, and Cynthia. We are grateful to you for all that you do and all that you are.

THE PRIVATE ROOTS
OF PUBLIC ACTION

1

---◅◦◦◦▻---

Introduction:
Citizenship and Unequal Participation

New Zealand was first—in 1893. Over the next century most of the world's nations followed: Norway in 1913; Brazil in 1932; Japan in 1945; Morocco in 1959; and Switzerland not until 1971. Kuwait has yet to act.[1]

Although not at the head of the pack, the United States was in the first wave of nations to enfranchise women on an equal basis with men. In the generations since the passage of the Nineteenth Amendment to the Constitution in 1920, America has been transformed in multiple ways, many of which touch on gender roles. Yet in spite of the profound changes in American society, men continue to be somewhat more active in politics than women are. Although women are more likely to go to the polls, with respect to other forms of political activity, men are more likely to take part.

The disparity in political activity is not enormous. On average, women engage in 1.96, and men in 2.27, political activities as measured by an eight-point scale that includes a variety of political

---

1. These dates are taken from Barbara J. Nelson and Najma Chowdhury, *Women and Politics Worldwide* (New Haven: Yale University Press, 1994), pp. 774–775; and Anne Firor Scott, "Woman Suffrage," *World Book Encyclopedia* (Chicago: World Book, 1986). In fact, the enfranchisement of women was not full in Switzerland's strongly federal system until 1990 when the Swiss Supreme Court ruled that the country's Equal Rights Amendment precluded the canton of Appenzell from restricting women's right to vote in communal and cantonal elections. Regula Stämpfli, "Direct Democracy and Women's Suffrage: Antagonism in Switzerland," in *Women and Politics Worldwide*, ed. Nelson and Chowdhury, p. 697.

acts.[2] A gender difference of 0.31 of a political act may seem paltry, but when we consider the impact across a large population, the effect mounts quickly. If we make the rough assumptions that there are 200,000,000 voting-age adults in the United States and that they are divided equally between men and women, then the participatory deficit translates each year into

2,000,000 fewer phone calls or letters to public officials from women than from men;

3,000,000 fewer women than men involved in informal efforts to solve community problems;

7,000,000 fewer campaign contributions from women than from men; and

9,000,000 fewer women than men affiliated with a political organization.

When translated into actual activity, we are talking about a distinction of potential consequence.

The gender disparity in citizen political participation forms the puzzle at the heart of this inquiry: why, after so many decades of suffrage and a revival of the women's movement in the late 1960s, has the gap not closed fully? This book constitutes an empirical answer to the question of why there is a residual deficit for women when it comes to political participation. We use quantitative data from several sources to shed light on matters that have more often been the subject of fertile speculation than of systematic evidence. The evidence for this investigation derives principally from two surveys, a national study of the attitudes, demographic characteristics, and voluntary commitments of Americans and a follow-up to this survey in which a number of our original respondents and, if married, their spouses were interviewed. Most surveys about citizens in politics lack critical variables—whether measures of various kinds of political participation or items about family life, experiences on the job, or voluntary activity outside politics. In contrast, our surveys were specifically designed to cover not only multiple political attitudes and activities but also multiple aspects

---

2. The scale is an overall measure of an individual's political activity in the recent past. Its components will be described fully in Chapter 3.

of non-political life that have either direct or indirect consequences for political participation. Thus our data permit us to consider each of the interlocking pieces of a complex puzzle. In short, we are able to conduct the most thorough inquiry ever undertaken into the origins of gender inequality in political participation.

The book is, most fundamentally, about the private roots of public action. Although we focus on gender differences in activity, we are concerned more broadly with the way that political participation is anchored in private life. The gender disparity in citizen participation is the result of inequalities with respect to a large number of factors. These inequalities, in turn, have their origins in a long, cumulative pattern of gender-differentiated experiences in the principal social institutions of everyday life—the family, school, workplace, voluntary associations, and church.[3] As we disentangle the multiple causes of the gender gap in participation, we shed light on both the links between the private institutions in which we nurture and are nurtured, learn, toil, play, and pray and the links between these institutions and engagement in public life. In solving our specific puzzle, we thus illumine more generally both the processes by which American citizens come to take part in politics and the role of social institutions in fostering inequalities. Although we consider the specific question of the sources of gender differences in political participation to be unequivocally important on its own, we are able to use it as an entrée to a deeper understanding of the connections between social institutions and public involvement.

Defining the Territory

What exactly do we mean when we say that we are concerned with the gender gap in *voluntary political participation?*[4] In order both to differentiate voluntary political activity from other forms of hu-

---

3. Our subject matter often places us on terrain where language is a politically charged issue. We sometimes use the single word "church" to refer to the multiplicity of religious institutions—mosques, temples, ashrams, synagogues, and so on—in our religiously pluralistic nation. We use this shorthand as a matter of style rather than to indicate a preference for Christianity.

4. This discussion draws almost directly from Sidney Verba, Kay Lehman Schlozman,

man endeavor and to acknowledge the fuzziness of the empirical boundaries that separate political activity from other domains of activity, we need to make clear just what we are studying.

By *political* participation we refer simply to activity that has the intent or effect of influencing government action—either directly, by affecting the making or implementation of public policy, or indirectly, by influencing the selection of people who make those policies. Some critics argue that our conception of politics should be broadened in either of two ways: to include all collective involvements that influence the life of the community, even those charitable and organizational activities that do not touch upon what is traditionally called the "public sector"; or to include all private relationships—for example, bosses and employees or parents and children—in which power is exercised.[5] As political scientists, we are, of course, sensitive to the impact on public life of voluntary efforts in the non-political domains of civic action, to the uses of power in private institutions, and to the extent to which the inequalities between women and men in the private realms of family, work, and church mirror inequalities in politics and have consequences for their lives. A large part of our inquiry concerns these very matters. Nevertheless, in order to differentiate the state, an institution with special characteristics in modern societies, from other social institutions, we use the term "political" in its conventional and more limited sense.

By *voluntary* activity we mean participation that is not obligatory—no one is forced to volunteer—and that receives, if any pay at all, only token financial compensation. Thus a paid position on a big-city school board or a senator's re-election campaign staff does not qualify under our definition.[6] The distinction between

---

and Henry Brady, *Voice and Equality: Civic Voluntarism in American Politics* (Cambridge: Harvard University Press, 1995), pp. 38–40.

5. Although historians are more likely than political scientists to call for a radical expansion of the term "political" to arenas of human action and relationship that have ordinarily not entailed government influence or involvement, scholars from both disciplines have made this argument. Among the many examples, see Kay Boals, "The Politics of Male-Female Relations: The Functions of Feminist Scholarship," *Signs* 1 (1975): 161–174; and Paula Baker, "The Domestication of Politics: Women and American Political Society, 1780–1920," *American Historical Review* 89 (1984): 646–647.

6. Max Weber distinguished between those for whom politics was an avocation and those for whom it was a vocation. The former enter political life as occasional politicians,

voluntary activity and paid work is not always clear. It is possible to serve private economic purposes through social and political activism: many people seek to do well while doing good. They undertake voluntary activity for which they receive no compensation—in their churches, in charities, in politics—in order to make contacts or otherwise enhance their jobs or careers. Furthermore, for many of those who participate in politics, the policy issues that animate their activity have consequences for their pocketbooks. Conversely, many people get involved in genuinely voluntary activity that is an extension of their paid employment. For example, an accountant may lend his or her professional expertise as part of unpaid service on a hospital or museum board. Those who work for non-profits or political organizations often extend their commitment with additional volunteer work in the name of the objectives pursued through their paid employment. In all these cases, the border between voluntary participation and paid employment is blurry.

Lastly, we focus on *activity*: we are concerned with doing politics, rather than with being attentive to politics. Although we shall have an ongoing concern with the place of politics in men's and women's lives—how much they know or care about it, whether they pay attention to it—we exclude from our definition of participation certain activities that might have been embraced by a more encompassing understanding. The umbrella of our definition, therefore, does not extend to following political events in the news or watching public affairs programs on television. We have also excluded communications—political discussions among friends, letters to the editor, calls to radio talk shows—in which the target audience is not a public official.[7]

---

who "cast a ballot or consummate a similar expression of intention, such as applauding or protesting in a 'political' meeting, or delivering [a] 'political' speech, etc."; the latter make politics their major vocation. Max Weber, "Politics as a Vocation," in *From Max Weber: Essays in Sociology*, ed. H. H. Gerth and C. Wright Mills (New York: Oxford University Press, 1946), p. 83. We are interested in those for whom politics is an avocation. It is, of course, possible that some for whom politics is a vocation do not earn the bulk of their income that way. However, as long as it is their main occupation, they fall outside of our volunteer category. Senators Jay Rockefeller and Edward M. Kennedy are full-time professionals, not volunteers, even though their incomes do not depend on a government salary.

7. In Chapter 4, however, we consider various activities at the border of political participation, including political discussion and following politics in the media.

Why Study Gender Differences in Participation?

Why bother to study the modest, but consistent, gender differences in political activity? One answer to the question focuses on politics. Through their participation, citizens communicate information about their preferences and needs to public officials and generate pressure on them to respond. Those who are inactive risk being ignored when policies are made. Moreover, beyond the possible impact on policy outcomes, participants gain additional benefits from taking part: recognition as full members of the community; education about the social and political world; and information, skills, and contacts that are useful in other social pursuits. Thus we care about group differences in political participation—between men and women, or between Blacks and Whites, or between lawyers and cashiers—because they represent a potential compromise in the democratic norm of equal protection of interests.

Another answer focuses on non-political institutions and the role they play in fostering political participation. Close analysis of the sources of the gender disparity in political activity sheds light on the way that non-political institutions shape political activity and, in particular, create disparities in activity between groups of citizens. We shall see how social inequalities are generated by processes of differential selection into institutions and by different experiences within institutions and how these social inequalities, in turn, result in participatory inequalities.

A third answer focuses on gender. In every society on this planet, gender is among the most important of social organizing principles.[8] Penetrating the gender gap in citizen political activity fills in part of the immense social canvas upon which differences between females and males figure importantly. As feminist scholars point out—and as the analysis of gender differences in experiences with various institutions confirms—domains of human ac-

---

8. See Sherry Ortner's discussion of twenty-five years of anthropological thought and evidence on this point in *Making Gender* (Boston: Beacon Press, 1996). See also the essays in *Toward an Anthropology of Women*, ed. Rayna R. Reiter (New York: Monthly Review Press, 1975).

tion vary in the extent to which men and women behave, and are treated, differently, and we cannot extrapolate directly from one setting to another.[9] Our analysis thus casts light on the larger question of the varying social processes that make sex differences matter in America.

The Sources of Unequal Participation: Some Hunches

Over the years, the colleagues, students, and friends to whom we have talked about our inquiry have suggested several possible explanations for the sources of the gender gap in political activity. These proposed solutions to the puzzle of unequal participation derive from several sources—the literature in political science, feminist theory, and, not least, common sense.

What might explain why, three generations after gaining full political citizenship, women continue to lag behind men in political activity?

- One answer that figures prominently in any informal or academic discussion of the gender gap in activity focuses on the many demands on women's *time*. Women, especially those with children at home and full-time jobs, simply do not have the time to take part in politics.
- A corollary to this hypothesis focuses on *psychic space* rather than on time. Raising children so absorbs available mental energy that mothers, especially those with toddlers under foot, are too preoccupied at home to pay attention to politics.
- Another approach emphasizes the role of the *patriarchal family* as a school for democratic citizenship. As long as men function as the undisputed head of household and women are unequal at home, women can never function equally as citizens.
- A different set of concerns points to the disparities between men and women in the *socioeconomic resources* that have long

---

9. See, for example, Elizabeth Wingrove's discussion of the varying structural and institutional roots of gender in "Interpellating Sex," *Signs* 24 (1999): 869–893.

been known to be associated with political participation. Since women are, on average, disadvantaged with respect to education, income, and occupational status, we would expect them to be less active politically.

• An alternative line of reasoning emphasizes processes of *discrimination* that operate directly to keep women out of politics and indirectly to pose barriers to the acquisition of the resources that facilitate political activity.

• The final suggestion centers on processes of childhood and adult *socialization* that create different environments for men and women and lead them to draw different conclusions about the relevance of politics to their lives. If women inhabit a less political world than men do—one that provides less exposure to informal political chat and other politicizing cues and offers fewer relevant political role models—then women are likely to infer that politics, like football, is not for them.

Each of these explanations for the disparity between men and women in political participation seems plausible. Several of them, however, remain at the level of conjecture—without the benefit of supporting evidence.[10] We are empiricists, and the principal enterprise of this inquiry will be to subject these explanations to the light of data.

What we find is that some of them, however compelling at the level of theory, are just plain wrong, and that no single one suffices to account for the gap in citizen political activity. Instead, the disparity in participation results from several factors. First, men enjoy an advantage when it comes to the single most important resource for political participation, formal education. In addition,

---

10. In "Women as Political Animals? A Test of Some Explanations for Male-Female Political Participation Differences," *American Journal of Political Science* 21 (1977): 711, Susan Welch made precisely the same point twenty-five years ago: "While many suggestions have been offered to explain why American women tend to participate in political activities slightly less than men, seldom have these explanations been subjected to a rigorous examination." Seventeen years ago, the situation had changed so little that Virginia Sapiro could make a similar observation. She referred to "the melange of hypotheses, findings, myths, and stereotypes commonly presented as descriptions of women's relationship to politics" in *The Political Integration of Women* (Urbana: University of Illinois Press, 1983), p. 79.

the non-political institutions of adult life—in particular, the work-place—function as an important source of the factors that foster participation. Because women are less likely than men to be in the work force, and because, even if employed full time, they are less likely to hold the kinds of jobs that provide these factors, gender differences in work force experiences loom large in our explana-tion of the disparity in political activity. Finally, women are less likely than men to be psychologically engaged with politics—that is, to be politically interested, informed, or efficacious—a deficit that contributes significantly to participatory inequalities. How-ever, when women are in an environment where women seek and hold visible public offices, they are more politically interested and informed, and disparities in psychological orientations to politics shrink.

The Liberal Tradition and Unequal Citizenship: From Coverture to Enfranchisement

In any political system, matters of citizenship—who qualifies as a citizen and what rights and responsibilities that status confers—in-evitably generate political controversy. In America, these issues have been played out against the background of a long tradition of liberal individualism stressing the inalienable rights of citizens. As a prefatory matter to understanding women and men as citizen ac-tivists in contemporary American democracy, let us review very briefly the history of women's citizenship status in America.

In the colonial period, the citizenship status of women—or, at least, of married, White women—was defined by the English com-mon law principle of *coverture*.[11] Under this doctrine, a married woman became, more or less, a legal non-person:

> It appears that the husband's control over the person of his wife is so complete that he may claim her society altogether; that he may reclaim her if she goes away or is detained by others; that he may

---

11. On *coverture,* see Linda K. Kerber's historical account of women's responsibilities as citizens, *No Constitutional Right to Be Ladies* (New York: Hill and Wang, 1998), pp. xxiii–xxiv, 11–15.

use constraint upon her liberty to prevent her going away, or to prevent improper conduct; that he may maintain suits for injuries to her person; that she cannot sue alone . . . In most respects she loses the power of personal independence and altogether that of separate action in legal matters.[12]

The doctrine of coverture would seem to be at odds with the emphasis upon individual rights that informed the political discourse of the Founding, the period during which the colonies became independent from England and established the constitutional order that continues to govern us today.[13] Given this Lockean liberalism, it is not surprising that at least some people thought to extend its principles to various excluded groups—among them, women. In a famous letter that used language suggestive of that in the soon-to-be-forthcoming Declaration, Abigail Adams wrote to her husband, John, during the spring of 1776 and admonished him to

Remember the Ladies, and be more generous and favourable to them than your ancestors. Do not put such unlimited power into the hands of the Husbands. Remember all Men would be tyrants if they could. If perticular [sic] care and attention is not paid to the Laidies [sic] we are determined to foment a Rebelion [sic], and will not hold ourselves bound by any Laws in which we have no voice, or Representation.

Two weeks later, he wrote in reply, "As to your extraordinary Code of Laws, 'I cannot but laugh.' "[14]

---

12. Edward Mansfield, *The Legal Rights, Liabilities, and Duties of Women* (Salem, Mass.: Jewett Co., 1845), p. 273, quoted in Jo Freeman, "The Revolution for Women in Law and Public Policy," in *Women: A Feminist Perspective*, ed. Jo Freeman, 5th ed. (Mountain View, Calif.: Mayfield Publishing, 1995), p. 366.

13. Kerber, *No Constitutional Right to Be Ladies*, p. 12. The contradiction between a liberal tradition and the denial of rights was what Gunnar Myrdal meant by *An American Dilemma: The Negro Problem and American Democracy* (New York: Harper and Row, 1944). For an extensive analysis of the way in which the treatment of citizenship issues in America reflects not only traditions of liberalism and republicanism but also the reinforcement of ascriptive hierarchy, see Rogers M. Smith, *Civic Ideals: Conflicting Visions of Citizenship in U.S. History* (New Haven: Yale University Press, 1997).

14. Document 2 in Anne Firor Scott and Andrew MacKay Scott, *One Half the People* (Urbana: University of Illinois Press, 1982), p. 54.

Little had changed with respect to women's status as citizens by the time of the first Women's Rights Convention, held in the upstate New York town of Seneca Falls in the summer of 1848.[15] That meeting produced an extraordinary document, one that served as a reminder of the tradition of Enlightenment liberalism so important to the American experience. The preamble to the Declaration of Principles that emerged from the convention appropriated verbatim the words of the Declaration of Independence until making a critical substitution: "We hold these truths to be self-evident: that all men and women are created equal." What followed was a series of grievances including that "He has made her, if married, in the eye of the law, civilly dead," and that "He has taken from her all right in property, even to the wages she earns." The manifesto concluded with a set of resolutions, including one asserting that "all laws . . . which place [woman] in a position inferior to that of man . . . [are] of no force or authority" and another calling for "the overthrow of the monopoly of the pulpit, and for securing to woman an equal participation with men in the various trades, professions, and commerce."[16] The one resolution that was deemed most radical at the time—and the only one that did not receive unanimous approval—was "the sacred right to elective franchise."

There is strong irony in the fact that the demand for the vote was so controversial, for the social, economic, legal, and religious changes demanded by the resolutions would, if realized, have brought about a much more far-reaching transformation than the enfranchisement of women ever did. During the protracted struggle for women's rights, the broad agenda for change implicit in the Seneca Falls Declaration grew progressively narrower until the vote became the paramount, if not the only, objective.

Long before women were permitted to go to the polls, however, they took part in politics—most notably in various nineteenth-

---

15. On the Seneca Falls Convention, see Eleanor Flexner, *Century of Struggle,* rev. ed. (Cambridge: Harvard University Press, 1975), chap. 5. On early attempts to establish rights for women see, in addition, William L. O'Neill, *Everyone Was Brave* (Chicago: Quadrangle Books, 1969); and Aileen S. Kraditor, *The Ideas of the Woman Suffrage Movement* (New York: Columbia University Press, 1965).

16. Document 3 in Scott and Scott, *One Half the People,* pp. 56–59.

century movements for social reform but also in the political parties.[17] Through their activity women developed important political skills—organizing, holding meetings, conducting petition drives, and even speaking in public. Especially through their involvement in the abolition movement, they also absorbed lessons applicable to their own circumstances as partial citizens.

After many years characterized by setback, frustration, and, not infrequently, internal division, woman suffrage was achieved on a national basis in 1920 with the passage of the Nineteenth Amendment to the Constitution—nearly a century and a half after both American independence and Abigail Adams's famous missive.[18] Ironically, women were excluded from the meeting at which the secretary of state of Tennessee signed the official papers making it the final state needed to ratify the amendment.[19] When women—or, at least, White women—were finally permitted to vote, their turnout was low and neither the positive outcomes promised by the suffragists nor the negative consequences feared by their antagonists materialized.[20]

---

17. On women's pre-suffrage political activity, see Suzanne Lebsock, "Women and American Politics," in *Women, Politics, and Change*, ed. Louise A. Tilly and Patricia Gurin (New York: Russell Sage Foundation, 1990), chap. 2; Rebecca Edwards, *Angels in the Machinery: Gender in American Party Politics from the Civil War to the Progressive Era* (New York: Oxford University Press, 1997); and Jo Freeman, *A Room at a Time: How Women Entered Party Politics* (Lanham: Rowman and Littlefield, 2000), pp. 33–45.

18. For a discussion that places women's suffrage in the context of the history of enfranchisement in America, see Alexander Keyssar, *The Right to Vote: The Contested History of Democracy in the United States* (New York: Basic Books, 2000), especially chap. 6. Before they were enfranchised on a national basis, women were permitted to vote in various states and localities, including New Jersey for a brief period just after the Revolution (pp. 20, 54, 174) and, beginning with Wyoming, in several states of the West in the late nineteenth century (pp. 183–187).

19. Clifton Daniel, ed., *Chronicle of the 20th Century: Ultimate Records of Our Time* (New York: Dorling Kindersley Publishing, 1995), p. 269.

20. Nevertheless, the stereotype of women as completely politically quiescent during the 1920s is inaccurate. See, for example, Nancy F. Cott, "Across the Great Divide: Women in Politics before and after 1920," Kristi Andersen, "Women and Citizenship in the 1920s," and Evelyn Brooks Higginbotham, "In Politics to Stay: Black Women Leaders and Party Politics in the 1920s," in *Women, Politics, and Change*, ed. Tilly and Gurin, chaps. 7–9; as well as Kristi Andersen, *After Suffrage* (Chicago: University of Chicago Press, 1996); and Anna L. Harvey, *Votes without Leverage: Women in American Electoral Politics, 1920–1970* (Cambridge: Cambridge University Press, 1998). For a particularly compelling discussion of women in party politics after suffrage, see Freeman, *A Room at a Time*. Freeman is especially concerned with what she calls "party women," not with suffragists or reformers.

After Suffrage: The Changing World of Gender Relations

Women's initial low turnout levels were a disappointment to those who had fought so hard for suffrage. Subsequent history, however, has demonstrated over and over that newly enfranchised groups do not immediately go to the polls at high rates. Besides, America was a very different place in 1920 when women won the vote than it is today. That year witnessed the first radio broadcast and the first coast-to-coast airmail service. The average employee earned roughly $1,200 a year, a figure that translates to approximately $9,400 in 1995 dollars.[21] Sinclair Lewis published *Main Street*. Babe Ruth was traded to the Yankees for the unprecedented sum of $125,000. And hemlines reached nearer to the knees than to the ankles, a daring fashion trend that permitted economizing on fabric.[22] Since then, America has changed in many ways, ranging from the ways we commute to work to the ethnic composition of the public. Many of these changes are relevant for addressing the puzzle we have posed: unequal participation between men and women.

Imagine the suffragists who struggled so valiantly to achieve the vote in 1920 returning for a visit and asking us to give them a succinct—if superficial—summary of what has transpired since their victory that would help them to get some purchase on the social processes that leave in their wake the disparity between men and women in political activity. At the outset, we would caution that the substantial changes in gender relations in a variety of domains must be understood in the context of other social trends that have complex, and often contradictory, implications for the place of women and men in economic, social, and political life. We would

---

21. These figures, which are approximate at best, are calculated from information contained in U.S. Bureau of the Census, *Historical Statistics of the United States, Colonial Times to 1970, Bicentennial Edition* (Washington, D.C.: U.S. Government Printing Office, 1975), p. 164, and U.S. Bureau of the Census, *Statistical Abstract of the United States: 1996*, 116th ed. (Washington, D.C.: U.S. Government Printing Office, 1996), p. 483.

22. The facts in this paragraph are taken from David Brownstone and Irene Franck, *Timelines of the 20th Century* (Boston: Little, Brown and Co., 1990), pp. 91–93; Daniel, *Chronicle of the 20th Century*, p. 268; and Ross Gregory, *Almanacs of American Life: Modern America, 1914 to 1945* (New York: Facts on File, 1995), p. 351.

also note that, while the consequences of these processes have been especially pronounced for women, it is not only women but men as well whose lives have been altered and whose opportunities have been expanded by the relaxation in traditional gender roles. And we would make clear that we were attempting, not to survey all of American society, but rather to concentrate on the domains that are most relevant to our understanding of gender differences in political activity.

We might then begin with politics itself and make clear that the breakthrough of enfranchisement has not been accompanied by equal political power for women. Still, the era since the revival of the women's movement in the late 1960s has witnessed a slow increase in the representation of women among political elites. In 1965, 3 percent of the members of the U.S. House of Representatives were women; by 2001, 14 percent were. At one time the surest route to Congress for a woman was over her husband's dead body; in the last two decades, however, the proportion of congressional widows among women in the House and Senate has diminished substantially. Women have generally fared better in seeking legislative than executive office, and, in a pattern that reflects what we shall see for the economy, the higher the rung on the political ladder, the lower the representation of women among elected or appointed public officials. In 2001, in contrast to their representation in the House, 22 percent of members of the state legislatures are women. Although there are thirteen women among the hundred members of the Senate, in contrast to many nations, including nations whose cultures look less kindly than our own upon the goal of gender equality, we have never had a female president.[23]

We might continue by noting the substantial changes in a domain that has always been strongly associated with political participation, educational attainment. Since the early years of the century, the aggregate educational level of the population has climbed substantially. In 1920, only about one teenager in six graduated from high school; today nearly nine out of ten do.[24] At the same

---

23. Information in this paragraph is taken from the Web site of the Center for American Women and Politics at Rutgers <http://www.rci.rutgers.edu/~cawp/facts>.

24. These figures, which are rough, are based on data in Gregory, *Almanacs of American*

time the educational disparity between women and men has narrowed, though not closed completely. In 1920, men earned 66 percent of the bachelor's degrees, 70 percent of the master's degrees, and 85 percent of the doctoral-level degrees. By 1990, these figures had fallen to 47 percent, 47 percent, and 63 percent respectively.[25]

Since the participatory factors acquired on the job figure importantly in our explanation of political activity, we would next highlight the most obvious and substantial change in American society: the entry of women into the work force. In 1920, labor force participation for women was 23 percent; by 1995, it had risen to 59 percent. Reflecting later school leaving and the institutionalization of retirement, labor force participation for men diminished from 85 percent to 76 percent over the same period.[26] Not only has women's work force participation increased steadily over the past several decades, but there has been a transformation in the kinds of women who are likely to have jobs outside the home. At one time, paid work was the domain of young, unmarried women and poor women, especially women of color. These generalizations no longer hold: in recent years, well-educated women are more likely to be in the labor force than women of more limited educational attainment; labor force participation rates of Black and White women are virtually indistinguishable; and married women are likely to be in the work force even if they have preschool children. Moreover, women are showing greater work force attachment, staying with their jobs rather than moving in and out of the work force.

Changes in other aspects of the economic status of women have been less dramatic and—at least on the basis of the expectations held in the heady days of the revival of the women's movement in

---

Life, p. 301, and U.S. Bureau of the Census, *Statistical Abstract,* p. 191. Although there is a strong association between political activity and educational attainment in any cross-section, rising educational attainment has not been accompanied by commensurate increases in participation. See Norman H. Nie, Jane Junn, and Kenneth Stehlik-Barry, *Education and Democratic Citizenship in America* (Chicago: University of Chicago Press, 1996).

25. U.S. Bureau of the Census, *Historical Statistics,* p. 385, and U.S. Bureau of the Census, *Statistical Abstract,* p. 191.

26. U.S. Bureau of the Census, *Historical Statistics,* p. 132; and U.S. Bureau of the Census, *Statistical Abstract,* p. 393.

the late 1960s—less predictable. Growing numbers of women have entered fields traditionally dominated by men; nevertheless, the sharing of job titles by men and women is still not the norm. At the same time that there are more female lawyers and engineers and more male flight attendants, the enormous expansion of positions in the traditionally female pink-collar ghetto implies that men and women in the labor force continue to do essentially different work.

The persistence of high, though diminishing, levels of gender segregation in job titles is matched by the persistence of high, though diminishing, levels of vertical stratification. That is, although women have begun to penetrate the highest echelons in many fields, in any particular occupation the most prestigious and highly paid positions tend to be held by men, a phenomenon that is often denoted by the metaphor of the "glass ceiling." Hence there are increasing numbers of women in middle management, but few women CEOs. This pattern obtains even in occupations dominated by women: although the librarian in your town library and the server at your local beanery are likely to be female, the Librarian of Congress and the waitstaff at the Ritz are not.

Coupled with the erosion of men's wages as the result of de-industrialization and global competition, these trends—women's greater work force attachment and widened opportunities for nontraditional employment and occupational success—have meant a diminution of the pay gap between the sexes. For decades the earnings of women working full time, year round hovered in the neighborhood of 60 percent of men's earnings. Since the early 1980s, a slow process of convergence has been at work such that women now earn, on average, just under three-quarters what men do.

The transformation implied by the entry of massive numbers of women into the work force has not been matched by a similar transformation in the private domain of the household, a sphere to which we shall pay ongoing attention throughout our analysis. In spite of a trend toward greater gender equality, women—even married women who are employed full time—continue to do most of the housework, a circumstance that leaves women with children and full-time jobs as the group with the least leisure time. Once again, we must place our observations in the context of other social processes. Escalating rates of divorce and births out of wedlock imply that growing proportions of children live with only one of their parents, ordinarily their mothers; the result is that, on average, children actually spend less time with their fathers—even though child-care responsibilities in two-parent families may be divided more evenly than in the past. The same trends affecting family structure have economic consequences as well. The growth in the number of single-parent households headed by women, and the erosion of government economic support for the needy, imply that the adult poor are disproportionately likely to be female—a tendency known as "the femininization of poverty."

In the sphere of religious activity—one that plays an important but complicated part in our analysis—the pattern of overall convergence in gender roles that we have seen for other domains does not obtain. Instead we see a denominationally specific set of changes with substantial progress toward equality between women and men in many denominations, little change in some denominations, and the self-conscious reassertion of traditional gender roles in a few. Although religious institutions long excluded women from clerical leadership and religious doctrine has customarily been invoked to buttress a traditional division of labor, women have consistently been more devout and more religiously active than men.

At the time of the passage of the Nineteenth Amendment, only a few denominations—among them the Congregationalists, the Unitarians, and a few holiness sects such as the Nazarenes[27]—permitted the ordination of women. After World War II, various denominations began to ordain women, and since the 1970s there has been rapid growth in the number of ordained women.[28] Orthodox faiths—among them Roman Catholics, Eastern Orthodox, Mor-

---

27. For the dates at which various denominations first permitted the ordination of women, see Catherine Wessinger, "Women's Religious Leadership in the U.S." in *Religious Institutions and Women's Leadership,* ed. Catherine Wessinger (Columbia: University of South Carolina Press, 1996), p. 4; and Mark Chaves, *Ordaining Women* (Cambridge: Harvard University Press, 1997), pp. 16–17.

28. Jackson W. Carroll, Barbara Hargrove, and Adair Lummis, *Women of the Cloth* (San Francisco: Harper and Row, 1983), p. 3.

mons, Muslims, and Orthodox Jews—have, however, resisted the trend and do not ordain women. Furthermore, in a few denominations, there has been a retreat from the general trend toward equality between men and women. In spite of the centrality of congregational autonomy in the Baptist tradition and the exercise of leadership by women in its early years, in 2000 the Southern Baptist Convention passed a resolution declaring that women should not serve as pastors in congregations.[29] Thus in the religious domain we see not only a very mixed set of outcomes but, in certain denominations, actual reversal of the dominant trend toward gender equality.

In short, given the opportunity to describe to the suffragists the evolution of gender roles since the passage of the Nineteenth Amendment, we would conclude by stressing the obvious: the United States is in many ways—including, but not confined to, matters of gender relations—a very different country from the one that gave women the vote in 1920, and we would underline the extent to which changes in what men and women do and the way they relate to one another are embedded in other social processes. We would also note that the changes do not affect all women—or all men—in the same way. Instead, men and women who differ in terms of their age, their race, and their social class have felt the consequences of these social processes differentially. Moreover, these changes are proceeding very unevenly—more rapidly in some domains than in others, sometimes stalled, occasionally even reversed.

Forced to deliver a bottom-line assessment, we would indicate that the overall trend is toward the reduction of inequalities between women and men. Nevertheless, we would point out that the convergence in roles and statuses has involved more movement by women than by men. In part this asymmetry reflects the fact that men have traditionally commanded a disproportionate share of

29. See Sarah Frances Anders and Marilyn Metcalf Whittaker, "Women as Lay Leaders and Clergy: A Critical Issue," in *Southern Baptists Observed,* ed. Nancy Tatom Ammerman (Knoxville: University of Tennessee Press, 1993), chap. 11; Carolyn DeArmond Blevins, "Women and the Baptist Experience," in *Religious Institutions and Women's Leadership,* ed. Wessinger, pp. 158–179; and "Southern Baptist Convention Passes Resolution Opposing Women as Pastors," *New York Times,* June 15, 2000, p. A-18.

that which is most valued in society—for example, money, power, status, or education, though not long life. Reducing inequality, therefore, would involve women's seeking more of what men have always enjoyed.[30] However, perhaps because whatever men are associated with tends to have higher status, men have been much more reluctant to embrace that which is worthy of emulation or enviable about women's traditional roles and concerns. For example, even when it is available, few men take advantage of paternity leave to care for a new baby or sick child.

Gender Differences in the United States and Elsewhere

While gender is an important, but far from the only, principle of social organization in every human society, the magnitude and pervasiveness of gender differences also vary across societies and cultures. In general, traditional societies tend to maintain more rigid boundaries between the sexes than do developed ones. Even among developed democracies, however, there is substantial variation.

Where do the multiple processes of social change just described leave the United States compared with the other nations it is presumed to resemble? Students of democratic politics often discuss "American exceptionalism" and note that, when developed democracies are arrayed with respect to some aspect of politics—for example, welfare state guarantees or the strength of the parties—the United States is on one end of the continuum. The circumstance is very different when it comes to equality between men and women.

Rank ordering a number of developed democracies with respect to ten measures of equality between the sexes and well-being for women puts the United States in first or last place only twice and shows no consistency across measures. The United States is in the upper ranks of the list with respect to the ratio of women to men in higher education, the share of unpaid housework done by men,

---

30. We should note that some of the convergence—such as that which is caused by the reduction in men's wages occasioned by the decline in the number of highly skilled industrial jobs—is the result of men's having less rather than women's having more.

the percentage of women in the work force, and the percentage of administrative and managerial workers who are female. The United States is in the middle of the list in terms of the extensiveness of contraceptive use, the ratio of women's to men's wages among non-agricultural workers, and the proportion of women among union members and members of the national legislature. The United States is tied with New Zealand for last place with respect to the provision of paid maternity leave.[31] In addition, while women everywhere are more likely than men to say that religion is very important to them, the disparity is far wider in the United States than elsewhere.[32]

As for our central concern, citizen political participation, the data are less complete: the measures are limited and fewer developed democracies are ranked. Nonetheless, one study shows the United States to compare favorably with other democracies in this domain. The gender gap in participation is narrower here than in other democracies.[33]

Thinking about Participation

As we shall discuss in Chapter 2, we cast a broad net in defining political participation and include under that rubric a variety

---

31. These data are derived from United Nations, *The World's Women 1995: Trends and Statistics* (New York: United Nations, 1995), tables 6, 7, 8, 10, 14; and Joyce P. Jacobsen, *The Economics of Gender,* 2nd ed. (Malden, Mass.: Blackwell Publishers, 1998), pp. 346–351. See also Naomi Neft and Ann D. Levine, *Where Women Stand* (New York: Random House, 1997). For most of these measures the comparison group is the following twenty countries: Australia, Austria, Belgium, Canada, Denmark, Finland, France, Germany, Ireland, Italy, Japan, the Netherlands, New Zealand, Norway, Portugal, Spain, Sweden, Switzerland, the United Kingdom, and the United States. Although there is little consistency in the ranking of countries across the various measures, the Scandinavian countries tend to be near the top of the list and Japan near the bottom.

32. The World Values Surveys for 1995 and 1996 compare Australia, Finland, Germany, Japan, Norway, Spain, Sweden, Switzerland, and the United States with respect to the proportion of respondents who said that religion is very important. Not only is the difference between women and men most pronounced for the United States, but American women and men are more than twice as likely as their counterparts in any other country to consider religion very important.

33. Carol A. Christy, *Sex Differences in Political Participation* (New York: Praeger, 1987), chap. 2. In addition, on the basis of data collected in the 1960s, Sidney Verba, Norman H. Nie, and Jae-On Kim, *Participation and Political Equality* (Cambridge: Cambridge

of forms of activity in which there is the intent or consequence of influencing government action—either directly, by affecting the formulation or implementation of public policy, or indirectly, by affecting the selection of public officials. Citizens in American democracy who have political objectives have many options for making their voices heard. We consider, of course, the most fundamental mechanism for holding public officials accountable, voting. But we also investigate other efforts to influence who will hold public office—either by working in, or making contributions to, electoral campaigns. We examine, in addition, several forms of activity aimed at having a direct impact on what policymakers do: contacting them directly; attending protests, marches, or demonstrations; getting involved in organizations that take stands in politics; taking part in informal efforts to solve community problems; and serving in a voluntary capacity on local governing boards such as school or zoning boards. Our understanding of participation thus encompasses activity at the local as well as the national level; unconventional as well as conventional activity; activity requiring money as well as activity demanding time; and activity undertaken with others as well as activity done alone.

An expansive understanding of what constitutes participation is especially important given our concern with gender differences in political activity. It is sometimes argued that, like traditional approaches in many academic disciplines, mainstream political science tends to overlook women's distinctive choices or contributions. In thinking about political participation, therefore, we should examine not only differences in degree but also differences in kind. By including in our purview non-electoral forms of participation—especially the organizational, protest, and grassroots community activity in which women have always taken part—we are able to subject to empirical scrutiny the claim that the gender gap in political activity has been exaggerated by an emphasis on particular modes of participation.

University Press, 1978), chap. 12, find that the disparity in participation between men and women is narrower in the United States than in Austria, India, Japan, the Netherlands, Nigeria, or the former Yugoslavia.

WHAT DIFFERENCE DOES PARTICIPATION MAKE?

One theme in recent political discourse is concern about declining civic engagement.[34] Discussions about the health of civil society are ordinarily conducted, however, as if the reasons for concern about levels of participation are self-evident. Rather than make such presumptions, it seems appropriate to make explicit why we believe that political participation matters. When we bother to ask, we see that there are three broad categories of reasons for caring about levels of political activity: the creation of community and the cultivation of democratic virtues, the development of the capacities of the individual, and the equal protection of interests in public life.[35]

First, contemporary concerns about low levels of political activity stem from the consequences of political participation—and voluntary activity more generally—for the community and democracy. When people work together voluntarily—whether for political or non-political ends—democratic orientations and skills are fostered: social trust,[36] norms of reciprocity and cooperation, and

---

34. On the erosion of civic engagement, see Robert D. Putnam, *Bowling Alone: The Collapse and Revival of American American Community* (New York: Simon and Schuster, 2000), as well as the much less compelling argument in Everett Carll Ladd, *The Ladd Report* (New York: Free Press, 1999).

35. This discussion of the various reasons for concern about equality in participation draws heavily upon Kay Lehman Schlozman, Sidney Verba, and Henry E. Brady, "Civic Participation and the Equality Problem," in *Civic Engagment in American Democracy*, ed. Theda Skocpol and Morris Fiorina (Washington, D.C.: Brookings, 1999), chap. 12. In proposing tripartite benefits from voluntary activity, we make no claims of either novelty or definitiveness. Rather we seek to position our work within an ongoing dialogue.

There are a number of helpful discussions about why we care about civic engagement, among them Jane J. Mansbridge, *Beyond Adversary Democracy* (New York: Basic Books, 1980), chap. 17; Geraint Parry, George Moyser, and Neil Day, *Political Participation and Democracy in Britain* (Cambridge: Cambridge University Press, 1992), chap. 1; Robert D. Putnam, *Making Democracy Work* (Princeton: Princeton University Press, 1993); Theda Skocpol, "Unravelling from Above," *American Prospect*, March/April 1996, pp. 20–25; Kenneth Newton, "Social Capital and Democracy," *American Behavioral Scientist* 40 (1997): 575–586; Bob Edwards and Michael W. Foley, "Social Capital and the Political Economy of Our Discontent," *American Behavioral Scientist* 40 (1997): 669–678; Mark E. Warren, "Democracy and Associations: An Approach to the Contributions of Associations to Democracy" (paper presented at the annual meeting of the Western Political Science Association, Los Angeles, 1998); Putnam, *Bowling Alone*, esp. sect. IV. We should make clear that there is variation across authors with respect to the rubrics used to categorize the salutary consequences of civic involvement.

36. This perspective draws from James S. Coleman's (1988) concept of social capital. "Social Capital in the Creation of Human Capital," *American Journal of Sociology* 94 (1988): 95–120. For a rare empirical test of this hypothesis, see John Brehm and Wendy

the capacity to transcend narrow points of view and conceptualize the common good.[37] Thus when there is a vigorous sector of voluntary involvement—and the strong associational foundation that underlies it—it becomes easier for communities, and democratic nations, to engage in joint activity and to produce public goods. Communities characterized by high levels of voluntary activity are in many ways better places to live: the schools are better; crime rates are lower; tax evasion is less common.[38] Moreover, a vital arena of voluntary activity between individual and state protects citizens from overweening state power and preserves freedom.

The other two reasons for concern about levels of political participation shift our attention from social to individual benefits. Understanding the individual benefits derived from political participation makes clear the basis for our concern with disparities in activity between individuals and between groups, rather than with levels of activity. Not only does the community gain when citizens take part but individuals grow and learn through their activity. Political participation builds individual capacities in several ways: those who take part learn about community and society; they develop civic skills that can be carried throughout their lives; and they can come to have a greater appreciation of the needs and interests of others and of society as a whole.[39]

Finally, and most importantly, we care about participation

Rahn, "Individual-Level Evidence for the Causes and Consequences of Social Capital," *American Journal of Political Science* 41 (1997): 999–1023.

37. Many commentators point out that the inevitable result of collective action is not necessarily to foster community and democracy. Some groups—for example, militias—hardly promote democratic values. Moreover, organizations of like-minded individuals beget conflict as well as cooperation. See, for example, the arguments and references contained in Michael W. Foley and Bob Edwards, "Escape from Politics? Social Theory and the Social Capital Debate" *American Behavioral Scientist* 40 (1997): 550–561; Sheri Berman, "Civil Society and Political Institutionalization," *American Behavioral Scientist* 40 (1997): 562–574; and Putnam, *Bowling Alone,* chap. 22. In fact, the evidence suggests that some kinds of trust foster political participation, and some do not. See Nancy Burns and Donald Kinder, "Social Trust and Democratic Politics," Pilot Study Report to the NES Board of Overseers, 2000 <www.umich.edu/~nes>.

38. For elaboration of this theme, see Putnam, *Bowling Alone,* sect. IV.

39. See, for example, Peter Bachrach, *The Theory of Democratic Elitism: A Critique* (Boston: Little, Brown, 1967); Carole Pateman, *Participation and Democratic Theory* (Cambridge: Cambridge University Press, 1970); and Geraint Parry, "The Idea of Political Participation," in *Participation in Politics,* ed. Geraint Parry (Totowa, N.J.: Rowman and Littlefield, 1972).

because of its consequences for equal protection of interests. Through the medium of political participation, citizens communicate information about their preferences and needs for government action and generate pressure on public officials to heed what they hear. We know, of course, that public officials act for many reasons—only one of which is their assessment of what the public wants and needs. And policymakers have ways other than the medium of citizen participation of learning what citizens want and need from the government. Nonetheless, since public officials are likely to be differentially responsive to citizens who exercise their participatory rights and those who do not, disparities in political involvement may compromise the democratic ideal of equal consideration of the wishes and needs of all citizens. The needs and preferences of those who are politically quiescent may get short shrift.

This logic makes clear not only why we care about participatory equality but why concern with women's participatory deficit is not simply another example of, to use a cliché, "adopting the male model." Scholars studying gender differences in a variety of aspects of human behavior converge in making an important point: that the appropriate way to think about gender differences is not necessarily to ask, "Why can't a woman be more like a man?"[40] We agree fully that, in many respects, women's ways of doing things—such as their greater willingness to make sacrifices on behalf of their children, their lower rates of violent crime, the grades they get in school—set a standard that men would do well to emulate.

The gender gap in political participation, however, puts women in a potential position of disadvantage. Not only are they deprived of the educational benefits that accrue from political participation, but they may lose out when public policy is made. Government policies ranging from the implementation of equal employment opportunity policy to Social Security survivors' benefits to abortion to the handling of domestic violence affect men and

---

40. Virginia Sapiro (*The Political Integration of Women*, p. 8) also refers to Henry Higgins's question in cautioning against adopting a male model and arguing that participation brings a range of benefits to women and to men (pp. 59, 85–86).

women differently. If public officials hear disproportionately from men, then the political needs and preferences of women may not be given equal weight in the political process. In short, we are concerned about the disparity in participation between men and women, not because we assume that the masculine pattern is the human pattern, but because we are concerned about the democratic norm of equal responsiveness to all.

Thinking about Gender

Because matters of gender constitute contested terrain in contemporary intellectual discourse, we would like to clarify our own stance by making a few initial distinctions.[41] In seeking to understand the roots of political participation and the social processes that create differences between women and men in political activity, we are focusing on *gender* and participation, not on *women* and participation or on *sex* and participation.

Presumably as a reaction to the near invisibility of the female half of the population in traditional academic analysis, contemporary discussions of "gender" are often really discussions of women. We are deeply beholden to feminist historians and theorists who have drawn our attention to long-neglected topics having particular relevance to women's lives—for example, the consequences of family relationships for political participation or the special impact of gender-segregated voluntary associations. This book, however, is about both women and men. And when we train empirical data on these matters, we find they are relevant for men's

---

41. Our understanding of the origins and meaning of differences between females and males has been shaped by the creative thinking of feminist theorists from several disciplines. Some works that we have found particularly helpful for our consideration of differences in political participation include: Erving Goffman, "The Arrangement between the Sexes," *Theory and Society* 4 (1977): 301–333; Candace West and Don H. Zimmerman, "Doing Gender," *Gender and Society* 1 (1987): 125–151; Carole Pateman, "Equality, Difference, Subordination: The Politics of Motherhood and Women's Citizenship," and Deborah L. Rhode, "The Politics of Paradigms: Gender Difference and Gender Disadvantage," in *Beyond Equality and Difference: Citizenship, Feminist Politics, and Female Subjectivity,* ed. Gisela Bock and Susan James (London: Routledge, 1992); Mary R. Jackman, *The Velvet Glove* (Berkeley: University of California Press, 1994); Roberta S. Sigel, *Ambition and Accommodation: How Women View Gender Relations* (Chicago: University of Chicago Press, 1996), chap. 1.

lives as well for women's. Nevertheless, because women were so long excluded from the world of public affairs, we too sometimes focus especially on women.

As a category of social analysis, the distinction between males and females has some useful properties. In contrast to, for example, social class, sex is dichotomous and, under most circumstances, readily observable at birth. In contrast to age, it is, except under extraordinary circumstances, immutable throughout the life cycle. Thus sex is temporally prior to any social outcomes with which it is associated, which means that the direction of causal relationships is unambiguous: while being female might cause a preference for playing with dolls rather than trucks among children or being a nursery school teacher rather than a professional boxer among adults, it is difficult to imagine the reverse, that playing with dolls or being a nursery school teacher causes one to become female. For these reasons, a great deal of social science analysis has used the dichotomous division on the basis of sex as an explanatory variable.

A concern with gender rather than sex points us in the direction of socially constructed rather than biologically determined differences.[42] A great deal of scholarship has debated the relative importance of biology and society in producing differences between males and females. We are agnostic as to the overall balance of nature and nurture. However, socially structured experience is undeniably germane to the domain of our concern, voluntary activity. It is impossible to investigate participation in general—or participatory differences between women and men, in particular—without regard to the expectations, opportunities, and life circumstances that operate so powerfully throughout the life cycle to shape who we are.

Thinking in terms of gender rather than sex orients us away from thinking in terms of dichotomous and immutable distinctions. We have already seen that the forces that produce gender differences have varied through history and across societies and

---

42. For an especially illuminating discussion of the place of sex and gender, biology, and social construction in explanation, see Cynthia Fuchs Epstein, *Deceptive Distinctions* (New Haven: Yale University Press, 1988), chaps. 1–3.

cultures. Moreover, they vary across the life cycle and across social contexts. Indeed, the social processes that create gender differences begin at birth—the first question asked about each of us is, usually, "Boy or girl?"—and continue through childhood and adolescence. Moreover, the social construction of differences between men and women does not end with the onset of adulthood but, rather, continues throughout the life cycle. Indeed, a large part of our overall story concerns the impact of adult experiences—especially adult experiences in the family, on the job, in organizations, and at church—on voluntary activity.

In addition, gender differences are contextual, their extent and nature varying across social domains.[43] The implications of being female rather than male are different within the sanctum of the family from what they are on a construction site, at a playground, at a supermarket, or in an elementary school classroom; and they are different across groups defined by other social characteristics—for example, social class and race or ethnicity.[44] Our analytical approach takes account of the contextuality of gender differences. We do not assume that we can extrapolate to politics from what we know about gender differences in church or at school. Moreover, we will explore the interrelationships among these domains, delineating the direct and indirect consequences of what happens in two arenas where gender differences matter profoundly, the home and the workplace, for a domain where they are much less central, citizen politics.

Using gender as a conceptual lens thus calls our attention to the

---

43. As Virginia Sapiro (*The Political Integration of Women*, p. 37) put it, "No single role is attached to being a man or a woman, rather, a constellation of roles, all revolving around the fact that one was born male or female."

44. We use the term "race or ethnicity" because African-Americans are usually referred to as a racial group and Latinos as an ethnic group. Where the context demands, we sometimes use the inelegant construction "race/ethnicity" in order to make clear the differentiation of race or ethnicity, on one hand, from gender, on the other.

There is no generally accepted nomenclature for the three groups on which we focus, and what the appropriate designations are is often a politically volatile question. We use the terms "African-Americans" or "Blacks" for one of the minority groups and "Latinos" for the other. We use the term "Anglo-Whites" to denote those who described themselves as White, but not as Latino or Hispanic. The locution is admittedly awkward. Since "White" is often usually juxtaposed to "Black" or "African-American" and "Anglo" to "Latino" or "Hispanic," however, the conglomerate term for the majority group seems appropriate.

heterogeneity among men and among women. Sometimes the differences among men and among women are greater than the differences between men and women. With respect to most human attributes, even ones with a physiological basis, it is useful to conceptualize the differences between females and males, not in terms of a dichotomy, but rather in terms of overlapping bell curves with different means. With respect to some of these characteristics—for example, vocabulary skill or musical ability—the difference between means is barely detectable and the degree of overlap substantial.[45] When it comes to other human qualities—for example, upper-body strength or rates of violent crime—the means are much further apart and the degree of overlap is much less.

An intrinsic part of our mode of analysis is, therefore, the recognition of the many ways that women and men differ among themselves that are relevant for political participation—for example, in terms of education, income, family circumstances, other voluntary commitments, and interest in and knowledge about politics. As we proceed we shall be aware of the way that differences among men and among women with respect to these attributes help to explain who takes part and who does not. We shall also be aware of the way that differences between men and women with respect to these attributes help to explain the fact that men are, on average, more politically active than women are. Furthermore, recognizing the diversity among women and among men focuses our attention on the intersections between gender and other social characteristics, most importantly, class and race, both of which are fundamental axes of cleavage in American politics and both of which are also associated with political participation.

As we shall elaborate at length in Chapter 2, our analytic strategy is informed by these understandings. In considering how social experience shapes orientations to politics, we are concerned not only with the crucial formative years of childhood and adolescence but also with adulthood. Moreover, in assessing the constraints and choices that create gender differences, we pay particular attention to variations across contexts and make no assumptions that

---

45. See the helpful discussion of this subject in Richard Lewontin, *Human Diversity* (New York: Scientific American, 1995), chap. 7.

what is true for one domain must obtain for others. Within each context—home, workplace, church, and so on—we examine the nature and extent of gender differences and investigate how those differences are created and maintained. In addition, we are cognizant that the differences among women and among men may overshadow the differences between them.

Gender as a Political Category in America

Our concern with the implications of unequal participation for the equal protection of interests in politics suggests that we should consider gender as not only a social but a political category and seek to locate gender differences in the terrain of political conflict in America. Group differences tend to become politically relevant and to become continuing fault lines of political conflict when group members are affected in similar ways by governmental policies; when group members are united by distinctive and shared preferences with respect to these policies; and when group identities find expression in the institutions that represent citizen interests in the political process, interest groups and parties. In short, if group members agree strongly with one another and disagree sharply with non-members on matters of deep political import, and if these divisions are embodied in the representative institutions of American democracy, then we expect group identity to become an axis of political cleavage.

It is easy to specify a variety of government policies on which women and men in America would seem to have different objective interests.[46] Some of these—for example, abortion, contraception, and pregnancy leaves—derive from women's reproductive capacities. Others—for example, the assignment of women to combat roles in the military, veterans' preference in civil service hiring, and the implementation of non-discrimination policies in employment and education—derive from a long tradition of de jure and de facto discrimination on the basis of sex in many realms

---

46. For a valuable framework for thinking about women's interests, see Virginia Sapiro, "When Are Interests Interesting? The Problem of Political Representation of Women," *American Political Science Review* 75 (1981): 701–716.

of life. And still others—for example, government support for child care, divorce law, and income maintenance for the poor—derive from the consequences of a division of labor in which women have traditionally taken responsibility for the care of home and children.

Although there is a long list of issues on which men and women might be expected to have different interests, their actual preferences reflect these expectations very imperfectly, if at all.[47] As politically relevant groups, women and men are divided along other fault lines—in particular, along lines of race and class. The result is that the differences in opinion among men and among women are more pronounced than the differences between the two groups. With respect to opinions on many policies that have a different impact on women's and men's lives—abortion, for example—the two groups are virtually indistinguishable.[48] In contrast to the absence of gender difference in opinions on such "women's issues" is the long-standing gender difference in opinions on a variety of issues involving violence. Compared with women, men are more likely to be willing to use force in international disputes, to support enhanced military expenditures, and to oppose gun control measures. More recently, a disparity between men and women has emerged on issues involving government assistance to the needy, with women more supportive than men of government assistance and services in a variety of areas. Even in the areas in which the

47. On gender differences in political preferences and behaviors, see Kathleen Frankovic, "Sex and Politics—New Alignments, Old Issues," *PS: Political Science and Politics* 15 (1982): 439–448; Daniel Wirls, "Reinterpreting the Gender Gap," *Public Opinion Quarterly* 50 (1986): 316–350; Kristi Andersen, "Gender and Public Opinion," in *Understanding Public Opinion,* ed. Barbara Norrander and Clyde Wilcox (Washington, D.C.: CQ Press, 1997), chap. 2; Carole K. Chaney, R. Michael Alvarez, and Jonathan Nagler, "Explaining the Gender Gap in the U.S. Presidential Elections, 1980–1992," *Political Research Quarterly* 51 (1998): 211–340; Karen M. Kaufmann and John R. Petrocik, "The Changing Politics of American Men: Understanding the Sources of the Gender Gap," *American Journal of Political Science* 43 (1999): 864–887; as well as the discussion and bibliographical references in M. Margaret Conway, Gertrude A. Steuernagel, and David W. Ahern, *Women and Political Participation* (Washington, D.C.: CQ Press, 1997), chaps. 1–5.

48. See, for example, Barabara Hinkson Craig and David M. O'Brien, *Abortion and American Politics* (Chatham, N.J.: Chatham House, 1993), chap. 7; and Everett Carll Ladd and Karlyn H. Bowman, *Public Opinion about Abortion* (Washington, D.C.: AEI Press, 1997), p. 13.

differences between masculine and feminine opinion are most pronounced, however, neither men nor women are united in their attitudes; the gap between the two groups is hardly a chasm. In contrast, as a political group, African-Americans are much more distinctive in their opinions, and the distance that separates the opinions of Blacks and Whites is greater than that which separates women and men.

With respect to the extent to which group identities are built into political conflict by institutions, many organizations—ranging from the American Legion to the American Nurses Association—that take part in American politics are dominated by members of one sex or the other. In spite of the fact that most of the organized interests in Washington politics are dominated by men, organizations that self-consciously represent women's interests are more common than organizations that make explicit claims on men's behalf.[49] In addition to general-purpose organizations such as the National Organization for Women are more than a hundred narrower groups that advocate on behalf of particular issues like domestic violence or pay equity or particular groups of women ranging from Mexican-American women to military widows to women college administrators to older women.[50] In contrast, men's interests are very well represented in the mainstream corporations, trade associations, unions, and professional associations that make up the overwhelming share of the organized interests in national politics. In short, while gender issues are part of the seemingly endless agenda of issues over which there is conflict in pressure politics, they do not form the core of that agenda.

Although pressure politics in America usually involves narrow constituencies and narrow issues, it is the political parties that or-

---

49. One issue that has generated advocacy by groups of men self-consciously acting on behalf of men is divorce. Father's groups have lobbied on the state level for reduced financial responsibilities to ex-wives and, especially, joint custody arrangements for children. See Herbert Jacob, *Silent Revolution: The Transformation of Divorce Law in the United States* (Chicago: University of Chicago Press, 1988), chap. 8.

50. On the organizations that represent women in Washington, see Kay Lehman Schlozman, "Representing Women in Washington: Sisterhood and Pressure Politics," in *Women, Politics, and Change,* ed. Tilly and Gurin, chap. 15; and Joyce Gelb and Marian Lief Palley, *Women and Public Policies* (Charlottesville: University Press of Virginia, 1996), chap. 3.

ganize into politics the conflicts between broad publics over the most fundamental issues dividing Americans. With respect to political parties, the gender gap has been widely observed since 1980. When it comes to both partisanship and candidate choice, women are somewhat more Democratic, and men are somewhat more Republican. In parallel fashion, over the last generation, the major parties have offered clearly defined alternatives on an array of policy matters having a special impact on women, including the Equal Rights Amendment, the implementation of civil rights laws, and abortion, with Democrats congenial to, and Republicans hostile to, policies that promote equal rights and changes in traditional gender roles.[51]

In spite of the intermittent presence of women's rights issues on the American political agenda over the past century and a half, and in spite of the differentiation between the contemporary parties on such issues, gender does not have the prominence of either class or race as an axis of cleavage in American politics. In terms of opinions, party preferences, and candidate choices, neither men nor women constitute the kind of cohesive group that African-Americans have been since the 1960s. Furthermore, although class groups are less readily identifiable than groups based on gender or race or ethnicity, class issues involving government assistance to working people and the needy and the regulation of business have never been long absent from the center of American politics. Moreover, the New Deal party coalitions that emerged during the 1930s built conflict over class issues into American politics. In contrast, gender issues have been a consistent sub-theme, but rarely if ever the main theme, of political conflict in America.

---

51. On the differences between Republicans and Democrats on women's rights issues and the way that the parties' current positions constitute a reversal of their historical positions, see Jo Freeman, "Whom You Know versus Whom You Represent: Feminist Influence in the Democratic and Republican Parties," in *The Women's Movements of the United States and Western Europe,* ed. Mary Fainsod Katzenstein and Carol McClurg Mueller (Philadelphia: Temple University Press, 1987), chap. 10; and Christina Wolbrecht, *The Politics of Women's Rights* (Princeton: Princeton University Press, 2000). On the politics of women's issues at the federal level during the middle of the twentieth century, see Cynthia Harrison, *On Account of Sex: The Politics of Women's Issues, 1945–1968* (Berkeley: University of California Press, 1988).

Explaining Gender Disparities in Participation

The specific enterprise of this book, explaining the gender gap in participation, is embedded in a larger enterprise, explaining participation. If we can do the latter successfully, we will be able to do the former.

EXPLAINING PARTICIPATION

In our understanding, political activity is fostered by a variety of characteristics that predispose an individual to take part. We focus on three sets of *participatory factors:* resources, recruitment, and orientations to politics.[52]

> *Resources.* Individuals will be more likely to take part in politics if they have resources that make it possible to do so: among them are the time to devote to activity; money to make contributions to campaigns and other political causes; and civic skills, those organizational and communications capacities that make it easier to get involved and that enhance an individual's effectiveness as a participant.
>
> *Recruitment.* Political activity is often triggered by a request—from a relative, a workmate, a fellow organization or church member or, even, a stranger who calls during dinner. Those who have the wherewithal to take part are more likely to do so if they are asked.[53]
>
> *Political Orientations.* Several psychological orientations facilitate political activity. Individuals are more likely to participate if they are politically interested, informed, and efficacious, and if they can make connections between their concerns—especially the concerns rooted in group identities—and governmental action.

---

52. This model of the sources of political participation draws heavily from Verba, Schlozman, and Brady, *Voice and Equality,* part III.

53. We also know that those who have characteristics that make it likely that they would take part and who have a history of past participation are more likely to be targeted by requests for activity. See Henry E. Brady, Kay Lehman Schlozman, Sidney Verba, "Prospecting for Participants: Rational Expectations and the Recruitment of Political Activists," *American Political Science Review* 93 (1999): 153–168.

Earlier we listed a variety of common-sense explanations as to why men are somewhat more active in politics than women are. It is easy to see how these expectations map onto our more systematic model. For example, the suggestion that women—especially women with children and full-time jobs—are too time-deprived to participate would be encompassed by the emphasis upon resources. Or the suggestion that women learn from an early age that politics is a masculine enterprise falls under the rubric of a focus on political orientations.

THE ROLE OF INSTITUTIONS

These participatory factors are accumulated throughout the life cycle in non-political institutions.[54] At home, in school, on the job, and in voluntary association and religious institutions, individuals acquire resources, receive requests for activity, and develop the political orientations that foster participation. In the course of our analysis, we shall examine each of these institutions in sequence. The relative emphasis that we give to each particular institution will be determined both by how central it is to our argument and, frankly, by how fully our data are able to address the relevant concerns.

Let us illustrate beginning with the *families in which we are born*. An individual's earliest political exposures begin at home. All other things equal, those whose parents took part in politics

---

54. In our concern with social institutions, we build on the foundations laid by many scholars of gender and participation, scholars who have examined whether having jobs, being married, and having children affect women's and men's political participation. See, for example, Kristi Andersen, "Working Women and Political Participation, 1952–1972," *American Journal of Political Science* 19 (1975): 439–453; Welch, "Women as Political Animals?"; M. Kent Jennings and Barbara Farah, "Social Roles and Political Resources," *American Journal of Political Science* 25 (1981): 462–482; Eileen McDonagh, "To Work or Not to Work: The Differential Impact of Achieved and Derived Status upon the Political Participation of Women, 1956–76," *American Journal of Political Science* 26 (1982): 280–297; Kristi Andersen and Elizabeth A. Cook, "Women, Work, and Political Attitudes," *American Journal of Political Science* 29 (1985): 606–625; Karen Beckwith, *American Women and Political Participation: The Impacts of Work, Generation, and Feminism* (New York: Greenwood Press, 1986); and Cal Clark and Janet Clark, "Models of Gender and Political Participation in the United States," *Women and Politics* 6 (1986): 5–25. And we take up the challenge, put forward by Andersen and Cook (p. 622), to look more closely at the detailed workings of adult institutions, particularly the workplace.

are more likely to do so themselves. Furthermore, the American dream of equality of opportunity to the contrary, an important legacy of the families into which we are born is that parental socioeconomic status is passed along in the educational opportunities that are made available to the next generation.

It is well known that what happens in *school* is crucial for political participation in adulthood. Formal education cultivates the communications and organizational skills that facilitate political activity and provides opportunities for civic training through participation in school government and other clubs and activities. Moreover, those who have high levels of formal education are in various ways better endowed with participatory factors: they are more likely to have jobs that pay well and provide opportunities for the exercise of civic skills; they are more likely to be involved in voluntary associations; they are more likely to be the targets of requests for political activity; and they are more likely to be politically interested and informed.[55] Because our data about early experiences in the family and in school are based on adult recall, our treatment of these early institutions will be less thorough than our treatment of the institutions of adulthood, and our conclusions will be tentative.

Our principal focus is on the institutions of adult life. Among them are the *families that we create as adults*. Family life has multiple, and contradictory, consequences for participatory factors. On one hand, especially if there is more than one earner, families generate income that is usually available to all family members. In addition, the household can be the site of political discussion and exposure to other political cues, and married couples often take part together or represent one another in politics. On the other, responsibilities for household maintenance and child care make major claims on the time available for other pursuits, including political activity. The *workplace* is a prime location for acquiring participatory factors. Earnings from work are the primary source of income for most Americans. Moreover, individuals develop civic skills and receive requests for political participation at work.

---

55. On the multiple effects of education for participation, see Verba, Schlozman, and Brady, *Voice and Equality*, chap. 15.

However, the hours spent on the job represent the single largest commitment of time in most adults' lives. Voluntary activity in *non-political organizations* and *religious institutions* also figures importantly in generating participatory factors. Like the workplace, both non-political organizations and churches function as sites in which civic skills are exercised and social networks generate requests for activity.

In considering the role of institutions in providing participatory factors, we shall distinguish between *selection* into institutions and *treatment* within institutions. Selection refers to the processes that predispose individuals with particular characteristics to end up in a particular institutional setting. Treatment refers to what happens to individuals in an institution—in particular, the processes that influence who among those selected into institutions acquires participatory factors.

ACCOUNTING FOR THE DISPARITY BETWEEN WOMEN AND MEN
Our model not only gives us a template for understanding participatory differences among individuals but guides us in explaining why men are somewhat more active than women. The gender gap in participation grows out of either or both of the following circumstances: where there is a difference between women and men in the level of a particular participatory factor or in the effect on activity of a factor, that is, the process by which it is converted into activity.

We should note that explaining the gender gap in participation is a different enterprise from explaining participation. Even if a particular factor has consequences for participation, it does not help us to understand the gender gap in activity unless there is a gender difference in the level or the effect of that factor. For example, activity in student government and other clubs in high school and affiliation with non-political organizations during adulthood turn out, not surprisingly, to be strongly associated with political activity. Nevertheless, there are no significant gender differences in the level of activity either in high school clubs or in adult organizations or in their effects on political participation. Hence they are useful for explaining participation but not for explaining the gender gap in participation.

Our model, however, tells us where to look for gender differ-ences in the participatory endowments that men and women de-rive from institutions. Several of the institutions we investigate contribute to and reflect the results of the social construction of differences between men and women.[56] Family life is, obviously, characterized by a powerful, though diminishing, division of labor on the basis of sex, with women taking a disproportionate share of the responsibility for home and children and men a disproportion-ate share of the responsibility for financial support. When it comes to participatory factors acquired at work, men are not only more likely than women to be in the work force, they are more likely to hold jobs that pay well and provide opportunities to develop civic skills. Religious institutions present a particularly complicated case. On one hand, in many denominations women were excluded from full participation in religious life until quite recently, and in some denominations they continue to be. On the other, women are more religiously active than men are—even in denominations that restrict their full religious citizenship.

Using evidence from surveys about individuals and couples, we are able to account for women's continuing deficit in political par-ticipation. A model that focuses on access to and treatment within the non-political institutions of everyday life—the family, school, workplace, non-political voluntary association, and church—dem-onstrates a circumstance of cumulative inequalities such that men are better endowed with most of the participatory factors that facilitate activity. That is, with few compensatory inequalities, men—especially Anglo-White men—are advantaged with respect to the resources, recruitment attempts, and political orientations that foster activity. The gender gap in participation can be ex-

---

56. Roberta Sigel makes a similar point in another way: "The written and unwritten, of-ficial and unofficial norms of the gender systems pervade all institutional structures, thereby limiting the options available to women and restricting their capacity to control their own lives" (*Ambition and Accommodation*, p. 16). We would add to Sigel's formulation that these norms shape the options available to men as well. Alice Eagly has developed a com-pelling model of the situational roots of sex differences, with attention to both women and men in *Sex Differences in Social Behavior* (Hillsdale, N.J.: Lawrence Erlbaum Associates, 1987). For an analogous approach to men, see Jack W. Sattel, "Men, Inexpressiveness, and Power," in *The Gender and Psychology Reader*, ed. Blythe McVicker Clinchy and Julie K. Norem (New York: New York University Press, 1998), pp. 498–504.

plained by gender differences in the stockpiles of participatory factors.

The disparity in political activity thus results much less from gender differences in the way that participatory factors are converted into activity than from gender differences in the levels of participatory factors, and not from a big difference in a single factor, but from the accumulated effects of deficits in a variety of factors. This constellation of circumstances implies that a simple question yields no simple answer. However, our complicated solution to the puzzle of unequal participation illumines the nature of political participation, the institutional domains of adult life, and the social processes that create gender differences in contemporary America.

2

⊸⊷⊶⊷⊸

Studying Gender and Participation:
A Brief Discourse on Method

To inquire about the origins of the participation gap between women and men is to ask a simple question that will yield a complicated answer. In this chapter we discuss both the methods we use to seek that answer and the way these methods grow out of our theoretical understanding of the substantive intellectual problem. Although we shall have occasion to do so later on, we do not at this point consider particular statistical techniques. Rather we present an overall strategy for studying the roots both of political activity and of gender in various contexts.

Our approach bears an obvious debt to the techniques used by quantitative researchers in the social sciences and a less obvious, but equally important, debt to feminist theorists. Our principal method—multivariate analysis of survey data using separate models for men and women—was chosen precisely because it allows systematic analysis of data to be informed by two important insights derived from feminist theory: that any investigation of differences between women and men must recognize the heterogeneity within these two groups and, thus, take into account the differences among women and among men; and that simply because a social process works in a particular way for men does not mean that it will work in the same way for women. The links between regression analyses conducted separately for men and women and these feminist insights are not immediately apparent. Therefore, part of our task in this chapter is to elaborate how our method—which is, in certain respects, unorthodox even for quantitative data analysts—incorporates these understandings.[1]

We hope that we can explain why our method constitutes a worthy—though certainly not the only worthy—approach, one that merits inclusion within the arsenal of diverse methods appropriately used to study gender. At the same time, we hope to convince social scientists who use quantitative methods of the utility of our approach for studying not only participatory differences among groups distinguished by other social characteristics—for example, race, ethnicity, or age[2]—but social group differences with respect to other social matters.

In order to assess whether men are more politically active than women—and, if so, in what ways and by how much—we need a data-gathering technique that will permit us to measure the political participation, in all its forms, of a large number of citizens; to compare women and men, while paying attention to the diversity within each group; and to generalize to the population as a whole on the basis of observations of a finite number of individuals. In order to explain the way the gap in political behavior is shaped by men's and women's distinctive experiences in a variety of institutions, we need analytical techniques that allow us to differentiate between social processes operating for women and for men, to distinguish processes of selection into institutions from experiences within institutions, and to link the effects of one institution to another.

The sections of this chapter do the following:

- Explain and justify the use of sample surveys as the appropriate source of evidence;

---

1. Charles Tilly emphasizes that what he calls bounded categories, like those our method is suited to study, deserve special attention because they provide clearer evidence for the operation of durable inequality, because their boundaries do crucial organizational work, and because categorical differences actually account for much of what ordinary observers take to be results of variation in individual talent or effort. See *Durable Inequality* (Berkeley: University of California Press, 1998), p. 6.

2. Because class boundaries in America tend to be relatively indistinct and class differences tend to fall along a continuum, we would not consider this an appropriate strategy for analyzing class differences.

- Explain and justify the use of multivariate analysis;
- Elaborate a particular analytical strategy involving separate regression equations and what we call outcomes analysis that we use to penetrate the origins of the disparity between men and women in participation;
- Describe the data on which we rely throughout this book.

Even readers familiar with matters such as random sampling and multivariate analysis—who might wish to skip the first two sections—should find that the final two sections (beginning with "Why Separate Analyses?") provide useful background for the conduct of our inquiry. Those who are less familiar with quantitative techniques should, in addition, find the first two sections helpful in understanding how and why we do what we do.

Why Sample Surveys?: Letting the Silent Speak

Students of political participation and feminist scholars share a concern with voice—and a desire to locate the silent and to discern what matters to them. Because it is predicated on the democratic principle of equal voice, survey research, one of the most commonly adopted methods in empirical research, is especially appropriate for our subject, understanding inequalities between men and women in political participation.

Book reviews of works in the social sciences often ask why it is necessary to wade through pages of statistical tables in order to get the message when a few, well-chosen stories about real people would be so much more insightful and interesting. True, a good story often makes a point much more vividly than a statistical table can. But a good story may also give a distorted view of what is typical. In fact, the best stories may be the least typical: the story about the stay-at-home dad, the female CEO of a multinational corporation, or the couple in which she repairs the car and he washes the bathroom floor is a lot more arresting than the opposite. To establish the range and distribution of behavior and to assess what is typical, some kind of systematic data collection is necessary.

Consider, for example, sexual harassment of students on college campuses. When attention was first being drawn to the problem, there were frequent mutterings to the effect that sexual harassment was, in fact, quite rare and that a mountain was being made out of a molehill. Moreover, stories would circulate—without names, of course, out of respect for the privacy of those involved—about the male graduate student harassed by a female professor, about the undergraduate who made a false accusation as a way of extracting a higher grade, or about the tenured professor who was fired for a misunderstanding about a minor infraction. Since then, numerous studies of sexual harassment have been conducted. They vary in the number of cases of harassment they find—often depending on the definition of harassment used and other features of the survey—but all agree that harassment of female students by male faculty is not uncommon.[3] Furthermore, they concur in finding that cases in which a female harasses a male, in which a purported victim knowingly lies about an incident, or in which a professor is sanctioned severely are, while not unknown, exceedingly rare. It is important both to deplore these atypical cases when they arise and to recognize that they are infrequent. Colorful anecdotes often obscure realities that systematic evidence can illumine.

To learn about the characteristics of a very large group of people, collecting information about everyone within a population is certainly not the cheapest—and, if current controversies about the decennial national census are any indication, not necessarily the most accurate—approach. However, as long as a sample is selected in such a way as to eliminate bias and as long as it includes a sufficiently large number of cases for inference, we can use it to generate information about patterns of behavior and belief for the larger population in which we are really interested, but that we do not directly observe.

Random sampling constrains the process by which subjects are

---

3. See Billie Wright Dziech and Linda Weiner, *The Lecherous Professor: Sexual Harassment on Campus*, 2nd ed. (Urbana: University of Illinois Press, 1990), chap. 1, as well as the summary of the literature in Kay Lehman Schlozman, "Sexual Harassment of Students: What I Learned in the Library," *PS: Political Science and Politics* 24 (1991): 236–239. We recognize that behavior on campuses may have changed since these studies were conducted. Nevertheless, any obsolescence in the data does not negate the point that anecdotes that are true but atypical can misrepresent reality.

selected so that there is a known relationship between the people selected to be studied and the population from which they are chosen, yielding—under ideal conditions, which are only approximated in reality—a circumstance such that each member of a population has an equal chance to be counted.[4] In order to generate a representative picture, it is essential not simply to select people who are easy to find and, especially, not to permit respondents to select themselves. If the subjects of study volunteer for that purpose—by, for example, clipping a questionnaire out of a magazine, by calling a phone-in poll, or by otherwise coming forward and making themselves available—the result is a potentially biased sample.

SURVEYS, EQUAL VOICE, AND GENDER POLITICS

Although surveys are an important tool for many kinds of social analysis, they are especially appropriate for our subject: the gender gap in participation. The random sample is a singularly democratic instrument, providing one of the few circumstances in which all citizens have an equal chance of being heard. Our study is predicated on the understanding that, in the real world of politics, voices are not equal. Some people take part in politics and make their wishes loud and clear; others are quiescent. Unlike the respondents to a survey, however, the set of people who express their views through the medium of citizen participation are not representative of the public as a whole. The social processes enhancing the likelihood that some will speak, and others will not, operate in such a way that those who take part are distinctive in many ways. In order to understand the extent of participatory inequality and the processes that create it, it is essential to map out the distribution of politically relevant characteristics—political preferences and needs as well as social characteristics—in the population as a

---

4. Even samples that aspire to randomness have biases that result from the difficulty of locating respondents and refusals by those who are located. The bias thus introduced by the fact that those who cannot be found and those who refuse to be interviewed are likely to have other special characteristics is a serious problem for those who do surveys. Nevertheless, random samples represent a more accurate procedure than less systematic means of selection. On these issues, see John Brehm, *The Phantom Respondents: Opinion Surveys and Political Representation* (Ann Arbor: University of Michigan Press, 1993).

whole. The ideal sample survey—and we must underline that actual surveys, at best, only approximate this ideal—allows us to establish the baseline from which to measure departures from democratic equality.

The random representative sample thus permits us to study individuals and groups who might not otherwise have a voice. Single mothers are a group with obvious needs for governmental assistance: they are disproportionately poor and, if they seek paid work, they may have difficulty finding transportation and will probably have difficulty finding affordable, high-quality day care. Yet as our data will make clear, they are almost totally politically inactive and are therefore invisible in the democratic process. Not only do our survey data allow us to establish that single mothers have low levels of participation, but they allow us to ask why— with often surprising results.

Although the sample survey is the appropriate tool when investigating participatory differences among groups of many kinds, it is particularly important when studying political differences between women and men. Many groups with distinctive political habits—for example, Cuban-Americans or African-Americans— are clustered geographically. Because they live in proximity to one another, their politics may be more easily visible. Group-based differences in issue commitments, propensity to go to the polls, and vote choices can be inferred from the political behavior of the district—levels of turnout, the candidates who are elected, and the issues to which they pay attention. But because women are not geographically separated from men, district-based evidence does not give clues to gender differences. And because men and women are such large groups, relatively small differences in attitudes or behavior have a greater potential political impact than differences of a similar magnitude between smaller groups—say, between Episcopalians and Jews.

We are by no means arguing, however, that sample surveys are the only useful technique for undertaking social inquiry. Surveys are justifiably criticized for failing to capture the historical and social context in which respondents' views are embedded. In addition, even when the questionnaire is long and the questions are well formulated—by no means always the case in political or commercial polls—surveys cannot capture the rich texture of individuals' thinking and experiences. Data from surveys thus gain greater resonance when supplemented by less superficial—but also less systematic—evidence gleaned from other sources: longer, open-ended interviews; participant observation; historical analysis; the media; art and literature; popular culture. Not only do such qualitative sources yield a deeper and more rounded picture of the complexity of social life, but they supply hypotheses worth testing, generating the questions we want to answer more systematically. We have drawn upon insights from qualitative sources in framing the problems that we address and in designing and analyzing our survey. In short, we are not simply methodological pluralists, relying on a set of favored techniques while tolerating others. On the contrary, we believe that the literature on gender and politics is deepened when informed by insights from many kinds of evidence.[5]

Why Multivariate Analysis?: Explaining Gender (Not Sex) Differences

As we made clear at the outset, we did not lack for explanations of the gender gap in civic activity when we began our analysis. Our initial hunches focused on differences between women and men in childhood and adult socialization, available leisure time, psychic space, the stockpile of socioeconomic resources, and power in the family. We also guessed that each of these hunches was likely to be not so much wrong, as incomplete. Each one draws our attention to a single cause, and research on political participation has always shown it to have multiple causes.[6] And as social groups, men and women are diverse with respect to many attributes, a number of

---

5. For an especially powerful example of this sort of multi-method work in the gender and politics literature, see Roberta S. Sigel's creative use of data from surveys and focus groups in *Ambition and Accommodation: How Women View Gender Relations* (Chicago: University of Chicago Press, 1996).

6. See, for example, Lester W. Milbrath and M. L. Goel, *Political Participation,* 2nd ed. (Chicago: Rand McNally, 1977); Steven J. Rosenstone and John Mark Hansen, *Mobilization, Participation, and Democracy in America* (New York: Macmillan, 1993); Sidney Verba, Kay Lehman Schlozman, and Henry E. Brady, *Voice and Equality: Civic Voluntarism in American Politics* (Cambridge: Harvard University Press, 1995); and M. Margaret Conway, *Political Participation in the United States,* 3rd ed. (Washington, D.C.: CQ Press, 2000).

which are relevant to political participation. Hence we need a research technique that allows us to consider many potential causal
factors; to weigh one against another; to see how, separately and
jointly, they lead to activity; and to assess their relative weight in
fostering participation.

MULTIPLE REGRESSION

Our main analytical tool is multiple regression, a statistical technique widely used to link multiple assumed causes, the independent or explanatory variables, to their effect on some outcome, the
dependent variable. In Chapter 6 we will give more detailed guid-
ance for reading regression tables. For those not familiar with multiple regression, let us, at this point, briefly outline some of its features.

As a statistical tool, multiple regression recognizes the fact that
social reality is messy and complex: we live in a multivariate
world. This technique allows us to deal with multiple overlapping
causes and to distinguish those causes that are systematic across
people and situations from those that are idiosyncratic to particular people and situations. Regression analysis considers a set of
possible systematic determinants of the dependent variable and as-
signs to each one a *regression coefficient,* which measures its effect
on the dependent variable, taking into account—controlling for—
the other factors included in the analysis. The regression coefficient, which is the crucial measure of a regression analysis, thus
tells us how much a change in an independent variable affects a
dependent variable, everything else remaining the same.

Our ability to isolate the effect of one explanatory variable on a
dependent variable while controlling for other possible causal or
confounding factors depends upon having all other potentially relevant variables in the analysis. If some explanatory variable is left
out, what looks like the effect of a particular causal factor may be
the result of an omitted variable that causes both the explanatory
variable and the dependent variable. To cite the textbook example:
there is a strong, positive relationship between shoe size and spelling ability among children. Do big feet produce good spellers in
the way that strong muscles might produce good weight lifters?
Once we recall that not only are eighth graders better spellers than

toddlers, but their feet are bigger, the mystery disappears. Age, which is related to both shoe size and spelling ability, was omitted from the original formulation. Multiple regression permits the consideration of many variables at the same time; however, if an important variable is omitted, an endemic problem in multivariate regression analysis, the causal story may be inaccurate.

Ignoring the issue of multivariate causality and the implications of omitted variables is often a source of misunderstanding in research on gender differences. As is well known, there are, in the aggregate, differences between men and women on many dimensions. There are also differences of similar or greater magnitude among women and among men on these same dimensions. The heart of our enterprise will be to understand how a variety of causes work together to foster political participation and thus what it is about being male or female that produces the disparity in political activity.[7] For example, studies concur in finding differences in socioeconomic status to be relevant to differences in civic and political involvement. As we shall see, however, men and women differ with respect to each of the components of socioeconomic status: levels of education, income, and work force status and, if employed, in the kinds of jobs they hold. When we use multivariate analysis to sort out the impact on participation of the various aspects of socioeconomic status, we find both that the component of socioeconomic status that matters most for participation is education and that gender differences in education, income, work force status, and occupation explain a significant portion of the gender gap in activity.

We must, however, take the discussion a couple of steps further. The researcher who fails to account for social class in explaining

---

7. We are squarely in the tradition of gender and political participation scholars like Susan Welch ("Women as Political Animals? A Test of Some Explanations for Male-Female Political Participation Differences," *American Journal of Political Science* 21 [1977]: 712), who long ago pointed out that many explanations for gender differences "might be working together," that these explanations were "neither contradictory nor mutually exclusive," and Virginia Sapiro, who worried about scholarship that focused on some adult roles and not others, generating a "selective" and potentially misleading set of conclusions in *The Political Integration of Women* (Urbana: University of Illinois Press, 1983), p. 61. Both Welch and Sapiro argued for multiple regression.

participatory differences between women and men has gotten the gender story wrong. Nonetheless, the analyst who sees gender differences fade when social class is introduced in a multiple regression and concludes thereby that gender is not important in relation to civic activity has also gotten the gender story wrong—for two reasons. First, the fact that the "real" origins of the gender gap in civic activity are rooted, in part, in socioeconomic differences does not change the fact that women are less politically active—with the consequence that public officials are hearing less from women and their political voices are muted. Second, even if socioeconomic differences are the driving force behind the gender gap in political activity, these disparities in class have a lot to do with gender. The processes that produce differences between men and women in education, income, and occupation are deeply entwined with social expectations and roles that are differentiated by gender. Our inquiry depends heavily on this understanding.

Why Separate Analyses?: Allowing for Different Processes for Women and Men

Most of the analysis in this book is based on separate regression equations for women and men. This approach, which is not standard in the field, goes to the heart of our research strategy.[8] Ordinarily a multivariate analysis that seeks to estimate the effect of gender on some outcome, the dependent variable, uses a single regression equation for the whole sample. Along with other information about each case in the analysis is a dichotomy measuring whether that individual is female or male. In the resulting equation, the size of the regression coefficient for gender is interpreted as a measure of the effect of gender on the dependent variable when other variables are taken into account. So, for example, an equation predicting earnings will have a substantial coefficient for gender, indicating that women have significantly lower earnings

8. In one of the earliest systematic examinations of gender and political participation, Susan Welch used separate regressions for women and men; for reasons of space, however, she was not able to present those regressions in her article. See "Women as Political Animals?," p. 719.

than men do. When work force experience—which is related both to gender and to earnings—is added to the analysis, the coefficient shrinks. That is, because women are more likely than men to have interrupted careers, when work force experience is introduced into the analysis, the effect of gender on earnings is diminished.[9]

This approach is quite valid, and we will use it from time to time when appropriate. However, it is predicated on the supposition that the social processes under examination operate in the same way for women and men. Returning to the example of predicting earnings, including women and men in a single analysis makes the assumption that education, work force experience, and the other factors introduced to explain earnings yield the same returns in earnings to men and to women. This assumption may not be warranted. Our common-sense understandings—and theorizing about gender—suggest that women and men often have different experiences within social institutions. Rather than make presumptions, we shall examine whether social processes work in the same way, or in different ways, for men and women.

An example from another field might clarify this logic. At one time, the trials required by the federal government to evaluate the safety and effectiveness of drugs included male subjects only, an approach that was criticized as discriminatory. Under federal law, most of these experiments must now have both male and female subjects. Nevertheless, the revised model for drug research has also been criticized, because the results of drug experiments are not analyzed separately for women and men. According to the critics, physiological differences between the sexes imply that men and women may respond differently to the proposed treatments. When data for women and men are combined, researchers cannot discern any significant differences between women and men in the proposed treatments' therapeutic value or side effects.[10]

In general, we use separate regression equations for women and men in order to differentiate the way that social processes work

9. For an important, early discussion of this issue, see Sapiro, *The Political Integration of Women*, pp. 58–59.

10. Robert Pear, "Research Neglects Women, Studies Find," *New York Times*, April 30, 2000, p. 16.

for the two groups. This approach allows us to search for the sources of gender differences and to locate the contexts within which gender differences are constructed.[11]

INCORPORATING HETEROGENEITY AMONG MEN AND AMONG WOMEN

We have stressed that men and women are very heterogeneous groupings—differentiated by age, race or ethnicity, social class, and many other attributes into sub-groups whose political and social experiences vary substantially. Multivariate analysis allows us to take this diversity into account by considering the role of gender in a framework that controls for many other social characteristics. However, just as we felt that we could not assume that the social processes that lead to political participation operate in the same way for women and men, we might ask whether they operate in the same way for young men as for elderly men or in the same way for women at home as for women in the work force. It is not feasible to elaborate the logic we have just outlined ad infinitum by comparing all sub-sets of women and men. However, we shall focus attention on a variety of sub-groups—for example, women and men of different educational levels, in different family and work situations, and with different religious and social views.

In particular, we shall devote attention to women and men differentiated by race and ethnicity. To consider together all women—or all men—without acknowledging the distinctive political and social experiences of Anglo-White, African-American, and Latina women—or men—is to neglect an important reality about America. We shall pay special attention to the intersection of two important social cleavages, on one hand, gender, and on the other, race or ethnicity, asking not only how Black, Latino, and Anglo-White women and men differ from one another but

---

11. Statistically sophisticated readers will recognize that the problem we discuss can also be solved by using interaction terms in a single equation, a strategy we adopt on occasion. Interaction terms measure the effect of a particular independent variable for given levels of another independent variable. Thus, in the earnings example, we could use a single equation with interaction terms to assess the impact of education on earnings separately for men and women.

whether the social processes we observe for men and women in general work the same way within these groups.

Why Linked Regressions?: Viewing Women and Men in Context

One weakness of surveys as a source of insight about human behavior is that they snatch the individual out of social context. The survey is an individualistic tool, and inferences drawn from surveys tend to treat respondents as unconnected individuals. Nevertheless, as we discussed in Chapter 1, gender differences are contextual, their extent and nature varying across social and cultural domains. What it means to be male rather than female differs depending upon the beliefs and values of others with whom we associate and the institutions with which we affiliate. By relating the individuals, and couples, who responded to our various surveys to institutional contexts—the home, the workplace, non-political organizations, and churches—we hope to transcend one of the limitations of the individually based survey.

The key to understanding gender differences in political activity is the impact of institutions on the acquisition by women and men of the factors that facilitate participation. For each institution, we model a two-stage process. The first stage entails *selection* into the institution, the processes—which may be different for women and men—by which individuals come to enter the work force or to be affiliated with a church or an organization. The second stage involves *treatment* within institutions, what those affiliated with institutions experience once they are there.[12] We can illustrate with reference to participatory factors acquired in religious institutions. Women, who are, on average, more religious than men, are more likely to be affiliated with and active in a church. Once in a congregation, however, men—who are more likely to be officers or on

---

12. We use the terms "selection" and "treatment" in a manner analogous to their use in experimental research. In experiments, there is a selection process by which people come to be experimental subjects and a treatment process within the experiment. For one of the first efforts to untangle issues of selection and treatment in the gender and political participation literature, see Kristi Andersen and Elizabeth A. Cook, "Women, Work, and Political Attitudes," *American Journal of Political Science* 29 (1985): 606–625.

the board—actually acquire a slightly larger stockpile of church-based participatory factors. These complex processes interact to produce a small advantage to women in participatory factors acquired in religious institutions, the net result of strong selection processes favoring women and weak treatment processes favoring men.

For each institution, we use multiple regression to understand both stages. First, we use regression to estimate the factors associated with selection into the institution. On the basis of the results of that process, we then use regression to model what happens there, the allocational processes that yield differences in participatory factors.[13]

LINKING INSTITUTIONS

Not only do we link selection and treatment processes for a single institution, but we link one institution to another and, eventually, to political participation. By using a chain of regression analyses—conducted separately for men and women so as to capture any gender differences in these institutional processes—in which the outcome of the process in one institution becomes an input into the process in another institution, we demonstrate how a process in one institution affects what happens in other institutions. For example, we show how the experiences of women and men within the family help to explain their differential work force and religious participation.

Our analysis of the origins of political activity—and of the gen-

---

13. In earlier work, we used even more complicated models to consider the possibility that treatment in an institution might depend on just how the person arrived in the institution in the first place. We explored this possibility with respect to the most obvious potential site where this kind of linkage might occur *and* with respect to the site where our data are the most capable of estimating such a model—the workplace. These more complicated models suggested that selection and treatment—even in the case of women and the workplace—are relatively independent processes.

Thus, throughout this book, we will use the simpler models that treat selection and treatment independently. We *will* link these stages through the resource endowments that one stage produces for use in the next stage. Surprisingly, perhaps, the stages we study here are linked via the resource endowments they produce and not because treatment in an institution depends on how the person arrived in the institution in the first place. See Kay Lehman Schlozman, Nancy E. Burns, and Sidney Verba, "What Happened at Work Today?: A Multi-Stage Model of Gender, Employment, and Political Participation," *Journal of Politics* 61 (1999): 29–54.

der difference in political activity—thus takes us through a chain of processes. In one set of links, we analyze how men's and women's family experiences affect entry into the work force, how experiences at work lead to the acquisition of civic skills and exposure to requests for activity, and, finally, how civic skills and requests for activity foster political participation. Multiple regression allows us to estimate the effect of processes at one stage on the next. The regression coefficient for an independent variable such as the number of hours spent working indicates how it influences a dependent variable, for example, the number of civic skills acquired on the job. The dependent variable then becomes the independent variable in the next link of the chain. The regression coefficient for work-based civic skills tells us how much each skill increases political activity.[14] Because the analyses are conducted separately, we can assess whether these processes operate differently for men and women and understand how institutions operate to create gender differences.

Why Outcomes Analysis?: Incorporating Both Level and Effect

This set of interlinked regressions provides the raw material for understanding the complex origins of the gender gap in participation. In the pair of regressions that culminates our analysis of the sources of the gender gap, the regression coefficients estimate, for men and for women, the impact of each of a variety of institutionally based factors on political participation. However, it is not enough to know the *effects* of these variables, that is, how much a given increase in a participatory factor like education, family income, or civic skills would boost women's or men's political activity. In order to disaggregate the disparity between men and women in participation into its components, we need to know about gender differences in the *levels* of participatory factors. That is, we need to know whether men and women differ in the amount of ed-

---

14. This is exactly what we meant when we said earlier that institutions will be linked through the endowments produced at one stage and used in the next stage. This linkage—and not the coefficient linkages in traditional Heckman selection processes—creates the connections between the institutions we examine here.

ucation, family income, or civic skills they command. We might think of these two components as the stock of an independent variable acquired by women and men and the rate of return for that variable in terms of political activity.

In order to incorporate consideration of both level and effect into our results, we perform what we call an outcomes analysis. Although we shall explain our method more fully when we introduce it in Chapter 10, at this point we wish to establish that it permits us to decompose the disparity between women and men in participation into its components. We show how gender differences in the level or the effect of each of the factors that foster participation—say, family income or activity in high school—make contributions of different sizes to the gender gap in activity.

The Citizen Participation Study

The principal empirical basis for this enterprise is the Citizen Participation Study, a multi-wave major survey of civic engagement in a variety of domains. The first stage consisted of over 15,000 telephone interviews with a random sample of the American public conducted during the last six months of 1989. These 20-minute screener interviews provided a profile of political and non-political activity as well as basic demographic information. Because the original telephone survey—which we call the Screener Survey—was a random sample, it provided the baseline from which to select a second sample that included disproportionate numbers from small groups in society, for example, Latinos or major campaign donors. In the spring of 1990, we conducted what we call the Main Survey—much longer, in-person interviews with a subset of 2,517 of the original 15,000 respondents chosen so as to produce a disproportionate number of political activists as well as African-Americans and Latinos. Since members of these groups were chosen according to known probabilities, the resulting sub-sample can be treated as a random sample—once appropriate case weights have been applied.[15] This survey, from which we derive most of the analysis in the book, is unusual in that it contains large numbers of

---

15. For further technical information about the construction of the sample, see Verba, Schlozman, and Brady, *Voice and Equality,* app. A.

respondents drawn from relatively small groups, while retaining the properties of a random sample.[16]

With respect to its substantive coverage, the Citizen Participation Study is unusually well suited for exploring gender differences in political activity: it includes an expansive definition of what constitutes participation, allowing us, for the first time, to subject to empirical test the contention that women and men specialize in different kinds of voluntary activity. In terms of political activity, the survey asked about an array of citizen activities: modes of participation that require money as well as those that demand inputs of time; unconventional as well as conventional activity; electoral activities as well as more direct forms of the communication of messages to public officials; and activities performed alone as well as those undertaken jointly. We can thus move beyond voting and electoral activity to encompass contacts with government officials; attendance at protests, marches, or demonstrations; involvement in organizations that take stands in politics; informal efforts to address community problems; and voluntary service on local-governing boards or regular attendance at meetings of such boards. In addition, we asked about volume of activity—not only whether respondents had engaged in the activity but how much they had done.

For the third wave, or the Follow-up, we conducted telephone interviews consisting of items about social characteristics and voluntary activity from the initial questionnaires as well as new items about family characteristics with 609 of the respondents from the second wave.[17] Once again, with the application of appropriate sampling weights, the data from the third wave—like the data from the second wave—can be treated as an ordinary random sample.

Of this third group, 382 were married at the time of the third in-

16. We use the oversamples to increase the reliability of our reports about the participation of these small groups. Thus our descriptive data for these groups rest on many more respondents than would ordinarily show up in a sample of 2,517 people. In addition, when we focus solely on the groups that were oversampled, we maintain the sample weights, but we increase the sample size in recognition of the fact that our analysis rests on more respondents than would appear in a typical random sample.

17. For the design of the third-wave questionnaire, we are grateful for the advice offered by a panel of experts in the field: Ted Huston, Jane J. Mansbridge, and Laura Stoker.

terview.[18] For married respondents we also conducted separate interviews with their spouses—using special techniques to ensure that the members of the couple could not monitor each other's answers.[19] The data from the Couples Survey provide basic information on the members of the couples sample who were entering our study for the first time and allowed us to get up-to-date information on the people interviewed in the first and second waves. In addition, we have independent reports from each spouse about family and household matters. Thus we are able to combine information from wife and husband to typify the family. We can also consider inconsistencies in reports from partners and incorporate any discrepancies into our characterization of the family.

In the course of our analysis, we will draw on these various samples. Their complexity gives us options. Although the number of variables in the Screener is limited, we can use its sample of 15,000 respondents when we require a great many cases. The second-wave sample, which is the principal basis for our analysis of the effects of secondary institutions, permits us to differentiate among

---

18. It is important to note that the respondent's marital status at the time of the second wave was not a criterion in interviewing spouses. We did not specifically select couples who were married in both waves, thus overrepresenting those with marriages of longer duration.

We considered interviewing the domestic partners of unmarried, heterosexual and homosexual respondents. However, there were simply too few respondents in these categories to pursue this approach. A study seeking to compare married couples and unmarried couples would need to follow a strategy analogous to the one that we followed: a large initial screener followed by oversampling of unmarried respondents living with partners of the same or opposite sex. Other techniques for generating large numbers of respondents, such as those used by Philip Blumstein and Pepper Schwartz (*American Couples: Money, Work, Sex* [New York: William Morrow, 1983]), in their insightful study of married and unmarried homosexual and heterosexual couples, sacrifice the capacities of a random sample.

19. We mailed respondents a series of cards—analogous to the cards used to inquire about family income in an in-person interview. These cards contained the answer alternatives for many items, especially sensitive ones. When answering a question, the respondent was directed to say the letter corresponding to the category of the response rather than to express the response in words. In this way, someone else in the room would have difficulty knowing what the respondent was saying to the interviewer over the phone. This approach added to the existing advantages of surveying couples by telephone: "By telephone, others present in the room cannot hear the questions and may have little information upon which to guess the meaning of the answers. Telephone interviews may feel more private, since third parties only hear one side." William S. Aquilino, "Effects of Spouse Presence during the Interview on Survey Responses Concerning Marriage," *Public Opinion Quarterly* 57 (1993): 375.

different kinds of women and men. With the third-wave Couples Survey, which places individuals in a wife-husband setting, we can observe patterns of interaction and assess the impact of family life on civic engagement. Ordinarily we rely on our own surveys because they offer the most complete information about voluntary involvement in political and secular life, about experiences in social institutions, and about the structures and beliefs that create gender differences. Occasionally, however, we introduce data from other national surveys when they have properties—for example, a large sample of young people or over-time data—that our own data do not.

DISTINGUISHING POLITICAL AND NON-POLITICAL ACTIVITY

The Citizen Participation Study contains an unusually detailed battery of questions about voluntary activity outside of politics— in churches, secular charities, and non-political organizations. We asked about the respondent's involvement in each of no fewer than twenty categories of organizations—fraternal groups, unions, political issue organizations, hobby clubs, neighborhood or homeowner associations, and so on. We followed up this organizational census with an extensive battery about the single organization that was most important to the respondent.[20] With respect to religious participation, we asked about not only attendance at religious services but also involvement in educational, charitable, and social activities associated with a church—apart from attendance at services. Systematic data on participation in these domains are very rare, and systematic data that permit comparisons between political participation and voluntary activity outside of politics have been, until now, non-existent.

Since it is novel to bring together data about participation in political and non-political realms, it is important both to distinguish them analytically and to recognize the fuzziness of the empirical

---

20. Because the interview was already very long, we decided to ask a series of follow-up questions about a single organization only. The "most important organization" is the one to which the respondent gives either the most time or the most money—or, if these are different organizations—the one that the respondent designated as "most important" to him or her.

boundary that separates them. We have defined political participation as activities that seek to influence either directly or indirectly what the government does. However, voluntary activity in both the religious and the secular domains outside of politics intersects with politics in many ways. First, as we shall see, participation in these spheres—for example, running the PTA fund drive or managing the church soup kitchen—can develop skills that are transferable to politics even when the activity itself has nothing to do with politics. In addition, these non-political institutions can act as the locus of attempts at political mobilization: church and organization members make social contacts and, in the process, become part of networks through which requests for participation in politics are mediated. Moreover, those who take part in religious or organizational activity are exposed to political cues and messages—as when a minister gives a sermon on a political topic or when organization members chat informally about politics at a meeting. Furthermore, churches and, especially, non-profit organizations undertake many activities—ranging from aiding the homeless to funding cancer research to supporting the symphony—that are also undertaken by governments here and abroad. Finally, both religious institutions and voluntary associations get involved in politics, and their attempts at influencing policy outcomes constitute a crucial source of input to public officials about citizen views and preferences.

These issues are especially complicated when it comes to organizational involvement. Support of an organization that takes stands on public issues, even passive support or support motivated by concerns other than government influence, represents a form of political activity. For example, a worker might join a union in order to keep a job and to enjoy the benefits of collective bargaining. Nonetheless, because unions are deeply involved in politics—lobbying legislatures, funding campaigns, and the like—to be a union member is implicitly to take part in politics. What makes the world of voluntary associations so complex for an inquiry like this one is the substantial variation among organizations in the extent to which they maintain an ongoing presence in politics and mix political and non-political means of furthering their members' interests. At one end of the continuum are organizations like the National Abortion Rights Action League or the National Taxpayers Union, for which political goals are intrinsic to organizational objectives and a high proportion of organizational activity is directed toward influencing political outcomes. At the other are organizations like a local bowling league or garden club that have little or nothing to do with politics.

When we discussed what we mean by "voluntary political activity" in Chapter 1, we made several important distinctions with respect to the domain of our concern. However, it is clear that, no matter how sophisticated our conceptualization of this terrain, what really matters are the actual measures. Therefore, as we proceed, we shall make our measures explicit and point out the discretionary decisions about the classification of specific activities that sit on the borders of what are analytically distinguishable domains.

Conclusion

We have outlined a strategy for understanding the many sources of the disparity between men and women in political participation. Our approach is predicated on the use of a tool that is invaluable in understanding social processes, the random sample, a tool that, because it gives a voice to those who are politically silent, is especially appropriate for studies of political activity. Because we are concerned with an outcome that has many causes, we use multivariate techniques. A series of multiple regressions allows us to assess the variables associated with selection into and treatment within a series of interlinked institutions and the effects of various institutionally based participatory factors on political activity. In order to understand whether these processes operate in the same way for women and men, we conduct these analyses separately for the two groups. Then, in order to demonstrate the relative weight of each of a variety of factors in causing the gender gap in participation, we combine the results of these analyses—which show the effects of various factors on men's and women's participation—with data about the levels of each of these factors that women and men command in an outcomes analysis.

This set of procedures illumines not only the origins of gender differences in political participation but also the social processes that result in gender differences in a variety of domains of everyday life. At one point in the not too distant past, it was common to distinguish "sex," which referred to physiologically determined attributes of males and females, from "gender," which referred to those that reflect the results of social and cultural expectations and experiences. A recent reference to "the gender of an unborn baby"[21] suggests that the distinction has fallen into desuetude in popular parlance. Nevertheless, to the extent that it remains an analytically useful one, we can summarize our approach by claiming that we are able to go from "sex" to "gender" using multivariate analysis.

We believe that this approach has utility beyond the problem we set out for ourselves here. First, it can be used to understand differences among groups having relatively clearly demarcated boundaries—for example, groups defined by race, religion, or age. Furthermore, it can be used to understand the complex roots of group differences with respect to other social outcomes beyond political participation. Nevertheless, we wish to reiterate that we do not consider ours to be the only viable method for comprehending the social construction of group differences. On the contrary, we maintain that it should be one important arrow in the quiver of approaches used by social scientists and suggest that we learn more about problems with complicated origins when multiple approaches are used.

21. Carol Saline, "Mothers, Daughters, Sisters," *Ladies' Home Journal,* November 1998, p. 300.

3

⚬⚬⚬

Civic Activity:
Political and Non-Political

If we are to understand the extent and sources of differential involvement of women and men in civic life, we must begin by mapping the terrain of civic action—how much and what kinds of voluntary participation take place. In this chapter, we look directly at activity: what men and women do in political and non-political civic life. In the one that follows, we consider the more subjective side of civic involvement: what people know and care about, what issue concerns they bring to civic involvement, and what values are expressed and gratifications are derived through voluntary activity. In these two chapters, we treat women and men as social categories and are concerned with describing, not explaining, gender differences in voluntary activity.

Gender Differences in Political Participation:
Early Findings

It is widely known that there are gender differences in political activity. One of the early findings that emerged from the systematic study of the behavior of citizens in American politics was that men were more likely than women to take part in political life.[1] These studies have come in for criticism on several grounds, all of which

---

1. See, for example, Angus Campbell, Philip E. Converse, Warren E. Miller, and Donald E. Stokes, *The American Voter* (New York: John Wiley and Sons, 1960), pp. 483–493;

61

we shall assess in the course of this inquiry.[2] First, scholars point out that small—and sometimes not statistically significant—differences were invested with too much importance.[3] Second, critics argue that these early studies ignored the pivotal role of differential access to political resources. Women may be less politically active, these critics argued, because they are disadvantaged with respect to the resources that facilitate political activity—that is, because they may have lower levels of education, earn less money, or have less free time.

Another line of reasoning holds that, if we really want to understand women's political activities, we should think not only in terms of "more or less" but also in terms of "different." We have already mentioned that the process of becoming involved in politics might be different for men and women. Gender differences in the patterns of citizens' lives might mean not only differences in the amounts of resources accumulated by women and men but also differences in the mix of resources in the respective stockpiles and in the utility of various resources for political activity. Studies

---

Robert E. Lane, *Political Life: Why People Get Involved in Politics* (New York: Free Press of Glencoe, 1959), pp. 209–216, 354, 355; Maurice Duverger, *The Political Role of Women* (Paris: UNESCO, 1955). In addition to the investigations of adult political behavior are socialization studies that have considered gender differences in children's political orientations. See, for example, Fred Greenstein, *Children and Politics* (New Haven: Yale University Press, 1965), chap. 6; Robert D. Hess and Judith V. Torney, *The Development of Political Attitudes in Children* (Garden City, N.Y.: Doubleday, Anchor Books, 1968), chap. 8; and Dean Jaros, *Socialization to Politics* (New York: Praeger, 1973), pp. 44–45, 81–82.

2. There are numerous assessments of this literature. See, for example, Susan Bourque and Jean Grossholtz, "Politics as an Unnatural Practice: Political Science Looks at Female Participation," *Politics and Society* 4 (1974): 255–266; Murray Goot and Elizabeth Reid, *Women and Voting Studies: Mindless Matrons or Sexist Scientism?* (Beverly Hills, Calif.: Sage, 1975); Susan Welch, "Women as Political Animals? A Test of Some Explanations for Male-Female Political Participation Differences," *American Journal of Political Science* 21 (1977): 712–714; and Vicky Randall, *Women and Politics: An International Perspective,* 2nd ed. (Chicago: University of Chicago Press, 1987), chap. 2.

3. For example, in the graphic presentations of their data in *The Development of Political Attitudes in Children,* Hess and Torney show only the truncated portion of the scale in which real values fall. Thus, although a scale measuring children's evaluations of presidential responsiveness can take on values ranging from 2 to 9, the y-axis of Hess and Torney's graph (p. 206) ranges only from 6.42 to 8.18. This practice has the effect of exaggerating the small—but very consistent—differences between boys and girls.

of political elites, for example, have shown that the traditional route to elected office for men, through careers in fields like law and business, is less typical for women, who often aspire to public office after experience in voluntary organizations.[4] There may be analogous differences with respect to the pathways to citizen activity. As indicated, in order not to obscure real gender differences in the processes of politicization we always use separate explanatory models for men and women.

Still another criticism, one that is especially germane to our concerns in this chapter, stresses "different" with respect to activity itself. This line of reasoning takes issue with the very definition of what constitutes political activity, arguing that overemphasis upon voting and other electoral activities leads scholars to underestimate women's political involvement because it ignores alternative modes of participation—for example, organization, protest, and grassroots community activity—in which women have always taken part. The necessary corrective is an understanding of political participation that would encompass modes of involvement less formal, less conventional, and less nationally centered than those documented in many surveys.[5]

---

4. On differential patterns of recruitment of political elites, see Jeanne J. Kirkpatrick, *Political Woman* (New York: Basic Books, 1974), chap. 4; Susan J. Carroll, *Women as Candidates in American Politics* (Bloomington: Indiana University Press, 1985), chap. 5; and Irwin N. Gertzog, *Congressional Women*, 2nd ed. (Westport, Conn.: Praeger, 1995), chaps. 2–3.

5. This general point is made by many authors. For an especially articulate and concrete exposition of this perspective, see Randall, *Women and Politics*, pp. 50ff.

It may be that the reason mainstream political science has developed a reputation for slighting nonelectoral forms of citizen participation is that the single best source of continuing survey data is the biennial American National Election Study, which—because it is anchored in national elections—naturally emphasizes voting and other forms of electoral participation. A number of the most important studies in the field of gender and political behavior use data from the American National Election Studies. See, for example, Kristi Andersen, "Working Women and Political Participation, 1952–1972," *American Journal of Political Science* 19 (1975): 439–453; Welch, "Women as Political Animals?" pp. 711–730; Kristi Andersen and Elizabeth A. Cook, "Women, Work, and Political Attitudes," *American Journal of Political Science* 29 (1985): 606–625; Karen Beckwith, *American Women and Political Participation: The Impacts of Work, Generation, and Feminism* (New York: Greenwood Press, 1986); Sue Tolleson Rinehart, *Gender Consciousness and Politics* (New York: Routledge, Chapman, and Hall, 1992).

Gender Disparities in Political Activity

When we expand the scope of what we mean by political participation, are there differences between women and men in the amount and kind of activity they undertake? Is the disparity between men and women in participation especially pronounced for electoral activity and negligible—or even reversed—for organization-based activity, protest, and informal local activity?

Figure 3.1 presents data on the proportion who engage in various political acts. What we see there does not fully confirm our expectations about gender differences in political participation. For each kind of activity except for attending protests, there is a gender difference, with women less active than men.[6] These gender differences range from almost imperceptible in the case of voting, working in campaigns, and serving in a voluntary capacity on a local government board, to statistically noticeable in the case of working informally to deal with a community problem, to somewhat larger in the case of making campaign contributions, contacting public officials,[7] and affiliation with—that is, membership in or contributions to—organizations that take stands in politics. To the extent that the percentage of citizens who engage in a particular political activity is a measure of how hard or easy that act is, the size of the gender gap is not related to the difficulty of participatory acts. In both absolute and relative terms, the gap is no larger for difficult acts such as working in a campaign, serving on a local board, or protesting than it is for making campaign contri-

---

6. For most of these measures, the time frame is the twelve months preceding the interview. However, for working in campaigns and making campaign contributions we asked about the preceding presidential election cycle beginning in January 1988. For two activities in which only a small proportion of respondents reported taking part, serving on local boards and protesting, we include activity over a two-year period.

7. It is worth noting that there is virtually no difference between women and men who get in touch with public officials with respect to whether the matter about which they contact the official is particularized (that is, germane only to themselves or their families) or a policy issue of more general concern. Discussing their most recent contact, 22 percent of the men and 21 percent of the women indicated that their most recent contact was about a particularized concern. The men (36 percent) were slightly more likely than the women (31 percent) to indicate that they knew the government official with whom they got in touch before they made the contact.

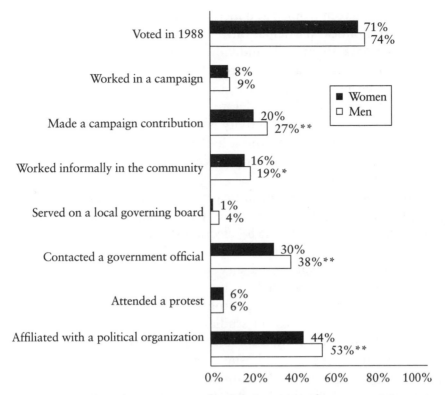

Figure 3.1 Political Participation by Gender. *Significant at <.05;
**significant at <.01. (Citizen Participation Study—Main Survey)

butions, contacting public officials, or being involved in a political
organization that takes stands in politics.

In addition, the gender differences do not disappear when we
expand the scope of participation beyond electoral participation.
These data suggest that women participate nearly as much as, but
not more than, men in community activity. In fact, there is a slight
advantage to men in the formal political activity of serving on a local government board as well as in more informal, ad hoc activities such as working with others in the community or getting involved in a political organization. This pattern does not hold,
however, for one other non-institutional activity—protesting—in
which women and men participate equally. In short, the small dif-

ferences between women and men persist even after we expand the scope of political participation.

When data about these individual political acts are aggregated into a single scale that ranges from 0 to 8, women perform, on average, 1.96 political acts; men, on average, 2.27. This difference can best be described as moderate, not cavernous. The gender disparity in overall political activity is roughly the same as the difference associated with one and a half years of additional schooling and about the same as the difference between African-Americans and Anglo-Whites.

We must add one important caveat to these data. As in all surveys, the figures for voter turnout are exaggerated. Data from polls taken just after the 1988 election show women to have been more likely than men to have gone to the polls: according to a large government-sponsored survey, 56.4 percent of men and 58.3 percent of women reported voting in 1988.[8] These figures are still inflated, but are closer to the actual turnout than the figures from our survey. Vote validation studies, which suggest that men are slightly more likely to misrepresent having gone to the polls than women are, help us to understand this reversal of the gender gap with respect to turnout.[9] Unfortunately, we have no analogous method of ascertaining the extent of, or gender bias in, over-reporting for other activities.[10] Nevertheless, a possible masculine tendency to claim credit should be borne in mind.

LOCAL AND NATIONAL

Interestingly, data not included in Figure 3.1 also call into question another political stereotype—the notion that women are local specialists. Each time a respondent indicated having engaged in a

---

8. See U.S. Bureau of the Census, *Statistical Abstract of the United States: 1990,* 110th ed. (Washington, D.C.: U.S. Government Printing Office, 1990), p. 262.

9. See Michael W. Traugott and John P. Katosh, "Response Validity in Surveys of Voting Behavior," *Public Opinion Quarterly* 43 (1979): 359–377.

10. However, the Cronbach's alphas for men's (.62) and women's (.63) participation scales are nearly identical, which suggests that, if men are exaggerating, they are exaggerating so systematically that the internal correlations among the items in the scale are remaining exactly the same.

political act, we asked a series of follow-up questions about the activity, including whether it was national, state, or local (that is, whether the candidate benefiting from a contribution was running for national, state, or local office; whether the issue in the protest was national, state, or local; or whether the public official contacted held national, state, or local office). Women were only slightly more likely than men to confine their political activity to sub-national politics: 53 percent of the women, as opposed to 49 percent of the men, who participated in any way beyond voting had no activity at the national level.

TIME AND MONEY TO POLITICS

We have considered what women and men do—how many are active in what kinds of activity—without paying attention to the volume of activity. Table 3.1 shows, for men and women who undertake various forms of political activity, how much they do: that is, the average number of hours or dollars contributed. Thus these data differ from the data in Figure 3.1 in that they show the amount of participatory input once the threshold of activity has been crossed, rather than the proportion who are active in a particular way. In Table 3.1, and most other tables thereafter, we indicate a statistically significant difference in means with a symbol, ⇔.[11] In these data, the striking contrast is not among the several kinds of political activity, but is rather between time and money as inputs. With respect to time, once active, women seem to give more hours to politics than do men who take part. When it comes to money, however, the pattern is quite different. In each of the three domains about which we asked—contributions to campaigns, to a political organization, and in response to a mail solicitation—among donors, men give more than women do. In short, gender differences in participation seem to have less to do with

11. This symbol ⇔ indicates that the difference between means is probably not the result of chance. Thus, there is less than one chance in twenty that the gender difference in the size of campaign contributions results from chance. The larger the difference between the mean for men and women, the larger the size of the groups on which the inference is based, and the smaller the variability within each group, the surer we can be in not rejecting the difference as real, rather than the result of a statistical fluke.

Table 3.1 Voluntary Contributions of Time and Money to Politics (among those who gave time or money)[a]

	Women		Men
Contributions to Political Campaigns			
Mean hours	7.9	⇔	7.2
Mean dollars	$223	⇔	$306
Contributions to Political Organization[b]			
Mean hours	3.2		2.8
Mean dollars	$227	⇔	$390
Other Political Activity			
Mean hours informal community work	3.7	⇔	2.2
Mean dollars in response to mail solicitation	$100		$136

Source: Citizen Participation Study—Main Survey.

a. Appendix A contains the valid number of cases for these and other measures used in the tables.

b. Main organization that takes stands in politics only.

⇔ Difference between women and men is statistically significant at the .05 level.

whether an activity is conventional or unconventional, formal or informal, electoral or direct than with whether the form of participatory capital is dollars or hours.

The (Un)Changing Gender Gap in Political Activity

Since the past quarter century has witnessed so many changes in gender roles, we were led to inquire whether the small but consistent gender gap that we saw in Figure 3.1 was wider in the past. Although the Citizen Participation Study does not permit us to address this question, a new data set, the Roper Trends in American Political Participation, contains information collected over two decades about Americans' participation in twelve kinds of political activity.[12] Figure 3.2 shows the average political activity of

---

12. From the end of 1973 to the middle of 1994, the Roper polling organization conducted ten polls each year, with about 2,000 Americans in each survey. Each poll asked an identical battery of twelve items covering many different types of political participation. We are grateful to Henry Brady, Andrea Campbell, and Robert Putnam, who acquired these data from Roper with support from the Pew Charitable Trusts and shared them with us. We

men and women from 1973 through 1994.[13] When we consider the over-time average for all twelve political activities in Figure 3.2a, two regularities are apparent. First, these data confirm the overall decline in political activity that others have documented.[14] In addition, they show a small but persistent gender gap in political activity that seems to have narrowed somewhat, though not dramatically, over the period.

Decomposing the scale for overall participation into its three constituent parts in Figure 3.2b–d replicates the patterns we have just described.[15] The gap is modest but persistent. Across the various kinds of activity, the lines for women and men move in tandem and almost never converge or cross. In summary, longitudinal data show the expected convergence between women and men, but the overall pattern is one of greater stability than of change.

---

are also very appreciative of the tremendous effort invested by Brady, Dorie Apollonio, and Laurel Elms—who created one large file of over 400,000 respondents from 204 studies—for making these data available. Special thanks to Laurel Elms who performed the data analysis and prepared Figure 3.2.

13. The twelve acts, grouped into the sub-categories shown in Figure 3.2, are as follows:

Political Work: attending a political rally or speech, working for a political party, being a member of some group like the League of Women Voters (which is also related to organizational work), and signing a petition (which is also related to direct communications).

Organizational Work: serving as an officer of some club or organization; serving on a committee for some local organization; making a speech (which has some relationship to direct communications as well); and attending a public meeting on town or school affairs (which, not surprisingly, also has a substantial relationship to political work).

Direct Communications: writing a letter to the newspaper, writing an article for a magazine or newspaper (which also has some relationship to organizational work), and writing your member of Congress or senator (which, as might be expected, also has some relationship to political work).

The twelfth activity is holding or running for office. For further description of the data and justification for the construction of the scales, see Henry E. Brady, Kay Lehman Schlozman, Sidney Verba, and Laurel Elms, "Who Bowls?: Class, Race, and Changing Participatory Equality" (paper presented at the annual meeting of the American Political Science Association, Boston, September 1998).

14. Steven J. Rosenstone and John Mark Hansen, *Mobilization, Participation, and Democracy in America* (New York: Macmillan, 1993), chap. 3, demonstrate a clear decline in many forms of political participation. See also Robert D. Putnam, *Bowling Alone* (New York: Simon and Schuster, 2000).

15. In addition, as shown in Figure 3.2b, the political work index reveals a two-year cycle that follows the biennial elections.

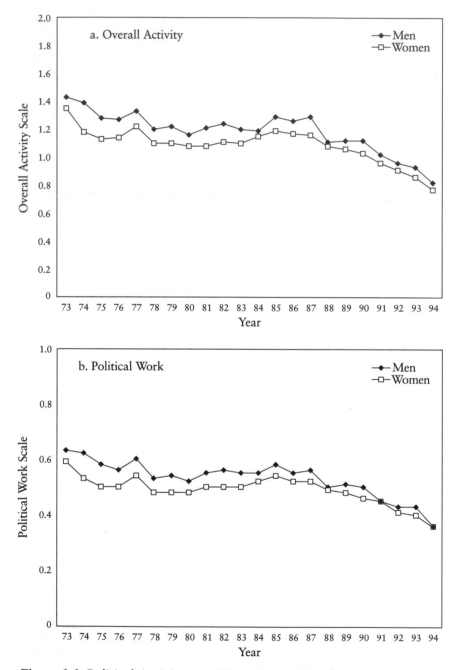

Figure 3.2 Political Activity over Time. (Roper Trends in American Political Participation Study)

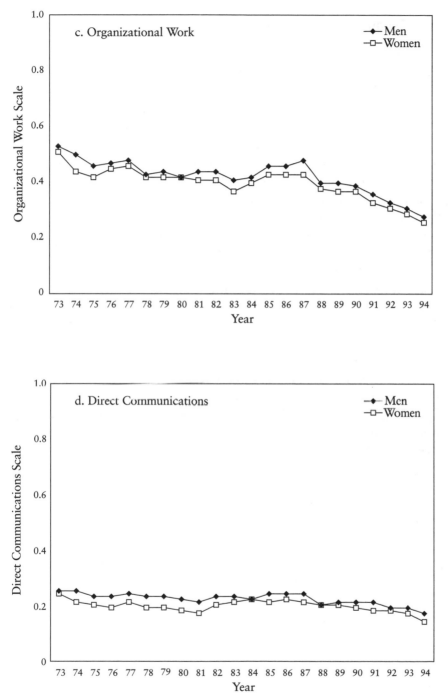

Organizational Involvement: Political and Non-Political

Tocqueville's observations on the peculiar American penchant for forming organizations are well known. "Americans of all ages, all conditions, and all dispositions constantly form associations . . . ," he wrote. "The Americans make associations to give entertainments, to found seminaries, to build inns, to construct churches, to diffuse books, to send missionaries to the antipodes; in this manner they found hospitals, prisons, and schools. If it is proposed to inculcate some truth or to foster some feeling by the encouragement of a great example, they form a society. Wherever at the head of some new undertaking you see the government in France, or a man of rank in England, in the United States you will be sure to find an association."[16] Associational life is fundamental to democracy everywhere. However, even more than in most democracies, voluntary associations in the United States shape the allocation of economic, social, and cultural benefits and contribute to the achievement of collective purposes.[17] In addition, they are more likely than associations elsewhere to be politically autonomous: less likely to be state-sponsored than in nations where corporatist structures dominate and less likely to be officially linked to political parties.

Our analysis probes deeply into the intertwining of political and non-political domains of life, and voluntary associations play a special role in that process. We have already mentioned that involvement in organizations that take stands on public issues is a significant form of political participation. Moreover, activity in non-political organizations figures in our story in two ways. It is itself an important mode of voluntary involvement. Through voluntary associations significant public purposes—from supporting the public schools to funding the symphony to providing meals for the homeless—are achieved. Furthermore, involvement in organi-

---

16. Alexis de Tocqueville, *Democracy in America* (New York: Alfred A. Knopf, 1948), vol. two, book II, chap. V, p. 106.

17. On this general issue, see the essays in *Between States and Markets: The Voluntary Sector in Comparative Perspective,* ed. Robert Wuthnow (Princeton: Princeton University Press, 1991).

zations, even those completely outside politics, operates in several ways to facilitate political participation.

Organizations figure especially importantly in the understanding of women's civic activity. In recent years, historians have produced a rich body of literature documenting the depth, diversity, and significance of women's long-neglected involvement in organizations.[18] More than a century before women acquired the vote, they came together in organizations devoted to good works: caring for the sick, teaching the young, housing orphans, and the like. Later on, their organizational purposes grew to encompass agitation on behalf of social causes—among them abolition, temperance, moral reform,[19] women's rights, and, still later, municipal sanitation and safety—and self-improvement through intellectual and literary pursuits. All this activity took place at a time when women were not only denied fundamental rights of citizenship but also excluded from most public institutions, among them higher education. These gender-segregated organizations provided almost the only avenue for public involvement for women. Moreover, after suffrage, organizational involvements were viewed as a crucial training ground for women who eventually sought elected office.

These organizational involvements had important consequences for women and for the community. This activity permitted them to exercise leadership, to develop their individual talents and intellectual faculties, to learn practical skills for entry into the public world—giving a speech, running a meeting, keeping the books,

---

18. The literature is vast. See, for example, Gerda Lerner, *The Majority Finds Its Past: Placing Women in History* (New York: Oxford University Press, 1979); Anne Firor Scott, *Making the Invisible Woman Visible* (Urbana: University of Illinois Press, 1984); Anne Firor Scott, *Natural Allies: Women's Associations in American History* (Urbana: University of Illinois Press, 1991); Paula Baker, "The Domestication of Politics: Women and American Political Society, 1780–1920," *American Historical Review* 89 (1984): 620–647; Paula Giddings, *When and Where I Enter: The Impact of Black Women on Race and Sex in America* (New York: Morrow, 1984); Nancy F. Cott, "Across the Great Divide: Women in Politics before and after 1920," in *Women, Politics, and Change*, ed. Louise A. Tilly and Patricia Gurin (New York: Russell Sage Foundation, 1990); and Debra C. Minkoff, *Organizing for Equality: The Evolution of Women's and Racial-Ethnic Organizations in America, 1955–1985* (New Brunswick, N.J.: Rutgers University Press, 1995).

The discussion in the following paragraphs draws heavily on Scott's analysis in *Natural Allies*.

19. "Moral reform" was the euphemism adopted to signify ending prostitution.

and the like—and to extend their social and communications networks. Experiences within all-female organizations prepared many women to operate in a wider world, including the world of politics. As Anne Scott put it, "For women—cut off as they were through most of the years considered here from the political party, the bench, the bar, the Congress, the city council, the university, the pulpit—voluntary associations became a place to exercise public influence otherwise denied them; in a sense they provided an alternative career ladder, one that was open to women when few others were."[20]

Scott's assessment makes clear that women's organizational activity contributed not only to their development but also to the improvement of the community and to the achievement of public purposes. We make a similar argument about the role of organizational involvement in providing activists with opportunities to learn civic skills, to become socially connected, and to be exposed to political cues and messages.

ORGANIZATIONAL AFFILIATION

In an electronic era, affiliation with an organization may be a matter of writing a check instead of membership in the traditional sense in which one joins the League of Women Voters or the Rotary. Therefore, in inquiring about organizational affiliation, we asked about both membership and financial contributions and consider either to be sufficient to signify organizational involvement.[21]

Because the world of organizations is so diverse with respect to the level of involvement with politics, we decided to rely on the perception of the respondent in distinguishing between political and non-political organizations. As indicated, respondents were asked about twenty different categories of organizations.[22] Each

---

20. Scott, *Natural Allies,* p. 177.

21. For an extended discussion of these measures, and the rationale for them, see Kay Lehman Schlozman, "Voluntary Associations in Politics: Who Gets Involved?" in *Representing Interests and Interest Group Representation,* ed. William Crotty, Mildred A. Schwartz, and John C. Green (Lanham, Md.: University Press of America, 1994), chap. 8.

22. We constructed the organizational categories so as to make them familiar to respondents and to help them to recall their organizational affiliations, and we almost never refer

time a respondent indicated affiliation with—that is, indicated membership in or contributions to—one of these twenty types of organizations, we followed up by asking whether the organization sometimes takes stands on public issues—either locally or nationally. We consider to be political any organization that, according to the respondent, takes stands. We should acknowledge that our scrutiny of actual interview protocols indicates respondents do sometimes make mistakes, usually by failing to perceive political stands taken by organizations that we know get involved in politics. By and large, however, the overall pattern of responses suggests that respondents make correct judgments about the organizations with which they are affiliated.[23] This definition thus focuses upon the official positions of the organization and ignores a great deal—about which we also inquired—of political relevance that may take place in an organizational context.

The important contribution by historians in calling attention to the vibrancy of women's organizations and the extensiveness of women's organizational affiliations has sometimes led to the inference that women are more organizationally active than men. Systematic data presented in Table 3.2 indicate that a great deal of activity does not necessarily imply more activity. Contrary to what might have been expected, women are slightly less likely than men

---

to specific organizational categories in our analysis. Rather we make extensive use of responses to the follow-up questions about the nature of the organization (for example, Does it take stands on public issues?) and the amount of activity (for example, Has the respondent been on the board?) within it.

23. For discussion of the technical issues involved in measuring organizational affiliation, see Sidney Verba, Kay Lehman Schlozman, and Henry E. Brady, *Voice and Equality: Civic Voluntarism in American Politics* (Cambridge: Harvard University Press, 1995), chap. 3 and app. B.

We should note that we constructed the twenty organizational categories in order to provide respondents with as clear an empirical referent as possible and not to separate political from non-political organizations. The categories varied substantially with respect to the proportion of those involved who indicated that the organization takes public stands. Ninety-four percent of respondents who reported involvement in an organization "active in supporting candidates in elections such as a party organization" indicated that the organization takes stands in politics. In contrast, only 18 percent of those reporting affiliation with a hobby, sports, or other leisure club said that the organization takes stands. By the way, there is no reason to assume that those respondents are imagining politics where it does not exist. The National Rifle Association is an example of a recreational organization that obviously takes stands in politics.

Table 3.2 Organizational Involvement

	Women		Men
Organizational Involvement[a]	77%	⇔	82%
Mean Number of Organizational Involvements	3.8	⇔	4.2
Organizational Activity[b]			
Attended meeting in past twelve months	49%		51%
Served on board or as officer in past five years	28%		29%
Gender Composition of "Most Important" Organization[c]			
All	17%		13%
Most	17		26
Mixed	60		56
Few	4		2
	98%		100%

Source: Citizen Participation Study—Main Survey.
a. Member or contributor.
b. Among those affiliated.
c. Share of organization members who are same sex as respondent.
   Overall distribution of responses is statistically significant with Chi-squared = 22.86624, $p < .001$.
   ⇔ Difference between women and men is statistically significant at the .05 level.

to be affiliated with any organization, whether political or non-political: 82 percent of the men, and 77 percent of the women, indicated involvement in an organization. Moreover, men have a slight advantage when it comes to the number of organizational involvements: they are affiliated, on average, with 4.2 different organizations compared with an average of 3.8 for women.

In many ways, what really matters is not simply affiliation with organizations but what happens there. In an era of mass mailing and telephone solicitation, there has been a transformation in the nature of organizational affiliations, much of which now consists in sending in one's dues and leaving to a staff of professionals the responsibility for the realization of organizational goals. While this form of affiliation may facilitate the accomplishment of joint purposes, it is probably not very effective in cultivating the civic endowments that are said to accompany active involvement. Once again, it was Tocqueville who noted the significance for democracy of the kind of face-to-face interaction that takes place when people meet in organizations: "Men have the opportunity of seeing one another; means of execution are combined; and opinions are maintained with a warmth and energy that written language can never attain."[24] Were he writing today Tocqueville might have added that the telephone, especially the telephone solicitation, is even more deficient than "written language" in conveying "warmth or energy."

Table 3.2 also presents data about more active forms of organizational involvement: attendance at meetings and service on the board. Among those who are affiliated with an organization, roughly half reported attending a meeting of at least one organization within the past twelve months and about a quarter indicated having served as an officer or on the board within the past five years. Although men are somewhat more likely to be affiliated with an organization, among those affiliated, there is almost no difference between women and men in terms of attending meetings or serving on the board.

In light of the emphasis on women's historical experience in organizations of women, we were interested in the gender composition of the organizations with which women and men affiliate. As shown in Table 3.2, while women were slightly more likely to report that the membership of their most important organization is made up entirely of people of their sex, men were actually slightly more likely than women to indicate that all or most of the members of their most important organization are of their sex. In Chapter 9, we investigate further the effects of the gender composition of organizations.

WHAT KINDS OF ORGANIZATIONS?
We can learn more about gender differences in organizational involvement by considering the kinds of organizations that men and women choose. As mentioned, our organizational census inquired about membership or financial contributions to no fewer than twenty kinds of organizations. As shown in Table 3.3, there is a great deal of variation across the kinds of organizations in the

24. Tocqueville, *Democracy in America*, vol. one, book I, chap. XII, p. 192.

Table 3.3 Organizational Affiliation and Activity

| | Percentage Affiliated | | Among Those Affiliated | | | |
| | | | Percentage Attended a Meeting[a] | | Percentage Board/Officer[b] | |
	Women	Men	Women	Men	Women	Men
Service, Fraternal	16 ⇔	21	46	51	27	22
Veterans'	14 ⇔	20	10 ⇔	20	6	5
Religious	14 ⇔	11	70 ⇔	53	24	26
Nationality, Ethnic	3	4	49	40	25	22
Senior Citizens'	14 ⇔	11	29 ⇔	18	11	9
Women's Rights	6 ⇔	2	38	20	17	2
Union	7 ⇔	17	44 ⇔	56	10	15
Business, Professional	19 ⇔	28	63	68	18	15
Political Issue	12 ⇔	16	16	22	6	5
Civic, Non-partisan	3	3	63	56	32	33
Liberal or Conservative	1	1	29	16	6	2
Candidate, Party	5	6	37	40	17	11
Youth	19 ⇔	16	45	38	13	19
Literary, Art, Study	6	5	81 ⇔	59	26	15
Hobby, Sports, Leisure	16 ⇔	27	52	53	20	16
Neighborhood, Homeowners'	11	13	65	68	14	12
Charitable, Social Service	45	43	15	12	6	4
Educational	27 ⇔	22	56 ⇔	43	12	9
Cultural	13	14	17	12	4	5
Other	4	5	31	32	9	16
Total	77 ⇔	82	49	51	22	23

Source: Citizen Participation Study—Main Survey.
a. Percentage who have attended a meeting within the past twelve months.
b. Percentage who have served as an officer or on the board in the past five years.
⇔ Difference between women and men is statistically significant at the .05 level.

proportion who indicated affiliation as well as similarity between women and men in the overall pattern of affiliation. For both groups, the most common organizational affiliation is with a charitable or social service organization, the least common with an organization that supports general liberal or conservative causes. In some cases, the gender disparities in organizational choice are to be expected: we are hardly astonished that men are more likely than women to be involved with a veterans' or a work-related organization. In others—for example, the fact that men are more likely than women to be involved with a hobby, sports, or leisure organization—the gender differences are more surprising. Table 3.3 also presents data, for those who are affiliated, about attendance at meetings and service on the board or as an officer of these various kinds of organizations. Once again, there is substantial variation across kinds of organizations—with no relationship between the proportion of respondents who are involved and the proportion of those involved who attend meetings or serve as officers.

ORGANIZATIONS THAT TAKE POLITICAL STANDS:
A CLOSER LOOK

Earlier, in Figure 3.1, we saw that men are more likely than women—by a margin of 53 percent to 44 percent—to indicate involvement in an organization that takes stands in politics. In fact, it turns out that the gender difference in overall organizational affiliation derives fully from the disparity in their affiliation with political organizations. When it comes to non-political organizations, a nearly identical proportion of women and men, 66 and 67 percent respectively, indicated involvement. Among those affiliated with an organization, 64 percent of the men and 57 percent of the women reported that at least one of their organizations takes stands in politics.

The difference in involvement in political organizations could have two different sources. Women and men could join different kinds of organizations. Or men might be more likely than women to see politics in more or less the same kinds of organizations. Table 3.4 repeats data from Table 3.3 about affiliations with different kinds of organizations and also shows the proportion of those affiliated who said that the organization takes stands in politics. These data suggest that both are at work but that the former operates more strongly than the latter: that is, that men and women are involved in different kinds of organizations, rather than that women are insensitive to political cues. However, these data do not provide a definitive solution to this puzzle. With the exception of women's rights organizations (with which 6 percent of the women and 2 percent of the men reported affiliation), the

Table 3.4 Affiliation with Organizations That Take Political Stands

	Percentage Affiliated		Percentage Saying Org. Takes Stands[a]	
	Women	Men	Women	Men
Service, Fraternal	16 ⇔	21	25 ⇔	35
Veterans'	14 ⇔	20	51 ⇔	64
Religious	14 ⇔	11	22 ⇔	33
Nationality, Ethnic	3	4	69	54
Senior Citizens'	14 ⇔	11	56 ⇔	67
Women's Rights	6 ⇔	2	76	86
Union	7 ⇔	17	57 ⇔	72
Business, Professional	19 ⇔	28	54 ⇔	63
Political Issue	12 ⇔	16	93	93
Civic, Non-partisan	3	3	51	69
Liberal or Conservative	1	1	93	96
Candidate, Party	5	6	90 ⇔	97
Youth	19 ⇔	16	16	21
Literary, Art, Study	6	5	13	19
Hobby, Sports, Leisure	16 ⇔	27	13 ⇔	21
Neighborhood, Homeowners'	11	13	55 ⇔	44
Charitable, Social Service	45	43	13 ⇔	19
Educational	27 ⇔	22	48 ⇔	37
Cultural	13	14	25	26
Other	4	5	39 ⇔	22
Total	77 ⇔	82	57 ⇔	64

Source: Citizen Participation Study—Main Survey.
a. Among those affiliated.
⇔ Difference between women and men is statistically significant at the .05 level.

categories for which women were more likely than men to report affiliation were those in which a relatively small proportion of those affiliated (regardless of gender) reported that the organization takes stands in politics: for example, youth groups, religiously affiliated organizations, and literary, discussion, or study groups. Within any particular organizational category, however, there seems to be some tendency for men to be more likely to view their organizations as being political. Still, within any particular category, men and women may be joining different kinds of organizations.

One further way to examine this puzzle is to consider the members of the single organization in which sufficient respondents reported membership to justify further analysis, the American Association of Retired People (AARP). Presumably reflecting the disproportionate number of women among the elderly, women were more likely than men to report affiliation with a senior citizens' organization but, among those involved in such a group, men were more likely than women to name the AARP, which admits members as young as fifty. Among AARP members, however, there was virtually no gender difference in terms of the proportion who recognize that the AARP takes stands: 80 percent of male, and 78 percent of female, AARP members indicated that the organization takes political stands. Among those affiliated with senior citizens' groups other than the AARP, 40 percent of the men and 27 percent of the women indicated that the organization takes stands in politics, suggesting that it is differences in organizational choices rather than in ability to perceive politics that is the source of the fact that men in senior citizens' groups are more likely to report that their organizations take stands on public issues.

Voluntary Activity outside Politics

Table 3.5 contains data for women and men on their voluntary activity in realms outside of politics in which women have sometimes been thought to predominate—non-political organizations and charities. These data suggest that there is virtually no gender difference when it comes to voluntary participation in the secular domain outside politics. Men and women are just about equally likely to be affiliated with an organization that does not take stands in politics, to have attended a meeting, or to have served on the board or as an officer in a non-political organization. Moreover, there is no significant gender difference in either the average number of non-political organizations with which the individual is affiliated or in the amount of time devoted to organizational activity among those who are affiliated with a non-political organization. With respect to charitable activity, women are very slightly more likely to have donated time. Moreover, among those who devoted time to charitable activity, there is almost no gender difference in the number of hours given. When it comes to the size of a

Table 3.5 Secular Activity outside Politics

	Women		Men
Non-Political Organization			
Affiliated	66%		67%
Attended meeting within past twelve months	38%		37%
Served on board or as officer within past five years	14%		15%
Mean number of non-political organizations	2.3		2.3
Mean number of hours given to most important org.[a]	2.7		2.6
Charity			
Gave time to charity	39%	⇔	35%
Gave money to charity	68%		69%
Mean number of hours given to charity[a]	4.48		4.53
Mean contribution to charity[b]	$248	⇔	$321

Source: Citizen Participation Study—Main Survey.
a. Among those who gave any time.
b. Among those who gave any money.
⇔ Difference between women and men is statistically significant at the .05 level.

charitable donation, however, a genuine disparity between women and men emerges—with men making significantly larger contributions.

In short, our expectations have, once again, not been met. With a single exception, there seems to be almost no difference between men and women in secular, non-political activity. That exception—that men give, on average, much larger charitable donations—parallels what we saw about giving to politics. Although gender differences in financial contributions have received very limited attention, they will figure later in our analysis.

Religious Activity

Religious institutions of astonishing number and variety form a second major component of civil society in America[25] and play an

25. For data see, among others, Andrew Greeley, "The Other Civic America," *American Prospect,* May–June 1997, pp. 68–73. For a review of the recent literature on the sociology of religion that places Americans' religious commitments in a comparative context, see Darren E. Sherkat and Christopher G. Ellison, "Recent Developments and Current Controversies in the Sociology of Religion," *Annual Review of Sociology* 25 (1999): 363–394. See also Johan Verweij, Peter Ester, and Rein Nauta, "Secularization as an Economic and Cul-

important, but complex, role in our story. Although the United States is known globally as the champion of materialism and consumption, what is less widely acknowledged is the depth of religious commitment in America. Compared with citizens in other countries, Americans are more likely to be religious—to report that they believe in God and that religion is important in their lives, to attend religious services regularly, and to be actively involved in a religious institution.[26]

Many of the points that have been made about organizational involvement obtain for religious activity as well. Although the United States does not have an established church and the constitutional separation between religion and state would seem to remove religious matters from political life, religion and religious institutions have long played important political roles. Many of the major political movements in American history—from abolitionism and temperance to civil rights and pro-life—have roots in religious beliefs and religious institutions.

Furthermore, like organizational participation, activity in religious institutions—churches, mosques, synagogues, temples, and so on—can operate in several ways to facilitate political participation. When undertaken in a religious institution, educational, charitable, or social activity that has nothing to do with politics develops skills that can be applied to political activity. Moreover, those active in religious institutions become enmeshed in social networks and become targets of requests for political participation. In addition, those who attend religious services or are otherwise active in a religious institution are exposed to political messages and discussions of public affairs. Finally, religious institutions themselves often take explicit stands on political issues. As in organizations, these processes have historically been especially important for women, who were denied entry to the major institutions of political, social, and economic life. However, while the organizations that played such a critical role in providing opportuni-

---

tural Phenomenon: A Cross-National Analysis," *Journal of the Scientific Study of Religion* 36 (1997): 309–324.

26. See, for example, the data in Verba, Schlozman, and Brady, *Voice and Equality*, p. 80; and Everett Carll Ladd, *The Ladd Report* (New York: Free Press, 1999), chap. 6.

ties for civic engagement to women were composed of women only, religious institutions are, of course, not segregated by gender.

Feminists have long been skeptical about established religious institutions—considering them to be oppressive to women and a barrier to equality between the sexes. For the three monotheistic religions that claim the loyalties of the overwhelming share of America's religiously affiliated citizens—Christianity, Islam, and Judaism—religious orthodoxy is strongly associated with traditionalism when it comes to relations between men and women. It is not simply that established religious institutions, like many social institutions, long excluded women from positions of leadership. Perhaps more important, religious doctrine has served as the justification for inequality in many other realms of life as well.[27] Around the world, religious tradition has been invoked to oppose political and social changes designed to widen opportunities for women.[28] Closer to home, the Christian Right appeals to biblical authority in support of a traditional division of labor between the sexes.[29]

As elsewhere in the world, women in contemporary America have confronted the patriarchal nature of most traditional religious institutions with a combination of exit, voice, and loyalty. It is well known that, among citizens of developed democracies, Americans are among the most religiously observant. Moreover, our own data confirm a tendency that is equally well known: that women are more likely than men to attend religious services and

27. See, for example, Katherine K. Young, "Introduction," in *Women in World Religions,* ed. Arvind Sharma (Albany: State University of New York Press, 1987), p. 31.

28. The role of religious institutions and orthodoxy in opposing equality between the sexes is an implicit theme uniting the essays in Barbara J. Nelson and Najma Chowdhury, *Women and Politics Worldwide* (New Haven: Yale University Press, 1994). Separate essays about countries as diverse as the Netherlands, Turkey, Bangladesh, Israel, Nigeria, and France each mention the multiple ways in which traditional religions have acted as a barrier to the social inclusion of women.

29. See, for example, William Martin, *With God on Our Side* (New York: Broadway Books, 1996), pp. 161–167. In the aftermath of the Second Great Awakening during the nineteenth century, there were links between evangelical Protestantism, the women's suffrage movement, and social protest on behalf of other causes, in particular abolition and temperance. (See Mary P. Ryan, *Womanhood in America* [New York: Franklin Watts, 1983], pp. 125–134.) Obviously, no such links characterized feminist politics in the late twentieth century.

to be active in their congregations. Thus women in America demonstrate deep loyalty to religious institutions. Nonetheless, there has been exit as well: some women—and some men—have gravitated away from religious institutions that make strict gender distinctions in the direction of less traditional denominations or congregations, or away from religious affiliation altogether.

In terms of voice, advocates of equal opportunity in religious practice have focused primarily in two areas: the ordination of women and theological and liturgical inclusivity. Religious denominations in America differ in many respects, among them their willingness to ordain women. The Congregationalists were the first to ordain women, in 1853, with the Universalists (1863) and Unitarians (1871) in their wake. It was not until well into the twentieth century that other major denominations followed along: African Methodist Episcopal Church (1948); Presbyterian and Methodist Episcopal (1956); Lutheran Church in America and American Lutheran Church (1970); Reform Jewish (1972); and Episcopal (1976).[30] The circumstance for Southern Baptists, who first ordained a woman in 1964, is complicated. The bottom line, however, is that Southern Baptists have ordained very few women, of whom only a small fraction serve as pastors in churches. In June 2000 the Southern Baptist Convention passed a resolution, which is not binding on congregations, that women should not serve as pastors.[31] The Eastern Orthodox, Roman Catholic, and Mormon churches—along with Orthodox Judaism and Islam—ordain men

---

30. Catherine Wessinger, "Introduction," in *Religious Institutions and Women's Leadership,* ed. Catherine Wessinger (Columbia: University of South Carolina Press, 1996), p. 4.

31. Southern Baptists are ordained by congregations—which are traditionally very autonomous—rather than by a central religious or affiliated educational institution. Nonetheless, disapproval of women as clergy, or even as deacons in congregational governance, is an important issue in the takeover of the Southern Baptist Convention by fundamentalists since the late 1970s. Congregations that have ordained women have faced various kinds of sanctions from local Baptist associations; in 1986 the Home Mission Board of the Southern Baptist Convention refused to give financial aid to churches that had called women pastors. See Nancy Tatom Ammerman, *Baptist Battles* (New Brunswick, N.J.: Rutgers University Press, 1990); Sarah Frances Anders and Marilyn Metcalf Whittaker, "Women as Lay Leaders and Clergy: A Critical Issue," in *Southern Baptists Observed,* ed. Nancy Tatom Ammerman (Knoxville: University of Tennessee Press, 1993), chap. 11; and "Southern Baptist Convention Passes Resolution Opposing Women as Pastors," *New York Times,* June 15, 2000, p. A-18.

only.[32] In general, the longer a denomination has ordained women, the higher the proportion of women clergy.[33] Because increasing numbers of women have been entering seminaries at a time when many denominations are having difficulty attracting male seminarians, the proportion of women clergy will surely rise in the future.[34] Since Black women have traditionally worked outside the home, have long been religiously active, and have been supportive of the feminist political agenda, it is surprising that there are very few female African-American preachers.[35]

Once ordained, women clergy face additional obstacles. As in many occupations, women clergy have less difficulty locating entry-level positions than in rising to higher levels of leadership and responsibility. There seems to be considerable opposition to having a woman as the senior or sole pastor of a church or synagogue, especially in a large, affluent congregation.[36] The result is that women clergy earn less than their male counterparts. In contrast to those in secular professions, clergy who are the objects of employment discrimination cannot seek relief under Title VII of the Civil Rights Act of 1964.[37]

The history of Christian denominations in America suggests that the gains currently being made by women may not be permanent. Historians of religion have discerned a pattern suggesting that when a newfound sect—of which there have been many in the United States—is in its initial, "charismatic" phase, women are given considerable autonomy and are permitted to preach. Later on, as the sect is institutionalized and bureaucratized, women's participation and freedom are curtailed.[38] Thus in the Church of

---

32. On protest by women within the Catholic Church, see Mary Fainsod Katzenstein, *Faithful and Fearless* (Princeton: Princeton University Press, 1998), pt. 3.

33. Edward C. Lehman, Jr., *Women Clergy: Breaking through Gender Barriers* (New Brunswick, N.J.: Transaction Books, 1985), p. 13.

34. Lehman, *Women Clergy*, pp. 10–13.

35. Robert Booth Fowler and Allen D. Hertzke, *Religion and Politics in America* (Boulder, Colo.: Westview Press, 1995), pp. 168–169. On the role of women in African-American churches, see Frederick C. Harris, *Something Within* (New York: Oxford University Press, 1999), chap. 9.

36. Lehman, *Women Clergy*, p. 41. See also Carroll, Hargrove, and Lummis, *Women of the Cloth*; and Sally B. Purvis, *The Stained-Glass Ceiling* (Louisville, Ky.: Westminster John Knox Press, 1995); and Wessinger, "Introduction."

37. Lehman, *Women Clergy*, p. 9.

38. Carroll, Hargrove, and Lummis, *Women of the Cloth*, pp. 21–27. See also Carolyn

the Nazarene, women constituted 20 percent of the clergy in 1908, but only 6 percent in 1973. Analogous figures for the Church of God are 32 percent in 1925 and 15 percent in 1996.[39] One of the consequences of the takeover of the Southern Baptist Convention by conservative forces in 1979 has been an especially marked decline in women in leadership positions.[40] In short, the current trend in the direction of reduced inequality between women and men in most American denominations could be reversed.

Especially germane to our concern in this inquiry is an aspect of religious gender hierarchy that has received much less attention, church governance. Religious denominations in America vary substantially with respect to whether individual congregations are autonomous and whether denominational authority rests in a religious hierarchy or in a representative body.[41] In most denominations women were not permitted either to vote or to speak at congregational or denominational deliberations before the Civil War.[42] As women gained voice in other domains of social life in the late nineteenth century, these arrangements began to be altered as well. Nevertheless, in many cases they persisted for another century: in the Lutheran Church Missouri Synod, women were permitted to vote and hold office only in 1969;[43] and it was not until 1970 that women were admitted as lay delegates to the Anglican General Convention.[44]

Still, in contrast to many domains of social life—including

De Armond Blevins, "Women and the Baptist Experience," in *Religious Institutions,* ed. Wessinger, p. 160.

39. Susie C. Stanley, "The Promise Fulfilled: Women's Ministries in the Wesleyan/Holiness Movement," in *Religious Institutions,* ed. Wessinger, p. 148.

40. Blevins, "Women and the Baptist Experience," pp. 170–177. The Danvers Statement issued in 1989 by the Southern Baptist Convention's Council on Biblical Manhood and Womanhood "decried 'feminist egalitarianism' and framed relationships between the sexes in terms of the 'loving, humble leadership of redeemed husbands and the intelligent, willing support of that leadership by redeemed wives.' " Margaret Lamberts Bendroth, *Fundamentalism and Gender: 1875 to the Present* (New Haven: Yale University Press, 1993), p. 1.

41. Wessinger, "Introduction," p. 9.

42. Virginia Lieson Brereton and Christa Ressmeyer Klein, "American Women in Ministry: A History of Protestant Beginning Points" in *Women of Spirit,* ed. Rosemary Ruether and Eleanor McLaughlin (New York: Simon and Schuster, 1979) pp. 302–303.

43. Gracia Grindal, "Women in the Evangelical Lutheran Church in America," in *Religious Institutions,* ed. Wessinger, p. 182.

44. Suzanne Radley Hiatt, "Women's Ordination in the Anglican Communion: Can This Church Be Saved?" in *Religious Institutions,* ed. Wessinger, p. 216.

politics—in which male dominance has engendered female withdrawal, women have not stayed away from church. As we have mentioned, it is widely known—and confirmed by the data that we shall review shortly—that women are more likely than men both to attend religious services regularly and to be religiously active. This pattern obtains even in denominations, like Roman Catholicism, in which women cannot be ordained, but is especially pronounced in mainline Protestant denominations and African-American churches.[45]

In spite of the role played by religious orthodoxy in legitimating traditional sex roles and the exclusion of women from the exercise of leadership in religious institutions, women's religiously based voluntary activity has often functioned as a source of confidence and autonomy. During the nineteenth century, churches often served as the only public institution beyond the home to which women had access, if not opportunities for leadership. During the nineteenth century, women taught Sunday school and, later on, formed various kinds of separate organizations such as altar guilds and missionary societies. While these good works fitted squarely into the traditional "women's sphere," they also nurtured bonds of friendship and developed competence among women.[46] Our ex-

---

45. In *The Emerging Parish* (San Francisco: Harper and Row, 1987), Jim Castelli and Joseph Gremillion point out (pp. 24–28) that the combined effects of Vatican II and the diminishing number of priests are to enhance the role of laypersons in parish administration and governance. Catholic parishes are particularly dependent upon the volunteer efforts of women (pp. 68–69), who constitute a majority of parish leaders but only a minority of those in influential positions (pp. 109–110). See also Virginia Sullivan Finn, "Ministerial Attitudes and Aspirations of Catholic Laywomen in the United States," in *Religious Institutions,* ed. Wessinger, p. 246. On "the tradition of female parishoners and male preachers" in Black churches, see Fowler and Hertzke, *Religion and Politics in America,* pp. 168–169.

The dominance of women in the pews and in church activity has sometimes given rise to concern about the masculine indifference to religion. Margaret Lamberts Bendroth (*Fundamentalism and Gender,* p. 3) describes the way that emerging fundamentalists in the early years of the twentieth century reversed the traditional Victorian formula that emphasized women's piety and made a case that it was "men, not women, who had the true aptitude for religion." In many ways, this early fundamentalist concern with Christian masculinity has echoes in the contemporary Promise Keepers organization. See Martin, *With God on Our Side,* pp. 349–353.

46. See Nancy F. Cott, *The Bonds of Womanhood* (New Haven: Yale University Press, 1977); Bendroth, *Fundamentalism and Gender;* Anne M. Boylan, "Evangelical Womanhood in Nineteenth-Century America: The Role of Women in Sunday Schools," in *Unspoken Worlds: Women's Religious Lives,* ed. Nancy Auer Falk and Rita M. Gross (Belmont, Calif.: Wadsworth Publishing Co., 1989), pp. 166–178; and Barbara Brown Zikmund,

amination of voluntary activity within religious institutions demonstrates that analogous processes are at work today.[47] The story we shall tell about the consequences of women's religious involvements is thus a complex and ambiguous one.

THE GENDER GAP IN RELIGIOUS ACTIVITY

As shown in Table 3.6, women are more religiously active than men: compared with men, they are more likely to be affiliated with a church, to attend services frequently, and to take part in other activities within a religious institution, and they give, on average, slightly, but not significantly, more time to church work. However, reflecting the traditional male domination of religious institutions, when it comes to lay positions of authority as board members or as officers within the congregation, among those who are active in their congregations, men are more likely than women to hold such leadership positions. There are small differences among Christian denominations in terms of the masculine advantage in congregational leadership, with Catholics reporting a wider gender gap than either mainline or evangelical Protestants.[48] In fact, however, what is striking in the data is the difference between Prot-

---

"Women's Organizations: Centers of Denominational Loyalty and Expressions of Christian Unity," in *Beyond Establishment: Protestant Identity in a Post-Protestant Age*, ed. Jackson W. Carroll and Wade Clark Roof (Louisville, Ky.: Westminster/John Knox Press, 1993), pp. 116–138.

47. Darren E. Sherkat and Christopher G. Ellison make a similar point in "Recent Developments and Current Controversies in the Sociology of Religion," *Annual Review of Sociology* 25 (1999): 368. See also Harris, *Something Within*, chap. 9.

48. There is dispute among students of politics on exactly how to differentiate mainline from evangelical Protestants. Our rule of thumb has been to omit from the table all respondents who call themselves simply "Christian" as well as Unitarians, Christian Scientists, and Mormons and to consider as mainline all Protestant denominations in the National Council of Churches. By this definition, all Methodists, Lutherans (including Missouri Synod), Presbyterians, Episcopalians, Congregationalists (United Church of Christ), and Quakers are categorized as mainline Protestants as are those who identified themselves with the American Baptist Association, the American Baptist Church, the National Baptist Convention of America, and the National Baptist Convention, U.S.A. Other Baptists, including members of the nation's largest Protestant denomination, the Southern Baptist Convention, are considered to be evangelical Protestants as are those respondents who named a variety of evangelical and pentecostal groups—for example, the Assemblies of God, Church of Christ, Church of the Nazarene, and the Pentecostal Church. Many of those who study Protestant denominations prefer the term "conservative Protestants" to "evangelical Protestants." Because this is a book about politics, we use the latter in order to avoid any confusion with conservative political ideology, as opposed to religious orientations.

Table 3.6 Religious Activity

	Women		Men
Affiliated[a]	74%	⇔	58%
Attends Religious Services			
Never or less than once a year	15%	⇔	22%
Weekly or more	38%	⇔	25%
Mean weeks per year	34	⇔	25
Active in a Religious Institution			
All respondents	29%	⇔	21%
Church-affiliated only	39%		35%
Mean Number of Hours per Week Given to Church Work	1.08		.99
Served on Board or as Officer within Past Five Years			
All respondents	21%	⇔	25%
Church-affiliated only	49%	⇔	61%
Mainline Protestants	58%	⇔	72%
Evangelical Protestants	52%		63%
Catholics	24%	⇔	42%

Source: Citizen Participation Study—Main Survey.
a. Belongs to a church or attends services regularly in the same congregation.
⇔ Difference between women and men is statistically significant at the .05 level.

estants and Catholics, whether male or female—with the Protestants considerably more likely than the Catholics to have served on the board or as officers within the past five years.[49]

In Table 3.7 we consider for religious activity another issue raised earlier: the distinction between giving time and giving money. Table 3.7 adds data about contributions to religious institutions to data reviewed earlier (in Tables 3.1 and 3.5) about the average number of hours and dollars given to political campaigns and causes and to secular charities. The striking contrast in these data is not among the three realms of voluntary activity, but rather between time and money as voluntary inputs. With respect to time, there is no consistent gender difference in the average number of hours dedicated to voluntary action among those who are

---

49. On the difference between Protestants and Catholics with respect to educational, charitable, and social activity in church, see Verba, Schlozman, and Brady, *Voice and Equality,* pp. 245–247, 320–325.

Table 3.7 Voluntary Contributions of Time and Money to Politics (among those who gave time or money)

	Women		Men
Mean Hours Contributed			
Political campaigns	7.9	⇔	7.2
Charity	4.4		4.4
Church	3.4	⇔	4.0
Mean Dollars Contributed			
Political campaigns	$223	⇔	$306
Charity	$248	⇔	$321
Church	$588	⇔	$697

Source: Citizen Participation Study—Main Survey.
⇔ Difference between women and men is statistically significant at the .05 level.

active. Surprisingly, once active, *men* give on average more hours to church than do women—even though women are more likely to be active in their churches. As we saw earlier, once active, *women* give more hours to politics than do men. With respect to money, however, the pattern is quite uniform. Among donors, men make larger contributions than do women in each of the three domains—even though they are more likely than women to be donors only in politics. These data underline our earlier observation about the importance of the distinction between hours and dollars as forms of participatory input.

What Kinds of Men? What Kinds of Women?

Our extended comparison of the participatory profiles of women and men should not be construed as implying that we think of these as undifferentiated groups. As we have pointed out, men and women differ among themselves in many ways, including along the most significant fault lines of conflict in American politics: class, race, religion, and political ideology. They also differ with respect to the work and family circumstances that, while less relevant for the substance of political conflict in America, are critical for the patterning of men and women's lives and daily activities.

In Figures 3.3, 3.4, and 3.5 we consider women and men differentiated by their education, their race or ethnicity, and their age.

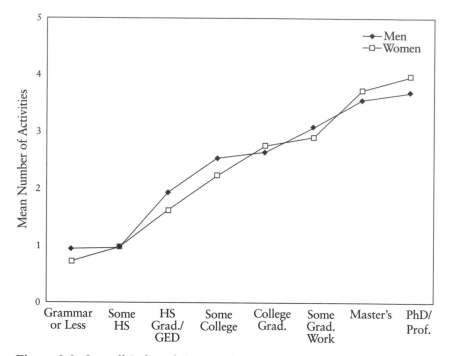

Figure 3.3 Overall Political Activity by Education. (Citizen Participation Study—Main Survey)

To simplify the presentation we show averages for the various sub-groups on the eight-point summary measure of political activity.[50] Since much of what is contained in these data will be investigated at length in later chapters, at this point we shall discuss these findings only briefly.

Men have, as expected, a somewhat higher mean than women on the scale of political activity. The gender gap in political participation is fairly consistent across sub-groups defined by their education, their race or ethnicity, or their age. Figure 3.3 shows, not surprisingly, that political participation increases sharply with educational level. In fact, education plays an important part in our

---

50. The acts are voting; working in a campaign; contributing to a campaign; contacting an official; taking part in a protest, march, or demonstration; being affiliated with an organization that takes stands in politics; being active in the local community; and serving as a volunteer on a local board.

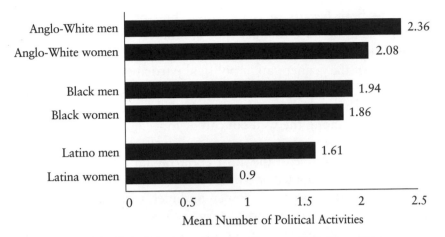

Figure 3.4 Overall Political Activity by Race or Ethnicity. (Citizen Participation Study—Main Survey)

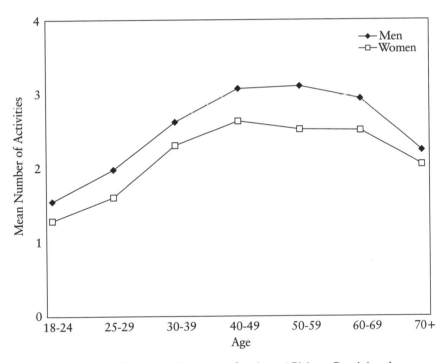

Figure 3.5 Overall Political Activity by Age. (Citizen Participation Study—Main Survey)

analysis—both because it is the single best predictor of political activity[51] and because the fact that men have, on average, higher levels of education than women do figures significantly in the explanation of the gender gap in political participation. As shown in Figure 3.3, while there is a disparity in participation between women and men who have not graduated from college, there is convergence among the well educated. Indeed, among those with graduate degrees, women are more politically active than men.

With respect to one of the most enduring fault lines of political cleavage in America, race or ethnicity, the magnitude of the disparity in participation between women and men varies across groups. The gap is quite narrow among African-Americans and especially wide among Latinos. In Chapter 11, we treat at length the multiple sources of participatory differences among groups defined by their gender and their race and ethnicity. At this point, we simply note the size of the group differences and the depressed rates of activity among Latinas.

With respect to age groups, our data conform to the well-established curvilinear pattern in which participation begins at a low level among young adults, rises through middle age, and declines thereafter.[52] Because younger women have come of age in an era of expanded opportunities for women, we might have expected the gender gap in activity to be wider among older people. But the pattern with respect to age is not especially clear, and the interpretation differs depending upon whether the absolute or the relative size of the disparity is considered. By either measure, however, the participatory difference between men and women seems to be smallest among the elderly. This pattern, which is consistent with data presented earlier in the chapter showing that the gender gap has not changed appreciably over the past quarter century, suggests that gender parity in political participation is not simply a

51. For an elaboration of the multiple roles played by education in fostering participation, see Verba, Schlozman, and Brady, *Voice and Equality,* chap. 15.

52. For a discussion of the relationship between age and participation and extensive bibliographical references, see Kay Lehman Schlozman, Henry Brady, Sidney Verba, Jennifer Erkulwater, and Laurel Elms, "Why Can't They Be Like We Were?: Life Cycle, Generation, and Political Participation" (paper presented at the annual meeting of the American Political Science Association, Atlanta, Ga., September 1999).

matter of time and patience. Waiting for recent, post-feminist generations to come of age will not automatically close the gap in political activity.

Perhaps the most significant feature of the data in these figures is that the differences in political activity between men and women are less substantial than the differences among women and among men. More striking than the gender differences are the well-known relationship between educational level and participation, the curvilinear relationship between age and participation, and the depressed levels of activity among Latinos, especially Latina women. To illustrate, the disparity in political participation between a woman with only a high school education and a woman with a college degree is six times the size of the gender gap in activity. This example is meant neither to dismiss as unimportant the disparity in political activity between men and women nor to deny that focusing on a summary measure obscures interesting differences among particular participatory acts. Nevertheless, these data make clear the importance of considering gender differences in the context of many other social differences.

WORK STATUS AND FAMILY STRUCTURE

We also wanted to explore group heterogeneity with respect to the family and work circumstances that play such a powerful role in patterning adult lives. The dictates of work and family operate differently for men and women. In the traditional division of labor, his responsibility was to support and hers to nurture. Hence, while we have no reason to expect any gender difference in the association between education and participation, we might expect different relationships between participation and work, marriage, and children for women and men. In particular, we might expect men who settle into full-time work, marriage, and fatherhood to become more active in politics. In contrast, we might anticipate that, for women, the same configuration of roles—marriage, children, and full-time paid jobs—would leave them so busy and frazzled by competing demands as to have no time left for participation. Women at home, who have traditionally provided a great deal of the legwork for volunteer efforts, would, presumably, have more time to get involved in politics.

Table 3.8 Overall Political Activity by Work and Family Circumstances (mean number of political acts)

	Women	Men
Work-Force Participation		
Full-time work	2.09	2.34
At home	1.82	2.65
Retired	2.21	2.39
Family Circumstances		
Unmarried	1.67	2.04
No children	1.80	2.03
Children	1.43	2.04
Married	2.21	2.44
No children	2.36	2.47
Children	2.12	2.42

Source: Citizen Participation Study—Main Survey.

Table 3.8, which shows the average political participation for men and women differentiated by their work force and family status, lends only partial confirmation to these hunches. Among women and among men, there is no significant difference in activity between the retired and full-time workers. Contrary to the common wisdom, however, women at home are significantly less politically active than are their counterparts who are either retired or in the work force full time.[53] With respect to family circumstances, among both men and women, those who are married are more politically active than those who are not. The presence of children, with the mother's marital status taken into account, is associated with lower levels of activity for women. Among groups of married and unmarried men, however, there is no relationship between participation and having children at home.

The low levels of participation among women who are at home bear further investigation. Table 3.9 extends our analysis of the re-

---

53. Although it is often assumed that women in the work force are less active as political volunteers, our findings are consistent with more than two decades of scholarship. See, for example, Andersen, "Working Women and Political Participation"; Welch, "Women as Political Animals?"; Andersen and Cook, "Women, Work, and Political Attitudes." For an exception, see Virginia Sapiro, *The Political Integration of Women* (Urbana: University of Illinois Press, 1983), chap. 6.

Table 3.9 Overall Political Activity of Married and Unmarried
Women (mean number of political acts)

	Full-time Work	At Home
Unmarried	1.80	1.19
No children	1.86	1.64
Children	1.71	0.60
Married	2.40	2.06
No children	2.49	2.27
Children	2.34	1.93

Source: Citizen Participation Study—Main Survey.

lationship of family circumstances to political activity by comparing women who are in the work force full time with those at home. Considering groups defined by their work force participation confirms our earlier finding that married women are significantly more politically active than unmarried women. When it comes to motherhood, only among unmarried women at home are children associated with significantly lower levels of political activity. Unmarried women with children and no jobs have strikingly low levels of participation—lower than for any group we have seen so far. With respect to work force status, the pattern is uniform: for any group defined by marriage and the presence of children, those who are in the work force full time are, on average, more active in politics than are those who are at home.

DESCRIBING GROUP DIFFERENCES/EXPLAINING
GROUP DIFFERENCES
In this section we have focused on the heterogeneity among women and among men. We have seen that many characteristics are associated with political participation and that some of these characteristics are even more strongly related to political activity than is gender. Men and women who, for example, are well educated, Anglo-White, middle-aged, or married are more active than are their counterparts who are less well educated, Latino, young, or unmarried.

We must underscore, however, that we are not making a causal argument. That is, we are not asserting that being Anglo-White—

or, for women, being in the work force full time—causes participation. An important part of the task for the remainder of our inquiry is explanatory—getting inside these relationships to find out why they obtain. For example, is it simply being in the workplace full time that leads to greater political activity among women? Or can we specify particular aspects of being on the job that confer participatory advantage? Or is it related to processes of selection such that women who are in the work force full time have other characteristics that predispose them to take part in politics? Similarly, we will ask, and ascertain, what are the distinctive characteristics and experiences of Latinos, especially Latina women, that lead them to have such low rates of participation.

The relevant questions are not all answered once the causal puzzle is solved, however. Specifying what it is about Latinas that predisposes them to political quiescence—for example, their low levels of education, income, and political interest—does not explain why Latinas have these characteristics. Furthermore, knowing that it is class characteristics rather than cultural distinctiveness that underlie Latinas' low levels of participation does not change the political fact that policymakers hear very little from them. Causal explanation is an important part of the intellectual agenda of this inquiry. From the perspective of the messages sent to public officials through the medium of citizen participation, however, what matters is the inequality of participation.

4

---⊗⊗⊗---

The Political Worlds of
Men and Women

Political activity is embedded in a larger set of orientations to the political world. Behind what individuals do in politics is how they think and feel about it: whether they know or care about politics, feel capable of having an impact, have a taste for political participation and the gratifications it can provide, or harbor policy preferences they wish to communicate to public officials. Later on we explore the ways in which these inclinations are related to political participation. In this chapter we investigate gender differences with respect to a diverse set of predispositions that shape the motivation and propensity to take part. We first consider gender differences in the set of orientations toward political life that foster activity, including political interest, efficacy, and knowledge, as well as other indicators of affect toward politics. Second, we consider gender differences in what is sought from political action: the gratifications attendant to participation and the policy issues behind it.

Psychological Involvement with Politics

Participation is closely linked to a variety of psychological orientations that would make someone *want* to take part in political life.[1]

---

1. In other works we have referred to this cluster of orientations to politics as "political engagement." In order to avoid any confusions with "civic engagement," a term frequently used in discussions about the decline in civil society, we now discuss "psychological orienta-

In the last chapter, we observed a noticeable but moderate participation gap between women and men. In this one, we see a wider
gap in psychological involvement with politics. Data from the Citizen Participation Study confirm the findings of various studies to
the effect that, compared with men, women are less interested in
and less knowledgeable about politics and less likely to feel politically efficacious.[2] Not only have differences in political involve-

---

tions to politics" along with the term "political engagement." The supplementary terminol-
ogy implies no change in the items we use to measure it. Portions of this chapter are based
on material from Kay L. Schlozman, Nancy E. Burns, Sidney Verba, and Jesse Donahue,
"Gender and Citizen Participation: Is There a Different Voice?," *American Journal of Political Science* 39 (1995): 39–54 (copyright 1995; reprinted by permission of The University of
Wisconsin Press), and Sidney Verba, Nancy E. Burns, and Kay L. Schlozman, "Knowing
and Caring about Politics: Gender and Political Engagement," *Journal of Politics* 59 (copyright 1997, *The Journal of Politics,* with permission of Blackwell Publishers): 1051–1072.
We are grateful for permission to reuse portions in revised form.

For descriptions of these various measures and how they are used in the literature see,
among others, Paul R. Abramson, *Political Attitudes in America: Formation and Change*
(San Francisco: W. H. Freeman, 1983), p. 135; Stephen Earl Bennett, *Apathy in America,
1960–1984: Causes and Consequences of Citizen Political Indifference* (Dobbs Ferry, N.Y.:
Transnational Publishers, 1986); and Lester W. Milbrath and M. L. Goel, *Political Participation: How and Why Do People Get Involved in Politics?* 2nd ed. (Chicago: Rand
McNally, 1977).

2. The gender differences in political efficacy have received somewhat more attention
than the differences in political information and interest. See Linda Bennett and Stephen
Earl Bennett, "Enduring Gender Differences in Political Interest," *American Politics Quarterly* 17 (1989): 105–122, for bibliographical references and an excellent literature review.
For discussions of gender and political efficacy, see Kristi Andersen, "Working Women and
Political Participation, 1952–1972," *American Journal of Political Science* 19 (1975): 439–
453; Sandra Baxter and Marjorie Lansing, *Women and Politics: The Visible Majority,* rev.
ed. (Ann Arbor: University of Michigan Press, 1983), pp. 41–52; Karen Beckwith, *Ameri-
can Women and Political Participation: The Impacts of Work, Generation, and Feminism*
(New York: Greenwood, 1986); Sue Tolleson Rinehart, *Gender Consciousness and Politics*
(New York: Routledge, 1992), pp. 132–134; Virginia Sapiro, *The Political Integration of
Women* (Urbana: University of Illinois Press, 1983); John W. Soule and Wilma E. McGrath,
"A Comparative Study of Male-Female Political Attitudes at Citizen and Elite Levels," in *A
Portrait of Marginality,* ed. Marianne Githens and Jewel L. Prestage (New York: David
McKay Company, 1977). Writing during an era in which gender roles of many kinds were
more distinctive, Angus Campbell, Philip E. Converse, Warren E. Miller, and Donald E.
Stokes, *The American Voter* (New York: John Wiley and Sons, 1960), pointed to greater
masculine political sophistication and involvement in politics. Michael X. Delli Carpini and
Scott Keeter discuss gender differences in political knowledge in *What Americans Know
about Politics and Why It Matters* (New Haven: Yale University Press, 1996), pp. 203–209.
On the holding of political opinions, see Ronald B. Rapoport, "Sex Differences in Attitude
Expression: A Generational Explanation," *Public Opinion Quarterly* 46 (1982): 86–96;
Ronald B. Rapoport, "Like Mother, Like Daughter: Intergenerational Transmission of DK
Response Rates," *Public Opinion Quarterly* 49 (1985): 198–208.

ment persisted over time,[3] but similar relationships—of varying degrees of strength—have been observed in a number of democratic countries, especially countries in which Catholicism is the dominant religion.[4] Table 4.1 presents data about gender differences in a number of aspects of psychological involvement with politics. A majority of these measures show statistically significant gender differences; in all but one of these cases women are less politically involved than men.

First, with respect to *political interest,* the data show men to have been somewhat more likely than women to report being very interested in national politics or, in the larger Screener sample, in politics in general. In a pattern that is repeated elsewhere in the table, there is no gender difference with respect to being very interested in local politics.[5]

Political information differs from other aspects of political involvement in being an objective rather than a subjective measure.[6] Thus the gender disparity in political knowledge cannot be the result of a masculine willingness to claim credit[7]—although it might reflect differential willingness to guess and, therefore, to inflate

---

3. See Delli Carpini and Keeter, *What Americans Know About Politics,* chap. 4; and Delli Carpini and Keeter, "Measuring Political Knowledge: Putting First Things First," *American Journal of Political Science* 37 (1993): 1179–1206.

4. Margaret L. Inglehart, "Political Interest in West European Women," *Comparative Political Studies* 14 (1981): 299–326.

5. In spite of the consistent finding in Table 4.1 of gender equality with respect to orientations to local politics and greater masculine engagement with national politics, in Chapter 3 we saw little gender difference in the tendency to specialize in local politics when it comes to actual political activity.

6. We were uncertain whether to include information along with political orientations measuring, for example, interest in politics. However, John Zaller *(The Nature and Origins of Mass Opinion* [Cambridge: Cambridge University Press, 1992]) argues convincingly that political knowledge—which he calls "cognitive engagement"—is a powerful predictor of political attitude formation and of the connectedness of an individual to the political process.

7. To illustrate men's greater willingness to give themselves credit: at any level of cognitive competence (as measured objectively by a ten-word vocabulary test developed by the National Opinion Research Center and used regularly on the General Social Survey), they are more likely than women are to say that they could make an effective presentation at a public meeting or write a convincing letter to a public official. In addition, vote validation studies indicate that men are slightly more likely than women to misrepresent having gone to the polls; see Michael W. Traugott and John P. Katosh, "Response Validity in Surveys of Voting Behavior," *Public Opinion Quarterly* 43 (1979): 359–377.

Table 4.1 Measures of Psychological Involvement with Politics[a]

	Women		Men
POLITICAL INTEREST			
Very interested in politics (Screener)	24%	⇔	29%
Very interested in national politics	29%	⇔	38%
Very interested in local politics	21%		22%
POLITICAL INFORMATION			
Mean number of correct answers (out of 10)	4.5	⇔	5.2
Correct answers to individual items			
Name of one U.S. senator	51%	⇔	67%
Name of second U.S. senator	30%	⇔	43%
Name of representative in Congress	32%	⇔	42%
Name of state representative	29%	⇔	34%
Name of head of the local public school system	40%	⇔	34%
Government spends more on NASA or Social Security	18%	⇔	40%
Meaning of Fifth Amendment	39%	⇔	52%
Origin of primaries—bosses or reformers	44%	⇔	49%
Meaning of civil liberties	77%	⇔	84%
Difference between democracy and dictatorship	85%	⇔	91%
Respondent above average in political information[b]	32%	⇔	42%
POLITICAL DISCUSSION			
Discuss national politics nearly every day	20%	⇔	31%
Discuss local politics nearly every day	16%	⇔	22%
Enjoy political discussion	26%	⇔	36%
SENSITIVITY TO POLITICAL CUES			
Say AARP takes stands in politics (AARP members)	79%		80%
Say clergy sometimes or frequently discuss political issues from pulpit (attenders)[c]	22%	⇔	28%
EXPOSURE TO THE MEDIA			
Watch news on television daily	57%		56%
Watch public affairs programs on television weekly	38%	⇔	45%
Read newspaper daily	55%	⇔	59%
Pay a great deal of attention to national politics	24%	⇔	40%
Pay a great deal of attention to local politics	36%		36%
POLITICAL EFFICACY			
Mean for efficacy scale	5.08	⇔	5.45
Government would pay some or a lot of attention			
National	40%		41%
Local	60%		64%
Feeling of being able to influence some or a lot of governmental decisions (political voice)			
National	19%		17%
Local	46%	⇔	53%

Sources: Citizen Participation Study—Main Survey and Screener Survey.

a. Appendix A contains the valid number of cases for these and other measures used in the tables.

b. Rating by interviewer.

c. Among those who attend religious services two or three times a month or more.

⇔ Difference between women and men is statistically significant at the .05 level.

scores.[8] We measure political information with a ten-item scale, five asking the names of public officials and five testing knowledge of government and politics. As shown in Table 4.1, for nine of the ten items, men are more likely to provide a correct answer. Compared with women, men answered, on average, almost one additional item correctly across the whole test—an information gain roughly equivalent to that acquired from an additional $2\frac{3}{4}$ years of schooling.[9]

Women are more likely than men to know the name of the head of the local school system. This single reversal is consistent with both what is known about political knowledge and what is known about women's experiences in politics.[10] The ability to acquire political information is often domain specific and selective,[11] based

---

8. For evidence and discussion of the problems that knowledge questions can pose for assessing knowledge of groups that are differentially inclined to guess, see Jeffrey J. Mondak and Belinda Creel Davis, "Asked and Answered: Knowledge Levels When We Won't Take 'Don't Know' for an Answer," Pilot Study Report Prepared for the National Election Studies Board of Overseers, February, 2000 <www.umich.edu/~nes>.

The fact that the Cronbach's alphas for men and women are not significantly different suggests that men's higher score on the information scale is not the result of a male propensity to guess.

9. In *What Americans Know about Politics*, pp. 157–161, 203–209, Delli Carpini and Keeter consider a large number of questions across several surveys and report simiar results.

The Screener Survey included two additional questions: one about which party has majority control in Congress and one about the age of voter eligibility. Fifty-six percent of men and 47 percent of women answered both correctly.

10. We also checked the 1967 and 1987 General Social Surveys, which contain a battery of questions testing knowledge of public officials. In these two surveys as well, men were more likely than women to be able to name all public officials—except for the head of the school system, for which women held the advantage. Delli Carpini and Keeter, *What Americans Know about Politics*, pp. 207–208, report on several other smaller surveys with analogous results.

11. Philip E. Converse, "Information Flow and the Stability of Partisan Attitudes," *Public Opinion Quarterly* 26 (1962): 578–599; John Zaller, "Analysis of Information Items in the 1985 NES Pilot Study," National Election Pilot Study Report, Ann Arbor, Mich., 1986; Shanto Iyengar, "Whither Political Information?" National Election Pilot Study Report, Ann Arbor, Mich., 1986; Shanto Iyengar, "Shortcuts to Political Knowledge: The Role of Selective Attention and Accessibility," and Philip E. Converse, "Popular Representation and the Distribution of Information," in *Information and Democratic Processes*, ed. John A. Ferejohn and James H. Kuklinski (Urbana: University of Illinois Press, 1990); Michael X. Delli Carpini and Scott Keeter, "An Analysis of Information Items on the 1990 and 1991 NES Surveys: A Report to the Board of Overseers for the National Election Studies," National Election Study Report, Ann Arbor, Mich., 1992; and Delli Carpini and Keeter, "Measuring Political Knowledge."

on preexisting information and the ease of incorporating new information. According to Shanto Iyengar, "people acquire information in domains about which they are already relatively informed."[12] School politics is the political realm that has traditionally been defined as an appropriate one for women and that has been most welcoming to them. Before the enfranchisement of women in 1920, a number of states and even more locales extended a partial suffrage to women for participation in local elections, especially school elections.[13] Moreover, school boards have traditionally been, and continue to be, the elected councils on which women have achieved their greatest representation.[14] Furthermore, women legislators have traditionally been overrepresented on education committees.[15] It is fully consistent with these patterns that women would be more likely than men to know the name of the head of the school system.[16]

Although taking part in *political discussion* constitutes an action rather than a psychological state, it seems reasonable to examine it in this context as an indicator of psychological involvement with politics.[17] Men are more likely than women to report that they discuss local and, especially, national politics every day or nearly every day. What is perhaps even more germane to our concerns, they were more likely to indicate enjoying, rather than avoiding, political discussion.[18]

---

12. Iyengar, "Shortcuts to Political Knowledge," p. 163.

13. Eleanor Flexner, *Century of Struggle: The Women's Rights Movement in the United States,* rev. ed. (Cambridge: Harvard University Press, 1975), pp. 179–180.

14. In 1994 women represented 20.8 percent of all state legislators and 42.2 percent of all school board members—according to data in Center for American Women and Politics, "Fact Sheet: Women in State Legislatures 1995," Eagleton Institute, Rutgers University, New Brunswick, N.J., 1995; and William Weisenburger, Kenneth E. Underwood, and Jim Fortune, "The Violence Within," *American School Board Journal* 182 (1995): 33–38.

15. Sue Thomas, *How Women Legislate* (New York: Oxford University Press, 1994), pp. 65–67.

16. We were curious to examine whether women's ability to name the head of the school system is related to the fact that they are somewhat more likely to have school-age children at home. Among respondents with school-age children at home, 49 percent of the women and 45 percent of the men named the school head correctly. A similar difference obtains for those with no school-age children at home: the figures are 37 percent and 32 percent for women and men respectively.

17. Inglehart, "Political Interest in West European Women," also uses political discussion as an indicator of political engagement with similar results.

18. Women's expressed propensity to avoid political discussions does not appear to be

The data show relatively little disparity when it comes to whether, among individuals similarly situated, there is a gender difference in *sensitivity to political cues,* that is, in the likelihood of perceiving the political content of messages in the environment. As we showed in Chapter 3, AARP members, whether male or female, are equally likely to know that the organization takes stands in politics. Some evidence in the opposite direction might be the fact that among regular church attenders, women are less likely to report that clergy in their church sometimes or frequently discuss political issues from the pulpit.

In terms of *exposure to the media,* the data replicate patterns we have already seen. There is no gender gap in terms of either watching news on television or paying attention to newspaper stories about local politics and community affairs. However, men are somewhat more likely to report watching public affairs programs on television, reading a newspaper daily, or, especially, paying attention to stories about national and world politics in the newspaper.

Gender differences in *political efficacy* are well known. Our data, which focus on the respondent's perception of being able to have an impact on politics, or what is sometimes called "external efficacy," show a relatively small gender disparity, with men having higher average efficacy scores. However, when the four items in the scale are considered separately, the differences are not especially consistent and, in contrast to what we have seen for other measures, are more pronounced for local rather than for national politics.[19]

We can highlight these findings about political orientations by focusing briefly on religion, a domain that we use throughout this book as a counterpoint to the arena of politics. Data about gender differences in religious attitudes and orientations contrast strikingly with the data just reviewed about gender differences in political orientations. As we have mentioned, Americans are more

---

based on fear. We asked respondents if they thought that they might get into trouble with the authorities for taking a public stand on controversial issues. There is virtually no gender difference in the replies: 20 percent of men and 23 percent of women reported being somewhat or very worried.

19. In fact, data not shown in Table 4.1 indicate that for each separate item women are more likely to choose the most extreme option, indicating a sense of having no voice.

Table 4.2 Religious Attitudes and Orientations

	Women		Men
Express a Religious Preference	96%	⇔	90%
Religious Attitudes (among those expressing a preference)			
Say religion is very important	67	⇔	49
Think Bible is God's word	56	⇔	42
Have had a "born again" experience (among Protestants and Catholics)	39	⇔	32
Support Prayer in Schools	60	⇔	50
Reasons for Church Activity (among those active)			
Civic reasons			
Make the nation better	67		68
Influence government	6		5
Charitable reasons			
Lend a hand to people in need	77		73
Religious reasons			
To affirm religious faith	80	⇔	69
Further goals of religion	56	⇔	50

Source: Citizen Participation Study—Main Survey.
⇔ Difference between women and men is statistically significant at the .05 level.

deeply committed religiously than are people in the democracies of Europe; in turn, American women are more deeply committed religiously than are American men. For a series of measures of religious attitudes and orientations, Table 4.2 presents findings that are consistent with the higher level of religious practice—attendance at religious services and activity in religious institutions—that emerged in Chapter 3.

On each of several measures, women express greater depth of religious belief and concern about religious matters: they are more likely to report that religion is very important in their life, that the Bible is God's word, and, if Christian, that they have had a "born again" experience. In addition, they are more likely to support school prayer.

We also find an interesting pattern in the responses to a battery of questions posed to church activists about their reasons for being active in their churches. There was no significant difference between women and men with respect to civic reasons, such as making the nation a better place to live, or charitable reasons, such as lending a hand to those in need. However, women were more likely than men to mention religious reasons, affirming their faith or furthering the goals of their religion. The data reinforce our understanding that men and women direct their concerns in somewhat different directions.

Gender Consciousness and Experience of Gender Bias

With respect to politics, we have focused on general orientations—knowing and caring about politics, thinking that one could make a difference politically—that serve as a background to political participation. There is another set of political orientations, however, that deserves consideration. As members of a group that is disadvantaged in various ways, women may experience discrimination on the basis of sex. In addition, they may develop a sense of group consciousness. Either of these might be associated with political activity. These are not the easiest matters to probe in the context of a mass survey.[20] Nevertheless, in the Citizen Participation Study we used a standard survey item in order to ask women and men whether they had ever experienced discrimination in jobs, school admissions, housing, or in other important things on the basis of their sex or gender. Because one individual might deem discriminatory an experience that another shrugs off, we consider this measure to be neither entirely objective nor entirely subjective.[21] In addition, to measure gender consciousness for women, we asked

---

20. On the measurement of group consciousness for women and its impact on political behavior, see, for example, Arthur H. Miller, Patricia Gurin, Gerald Gurin, and Oksana Malanchuk, "Group Consciousness and Political Participation," *American Journal of Political Science* 25 (1981): 494–511; Ethel Klein, *Gender Politics* (Cambridge: Harvard University Press, 1984); Patricia Gurin, "Women's Gender Consciousness," *Public Opinion Quarterly* 49 (1985): 143–163; Kay Deaux and Marianne LaFrance, "Gender," in *The Handbook of Social Psychology*, 4th ed., ed. Daniel T. Gilbert, Susan T. Fiske, and Gardner Lindzey (Boston: McGraw Hill, 1988), pp. 788–827; Elizabeth Adell Cook, "Measuring Feminist Consciousness," *Women and Politics* 9 (1989): 71–88; Sue Tolleson Rinehart, *Gender Consciousness and Politics* (New York: Routledge, Chapman, and Hall, 1992); and Iris Marion Young, "Gender as Seriality: Thinking about Women as a Social Collective," *Signs* 19 (1994): 713–738.

21. The increasingly rich literature on the measurement and consequences of discrimination makes arguments that are important to keep in mind when interpreting these measures.

them whether they felt closer to women than to men; whether they thought that there are problems of special concern to women that they need to work together to solve; and, if so, whether they thought that the government should be doing more about these problems. Analogous questions were posed to all respondents about discrimination on the basis of race or ethnicity. In addition, African-Americans and Latinos were asked questions about feeling close to other group members, thinking that they had joint problems, and the government's responsibility to assist in solving shared problems.

In Table 4.3 we present data about these group orientations. Because responses to these questions are difficult to interpret in isolation, for comparative purposes we include data about the parallel questions having to do with race or ethnicity. Not surprisingly, as shown in the top portion of Table 4.3, there are, overall, fewer reports of gender bias than of racial or ethnic bias from Blacks or Latinos respectively. Although women are more likely than men to have reported experiencing sex discrimination, only a small proportion of either group—11 percent of women and 6 percent of men—indicated experiencing this kind of discrimination. When it comes to racial or ethnic discrimination, as we would expect, compared with Anglo-Whites, minority group members are more likely to report having experienced bias, and African-Americans, especially African-American men, are more likely than Latinos to report having experienced racial or ethnic bias. In addition, Black women and Latina women each report at least twice as much racial or ethnic bias as gender bias.

In the bottom portion of Table 4.3, we report data on the three measures of group consciousness: whether respondents feel close

---

Early and often-cited work on this topic suggests that some women may deny discrimination, even when discrimination exists. See Faye Crosby, "The Denial of Personal Discrimination," *American Behavioral Scientist* 27 (1984): 371–386. More recently, multi-item measures have been developed to measure both generalized and particular experiences with discrimination. See, for example, Tyrone A. Forman, David R. Williams, and James S. Jackson, "Race, Place, and Discrimination," *Perspectives on Social Problems* 9 (1997): 231–261; Ronald C. Kessler, Kristin D. Mickelson, and David R. Williams, "The Prevalence, Distribution, and Mental Health Correlates of Perceived Discrimination in the United States," *Journal of Health and Social Behavior* 40 (1999): 208–230; and Lee Sigelman and Susan Welch, *Black Americans' Views of Racial Inequality* (Cambridge: Harvard University Press, 1991).

Table 4.3 Group Orientations: Experiences of Discrimination and Group Consciousness

A. Percentage Who Say They Experienced Discrimination on the Basis of Sex and Race or Ethnicity

	On Basis of Sex	On Basis of Race or Ethnicity	On Basis of Either or Both
Women	11%	6%	14%
Anglo-White women	11	3	13
Black women	10	20	23
Latina women	7	19	21
Men	6	9	11
Anglo-White men	6	7	9
Black men	6	30	31
Latino men	5	16	19

B. Expressions of Group Consciousness by Gender and Race or Ethnicity

	Feel Close to Others in the Group	Believe They Have Problems in Common	Government Should Help
Feel about Women			
All women	10%	81%	78%
Anglo-White women	10	81	77
Black women	11	84	86
Latina women	13	77	82
Feel about Blacks			
All Blacks	16	87	88
Black women	15	86	89
Black men	17	88	88
Feel about Latinos			
All Latinos	14	80	82
Latina women	14	82	84
Latino men	14	78	78

Source: Citizen Participation Study—Main Survey.

to other group members; whether they think that there are problems of special concern to group members which they need to work together to solve; and, if so, whether the government should be doing more about these problems. In general, with respect to these measures, the similarities across groups are more striking than the differences. Only a modest proportion in each group report feeling particularly close to other group members.

Only a small minority of women say they feel especially close to other women, but 81 percent indicate that they believe women have common problems and, of them, 78 percent believe that the government has some responsibility to help out.[22] Similar proportions of African-Americans reported feeling especially close to other African-Americans and believing that African-Americans face joint problems. However, a somewhat higher proportion of African-Americans, 88 percent, indicated that the government should be involved in solving these problems.

Gender Differences in Political Voice?

We have examined gender differences with respect to a number of predispositions that provide background for political participation. Our next task is to get closer to political activity in order to explore the values and preferences that give to political activity its raison d'être. In this section, we consider gender differences in the rewards that activists seek in taking part and in the issue concerns they bring to their participation.[23] We ask whether women and men derive different gratifications from their activity and whether their activity is inspired by different sets of policy priorities.

Over the past two decades, political scientists have cast considerable light on the question of whether there are gender differences in political voice. A number of theoretical perspectives have been developed with respect to the issue of whether we should expect women and men to display different orientations to politics.[24] In

---

22. For a comparison between the gender and racial attachments of Black women, see Claudine Gay and Katherine Tate, "Doubly Bound: The Impact of Gender and Race on the Politics of Black Women," *Political Psychology* 19 (1998): 169–184.

23. This portion of the chapter draws very heavily from "Gender and Citizen Participation," of which Jesse Donahue was a co-author.

24. See, for example, Jean Bethke Elshtain, *Public Man, Private Woman* (Princeton: Princeton University Press, 1981); Virgina Sapiro, "When Are Interests Interesting?: The Problem of Political Representation of Women," *American Political Science Review* 75 (1981): 701–716; Mary G. Dietz, "Citizenship with a Feminist Face," *Political Theory* 13 (1985): 19–37; Joan C. Tronto, "Beyond Gender Difference to a Theory of Care," *Signs* 12 (1987): 644–663; and Sara Ruddick, *Maternal Thinking: Toward a Politics of Peace* (Boston: Beacon Press, 1989).

terms of empirical findings, at the level of the mass public, scholars have focused upon gender differences in partisan identification and vote choices as well as in political attitudes.[25]

In the aftermath of the 1980 election—when men gave 53 percent, and women gave 49 percent, of their votes to Ronald Reagan—scholars as well as observers in the media discovered the gender gap.[26] Since then, women have consistently been somewhat more Democratic than men in both their electoral choices and their party leanings. This circumstance is ordinarily interpreted as the result of women's distinctive preferences. Longitudinal data, however, make clear that it is men's, not women's, partisanship and vote choices that have changed. While men have moved toward the Republicans, thus creating the gender gap, women's preferences have, in the aggregate, remained largely unchanged.[27]

When it comes to attitudes on issues, the results of public opinion surveys, in which members of the mass public are asked to respond to a series of issues pre-selected by the researcher, have long shown interesting, and perhaps unexpected, patterns of gender difference. With respect to "women's issues"—that is, issues like

25. See, for example, Kathleen A. Frankovic, "Sex and Politics—New Alignments, Old Issues," *PS: Political Science and Politics* 15 (1982): 439–448; Ted Goertzel, "The Gender Gap: Sex, Family Income, and Political Opinions in the 1980s," *Journal of Family and Military Sociology* 11 (1983): 209–222; Ethel Klein, "The Gender Gap: Different Issues, Different Answers," *Brookings Review* 3 (1985): 33–37; Pippa Norris, "The Gender Gap: America and Britain," *Parliamentary Affairs* 38 (1985): 192–201; Robert Y. Shapiro and Harpreet Mahajan, "Gender Differences in Policy Preferences: A Summary of Trends from the 1960s to the 1980s," *Public Opinion Quarterly* 50 (1986): 42–61; Daniel Wirls, "Reinterpreting the Gender Gap," *Public Opinion Quarterly* 50 (1986): 316–330; Pamela Johnston Conover, "Feminists and the Gender Gap," *Journal of Politics* 50 (1988): 985–1010; Henry C. Kenski, "The Gender Factor in a Changing Electorate," and Arthur Miller, "Gender and the Vote: 1984" in *The Politics of the Gender Gap*, ed. Carol M. Mueller (Newbury Park, Calif.: Sage Publications, 1988); Susan Welch and Lee Sigelman, "A Black Gender Gap?" *Social Science Quarterly* 70 (1989): 120–133; Mary E. Bendyna and Celinda C. Lake, "Gender and Voting in the 1992 Presidential Election," in *The Year of the Woman: Myths and Realities,* ed. Elizabeth Adell Cook, Sue Thomas, and Clyde Wilcox (Boulder, Colo.: Westview Press, 1994); Kristi Andersen, "Gender and Public Opinion," in *Understanding Public Opinion,* ed. Barbara Norrander and Clyde Wilcox (Washington, D.C.: CQ Press, 1997), chap. 2; and Karen M. Kaufmann and John R. Petrocik, "The Changing Politics of American Men: Understanding the Sources of the Gender Gap," *American Journal of Political Science* 43 (1999): 864–887.

26. Gallup Poll figures given in Harold W. Stanley and Richard Niemi, eds., *Vital Statistics on American Politics, 1999–2000* (Washington, D.C.: CQ Press, 2000) p. 119.

27. On this point, see Andersen, "Gender and Public Opinion"; and Kaufmann and Petrocik, "The Changing Politics of American Men."

women's rights, abortion, or during the 1970s, the Equal Rights Amendment (ERA) that affect men and women differently—the gender differences in opinion are narrow and inconsistent. The disparities in opinion are somewhat more marked with respect to what are sometimes called "compassion issues," such as support for government welfare guarantees. The differences are wider still and more consistent when it comes to a series of issues—ranging from gun control to support for military intervention in international conflicts—that involve violence or coercion.

We have also learned a great deal about gender differences in the orientations and agendas of political elites. Recent studies of public officials—especially legislators in both the state houses and the U.S. Congress—concur in finding that it makes a difference when women hold office.[28] Compared with their male fellow partisans, female representatives tend to have distinctive attitudes: they are more liberal with respect not only to the issues on which there has traditionally been a gender gap in public opinion among citizens but also to a much broader array of policy concerns, including the relatively abbreviated list of issues that might be deemed women's issues. Moreover, their attitudes are reflected in their behavior and legislative priorities. Most notably, women legislators are more

---

28. Complementary perspectives and extensive bibliographical references can be found in, among others, Rita Mae Kelly, Michelle A. Saint-Germain, and Jody D. Horn, "Female Public Officials: A Different Voice?" in *American Feminism: New Issues for a Mature Movement,* ed. Janet K. Boles (Newbury Park, Calif.: Sage Publications, 1991); Susan Welch and Sue Thomas, "Do Women in Public Office Make a Difference?" in *Gender and Policymaking,* ed. Susan J. Carroll, Debra Dodson, and Ruth B. Mandel (New Brunswick, N.J.: Center for the American Woman and Politics, Eagleton Institute of Politics, Rutgers University, 1991); Ruth B. Mandel and Debra L. Dodson, "Do Women Officeholders Make a Difference?" in *The American Woman, 1992–93: A Status Report,* ed. Paula Ries and Anne J. Stone (New York: W. W. Norton, 1992); Susan Gluck Mezey, "Increasing the Number of Women in Office: Does It Matter?" in *The Year of the Woman: Myths and Realities,* ed. Elizabeth Adell Cook, Sue Thomas, and Clyde Wilcox (Boulder, Colo.: Westview Press, 1994); Lyn Kathlene, "Alternative Views of Crime," *Journal of Politics* 57 (1995): 696–723; Thomas, *How Women Legislate;* Cindy Simon Rosenthal, *When Women Lead* (New York: Oxford University Press, 1998); and Beth Reingold, *Representing Women* (Chapel Hall: University of North Carolina Press, 2000). On the issue of why we would expect gender differences to be more pronounced among policymakers than among members of the mass public, see Paul Schumaker and Nancy Elizabeth Burns, "Gender Cleavages and the Resolution of Local Policy Issues," *American Journal of Political Science* 32 (1988): 1070–1095.

likely to support and to champion measures concerning women, children, and families.[29]

Although political scientists have made substantial progress in probing the differences between men and women in the attitudes and choices of voters or political elites, we know much less about whether men and women speak with distinctive political voices when they participate as citizens and communicate to public officials about their needs, preferences, and priorities. Both the nature of the sample and the interview schedule of the Citizen Participation Study make it particularly useful for examining what activists seek when they take part. In contrast to ordinary random samples of the public, which net very few cases of those who undertake rare activities—respondents who, for example, have attended a protest or worked in a campaign within the recent past—the Citizen Participation Study deliberately oversampled activists. In addition, whenever a respondent indicated having been active in a particular way, we asked a series of questions designed to measure the relative importance of a range of possible rewards in animating the activity. We also inquired whether there was any issue or problem, "ranging from public policy issues to community, family, and personal concerns," that led to the activity. We later coded the verbatim answers into categories of issue concerns. These data permit us to investigate the roots of citizen activity in terms of the gratifications attendant to their participation and the issue concerns behind it.

The Rewards of Participation

The fact of political participation, for women or for men, is often considered a paradox. From a rational choice perspective, joint activity on behalf of shared objectives is, under ordinary cir-

---

29. As the proportion of women in the legislatures has increased over the past two decades, these patterns of gender difference among legislators have assumed a complex form. In certain ways, women legislators are entering the mainstream: beginning to be represented among committee chairs and legislative leaders and branching out from the small number of committees onto which they were once ghettoized. At the same time women are diverging from the masculine standard in their policy preferences and legislative priorities. On this theme, see, in particular, Thomas, *How Women Legislate,* chaps. 2–3.

cumstances, irrational. The logic is as follows: since governmental policies are collective goods—affecting citizens whether or not they are active in promoting or opposing them—the rational, self-interested individual has no incentive to invest scarce resources in political participation. Because the efforts of any single individual are unlikely to have a significant effect on whether the desired policy outcome is achieved, the rational individual will hitch a free ride on the activity of others and thus reap the benefits of the preferred policy without expending resources on its attainment. The result is that rational, self-interested individuals will refrain from taking part.

Nonetheless, millions vote and take part in other ways. Many solutions have been given to this puzzle; most of them focus on the range of selective, usually self-interested, gratifications that political activity can provide.[30] In the Citizen Participation Study, we took a simple, somewhat novel, approach to this issue. We looked at it from the perspective of the activists by asking them how *they* interpret their participation; in particular, how they recall the reasons for their activity.[31]

Although we might entertain contradictory hypotheses about differences between women and men in their retrospective understandings of the reasons that led to activity, inferences from a variety of studies suggest that women would be more likely than men to cite civic concerns and less likely than men to indicate seeking material rewards. For example, in her study of delegates to the 1972 presidential nominating conventions, Jeane Kirkpatrick found women delegates in both parties to be less ambitious for

---

30. More recently, rational choice scholars have focused on the role of information and reputation in generating action. See, for example, Dennis Chong, *Collective Action and the Civil Rights Movement* (Chicago: University of Chicago Press, 1991); Susanne Lohmann, "Information Aggregation through Costly Political Action," *American Economic Review* 84 (1994): 518–530; and Susanne Lohmann, "The Dynamics of Information Cascades: The Monday Demonstrations in Leipzig, East Germany, 1989–1991," *World Politics* 47 (1994): 42–101.

31. For a detailed analysis of the issue, including a discussion of the methodological issues associated with asking respondents to reconstruct their reasons for activity and extensive bibliographic references, see Kay Lehman Schlozman, Sidney Verba, and Henry Brady, "Participation's Not a Paradox: The View from American Activists," *British Journal of Political Science* 25 (1995): 1–36.

elective office than their male counterparts.[32] In addition, the literature on social feminism and women's involvements in the period just before the granting of suffrage emphasizes the extent to which that work was charitably oriented and motivated by community-spirited value orientations.[33] Furthermore, in her study of state legislators, Kirkpatrick found women in the state houses to be more comfortable with a conception of politics as an arena characterized by problem solving in search of the common good rather than by self-interested conflict.[34] Raymond Bauer, Ithiel de Sola Pool, and Louis Anthony Dexter echo this understanding of a distinctively female approach to politics in their patronizing 1963 characterization of "The Ladies from the League."[35]

We consider four kinds of motivations: selective benefits of three types—material benefits, social gratifications, and civic gratifications—as well as the desire to influence a collective policy. *Selective gratifications* may be material or intangible. *Material benefits,* such as jobs, career advancement, or help with a personal or family problem, were the lubricant of the classic urban machine. They continue to figure importantly in contemporary discussions of congressional constituency service and incentives for joining organizations. *Social gratifications,* such as the enjoyment of working with others or the excitement of politics,[36] cannot be enjoyed apart from the activity itself. Without taking part, there is no way to partake of the fun, gain the recognition, or enjoy other social benefits. Similarly, *civic gratifications,* such as satisfying a sense of duty or a desire to contribute to the welfare of the community also derive from the act itself. In this case, however, we are concerned

---

32. Jeane J. Kirkpatrick, *The New Presidential Elite* (New York: Russell Sage, 1976).

33. See, for example, Flexner, *Century of Struggle;* Paula Baker, "The Domestication of Politics: Women and American Political Society, 1780–1920," *American Historical Review* 89 (1984): 620–647; and Aileen S. Kraditor, *The Ideas of the Woman Suffrage Movement* (New York: W. W. Norton, 1968).

34. Jeane J. Kirkpatrick, *Political Woman* (New York: Basic Books, 1974), pp. 143–145.

35. Raymond A. Bauer, Ithiel de Sola Pool, and Louis Anthony Dexter, *American Business and Public Policy* (Chicago: Aldine, 1963), chap. 27.

36. Because activities undertaken alone can be exciting, excitement is not technically a "social" gratification. However, this is a gratification cited relatively frequently across acts, and it seems to fit in with the other reasons we call "social," all of which involve gratifications derived from an association with others.

Table 4.4 Gratifications from Political Participation (proportion mentioning gratification as "very important")

	Material		Social		Civic		Policy	
	Women	Men	Women	Men	Women	Men	Women	Men
Vote	8%	8%	22%	21%	90% ⇔	87%	49%	53%
Work in a Campaign	25	24	47	50	85	84	44	52
Campaign Contribution	14	20	28	18	79	80	47	46
Particularized Contact	86 ⇔	67	26	22	43	38	17	21
Contact on a National Issue	16 ⇔	32	10	13	87	88	80	79
Informal Community Activity	16	16	33	32	83 ⇔	76	35	37

Source: Citizen Participation Study—Main Survey.
⇔ Difference between women and men is statistically significant at the .05 level.

that social norms give respondents an incentive to emphasize the desire for these psychological rewards in order to please the interviewer. Although there is no reason to expect respondents to exaggerate the social gratifications attendant to voluntary activity, they might overstate the extent to which they were motivated by civic concerns. *Collective outcomes* are the enactment or implementation of desired public policies or the election of a favored candidate.[37]

Table 4.4 reports the proportion of activists who say that a gratification in one of the four categories was very important in their decisions to undertake six kinds of activity: vote, work in a campaign, make a campaign contribution, contact an official on a matter affecting themselves or their families, contact an official about an issue affecting the nation, and become active with others in an informal community effort. There are some gender differences in Table 4.4 that reach statistical significance. However, the differences are neither very substantial in magnitude nor consistent across gratifications or political acts. In fact, what is most apparent about Table 4.4 is how little difference there is between men and women in the gratifications cited.

Much more striking are the differences across political acts. In discussing voting, respondents—whether male or female—referred frequently to civic rewards and only rarely to material ones. With respect to the gratifications attendant to working in a campaign, social gratifications assume greater prominence—again for both women and men. What this means is that it is the nature of the act rather than the sex of the participant that determines the rewards

---

37. From the perspective of the theorists of collective action, respondents who cited a desire to influence government policy are irrational. Instead, what they could derive is what James Q. Wilson, on whose typology of organizational gratifications we draw heavily, calls "purposive" gratifications, "intangible rewards that derive from the sense of satisfaction of having contributed to the attainment of a worthwhile cause." See *Political Organizations* (New York: Basic Books, 1973), p. 34.

We group these intangible rewards under the rubric of civic gratifications and consider the "irrational" desire to affect policy separately. David Knoke follows a similar approach when he specifies a separate dimension for "lobbying incentives" in "Organizational Incentives," *American Sociological Review* 53 (1988): 311–329; as does John Mark Hansen, who discusses "political collective benefits" in "The Political Economy of Group Membership," *American Political Science Review* 79 (1985): 79–96.

associated with it. Since men and women choose to engage in the same kinds of participatory acts, the consequent rewards accruing to them are necessarily similar.

The Issue Agenda of Participation

One of the striking features of the data in Table 4.4 is the large proportion of activists, both women and men, who mention the chance to influence government policy as a reason for their activity—despite the fact that theories of rational choice would argue that it is irrational for them to do so.[38] As we might expect, for most of those who contact a government official directly, there is some policy issue at stake. However, we also find that about half of the voters and campaign workers also mention a policy concern associated with their activity. In short, activists do hope to further a public purpose through their activity.

Our principal concern, of course, is whether men and women differ systematically in the issues and problems they bring into political life. Earlier we mentioned the results of studies of the gender differences among legislators with respect to their discretionary activities—cosponsoring bills, attending committee meetings, making speeches, and so forth. In contrast to casting roll-call votes, these are activities that afford a legislator considerable control over the issue agenda. With respect to these discretionary activities, studies show that women are more likely than men to place a high priority on issues relating to children, to families, and to women. These results seem especially germane to our concerns here because—like legislators undertaking discretionary activities, but unlike legislators casting roll-call votes or respondents to a public opinion poll, who must decide about a pre-selected set of issues—citizen activists choose freely the issue baskets in which to place their participatory eggs. In one respect, however, we might expect differences between citizens and legislators when it comes to the content of their discretionary agendas. Women legislators

---

38. See Sidney Verba, Kay Lehman Schlozman, and Henry Brady, *Voice and Equality: Civic Voluntarism in American Politics* (Cambridge: Harvard University Press, 1995), chap. 5, for a discussion.

self-consciously assume that part of their legislative responsibility is to represent women.[39] Presumably, most women activists do not feel a similar responsibility.

THE SCOPE OF THE AGENDA

Given women's traditional role within the family as well as the particularistic orientation to politics that has been ascribed to them since the Greeks, we might expect women to bring to politics more personal or family concerns. We can investigate this surmise by considering the scope of the issues behind political activity. Each time a respondent indicated having engaged in a particular activity, we inquired whether there was any particular issue or problem—"ranging from public policy issues to community, family, and personal concerns"—that led to the activity. Across the totality of more than 3,600 political acts discussed by our respondents, in 63 percent of cases respondents provided a comprehensible, "codable" answer about the policy concerns that animated the activity.[40] Analyzing the substantive concerns behind this "issue-based activity" allows us to characterize the participatory input from various groups—including men and women.

Since we wish to assess whether women and men differ in the likelihood of mentioning a concern limited to the individual and the family rather than issues with a broader referent, we focus, at the outset, on contacts with public officials, the only activity for which sizable numbers of respondents said that their concern was narrowly personal. (With regard to all other participatory acts, for the overwhelming majority of activists, the referent was broader.) It turns out that there is remarkable similarity between men and women who get in touch with public officials with respect to whether the matter raised is germane only to themselves or their

39. See, for example, Karin L. Tamerius, "Does Sex Matter?: Women Representing Women's Interests in Congress" (paper presented at the annual meeting of the Midwest Political Science Association, Chicago, 1993); Thomas, *How Women Legislate;* and Michelle Swers, "From the Year of the Woman to the Republican Ascendancy: Evaluating the Policy Impact of Women in Congress" (Ph.D. dissertation, Harvard University, 2000).

40. Only 47 percent of voters—in contrast to 84 percent of those active in their communities, 87 percent of contactors, and 95 percent of protesters—cited at least one identifiable public policy issue as the basis of their activity.

Table 4.5 The Issues That Animate Political Participation[a]

	Women		Men
Basic Human Needs	10%		9%
Taxes	12	⇔	15
Economic Issues (except taxes)	9		11
Abortion	14	⇔	7
Social Issues (except abortion)	2		2
Education	20	⇔	13
Children or Youth (except education)	5		4
Crime or Drugs	9		7
Environment	8		10
Foreign Policy	5	⇔	8
Women's Issues	1		b
Number of Respondents	1,327		1,191
Number of Issue-Based Acts	1,162		1,235

Source: Citizen Participation Study—Main Survey.

a. Entries are the proportion of issue-based participation motivated by concern about particular issues.

b. Less than 1 percent.

⇔ Difference between women and men is statistically significant at the .05 level.

families or a policy issue of more general concern. Discussing their most recent contact, 22 percent of the men and 21 percent of the women indicated that the subject was a matter of particularized concern. Thirty-five percent of the female contactors indicated that the issue affects the whole community and 25 percent that it affects the entire nation (or the whole world); the analogous figures for male contactors are 38 percent and 22 percent respectively.

THE CONTENT OF THE AGENDA

More important than the scope of the policy concerns behind political activity is their subject matter. After all, issue-based citizen participation serves as an important—though hardly the only—vehicle for communicating information to policymakers about what is on the minds of members of the public. In order to ascertain whether we could discern distinctive male and female voices with respect to policy concerns, we tried an experiment. We printed separate lists for women and men of the "word bites" that were recorded by interviewers when respondents described the issues behind their contacts with public officials. Except for one identifying marker—a respondent who used gendered language in referring to a spouse—it was impossible to differentiate the men's list from the women's. In short, simply by scanning, we could not distinguish distinctive sets of priorities. We have reproduced the two lists in the appendix to this chapter and invite you to repeat our experiment.

Clearly, more systematic analysis is needed. Table 4.5 compares women and men respondents with respect to the issue concerns that animate their participation. The issue-based political act is the unit of analysis, and the figures represent the proportion of all issue-based activity for which the respondent mentioned, among other things, a particular set of policy concerns.[41] In consider-

---

41. In coding the open-ended responses we created over sixty relatively narrow categories. In analyzing the data, we have combined these narrow categories in various ways. The components of the categories in Table 4.5 are as follows:

Basic human needs: various government benefits (welfare, AFDC, food stamps, housing subsidies, Social Security, Medicare, and Medicaid); unemployment (either as an economic issue or in terms of the respondent's own circumstances); housing or homelessness; health or health care; poverty or hunger; aid to the handicapped or handicapped rights.

Taxes: all references to taxes at any governmental level.

Economic issues: local or national economic performance; inflation; budget issues or the budget deficit; government spending; other economic issues.

Abortion: all references to abortion whether pro-life, pro-choice, or ambiguous.

Social issues: traditional morality; pornography; family planning, teenage pregnancy, sex education, or contraception; school prayer; or gay rights or homosexuality.

Education: educational issues (for example, school reform, school voucher plans); problems or issues related to schooling of family members; guaranteed student loans.

Children or youth: recreation for children or youth; day care; other issues affecting young.

Crime or drugs: crime; gangs; safety in the streets; drugs.

Environment: specific environmental issues (for example, clean air, toxic wastes) or environmental concerns in general; wildlife preservation; animal rights.

Foreign policy: relations with particular nations or foreign policy in general; defense policy or defense spending; peace, arms control, or international human rights issues.

Women's issues: women's rights; domestic violence; rape; women's health and reproductive issues (excluding abortion).

Note that the categories vary in the extent to which they encompass respondents with quite different issue positions. For example, activists on the abortion issue are polarized in their opinions. In contrast, activists who cited concerns about the environment tend to be in overall agreement with one another. Their opposition might come from activists with concerns about economic development and performance.

ing Table 4.5, it is important to recall that public officials have many ways to learn about citizen concerns and preferences—among them, the media, public opinion polls, and communications from organized interests—only one of which is through political participation. It is also important to remember that the set of issue concerns expressed reflects the particular time when the data were collected, 1990: between two Supreme Court decisions that broadened the ability of the states to regulate abortion, *Webster* v. *Reproductive Health Services* (1989) and *Planned Parenthood* v. *Casey* (1992), and before the Senate confirmation hearings on Justice Clarence Thomas, which drew attention to the issue of sexual harassment.

When it comes to the actual issues associated with activity, both groups bring a diverse set of issue concerns to participation, and their issue agendas are similar, though not identical. Although the differences are not always statistically significant, men are slightly more likely to mention economic matters, including taxes, the environment, and foreign policy; women are slightly more likely to mention crime and drugs. With respect to two issues, education and abortion, the gender differences are more substantial. Twenty percent of women's issue-based activity, in contrast to 13 percent of men's, is animated, at least in part, by concern about educational matters.[42] When it comes to abortion, the analogous figures are 14 percent and 7 percent respectively. The greater weight that educational matters have in women's bundle of issue concerns is striking, for—unlike, say, gun control—women and men have not

---

It should also be noted that the categories in Table 4.5 are not exhaustive. Issue concerns ranging from gun control to drunk driving have been omitted from the table. If the universe of issue concerns had been included, the figures in each column would add to more than 100 percent. A single political act is often inspired by more than one issue concern. The contactor who expressed concern about "public housing, teenage pregnancy, and the child care bill" would have been coded as mentioning three separate issues.

42. In the first wave of their panel study, Jennings and Niemi found husbands to be generally more politically active and interested than their wives, except with respect to involvement in school matters. M. Kent Jennings and Richard G. Niemi, "The Division of Political Labor between Mothers and Fathers," *American Political Science Review* 65 (1971): 69–82. This pattern appeared decades later in the next generation of married couples as well. M. Kent Jennings, "Participation as Viewed through the Lens of the Political Socialization Study" (paper presented at a conference on "Political Participation: Building a Research Agenda," Center for the Study of Democratic Politics, Princeton University, October 2000).

traditionally held different opinions on educational issues. In addition, unlike abortion, educational issues do not have a special impact on women. Instead, education falls into the domain of issues of care that were the traditional bailiwick of the social feminists and that have traditionally taken precedence among the priorities of women legislators.[43]

Because the availability of abortion is germane to women's lives in a way that it is not relevant to men's, it is perhaps not surprising that women give greater relative weight to the issue of abortion in their issue-based activity than do men. It is necessary to recall, however, that these figures conflate activists who are pro-choice with those who are pro-life. Elsewhere in our questionnaire we asked a standard survey question about attitudes toward abortion. That item showed that Americans are divided in their opinions. The center of gravity leans decidedly in the direction of support for the availability of abortion—with men somewhat more pro-choice than women.[44] Nevertheless, for both women and men, activity on abortion comes disproportionately from the pro-life side.[45] Thirty-five percent of women expressed pro-life views in response to the survey question; yet 53 percent of the portion of women's political activity that is motivated by concern about the abortion issue emanated from respondents who reported pro-life attitudes. For men the figures are 26 percent and 43 percent respectively.[46] Women in the legislatures—who, unlike women activ-

---

43. Thomas, *How Women Legislate*, pp. 94–95.
44. The data are as follows:
   (1) A woman should always be able to obtain an abortion as a matter of choice.
   (7) By law abortion should never be permitted.

	1	2	3	4	5	6	7
Men	40%	11	9	13	6	10	10
Women	36%	9	8	12	7	9	19

45. In order to ensure that the direction of opinion on abortion expressed in the survey item could be used as a guide to the direction of opinion expressed through activity on abortion, we conducted the following experiment. We coded the actual verbatims for abortion activists as to whether the activity was pro-life, pro-choice, or ambiguous in direction. In no case that a direction was specified in connection with abortion-related activity did that direction contradict the opinion elicited by the survey item.

46. It is also worth noting that abortion figures more importantly in the activity of those

ists, place women's rights issues among their policy priorities—are not as divided in their attitudes about abortion as are women in the mass public and are distinctly less pro-life in their opinions than their fellow legislators who are male.[47]

In contrast to the circumstance with respect to abortion, there is no division of opinion among those who mentioned women's issues. All the messages on the subject indicated support for women's rights or greater attention to problems such as rape or domestic violence. (Interestingly, not one respondent mentioned sexual harassment in these 1990 interviews.) What is most noteworthy, however, is just how rarely these issues were raised in connection with activity. Women discussed these issues in connection with 1 percent of their issue-based activity, and men barely mentioned them at all. The silence when it comes to women's issues is particularly striking because, at just the time the interviews were being conducted, Congress was considering a civil rights bill—later vetoed by President George H. W. Bush—that would have made it easier to prove discrimination, including gender discrimination, on the job. Thus the absence of activity animated by concern about women's rights issues cannot be explained as merely reflecting a political agenda devoid of relevant policy matters.

What is most apparent is not that the government hears more from women than from men about women's issues or that the content of the messages is uniformly in support of equality between the sexes, but rather that public officials hear so little on the subject from citizens. Of course, they may hear more on this topic from the women's rights organizations—with which 6 percent of the women in the sample are affiliated—that are so active in politics. Nevertheless, except for abortion, a subject about which women, and men, are divided in their opinions, policymakers hear remarkably little from citizens about women's issues.

Presumably these results would have been different had the data

---

who are pro-life than of those who are pro-choice: abortion was mentioned in connection with 24 percent of the issue-based activity of pro-life women and 12 percent of the activity of pro-life men; in contrast, abortion was discussed in relation to 11 percent of the activity of pro-choice women and 6 percent of the activity of pro-choice men.

47. Thomas, *How Women Legislate,* p. 65.

been collected fifteen years earlier, when there was widespread public contention over the ERA. At that point the messages would have been more frequent and opinion on the subject would have been divided. Still, it is noteworthy how little space on the public's agenda these issues occupy.

PARTICIPATORY AGENDAS: A FURTHER PROBE

We can probe further by considering the participatory agendas of men and women who differ in terms of their class and their family circumstances.[48] We begin with socioeconomic advantage, and the findings are complex. In Table 4.6 we compare men and women who are relatively advantaged (who have had at least a year of college education and whose family incomes were $50,000 or more) with those who are much less advantaged (who have no more than a high school education and whose family incomes were no more than $20,000).[49] Educational concerns figure importantly in the issue-based activity of both advantaged and disadvantaged respondents. Once again, however, they occupy greater space in women's activity than in men's. Abortion weighs more heavily in the issue-based activity of the advantaged, for whom there is no gender gap, than in the activity of the disadvantaged, for whom there is a gender disparity in abortion-related activity.

Disadvantaged respondents, both female and male, are more concerned with issues of basic human need. Among the advantaged there is no difference between women and men in the extent to which these issues figure in issue-based activity. In contrast, among the disadvantaged issues of basic human need occupy much more space in the bundle of issue concerns for women than for men. A similar pattern obtains for issues associated with drugs

---

48. In Chapter 11, we consider the participatory agendas of women and men differentiated on the basis of race or ethnicity.

49. In Table 4.6, and other tables in which we compare various sub-groups of men and women, we omit measures of statistical significance because it is not clear which groups we most want to compare. For example, in Table 4.6 it is noteworthy both that the activity of advantaged women is *less* likely to be motivated by concerns about taxes than is the activity of advantaged men and that the activity of advantaged women is *less* likely to be motivated by concerns about taxes than is the activity of disadvantaged women.

In constant 2000 dollars, a 1989 family income of $50,000 would be roughly $66,000 and an income of $20,000 would be roughly $26,500.

Table 4.6 Socioeconomic Advantage and the Issues That Animate Political Participation[a]

	Advantaged[b]		Disadvantaged[c]	
	Women	Men	Women	Men
Basic Human Needs	9%	9%	27%	12%
Taxes	8	16	13	15
Economic Issues (except taxes)	14	15	4	5
Abortion	13	12	6	0
Social Issues (except abortion)	1	1	6	0
Education	24	14	17	8
Children or Youth (except education)	5	3	9	5
Crime or Drugs	8	5	15	6
Environment	5	10	0	4
Foreign Policy	7	9	2	4
Women's Issues	2	d	0	0
Number of Respondents	197	228	297	182
Number of Issue-Based Acts	326	338	113	72

Source: Citizen Participation Study—Main Survey.

a. Entries are the proportion of issue-based participation motivated by concern about particular issues.

b. Advantaged: At least one year of college and family income at least $50,000.

c. Disadvantaged: No college education and family income less than $20,000.

d. Less than 1 percent.

and crime. Concern about crime and drugs figures much more importantly on the agenda of issues that inspire activity among disadvantaged women than among disadvantaged men or among the advantaged of either sex.[50]

A special concern with single mothers led us to investigate the

---

50. We also examined the open-ended responses about informal community activity to see if we could discern gender differences in the way in which people go about solving problems. We looked at informal local political involvement because it is the kind of participation in which the participants can define both the agenda and the process of problem solving. We coded these responses by whether the individual took an approach to the problem that employed the people in the community to solve the problem as opposed to asking the police or the government to solve a problem.

There was no gender difference in the approach that people took to solving problems. Women were no more likely than men to try to work with others to develop a cooperative solution. However, almost all of the people who approached problems this way were talking about neighborhood crime watches. There are very few cases of people trying to work participatory agendas of parents with children living at home.[51] In light of what we have seen so far, the findings in Table 4.7 are not unexpected. Consistent with the results we have already reviewed, concerns about education or about crime or drugs weigh less heavily—and concerns about taxes more heavily—in the activity of married fathers than of mothers, whether single or married.[52] Reflecting their economic circumstances, single mothers are much more likely than their married counterparts to mention matters of basic need in connection with their issue-based activity. However, the most striking finding in Table 4.7 is not that public officials hear about different issues from single mothers than from married parents of either sex but rather that public officials hear so little from single mothers. The rate of issue-based activity among married mothers and fathers is nearly twice that among single mothers. In short, what is distinctive about the participation of single mothers is not its issue content but its rarity.

Agendas for Women—Agendas for Men

Because we were struck at how little activity—pro or con, by women or by men—is animated by concern about women's issues, we decided to focus more explicitly on gender issues in the Follow-up study that we conducted in 1994. We asked two open-ended

---

together with their neighbors to do things like create after-school programs for children or clean trash off of the local streets. Thus the open-ended data do not provide enough information to examine potentially more subtle differences between men and women.

51. We do not include single fathers in Table 4.8 because there were too few in our sample to permit analysis.

52. We were curious to investigate further the fact that, across all the groups we have considered, issues surrounding the young and their education weigh especially heavily in the bundle of issue concerns of women. In order to understand whether women's special concern with children's issues is the exclusive bailiwick of mothers or whether women activists pay greater attention to these issues regardless of whether they have children, we undertook a multivariate analysis. The results of this analysis suggest that there is always a small difference between men and women when it comes to participation animated by concerns about children and education, a difference that is larger for respondents with children than for those without. The largest effect, however, is not a gender-based effect indicating something about a differential propensity to take on—or to be assigned—responsibility for being caring and active when it comes to children. Instead, the most substantial impact derives from the fact of having school-age children—not just children but school-age children—in the first place.

Table 4.7 Parenthood and the Issues That Animate Political Participation[a]

| | Mothers | | Fathers |
	Single	Married	Married
Basic Human Needs	16%	6%	11%
Taxes	13	13	18
Economic Issues (except taxes)	12	6	11
Abortion	11	14	8
Social Issues (except abortion)	2	1	2
Education	22	25	13
Children or Youth (except education)	7	7	5
Crime or Drugs	16	10	5
Environment	4	6	8
Foreign Policy	7	3	7
Women's Issues	5	1	b
Number of Respondents	184	430	405
Number of Issue-based Acts	116	485	494

Source: Citizen Participation Study—Main Survey.

a. Table lists the proportion of issue-based participation motivated by concern about particular issues.

b. Less than 1 percent.

questions: one about whether there are any problems on which women need to work together in order to solve and an analogous one about problems men need to work together to solve. Because the question was open-ended, the issues mentioned came spontaneously from the respondents. However, the questions clearly directed the respondent to focus on gender. It is important to note that these data were collected a few years after those just reviewed, and the intervening years witnessed the Hill-Thomas hearings in the Senate, which brought attention to the issue of sexual harassment in the workplace, and the replacement of George H. W. Bush by Bill Clinton as president and, concomitantly, the replacement of Barbara Bush by Hillary Rodham Clinton as first lady.

The resulting data give us four possible sets of issues:

Issues that *women* believe require common action by *women;*
Issues that *men* believe require common action by *women;*
Issues that *women* believe require common action by *men;*
Issues that *men* believe require common action by *men.*

Not surprisingly, men and, especially, women see women as being more likely than men to have problems that they need to work together to solve: 64 percent of the men and 74 percent of the women mentioned an interpretable issue requiring joint action by women; in contrast, 49 percent of the men and 52 percent of the women mentioned an interpretable issue requiring joint action by men.[53]

Table 4.8 summarizes the issues that were mentioned most frequently. Several points are worth noting. Especially striking is the relative salience both to men and to women of matters pertaining to equality for women in the workplace—a category that includes reference to, for example, equal pay, sex discrimination on the job, unequal chances for advancement, and the glass ceiling.[54] Thirty-five percent of the women and 26 percent of the men mentioned this issue as one on which women should work together—a quite high proportion for an open-ended question of so general a nature. No other issue draws this kind of spontaneous mention. In addition, a smaller, but still noticeable, number of both men and women referred to issues of sex discrimination and equal treatment for women without specifying a particular domain such as the workplace or the home.

Abortion was also mentioned frequently—by 14 percent of the women and 21 percent of the men—as a problem on which women should work together. Given the greater prominence of abortion on the participatory agendas of activists, it is notable that matters of workplace equality weigh more importantly in respondents' conceptions of what women need to work on together. A clue to the source of this seeming discrepancy may be in the extent to which the brief word bites describing concern about workplace equality are devoid of references to political solutions. Although

---

53. Roberta S. Sigel conducted focus groups with men and reports that gender relations was simply not a topic that engaged the attention of the men, a finding that is compatible with the results reported here. See *Ambition and Accommodation: How Women View Gender Relations* (Chicago: University of Chicago Press, 1996), p. 143.

54. The entries in the cells are the proportion of all respondents, including those who think that women or men have no shared problems, who mentioned a particular theme. The percentages reported in the cells do not include the small number of cases in which a particular topic was discussed but opposition to equality for women was expressed: for example, comments to the effect that "women get all the breaks at the office these days," or "women need to work on giving their husbands the respect they deserve."

Table 4.8 What Women Need to Work on Together—What Men Need to Work on Together

	Women Need to Work on This Problem Together		Men Need to Work on This Problem Together	
	Women's Reports	Men's Reports	Women's Reports	Men's Reports
Mention Any Problem	74%	64%	52%	49%
Problems Related to Equality for Women				
Equal treatment in the workplace[a]	35	26	5	7
Equal treatment in other domains[b]	9	11	4	8
Problems Related to Children and Family				
Child care	15	8	5	2
Other issues involving children	7	1	1	1
Problems in Relations between Men and Women				
Violence or harassment[c]	11	9	4	5
Men's "attitude problem"[d]	e	e	19	16
Problems Related to Abortion				
(either pro-choice or pro-life)[f]	14	21	1	1

Source: Citizen Participation Study—Follow-up Survey.

a. Includes references to equal pay; sex discrimination at work; better jobs; glass ceiling; need for men to treat women as equals in the workplace, not be threatened by women co-workers.

b. Includes references to sex discrimination and equal treatment (when no specific referent such as workplace or family is apparent); to men's need to respect women, to treat them as equals, or not to be threatened by them; and to sex-role stereotyping and sex-role socialization.

c. Includes references to sexual harassment; spouse abuse or domestic violence; and other references to violence against women including rape.

d. Includes references to the need for men to be more sensitive or less aggressive, curb their egos, be less macho or chauvinistic, take more responsibility.

e. Less than 1 percent.

f. The data do not allow us to distinguish the direction of abortion views.

the nature and implementation of civil rights laws have enormous potential consequences for the establishment of equal opportunity on the job, it may be that workplace discrimination—like child care and joblessness—are not fully politicized but are instead construed as problems that individuals can solve on their own. In contrast, both sides in the abortion controversy are only too aware of the political nature of the conflict.

Another subject that arose frequently is children and child care. In discussing problems of joint concern to women, women were especially likely to bring up child care and other issues concerning children: 15 percent of the women mentioned child care and 7 percent referred to other issues involving children as issues on which women should work together; 5 percent mentioned child care, and 1 percent brought up other children's issues, as concerns for men's joint action. Of the men, only 8 percent discussed child care and 1 percent referred to other child-related issues as something on which women ought to work together; 2 percent of the men mentioned child care, and 1 percent mentioned other children's issues, as matters on which men need to work together.

What is noteworthy is the extent to which these are deemed, by both men and women, as problems on which women, but not men, should work together. It is hardly surprising that abortion is considered a problem requiring joint action by women. After all, one side in the abiding political controversy frames the issue in terms of a "woman's right to choose." Similarly, with respect to equality for women, both men and women might reasonably assume that the burden for collective action in addressing inequality should be on the shoulders of the group that has the most to gain from it—the group seeking equality rather than the group that enjoys superior status. However, it is not clear why this principle should obtain for children, who are usually construed as being the joint responsibility of both parents.

The pattern continues when it comes to a final set of loosely related issues, various aspects of the relations between men and women. The issue of male violence or harassment of women—sexual harassment, spousal abuse, and other manifestations of violence against women, including rape—is, once again, more likely to be considered by both women and men as an issue on which women have to work together, even though it would seem that changing male behavior is the key to making progress. Only when it comes to men's "attitude problem"—the need for men to be more sensitive or less aggressive, to curb their egos, or to be less macho—is the problem construed as men's work. Thus to the extent that they think about these problems at all, men and women seem to view problems that men and women might be considered to share—issues surrounding children or relations between the sexes—as women's responsibility to solve.

Conclusion

We have found unmistakable gender differences in a variety of orientations toward politics—differences that are, in fact, somewhat more pronounced than the relatively small disparity in actual participation that was discussed in Chapter 3. We found that, in a variety of ways, men are more likely than women to register psychological involvement with politics, especially national politics: to be politically interested and informed; to feel that they can make a difference if they take part; to discuss politics on a regular basis; and to follow politics in the media. In contrast, women are more likely than men to manifest deep religious commitment and to consider religion to be important in their lives, a gender difference that corresponds to the gender difference in religious activity that we saw in Chapter 3. We shall have occasion to revisit the matter of the disparity between men and women in these psychological orientations to politics over the course of this inquiry.

With respect to matters more proximate to political activity— the rewards that derive from it and the issue concerns that animate it—we found much less evidence of a distinctive political voice. In terms of the gratifications attendant to participation, we found overall similarity between women and men. What was striking was not any systematic patterning by gender but rather the differences among political acts as well as the extent to which respondents cited civic and policy benefits in their retrospective understandings of their activity.

When we examined the issues that activists bring to their participation, we also found a great deal of similarity in the overall contours of men's and women's policy agendas. Both groups carry a diverse set of policy matters to their activity, and their relative priorities are quite similar. However, we also found evidence of subtle differences between women and men when it comes to the content of participation.

Where we found gender differences in the issue concerns that animate political activity, they come closer to replicating the distinctive policy priorities of men and women legislators than to mapping the issues on which there is the greatest gender disparity in the attitudes of the mass public. Educational issues, in particular, weigh more heavily in the concerns of women activists, a result that holds even when we consider groups defined by their socioeconomic and family circumstances. This finding mirrors that of the studies of the discretionary priorities of women in legislatures. Abortion also occupies greater space among the issue concerns of female than male activists. This is an issue that divides women—and men—resulting in polarized conflict between pro-life and pro-choice activists of both sexes, a pattern that differs from that among legislators, among whom men are distinctly more pro-life than women are.

Our concern with policy issues leads us to recognize another problem with posing the questions of gender difference in such stark terms. A theme throughout this volume is the significance of the cleavages of class, race, family status, and the like that differentiate women's—and men's—experiences. We found that men's and women's agendas for political action were differentiated along lines of socioeconomic advantage. Thus, not only must we ask, "With respect to what do men and women differ?" but we must ask "Which men? Which women?"

Appendix: Issues Associated with Contacts to Public Officials

The following are verbatim transcriptions of what was recorded in face-to-face interviews when respondents mentioned issues or problems in association with contacts to public officials. In order not to make obvious which group of answers are women's and which are men's, in one case we substituted "spouse" for "husband" or "wife." Otherwise, we have not added words to what interviewers recorded. Can you differentiate women's voices from men's?

CONTACT ISSUES MENTIONED BY ONE GROUP

Laws for the citizens' rights to defend themselves (2nd Amendment).

I wanted N.Y. to get their first Black mayor.

It was concerning a problem with HUD.

Policy—environmental concerns.

My daughter works in the office with him, and I happened to meet him in person.

Appointment of commissioner of health.

Women's right to choose.

I was assaulted. Mental health, a cut in Albany—wrote a letter in protest.

Housing for the elderly was also another important issue on my mind.

Transportation issue.

Community concern about Westchester county airport, the noise level there.

Public housing, teenage pregnancy, the childcare bill.

Environmental issue—concerned about building too close to reservoirs.

A local boy from our high school asked me to write a letter of recommendation for the service academy (I graduated from there).

Good friends, purely social. We have different political views but are good friends. I told him to tell Bush he was an asshole.

Requested support to be able to organize this cultural exchange between Uruguay and U.S.

Personal concerns, issues on job—as matter of fact, our labor contract; there are several things in dispute, e.g. random drug testing.

Once again, Bush failed to keep his promises to NRA & other groups; concern with gun control.

Community affairs, the drug problems, kids' problems in
community, graffiti, gang membership.
Community problems; planning and gang violence.
Business policies, I was questioning him about certain votes
concerning insurance policies.
Gun ban in California.
A community project for AIDS.
Malathion spraying in residential areas.
Because I felt I been discriminated against. After I passed a
test they lower the points so that another person could get
the job & promotion.
More liberal attitudes about legalization of sex clubs and a
more liberal attitude on the legalization of nude beaches.
A new development right next door to us.

CONTACT ISSUES MENTIONED BY THE OTHER GROUP

Professional problem.
A plan to redevelop our area with large skyscrapers of
muled(?) use taxes, taxes on something.
Crime prevention issues.
The poor subway system—they're unsafe and a disgrace.
I was contacting the IRS for personal reasons.
Preservation of local neighborhood & improving local school
boards.
Transfer a principal of a school to another school—did not
want this to happen.
It was about the state cutting the budget for mental health
services.
It was the drug problem in this building and on the block.
Community; deli across the street—crowds, noise, parking
problems, loud radios; new owners of deli, problems in
area.
Personal concerns.
NY driver's license request.
Didn't like what was going on with the poor in my area,
wanted to discuss with her things that could be done.
An issue pertaining to a school yearbook.

No issues, I was just establishing contact.

For my sister-in-law (widowed) to get benefits for her and kids, Social Security.

Trying to get a family member out of Russia.

Got my mother's Medicare messed up.

They took two men from channel 52 off the air so I sent Alan Cranston a letter so he can put the two men back on Channel 52.

About zoning problems in Glendale.

Banking, something to do with putting a cap on interest rates.

It was regarding a law that we didn't think would work for us.

Regarding my [spouse's] profession.

It was on child care and education—it was a note sent on a particular issue.

The public policy issue involving the entire alignment of school district boundaries as it relates to race.

Mosquito problem in standing water on my street.

It was a personal concern. The water dept. had me down for $2,500 for a 4-flat building with only 5 people and I sent this problem to him.

The oil industry.

This was a post-card campaign to the congressman stating I did not want my tax dollars to go to defense.

Which is which? The men's answers are listed first; the women's answers follow.

5

⚯

The Legacy of Home
and School

We now begin a major section of our inquiry in which we examine a variety of social institutions—the homes in which we grow up and those we create as adults, schools, workplaces, organizations, and religious institutions—and consider how they function to foster civic involvement. We focus on the creation of gender differences in the factors that facilitate participation—various kinds of resources, psychological orientations to politics, and the social connections that generate requests for political activity—through processes of differential selection into institutions and differential treatment within institutions. A complex set of social processes by which girls and boys and women and men respond to different expectations, assume different roles, and have different experiences at home, at school, on the job, in organizations, and in church produces a circumstance such that they acquire quite different bundles of participatory factors.

Before moving on, in later chapters, to the institutions of adult life, we begin our exploration of the social processes that create gender differences in political activity with a brief look at pre-adult experiences in the family and at school. Our treatment of family and school will be more cursory than our treatment of experiences in adult institutions. We do so, in part, because the distance separating pre-adult experiences and adult political involvement is substantial and, in part, because our data—based on adult recollections of early experiences—are weaker than our data on adult experiences. Nevertheless, it is good to begin, more or less, at the beginning.

Political Cues in the Family

The search for the early lessons that might shape political involvement—and shape the involvement of women and men—takes us first to the family. Students of political socialization have focused on the transmission of political ideals and habits across the generations and have explored the implications of the nature of authority relations within the family for the character of the regime in places as disparate as Norway, Japan, and Nazi Germany. Closer to home, socialization studies conducted in the United States have considered the emergence in childhood of gender differences in orientations to politics.[1]

Political socialization explanations are particularly hard to test. The principal difficulty is that, even when there are clear and readily interpretable gender differences among the young, and often there are not, direct links between the predilections of the young and the behavior of adults are impossible to establish—especially in the absence of longitudinal studies that trace individuals over the life cycle.[2] Even if such data are available, it is difficult

---

1. See, for example, Fred Greenstein, *Children and Politics* (New Haven: Yale University Press, 1965), chap. 6; Robert D. Hess and Judith V. Torney, *The Development of Political Attitudes in Children* (Garden City, N.Y.: Doubleday, Anchor Books, 1968), chap. 8; Dean Jaros, *Socialization to Politics* (New York: Praeger, 1973), pp. 44–45, 81–82; Lynne B. Iglitzin, "The Making of the Apolitical Woman: Femininity and Sex-Stereotyping in Girls," in *Women in Politics,* ed. Jane S. Jaquette (New York: John Wiley, 1974); and Anthony M. Orum, Roberta S. Cohen, Sherri Grassmuck, and Amy Orum, "Sex, Socialization, and Politics," in *A Portrait of Marginality,* ed. Marianne Githens and Jewel L. Prestage (New York: David McKay, 1977), chap. 2.

For especially helpful discussions of the literature on gender and socialization, see Sue Tolleson Rinehart, *Gender Consciousness and Politics* (New York: Routledge, Chapman, and Hall, 1992), pp. 21–27, and Virginia Sapiro, *The Political Integration of Women* (Urbana: University of Illinois Press, 1984), pp. 36–45. And for a more recent evidence on the power of childhood socialization, see M. Kent Jennings and Laura Stoker, "The Persistence of the Past: The Class of 1965 Turns Fifty" (paper presented at the annual meeting of the Midwest Political Science Association, April 1999); and M. Kent Jennings, Laura Stoker, and Jake Bowers, "Politics across Generations: Family Transmission Reexamined" (paper presented at the annual meeting of the American Political Science Association, September 1999).

2. The major exception to the absence of long-term socialization studies is the Political Socialization Project, which has now traced political effects across three generations. This remarkable set of studies does find clear long-term—though moderate—effects of political

to make causal connections. The processes involved are largely implicit. Although children are exposed to many direct messages mandating appropriate behavior for boys and girls as they grow up, much of the learning, especially in the domain of politics, is indirect—communicated and absorbed unconsciously. Thus it is hard to be certain exactly what it is about the childhood experience that produces a particular outcome among adults.[3]

Our own data turn upside down the usual problem with socialization studies. Ordinarily, compelling information about youthful experiences cannot be linked to adult politics. We have rich information about the lives, especially the political lives, of our respondents but are forced to rely on weaker, retrospective data about their pre-adult experiences. We asked our respondents about politicizing experiences in the home during adolescence and school experiences in high school and college. These reports are, at best, a superficial scratching of the surface. Moreover, they suffer from problems of memory, including the possibility that the account of the past is tainted by the current situation; in particular, recollections of past experiences in politics might be more salient and

---

involvement by parents on the political activity of their offspring. Although they find similar effects for school participation, they do not deal with gender differences in these effects. M. Kent Jennings, "Participation as Viewed through the Lens of the Political Socialization Study" (paper presented at the conference on "Political Participation: Building a Research Agenda," Center for the Study of Democratic Politics, Princeton University, October 2000).

3. Psychologists have recently trained their attention on childhood to develop an understanding of the development of tastes for academic fields and occupations. Scholars have been focusing especially on the messages that parents and teachers send to children about girls' and boys' competencies within specific domains, like math or English. These results are compelling and offer, in conjunction with recent work on development over the life course, strong suggestions about the ways in which early messages can shape tastes over a lifetime. See, especially, Jacquelynne S. Eccles, "Understanding Women's Educational and Occupational Choices," *Psychology of Women Quarterly* 18 (1994): 585–609; Allan Wigfield, Jacquelynne S. Eccles, and Paul R. Pintrich, "Development between the Ages of 11 and 25," in *Handbook of Educational Psychology*, ed. David C. Berliner and Robert C. Calfee (New York: Macmillan, 1996), pp. 148–185; Jacquelynne S. Eccles, Janis E. Jacobs, and Rena D. Harold, "Gender Role Stereotypes, Expectancy Effects, and Parents' Socialization of Gender Differences," *Journal of Social Issues* 46 (1990): 183–201; Janis E. Jacobs and Jacquelynne S. Eccles, "The Impact of Mothers' Gender-Role Stereotypic Beliefs on Mothers' and Children's Ability Perceptions," *Journal of Personality and Social Psychology* 63 (1992): 932–944.

vivid to the respondent who is currently active in politics. This serious limitation must be borne in mind.

In searching for the roots of adulthood in earlier experiences in the home, a focus on gender—rather than on, say, race—has a distinct analytical advantage. Male and female babies are born, presumably randomly, into all kinds of families. Since female and male children appear equally in families of all social statuses, any gender difference in memories of family political engagement must be linked to gender rather than to some other family characteristic—for example, race, class, or religion. In contrast, if we were comparing memories about political discussions at home among Anglo-White, African-American, and Latino respondents, we would have much more difficulty disentangling the effects of race or ethnicity from the consequences of the other ways in which their families would have differed—in terms, say, of class or religion.

Although the families of boys and girls do not differ in as many respects as the families in which Anglo-Whites, African-Americans, and Latinos come of age, we should not exaggerate the extent to which girls and boys grow up in identical families. Surely, we would expect the mix of sons and daughters in a family to have consequences—including a possible effect on its dinner table conversations. Although we know of no systematic evidence to support our conjecture, it is plausible to suppose that conversations about sports—and, possibly, politics—are more common in families with sons than in families with daughters. It is also possible that parents discuss different topics when the boys are around than when the girls are on the scene.

We were interested in the extent to which our respondents were exposed to politicizing experiences at home during adolescence—around the time they were sixteen. In particular, we asked whether there was ever discussion of politics in their home and whether their mothers or their fathers were active in politics. What is striking about the data, shown in Table 5.1, is the absence of any difference between males and females. Men are no more likely than women to report that they heard political discussion in the family or that either parent was politically ac-

Table 5.1 Reports of Political Experiences at Age Sixteen[a,b]

	Women	Men
Political Discussions at Home		
Frequent	20%	19%
Sometimes	40	40
Almost never	40	41
	100%	100%
Mother's Political Activity		
Very active	7%	7%
Somewhat active	25	27
Not at all active	67	65
	99%	99%
Father's Political Activity		
Very active	12%	13%
Somewhat active	29	30
Not at all active	59	57
	100%	100%

Source: Citizen Participation Study—Main Survey.

a. Appendix A contains the valid number of cases for these and other measures used in the tables.

b. Examination of the Chi-squared statistics suggests that the gender differences in the distribution of responses for all three political experiences in question are not statistically significant.

tive.[4] Thus these scant data—which barely touch the possibilities of politically relevant experiences at home—yield no evidence that the roots of gender differences in adult political involvement lie in the childhood home.

The Legacy of Schooling

All studies of political activity emphasize the strength of the association between formal education and political participation. When the relationship between education and activity is investigated, it turns out that education has multiple effects, both direct and indi-

---

4. Since there is a different age distribution for men and women, we compared the memories of home political discussion within age groups and, once again, found no systematic difference.

rect, on participation. Indeed, education enhances nearly every single one of the participatory factors.[5] Because formal education tends to inculcate the kinds of verbal, organizational, and bureaucratic skills that are useful in political activity, the well educated are likely to find it easier to take part politically. Those who are well educated also tend to have the kinds of jobs that command high incomes and provide opportunities for the further development of civic skills. Moreover, the well educated are more psychologically engaged with politics—more politically interested, knowledgeable, and efficacious. In addition, they are more likely to be involved in non-political activities in organizations and religious institutions where they can exercise leadership and develop civic skills, become targets for requests for political activity, and be exposed to other political stimuli.[6]

The past several decades have witnessed considerable gains in the educational attainment of American adults and, more recently, some convergence in the relative educational attainment of women and men. For nearly two centuries—from the founding of Harvard College in 1636 until Oberlin College opened its doors on a coeducational basis in 1833—higher education in the United States was an exclusively masculine enterprise. Until recently, men have been much more likely than women to attend college and, especially, graduate school. As shown in Figure 5.1, the disparity widened in the 1950s—presumably as a result of early childbearing for women and the educational benefits to men from the G.I. Bill. Perhaps reflecting the impact of Title IX of the Educational Amendments—which outlawed sex discrimination in education—during the late 1970s women made extraordinary progress in

---

5. On the multiple roles of education in fostering participation, see Sidney Verba, Kay Lehman Schlozman, and Henry E. Brady, *Voice and Equality: Civic Voluntarism in American Politics* (Cambridge: Harvard University Press, 1995), chap. 15.

6. Interestingly, however, the massive increase in the levels of education of the American public in the second half of the twentieth century has not been accompanied by commensurate changes in the aggregate level of participation. In *Education and Democratic Citizenship in America* (Chicago: University of Chicago Press, 1996), Norman H. Nie, Jane Junn, and Kenneth Stehlik-Barry argue that, when it comes to participation, it is relative position in the educational hierarchy that matters.

higher education. In the late 1990s, the earlier situation had reversed, and women in this group have been more likely than men to be enrolled in college. Moreover, because women are more likely to return to college as "non-traditional students"—often on a part-time basis—as early as 1980, women formed a majority of college students and, by the mid-1980s, a majority of graduate students.[7] In 1990, the year of our survey, women constituted 55 percent and men 45 percent of enrolled college students.[8] Even so, as shown in Figure 5.2, men will continue to enjoy an aggregate educational advantage for some time to come, the result of educational differences in older generations.

At the other end of the educational hierarchy, there has been convergence as well. At the same time that men were traditionally more likely than women to go to college, they were also more likely to leave school early—presumably in order to go to work. As of 1960, 42.5 percent of women twenty-five years old and over—and 39.5 percent of their male counterparts—had completed four years of high school or more. Although males still drop out at somewhat higher rates than females, the vast majority of students of both sexes now graduate from high school, and the difference between women and men has become attenuated. In 1990 the proportion of adults with a high school degree was identical for women and men.[9]

However, the overall educational distribution for men and women reflects more than whatever educational differences there are between men and women in successive cohorts. It is well known that women live longer, on average, than men do, with the result that women are overrepresented among the elderly. Since one of the most striking social transformations of the post–World War II era in America has been the increase in educational attain-

---

7. Although the gap has closed substantially over the past thirty years, men continue to outnumber women as students in the most prestigious graduate programs—law school, medical school and doctoral programs.

8. *The Digest of Educational Statistics* (Washington, D.C.: U.S. Department of Education, 1991), table 187.

9. *Statistical Abstract of the United States* (U.S. Bureau of the Census, on-line database <www.census.gov>), table 264.

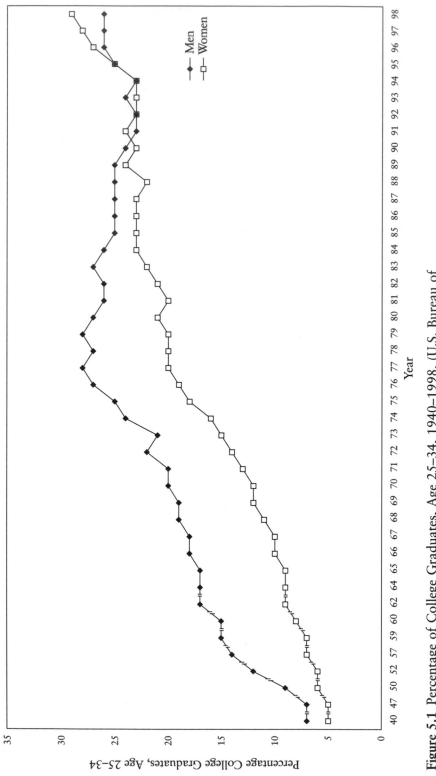

Figure 5.1 Percentage of College Graduates, Age 25–34, 1940–1998. (U.S. Bureau of the Census, Current Population Survey, data from March of each year)

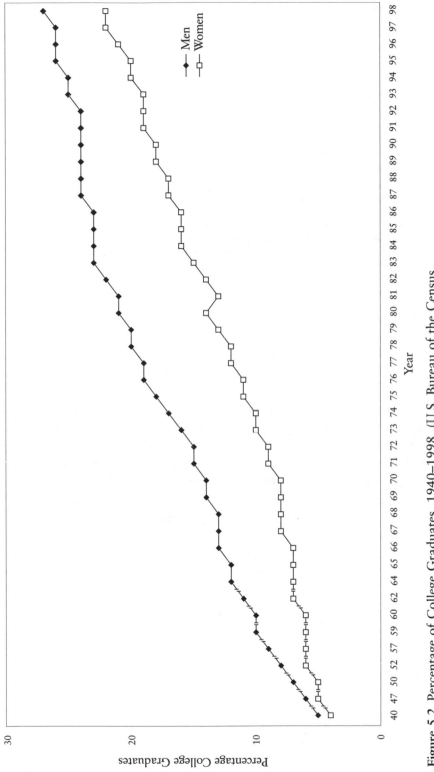

Figure 5.2 Percentage of College Graduates, 1940–1998. (U.S. Bureau of the Census, Current Population Survey, data from March of each year)

Table 5.2 Educational Attainment[a]

	Women	Men
Grammar School or Less	5%	5%
Some High School	11	8
High School Graduate or GED	38	34
Some College	25	24
College Graduate	12	14
Some Graduate Study	4	4
Master's Degree	5	7
Doctorate or Professional Degree	1	4
	100%	101%

Source: Citizen Participation Study—Screener Survey.

a. Overall distribution of responses is statistically significant with Chi-squared = 37.59277, $p < .0001$.

ment, the elderly are much less well educated than their children and grandchildren. Thus even if there were no gender gap for education within each generation, there would be no guarantee of educational parity between men and women in the adult population as a whole.

The result of this complex set of processes is reflected in the data gathered for our study. As shown in Table 5.2, among the more than 15,000 respondents to our Screener Survey, which was conducted in 1989, men enjoy a modest educational advantage— especially in the upper ranges. Compared with women, men are somewhat more likely to have graduated from college and considerably more likely to have a graduate degree.[10] Women's aggregate educational deficit, which results from both gender differences in educational attainment in older cohorts and from women's overrepresentation among the elderly, a cohort having limited edu-

---

10. Data from the 1990 Census show our Screener Survey to have oversampled the well educated. Nevertheless, they confirm the magnitude of the gender difference in educational attainment. According to the census, at the time of our survey, 18.4 percent of women, and 24.5 percent of men, had graduated from college. These data show gender parity when it comes to high school graduation: 77.5 percent of women and 77.7 percent of men had a high school diploma.

cational attainment, has important consequences for the gender gap in political participation.

THE SCHOOL AS A POLITICAL TRAINING GROUND

Over and above the multiple indirect effects of education upon political activity, experiences in school might operate more directly to influence adult participation in politics: schools offer courses designed to foster political information and skills as well as participatory values; and they offer opportunities for voluntary involvement in clubs and activities that can develop participatory skills and a taste for voluntary involvement. We asked our respondents a battery of items designed to ascertain the extent to which their high schools—and, if relevant, their undergraduate colleges—acted as a training ground for future political participation. With respect to high school, we asked whether:

The respondent had any courses that required students to pay attention to current events;
The respondent was active in school government;
The respondent was active in other school activities—such as school clubs or the student newspaper;
The respondent was active in sports.

The top portion of Table 5.3 presents the responses to these items. In light of the unreliability of answers to questions that ask about experiences that happened in the past, and sometimes in the distant past, the pattern of responses is encouraging. Not unexpectedly, the most substantial gender difference appears with respect to sports. Thirty-seven percent of the men, but only 20 percent of the women, indicated having been very active in sports in high school. As we would expect, there is, in contrast, no significant gender difference in the frequency of reports of having taken a course focusing on current events. There is evidence that girls are more active in extracurricular clubs. This pattern suggests that neither men nor women were systematically more likely to exaggerate in recalling their past involvements and lends credibility to our data.

The greater involvement of girls in high school activities and or-

Table 5.3 Experiences in High School

A. Reports by Adults about High School

	Women		Men
Took a course in civics	78%		79%
Very active in high school government	8		7
Very active in high school clubs	24	⇔	16
Very active in sports	20	⇔	37

B. Reports by High School Seniors, 1976–1996

	Girls		Boys
Took part in student government	13%	⇔	8%
Active in academic clubs	15	⇔	10
Active in student publications	14	⇔	8
Active in school athletics	27	⇔	43

Source: A–Citizen Participation Study—Main Survey; B–Monitoring the Future Survey, 1976–1996.
⇔ Difference between women and men is statistically significant at the .05 level.

ganizations is confirmed by data, shown in the bottom portion of Table 5.3, from the Monitoring the Future Study, which has surveyed a large number of high school seniors every year since 1976.[11] Unlike the data in the top portion of the table, these data are not retrospective but are based on the contemporary reports of seniors. Since there is very little variation from year to year, we present the averages for the two decades between 1976 and 1996. The data point to a modest, but significant, gender difference in school activity. Except for athletics, girls are more involved in several kinds of high school activity, including school government. If such experiences are associated with political participation among adults—either because they inculcate participatory skills that are carried into adulthood or because those with activist tendencies tend to take part even when young—the data show a slight advantage to girls.

---

11. Although the yearly surveys each sample a large number of students, every item is not asked on an annual basis. We have aggregated the surveys over the entire period. Each entry in the lower portion of Table 5.3 is based on at least 25,000 cases.

COLLEGE EXPERIENCES

We posed a similar set of questions about college experiences to respondents who had attended college. Table 5.4 presents the responses along with, for the same set of respondents, the data on their high school experiences. That is, Table 5.4 summarizes, in the top portion, the college experiences of those who attended college and, in the bottom portion, the high school experiences of the same set of people.

These data permit us to make several kinds of comparisons. Referring back to the top portion of Table 5.3, which presented data for all high school graduates, we can see that college-bound high school students were consistently more likely to report having been active in various kinds of high school activities. The disparity holds for high school government, other high school activities, and even high school sports. Among those who eventually went on to college, men were more active than women in high school sports and women more active than men in high school organizations and clubs. In addition, the pattern of female advantage in participation in high school student government that emerged in the Monitoring the Future data appears in ours as well. Comparing the top and bottom parts of Table 5.4, we note that these respondents indicated lower levels of school-based activity of all kinds in college than in high school.

Table 5.4 School Experiences of Those Who Attended College

	Women		Men
A. Experiences in College			
Very active in college student government	5%		4%
Very active in college clubs	13		12
Very active in college sports	6	⇔	14
B. Experiences in High School of Those Who Eventually Attended College			
Very active in high school government	13%	⇔	9%
Very active in high school clubs	34	⇔	22
Very active in sports	24	⇔	43

Source: Citizen Participation Study—Main Survey.
⇔ Difference between women and men is statistically significant at the .05 level.

When it comes to gender differences in activity during the college years, the data in Table 5.4 only partially replicate the findings for high school. Men are, once again, more likely to report athletic activity. For both student government and other clubs and activities, there is rough parity between women and men, a pattern that represents a departure from what we saw for high school.

Thus to the extent that school-based activities are associated with later political participation—either because they indicate a taste for getting involved or because they provide training for future voluntarism—men are more likely than women to be active in sports both in high school and in college. Women are more likely than men to be active in clubs and organizations in high school but not in college.

A Note on Political and Religious Engagement

We have seen that the domain of religion reverses the pattern of greater male involvement characteristic of the domain of politics. In contrast to politics, women are more active than men in religious institutions and are more likely to consider religion important in their lives. Because the difference between the arenas of politics and religion figures importantly in our analysis, it is noteworthy that this pattern is visible in the pre-adult years. Table 5.5, which presents data for 1976–1996 from the Monitoring the Future surveys, shows that, although there is little gender difference in concern about "community and social issues," high school boys are considerably more likely than girls are to be interested in "what is going on in government." Furthermore, consistent with what we saw for adults, girls are more likely than boys to say that

Table 5.5 Interests and Commitments during the High School Years

	Girls		Boys
A lot of or very great interest in politics	25%	⇔	40%
Think quite often about community and social issues	25	⇔	28
Religion very important in their life	32	⇔	24

Source: Monitoring the Future Survey, 1976–1996.
⇔ Difference between girls and boys is statistically significant at the .05 level.

religion is important in their lives. In short, the pattern among adults such that men are more involved with politics and women with religion develops early and is apparent among high school graduates.

The Legacy of Home and School: Summary

Perhaps the single most important legacy of the pre-adult years is formal education itself, which—as we shall see later—functions in many ways to foster political participation. We noted several trends that have implications for the overall educational level of the public and for gender differences in educational achievement within successive cohorts and within the population as a whole. First, since World War II, a massive increase in higher education has raised the overall level of education within the population as successive generations of better- and better-educated young people come of age and replace less well educated older generations. Differences in the age structure of the male and female populations—the result of the fact that, on average, women live longer than men—contribute somewhat to the gender gap in average educational levels. In addition, men have traditionally dominated in enrollments in higher education, especially at the highest levels. Since the 1970s women have made substantial gains in higher education—to the point that women outnumber men among college and graduate students. Nonetheless, in the population as a whole, men are more likely than women to have college and graduate degrees. Finally, the traditional gender gap in rates of high school graduation—with girls more likely to graduate than boys—has also diminished. The net effect of these processes is, in the aggregate, a small masculine education advantage.

When it comes to socialization experiences, we found little evidence of differential experiences at home. Girls and boys are as likely to remember hearing political conversation. In high school, though, there does appear to be a gender difference in extra-curricular activities. While boys are more likely to be involved in athletics, girls are more likely to be active in school government and other organizations, a difference with potential consequences for participation.

6

——⚛——

Domestic Tranquility:
The Beliefs of Wives and Husbands

Having glanced at the legacy of childhood, we now focus much more intensively on the role played by the institutions of adult life—the home, the workplace, voluntary associations, and religious institutions—in nurturing civic activity. We begin with the families we create as adults.[1]

On the presumption that the child is parent to the adult, in Chapter 5 we focused briefly on political transmission across the generations. In our attempt to learn how political values and predispositions are shaped by what happens at home, we now consider the family as experienced by married adults. In this chapter, we explore beliefs about appropriate gender roles and attitudes toward political issues. We ask whether birds of a feather flock together or opposites attract. That is, when it comes to beliefs about political and social matters, do couples tend to agree or disagree?

In the next chapter we spell out some basic features of the household as a social system, exploring the extent to which, on any particular dimension, husbands and wives are equal or unequal and, if the latter, which spouse is advantaged. Later on, we consider the role of other institutions and their links to political life. Finally, in Chapter 12 we return to the subject of the household and investigate the implications for political activity of in-

---

1. For a helpful review of literature on women and men in their adult families, see Nancy E. McGlen and Karen O'Connor, *Women, Politics, and American Society* (Englewood Cliffs, N.J.: Prentice Hall, 1995), pp. 246–293.

equality with respect to various aspects of domestic life, always keeping open the possibility that the effects need not be the same for wives and husbands.

Studying Couples

The data in this chapter are drawn from the Follow-up study to the Main Survey in which nearly 400 married couples were interviewed by telephone. This survey replicated many of the questions about civic activity and demographic information that had already proved key to the analysis of the main study. In addition, this survey went beyond the concerns of the main study in order to investigate a variety of aspects of gender politics, gender relations, and household arrangements. We asked a number of attitude questions about these issues as well as a long battery about the household division of labor. In particular, we examined the household as a social system in order to understand how couples apportion access to economic resources, political authority, and social status within the home.

These data about couples are unusual—probably even unique—in combining measures of political commitments and behaviors with measures of domestic management and hierarchy at home. They permit us to build links not only between spouses but also between the worlds of home and politics. Eventually, we shall use them to examine the proposition that inequality at home begets inequality in citizen politics. However, these data are of such intrinsic interest that we review them in some detail in this chapter and the next.

Household Cultures: Beliefs about Gender Roles at Home

There has long been a tension within the social sciences—dating back to differences between the successors to Marx and Weber—over whether social action springs from material conditions or whether values and beliefs have an independent influence on be-

Table 6.1 Beliefs about Equality in the Household[a]

		Agree Strongly	Agree Somewhat	Disagree Somewhat	Disagree Strongly		Total
TRADITIONAL FEMININE ROLES							
An employed mother is able to establish just as warm and secure a relationship with her children as a mother who is at home full time.	Wives	28%	47	21	5	=	101%
	Husbands	11%	45	34	10	=	100%
A mother of young children should work only if the family needs the money.	Wives	18%	35	35	13	=	101%
	Husbands	11%	39	39	11	=	100%
DIVISION OF LABOR							
Husbands and wives should share household chores equally.	Wives	34%	56	10	b	=	100%
	Husbands	24%	66	10	b	=	100%
FAMILY DECISIONS							
It's best if just the husband is in charge of making family decisions.	Wives	2%	5	35	58	=	100%
	Husbands	2%	5	67	26	=	100%
Even if the wife works, the man should have the major responsibility for the couple's financial decisions.	Wives	10%	23	42	26	=	101%
	Husbands	9%	26	52	12	=	99%

Source: Citizen Participation Study Follow-up—Couples Survey.
a. Appendix A contains the valid number of cases for these and other measures used in the tables.
b. Less than 1 percent.

havior. Recent scholarship has argued that ideas about gender roles operate on their own to shape family life—above and beyond the influences of relative resources—and thus affect the behavior of both men and women.[2] Working from a similar perspective, political scientists have argued that ideas about women's proper roles have an impact on women's political behavior.[3]

We begin our characterization of American couples by considering husbands' and wives' views about equality at home—not only the content and origin of these attitudes but the extent to which these opinions are shared by the members of a couple. Reflecting our concern with the implications for participation of domestic inequalities, we asked several questions about attitudes toward equality between husbands and wives at home: questions about traditional female roles, in particular, about family versus career; about the division of household chores; and about how family decisions ought to be made.[4] These data allow us to understand not just what wives and husbands think about these matters but whether they agree with one another.

Table 6.1 shows, across all these items, substantial similarity between the responses of the husbands and the wives and commitment to gender equality at home.[5] Nine-tenths of husbands and wives believe that household chores should be shared equally; and

2. See, for example, Julie Brines, "Economic Dependency, Gender, and the Division of Labor at Home," *American Journal of Sociology* 100 (1994): 652–688; Linda Thompson and Alexis J. Walker, "Gender in Families," *Journal of Marriage and the Family* 51 (1989): 845–871; and Candace West and Don Zimmerman, "Doing Gender," *Gender and Society* 1 (1987): 125–151.

3. Virginia Sapiro, *The Political Integration of Women* (Urbana: University of Illinois Press, 1983); and Sue Tolleson Rinehart, *Gender Consciousness and Politics* (New York: Routledge, Chapman, and Hall, 1992).

4. For helpful comparisons among various ways to measure ideas about appropriate roles for women and men, see Irene Hanson Frieze and Maureen C. McHugh, eds., *Psychology of Women Quarterly, Special Issue: Measuring Beliefs about Appropriate Roles for Women and Men* 21 (1997): 1–170; and, for a broad conceptual review placing measures like the ones used here in the context of the range of psychological work on gender, see Kay Deaux and Marianne LaFrance, "Gender," in *The Handbook of Social Psychology,* ed. Daniel T. Gilbert, Susan T. Fiske, and Gardner Lindzey (Boston: McGraw-Hill, 1998), pp. 788–827.

5. Ted L. Huston and Gilbert Geis, "In What Ways Do Gender-Related Attributes and Beliefs Affect Marriage?" *Journal of Social Issues* 49 (1993): 93, find this same similarity between husbands and wives. Data from the Detroit Area Study indicate that the views

more than 90 percent of wives and husbands disagree with the idea that men should make the family decisions. There is one exception to this pattern—the question about whether the mother of young children should work only if the family needs the money, on which opinion divided just about evenly among both men and women. We should note that with respect to the other measures, wives tend to hold their pro-equality views more strongly than do husbands and are, therefore, more egalitarian.

These data, which compare all husbands with all wives, leave many questions unanswered: whether these egalitarian views translate into an egalitarian division of labor at home; whether these views have consequences for attitudes and behaviors outside the house; and whether the members of married couples agree with each other on these subjects. Table 6.2 reports an index of agreement on these matters by husbands and wives taken as couples.[6] With the exception of the question about whether an employed mother can establish secure relations with her child, there is a statistically significant association between the views of the members of couples on these matters.

By comparing the measures of association just reviewed with those obtained when we measure the association between attitudes on related issues for individuals, we can place these findings in context. That is, we can ask whether there is more consistency between the views of a husband and wife on a single issue or between the views held by the wife (or the husband) on the related issues. Table 6.2 shows that, in general, there is more consistency between a single individual's opinions on related subjects than between spouses' opinions on a single issue. When we compare the average of the measures of association of pairs of attitudes

---

of women have moved in a more egalitarian direction over the past three decades. See Arland Thornton and Deborah Freedman, "Changes in the Sex Role Attitudes of Women, 1962–1977: Evidence from a Panel Study," *American Sociological Review* 44 (1979): 831–842.

6. The couple is the unit of analysis, and the measure is the gamma coefficient for the association between the answers given by the two members of the couple. In conducting this analysis, we essentially treat the attitude of the husband as a characteristic of the wife (and vice versa). Thus the gammas represent the degree of association of two attributes of a respondent: either the respondent's attitudes on two different subjects or the respondent's attitude and the spouse's attitude on the same subject.

Table 6.2 Consistency of Beliefs about Equality in the Family

| | Association (Gamma) of Wife's View with Husband's View[a] | | Association (Gamma) of Pairs of Views of | |
			Wives	Husbands
TRADITIONAL FEMININE ROLES				
Secure relationship[a]	.13	Secure relationship and Woman work[a,b]	.42***	.35**
Woman work[b]	.17**			
	.23			
FAMILY DECISIONS				
Husband decide[c]	.24**	Husband decide and Financial decisions[c,d]	.48***	.30***
Financial decisions[d] even if wife works	.25***			

Source: Citizen Participation Study Follow-up—Couples Survey.
a. Secure relationship: Agree that a working mother can have a warm and secure relationship with a child.
b. Woman work: Disagree that a woman should not work if it interferes with family responsibilities.
c. Husband decide: Disagree that husband should make decisions.
d. Financial decisions: Disagree that husband should make major financial decisions.
*Significant at <.05.
**Significant at <.01.
***Significant at <.001.

within the individual (whether wife or husband) with the average of the measures of association between one spouse and the other, we find that both husbands and wives—but especially wives—show greater internal consistency than consistency across the members of a couple. Still, the fact that three of the four measures of association between the husband's and the wife's attitudes are statistically significant bespeaks considerable agreement within couples on matters pertaining to gender roles.

EGALITARIANS AND TRADITIONALS
To obtain a better understanding of the origins and consequences of views about gender roles, we summed up the answers of each

spouse to the five questions listed in Table 6.1, yielding a *gender equality* score for wives and for husbands. These scores are lower for "traditionals" who reject equal roles for women—that is, who think that women belong at home and that husbands ought to make the decisions—and higher for "egalitarians," who take the opposite point of view.[7] As expected, there is moderate agreement within couples.

On the basis of these scores, we stratified the respondents into three roughly equal groups. Table 6.3 shows that there are real differences in the social characteristics of those who hold egalitarian or traditional views on gender equality and that these differences are much more pronounced among the wives. Among wives, those of a more egalitarian disposition on gender issues are, not surprisingly, better educated than are the traditionals. They are also more likely to be in the work force full time and, if employed, considerably more likely to have a high-level job, that is, a job requiring a high level of education or on-the-job training.[8] In addition, egalitarian wives are less likely to be over sixty than are traditional wives. In general, the same pattern holds for husbands as well. However, traditionals and egalitarians among the husbands differ

---

7. Note that the highest values on the scale are for those who support egalitarian roles. The items on the scale do not capture a circumstance of role reversal—by asking, for example, whether a husband should give up his job when it interferes with his role as a husband and father.

We used a regression-based measurement model to remove some of the measurement error from the resulting measures.

8. The job-level variable is a five-category variable based on the answers to the following two questions: How much formal education does somebody need to do a job like yours/the one you had? How long does a person have to spend in training on the job to be able to handle a job like yours? The lowest-level job requires no more than a high school diploma and no more than a month on the job for mastery. At the other end of the scale are jobs that require either a college degree and at least two years on the job or a graduate degree. Examples of occupations at each level include:

1. Dishwasher, janitor, cashier
2. Bank teller, mail carrier, machine operator
3. Electrician, machinist, construction inspector
4. Insurance agent, engineer, elementary school teacher
5. Physician, architect, attorney

See Sidney Verba, Kay Lehman Schlozman, and Henry Brady, *Voice and Equality: Civic Voluntarism in American Politics* (Cambridge: Harvard University Press, 1995), p. 564, for further information about this variable.

Table 6.3 Characteristics of Egalitarians and Traditionals on Gender Roles

	Wives		Husbands	
	Egalitarian	Traditional	Egalitarian	Traditional
Age				
35 and under	26%	21%	19%	19%
60 and over	8	20	22	19
Education: B.A. or more	41	21	44	39
Working Full Time	55	43	77	77
Job Level				
Top two	54	27	45	49
Bottom two	33	60	29	40
Party				
Democrat	43	27	32	28
Republican	27	43	32	48
Attend Church Weekly	22	57	29	34

Source: Citizen Participation Study Follow-up—Couples Survey.

less in these characteristics than do their ideological counterparts among the wives.

When it comes to party affiliation and religious attendance, the disparities between the egalitarians and traditionals are quite striking—once again, especially among the wives. Those who support more traditional definitions of gender roles are more likely than their egalitarian counterparts to identify as Republicans and to attend religious services regularly. Thus although our measures of attitudes on gender roles were deliberately constructed to refer to the family, rather than to political matters, views on these subjects are closely intertwined with politics. Especially notable is the fact that over half the traditional wives attend church weekly, while less than a quarter of the egalitarian wives do. The disparity is much smaller among men.[9]

These data cannot, of course, illumine the nature of the social processes that produce these differences. We cannot discern whether the association between traditional views on gender roles

---

9. On the connections between religiosity, attitudes, and political behavior among women, see Anna Greenberg, "Race, Religiosity, and the Women's Vote," *Women and Politics* 22 (2001): 59–82.

and, for wives, being a Republican, attending religious services or being a homemaker results from a *selection* effect such that the kinds of married women who become Republicans, go to church, or choose not to enter the work force are also the kinds of women who hold traditional views; or whether it reflects a *treatment* effect such that the experience of being a Republican, a churchgoer, or a homemaker influences attitudes toward gender equality.[10] These considerations do not arise when it comes to age: it is unlikely that the kind of people who live to age sixty-five are also the kinds of people who hold traditional views.

UNDERSTANDING BELIEFS ABOUT GENDER ROLES

We can get a clearer understanding of the characteristics associated with egalitarian or traditional attitudes by using regression analysis. Our concern is with the way that, all else being equal, various factors operate to predict views on gender roles as measured by our scale. To do so, we turn to multivariate analysis. For those who are unfamiliar with multiple regression, the appendix to this chapter explains the purposes of this technique and provides information about how to interpret a regression table.

Table 6.4 presents the results of separate regressions for wives and husbands that explore the relationship of egalitarian attitudes toward gender relations to a variety of personal and family characteristics. Among wives, those with higher job levels are more egalitarian when it comes to gender relationships. Moreover, in a pattern that has echoes in the cultural politics of our era, wives who consider themselves to be Republicans and who consider religion to be important in their lives are less egalitarian in their attitudes. The results are somewhat different for husbands. Consistent with what we saw in Table 6.3, the explanatory variables are much less powerful in accounting for male attitudes on gender equality. Interestingly, neither education nor religiosity is related to husbands' views on gender equality. For husbands, being a Re-

---

10. Although we are unable in this context to disentangle these processes in explaining beliefs about gender roles, the differences between selection effects and treatment effects will figure importantly later on when we discuss experiences in the workplace, in nonpolitical organizations, and in religious institutions.

Table 6.4 Predicting Egalitarian Gender Attitudes for Wives and Husbands (OLS regression)

	Wife		Husband
EDUCATION AND WORK STATUS			
Education	0.16		0.03
Hours of Work	0.22*	⇔	−0.04
Job Level	0.21*		0.22*
FAMILY INCOME			
Family Income	0.17		−0.02
Percentage of Family Income Respondent Brings In	−0.06		−0.16
POLITICS AND RELIGION			
Party Identification[a]	0.17**		0.12*
Importance of Religion	−0.15*	⇔	0.08
OTHER VARIABLES			
Age	−0.41*	⇔	−0.26
Preschool Children	0.02	⇔	0.10*
Years of Marriage	0.25**	⇔	0.15
Constant	2.21***		2.36***
Adjusted R-squared	0.15		0.05

Source: Citizen Participation Study Follow-up—Couples Survey.
a. Party identification is measured by a seven-point scale ranging from strong Republican to strong Democrat.
*Coefficient significant at <.05.
**Coefficient significant at <.01.
***Coefficient significant at <.001.
⇔ Difference in the coefficients for men and women is significant at <.05 (by t-test) or one coefficient is significant at <.05 and the other is not.

publican is associated with less egalitarian views. We should reiterate that we do not wish to attribute causality to the associations we find.

Table 6.5 combines the views of wife and husband to form an additive index of egalitarianism for the married couple. The results highlight the extent to which a couple's views on gender roles are related to the characteristics of the wife: if the wife is highly educated, works long hours on the job, and does not consider religion to be important in her life, a couple will, on average, have a more egalitarian view of gender roles. None of the husband's characteristics is related to the couple's gender ideology, however.

Table 6.5 Predicting Couples' Views on Gender Equality in the Family (OLS regression)

WIFE'S CHARACTERISTICS	
Education and Work Status	
Wife's education	2.13***
Wife's hours at work	1.37**
Wife's job level	0.54
Politics and Religion	
Wife is Democrat[a]	0.40
Importance of religion to wife	−1.60***
HUSBAND'S CHARACTERISTICS	
Education and Work Status	
Husband's education	−0.23
Husband's hours at work	0.52
Husband's job level	0.05
Politics and Religion	
Husband is Democrat[a]	0.26
Importance of religion to husband	0.46
FAMILY CHARACTERISTICS	
Family Income	−0.15
Percentage of Income Wife Brings In	−0.16
Preschoolers	0.49*
Years of Marriage	0.67
Age of Wife[b]	−0.63
Constant	4.26***
Adjusted R-squared	0.27

Source: Citizen Participation Study Follow-up—Couples Survey.

a. Party identification is measured by a seven-point scale ranging from strong Republican to strong Democrat.

b. Because of the high correlation between wives' and husbands' age, we include only the wife's age here.

*Coefficient significant at <.05.

**Coefficient significant at <.01.

***Coefficient significant at <.001.

Household Cultures: Political Attitudes

For many reasons we might expect husbands and wives to be like-minded when it comes to political matters. For one thing, they share many attributes that are traditionally related to political commitments and behavior: most notably, class and residential location and, usually, ethnicity and religion. Thus they have in common many of the circumstances that shape political views. Furthermore, they may have had similar views from the outset—either because they explicitly selected one another on that basis or because underlying their relationship is agreement on broader sets of values in which political views are embedded. In addition, we might reasonably expect that living together would yield convergence in views.

Nevertheless, members of a couple differ in ways that are relevant for politics. Obviously, they differ in that one is male and the other female, but they may also differ in other respects, in particular in terms of their relation to the work force. Besides, political opinions are never simply the product of social circumstances. Hence we also have reason to expect members of a couple to go their own ways politically.

How similar are the views of wives and husbands? Table 6.6 summarizes the responses of husbands and wives to a series of questions about political attitudes, all of which were formatted as seven-point scales. Three of the items offer a choice between support for government assistance and preference for self-reliant solutions: the standard question used to gauge New Deal liberalism, which asks whether the government should provide all citizens with an adequate job and standard of living or let each individual get ahead on his or her own; a question about whether the government should provide day care to those who need it or whether families should be responsible for arranging day care on their own; and an item about whether the government should help improve the social and economic position of women or whether women should help themselves. We also asked about attitudes toward abortion and school prayer. Finally, we asked the standard battery of questions used to ascertain party identification. When we compare the responses, we find, not unexpectedly, that wives, taken together, are more favorably disposed than husbands, taken together, to various forms of government assistance—in providing jobs and a decent standard of living, in providing day care, and in helping women. They are also more likely to think of themselves as Democrats. However, they are not uniformly more liberal than husbands: consistent with other studies, they are somewhat more

Table 6.6 Policy Attitudes of Husbands and Wives

	1	2	3	4	5	6	7	
GOVERNMENT ASSISTANCE								
Government in Washington should see that all have a job and a good standard of living.								Government should let each person get ahead on own.
Wives	7%	7	20	21	22	12	11 = 100%	
Husbands	2%	4	11	20	19	17	26 = 99%	
Government should provide child care for those who need it.								Families should be responsible for arranging child care.
Wives	16%	13	17	18	9	12	15 = 100%	
Husbands	12%	11	15	18	13	13	18 = 100%	
Government should help improve the social and economic position of women.								Women should help themselves.
Wives	14%	16	14	28	10	8	11 = 101%	
Husbands	11%	12	13	27	15	11	11 = 100%	

	Obtain abortion as a matter of personal choice.						Abortion should never be permitted.
SOCIAL ISSUES							
Wives	41%	10	5	8	6	19	12 = 101%
Husbands	46%	10	9	8	9	10	9 = 101%

	Religion does not belong in the schools.						Public schools should be allowed to start the day with a prayer.
Wives	15%	4	3	10	8	12	48 = 100%
Husbands	16%	2	6	8	10	11	46 = 99%

	Strong Democrat						Strong Republican
PARTY IDENTIFICATION							
Wives	18%	16	14	11	7	15	19 = 100%
Husbands	17%	13	10	13	8	17	23 = 101%

Source: Citizen Participation Study Follow-up—Couples Survey.

Table 6.7 Agreement[a] between Wives and Husbands on Political Matters

ECONOMIC AND WELFARE POLICY ISSUES	
Government provide jobs and good standard of living	.31**
Government help provide child care	.33**
Government improve position of women	.15**
Mean Association	.26
MORAL AND RELIGIOUS ISSUES	
Abortion	.50**
Prayer in the public schools	.48**
Morality attitudes	.49**
Mean Association	.49
GENERAL POLITICAL AND RELIGIOUS COMMITMENT	
Interest in politics	.39**
Importance of religion	.59**
PARTY IDENTIFICATION	.55**

Source: Citizen Participation Study Follow-up—Couples Survey.
a. Gamma between wives' and husbands' answers.
**Significant at <.01.

likely to take a pro-life position on abortion and to support prayer in the schools.[11]

While many surveys include much greater numbers of married men and women among their respondents, the special attribute of our survey is that it permits us to link members of couples to one another. Table 6.7 shows a clear relationship (as measured, once again, by the coefficient of association, gamma) between the positions of the members of couples. All the relationships are positive and statistically significant.[12] It is worth noting that, with respect to the policy issues, wives and husbands are more likely to agree on social issues like abortion and prayer in the schools than on the

11. These results reflect the findings of other surveys. For data and bibliographical suggestions, see M. Margaret Conway, Gertrude A. Steuernagel, and David W. Ahern, *Women and Political Participation* (Washington, D.C.: CQ Press, 1997), chaps. 3–5.

12. For a study that links the attitudes of wives and husbands and shows how they evolve over time, see M. Kent Jennings and Laura Stoker, "Political Similarity between Husbands and Wives" (paper presented at the annual meeting of the American Political Science Association, Washington, D.C., September 2000). They find, as we do, a good deal of similarity between spouses.

various measures of support for government assistance.[13] The consistency between spouses on these social issues, which is matched by consistency on party identification, is more pronounced than what we saw earlier for attitudes toward gender roles in Table 6.2.[14] It is also interesting to note that there is more consistency between husbands and wives in their evaluations of the importance of religion in their lives than in their interest in politics.[15]

In an attempt to probe further the extent to which attitude consistency is a family matter or an individual matter, we took advantage of the fact that our data permit us to link the attitudes of married couples to one another and conducted a factor analysis of the attitudes of husbands and wives.[16] That is, we sought to investigate patterns of political attitude positions, seeking to discern whether

---

13. The scale measuring traditional morality asked the respondent to judge whether each of the following is "morally wrong from your own personal point of view":
   1. For a man and a woman who are not married to live together
   2. A homosexual relationship between consenting adults
   3. A married man having an occasional fling with another woman
   4. A married woman having an occasional fling with another man
   5. Pornography in movies

14. For similar data showing the relationship between the attitudes of spouses, see M. Kent Jennings and Richard G. Niemi, "The Division of Political Labor between Mothers and Fathers," *American Political Science Review* 65 (1971): 69–82. Robert Huckfeldt and John Sprague also find that couples overwhelmingly agree on their vote choice. See *Citizens, Politics, and Social Communication* (Cambridge: Cambridge University Press, 1995), p. 199.

15. Jennings and Stoker, "Political Similarity Between Husbands and Wives," find a similar pattern whereby husbands and wives agree more on moral and religious matters than on other political issues.

16. Factor analysis explores the ways in which a set of variables vary together. Here it asks, in an exploratory fashion, which of the attitudes in Table 6.8 travel together. The technique is a descriptive one, initially developed to enable researchers to take large quantities of data (like the attitude measures we have in this table for each of the members of the couples in our data) and describe them in terms of a small set of underlying dimensions (or, more technically, in terms of the dimensions along which the set of variables covary). Factor analysis uses several rules to choose a way to describe the dimensions in the data; it only considers dimensions that capture a relatively large proportion of the covariance; and it requires that the researcher make several choices about the details of the analysis—among them, whether the dimensions to choose are ones that themselves are correlated. We present results for uncorrelated dimensions (or factors) chosen according to what is called a varimax rotation. A varimax rotation specifies a particular goal for the analysis, not to maximize the variance in the coefficients for a particular variable across the underlying dimensions but rather to maximize the variance in the coefficients for all variables on a particular dimension. Other goals than the one we chose—and thus other rotations—yield quite similar results.

Table 6.8 Dimensions of Attitudes of Husbands and Wives: Factor Analysis (varimax rotation)

	Wife's View: Economic Issues	Joint View: Moral and Religious Issues	Husband's View: Economic Issues
ECONOMIC AND WELFARE POLICY ISSUES			
Wife's View			
Government should provide jobs	0.80	0.06	0.15
Government should provide day care	0.76	0.18	0.25
Government should provide assistance to women	0.84	0.14	0.02
Husband's View			
Government should provide jobs	0.37	0.13	0.64
Government should provide day care	0.18	0.05	0.80
Government should provide assistance to women	−0.04	0.13	0.85
MORAL AND RELIGIOUS ISSUES			
Wife's View			
Support abortion rights	0.23	0.71	0.05
Oppose school prayer	0.03	0.72	0.09
Husband's View			
Support abortion rights	0.27	0.53	0.20
Oppose school prayer	−0.01	0.80	0.04

Source: Citizen Participation Study Follow-up—Couples Survey.

individuals show consistency with respect to related political issues or whether wives and husbands show consistency with respect to the same political issue. Table 6.8 shows the results of this analysis. Three factors emerge from the ten attitude items (five for each spouse). The second factor brings together attitudes of both members of the couple on matters having a religious or moral dimension: prayer in the schools and abortion. The first and third link together attitudes within individuals: the first one bringing together the attitudes of the wife toward several aspects of government assistance; and the third one these same attitudes of the husband. That couples are more likely to agree with one another with respect to social issues than with respect to issues that engage concerns surrounding government assistance accords with many other bits of evidence demonstrating that religious commitments take precedence over political ones as a source of cohesion within couples.

Summary: The Culture of the Household

We have found much more evidence that birds of a feather flock together than that opposites attract. Married couples express fairly egalitarian views when it comes to gender roles, and the partners demonstrate a fair amount of agreement with each other on these issues as well as on policy matters involving government assistance. When it comes to two social issues having a religious dimension—abortion and school prayer—and party identification, couples are even more likely to be like-minded. In fact, this chapter has presented various bits of evidence suggesting how central religion and religiosity are to couples.

Even though issues involving gender roles are germane to men's lives as well as to women's and even though some of our measures refer to men's roles in the household—especially with respect to decision making—as well as to women's, our discussion has uncovered evidence that these matters are more salient to wives than to husbands. Moreover, their views on these issues form a more coherent bundle internally and are more closely related to their political and religious commitments. In addition, the wife's characteristics are more tightly connected to the couple's opinions on these subjects than are the husband's.

Appendix: A Note on Reading a Regression Table

In Chapter 2, we discussed at some length the importance of multivariate analysis in assessing the relative weight of various factors in predicting complex social phenomena. There we offered a brief introduction to the statistical technique we ordinarily use, multiple regression. We also explained that, in order to ascertain whether the factors under scrutiny operate in the same way for the two groups, we usually conduct separate regressions for women and men—or, as in this case where we are using the data about couples, wives and husbands.

A multiple regression analysis focuses on a dependent variable, the phenomenon that we seek to understand, and a set of independent variables that are presumed to be associated with it. When there is a causal relationship between two factors, the regression is set up so that the independent variable is the cause and the dependent variable is the effect. Because we cannot always be certain of the causal ordering of the variables with which we deal, we often frame our discussion—as we do in this case—in terms of the relationship (or association) between the independent and dependent variables.

In selecting independent variables, it is crucial to include all the potentially relevant factors for which there are measures. In Table 6.4 the dependent variable is the scale of attitudes toward gender equality that we constructed on the basis of responses to five questions—with higher scores signifying more egalitarian views. This scale obviously has an arbitrary metric. In some cases, however, the dependent variable will be measured in "natural" units—for example, the number of dollars contributed to a campaign or the number of participatory acts. The independent variables in this analysis include certain characteristics of the individual (whether husband or wife) including education, job level, the number of hours spent working in an average week, party identification, the importance of religion to the respondent, and age, as well as certain characteristics of the couple—their family income, the proportion of the family income that is brought in by the respondent, whether they have preschool children, and the number of years they have been married.

Let us consider the information reported on the table. For each independent variable, we report an unstandardized *regression coefficient* that measures the association between that independent variable and the dependent variable with the other independent variables taken into account. In order to facilitate comparisons across different independent variables that are measured in different metrics and that have different ranges, we have transformed all the independent variables to have a range of 0 to 1. The coefficient tells us how much increase in the dependent variable would result, all else equal, if an individual went from the lowest to the highest point on the scale measuring a particular independent variable. Consider, for example, the respondent's party identification, which is measured on a seven-point scale ranging from strong Republican to strong Democrat. The coefficient of .17 for wives indicates that, if we compared two wives who were identical with respect to each of the independent variables—that is, who had the same age, same family income, and so on—except that one was a strong Republican and the other a strong Democrat, we would expect the latter to be .17 points higher on the gender equality scale.[17]

Although the regression coefficient measures the strength of the relationship between the dependent variable and a particular independent variable, we cannot draw conclusions until we have ruled out the possibility that the relationship is the result of chance. To do so, we need to pay attention to the *level of significance* of the *t*-statistic. The regression coefficient measures the average association between an independent variable and the dependent variable, not the association for each and every individual in the analysis. If there is a wide variation in that association from individual to individual, the effect of the independent variable is less certain.[18] The asterisks next to the coefficients show the statistical significance of *t*, the probability that the association between a particular independent and the dependent variable is the result of chance. Thus,

---

17. The meaning of a regression coefficient is dependent upon the range of the independent variable. Therefore, we provide that information for each variable in Appendix B.

We have mentioned that the transformation of the independent variables to a 0-to-1 range permits us to make comparisons among independent variables. We should note, however, that since the regression coefficient for each independent variable measures the effect of moving from the lowest to the highest score on that variable, the choice of the low and high points of the independent variable imposes a degree of arbitrariness on the results. For instance, the educational variable in the couples study has six categories ranging from no more than an eighth grade education to graduate training. Had we reduced the number of categories and made the highest category "B.A. or more," the results would have been different.

18. To elaborate further, the standard error of the regression coefficient measures the variation in the effect of the independent variable. Low standard errors indicate limited variation—and high standard errors indicate a great deal of variation—across individuals in the relationship between the dependent and independent variables. Thus the term "standard error" is misleading: it does not measure whether the data contain mistakes—though all data do; rather it measures whether the estimates made by the regression coefficients hold across a large portion of the sample. The higher the ratio between the regression coefficient (B) and the standard error (SE B), the lower the probability that the association between the independent and dependent variables is the result of chance and the less variability in the relationship in our data. This ratio is the *t*-statistic. We report the standard errors for all regression coefficients in Appendix C.

there is less than one chance in a hundred that, for wives, the relationship between partisanship and egalitarian views is the result of chance. Researchers differ in the level of statistical significance they set for not rejecting a hypothesis as the result of a statistical fluke—with significance at .05 or .01 as common thresholds. In any case, the more asterisks, the lower the probability that any relationship is the product of chance.

As we pointed out in Chapter 2, we analyze the data separately for husbands and wives in order to assess whether the process works differently for the two groups—that is, whether there are *significant differences between wives and husbands* in the strength of the association between a particular independent variable and the dependent variable. When the regression coefficients are significantly different for husbands and wives, we call attention to this difference by using the same convention we have used to indicate statistically significant differences in group means: ⇔.[19] It is important to distinguish between the significance of a particular coefficient for husbands or wives and the significance of the difference between the coefficients for wives and husbands. For example, in Table 6.4 we see that, for both husbands and wives, job level is significantly related to support for gender equality. However, because the relationships are essentially the same for the two groups, the coefficients on job level for husbands and wives are not significantly different. In contrast, there is a statistically significant difference between the coefficients for wives and husbands when it comes to the importance of religion in one's life. For wives, but not for husbands, considering religion to be important is significantly associated with traditional views on relations between the sexes. Therefore, in this case, the regression coefficient is significant for one group but not the other, and there is a significant difference between the regression coefficients for husbands and wives.

Sometimes we wish to assess the extent of the gender difference in the dependent variable that remains after the various independent variables have been taken into account. The *constant* mea-

---

19. We do so when the difference between the coefficients for wives and husbands is significant at the .05 level (assuming different variances).

sures the score on the dependent variable—in this case, attitudes toward gender equality—that wives and husbands would have after taking into account the factors introduced into the equation. By comparing the difference between the constants for husbands and wives, we can understand the extent of the gender difference—net of the effects of the independent variables in the regression analysis. In Table 6.4, the constants are not significantly different, indicating that once the various factors are taken into account, wives and husbands do not differ in their attitudes toward gender equality.

7

Domestic Hierarchy:
The Household as a Social System

Is the verbal commitment to equality that emerges so clearly from our interviews with couples matched by deeds? Having considered what husbands and wives say, we next examine what they actually do. In this chapter, we peek behind the closed doors of the home in order to understand how the domestic lives of couples are organized. Drawing on Weber's insight that societies are stratified on multiple bases, we construe the household as a miniature social system and investigate several kinds of hierarchy at home.[1] That is, we conceptualize the household as a micro-economy, a micro-polity, and a micro-society. We explore household structure not only because domestic arrangements are intrinsically interesting—although, surely, they are—but also because the organization of the household and the allocation of time, money, power, and respect within it have possible implications for civic involvement. Our eventual goal will be to examine the argument that is made, without benefit of systematic evidence, that inequalities in domestic arrangements prevent women from becoming full citizens within the polity. Here we use the data about married couples to investigate the inequalities within the household that might have an impact on women's and men's participation in politics. Later on in Chapter 12 we confront head-on the implications of domestic hierarchies for politics.

---

1. Max Weber, "Class, Status, and Party," in *From Max Weber: Essays in Sociology,* ed. H. H. Gerth and C. Wright Mills (New York: Oxford University Press, 1958).

Our analysis thus focuses on aspects of resources and family social structure that might have an impact on political activity. In terms of resources, constraints with respect to either time or money might depress participation. That is, differing positions in the labor market or differing responsibilities at home might leave husbands and wives with different stockpiles of leisure time or personal income, resources that might facilitate political activity.

When it comes to family social structure, role differentiation and patterns of authority within the family might affect political activity in either or both of two ways. First, those who do not share fully in authority over family decisions or who find that they do not enjoy equal respect might extrapolate from their experiences and feel less efficacious in the political realm. In addition, those who assume the burden of running the household and raising children might receive the implicit message that their energies should be focused inward on the home rather than outward on the public world.

Household Economy: Who Brings in Money? Who Gives Time?

The household is a miniature economy in which resources are generated internally through domestic production and externally by family members who are employed outside. More and more, the acquisition of external resources depends on the paid work of both wives and husbands. Within the economy of the family, time is also allocated to domestic activities. We begin by considering the division of labor within households—both because who does what at home is an important aspect of American society and because domestic arrangements have potential implications for politics.

WHO EARNS THE HOUSEHOLD INCOME?

We have pointed out that one of the most substantial and seemingly enduring of the changes wrought over the past half century is the entry of women into the work force, a trend that is evident in

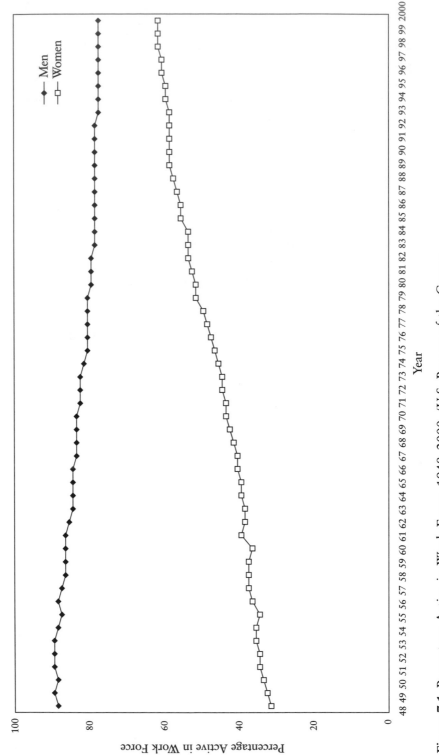

Figure 7.1 Percentage Active in Work Force, 1948–2000. (U.S. Bureau of the Census, Current Population Survey, data from March of each year)

Figure 7.1. In 1940, 27.4 percent of all women, and a mere 16.7 percent of married women, were in the labor force.[2] With the absorption of a substantial portion of the male labor force into the armed forces during World War II, the proportion of women in the work force increased quickly, reaching 35.0 percent of all women, and 25.6 percent of married women, by 1944. Much less noted than the well-known demobilization of women from the work force that accompanied the demobilization of the troops is the fact that, even in the immediate aftermath of the war, women's work force participation never again dipped to its pre-war levels. What ensued was a fairly steady increase in the proportion of women in the labor force—even during the household- and child-rearing–intensive Baby Boom years of the 1950s. This process of movement into the work force was especially pronounced for married women, whose rates of work force participation slowly converged with the traditionally higher rates for single women. By 1995, 58.9 percent of all women—including 61.0 percent of married women and 66.8 percent of single women—were in the work force.[3] With later school leaving and the institutionalization of retirement, men's work force participation declined somewhat over the same period. Because elderly men are relatively likely to be married, this process of gradual decline was especially noticeable among married men. By 1995, 75 percent of all men, and 77.5 percent of married men, were in the work force.

In a parallel development, the gender gap in wages—which for decades had hovered at roughly 59 percent—began to close very slowly in the 1980s, a process that reflected both real gains by women, especially women in non-traditional occupations, and the stagnation of men's wages in an era of deindustrialization and downsizing. By early 1997 women working full time, year round, earned 74 cents for every dollar earned by their male counter-

---

2. Figures in this paragraph are taken from U.S. Bureau of the Census, *Statistical Abstract of the United States: 1984*, 104th ed. (Washington, D.C.: U.S. Government Printing Office, 1983), p. 413; and U.S. Bureau of the Census, *Statistical Abstract of the United States: 1996*, 116th ed. (Washington, D.C.: U.S. Government Printing Office, 1996), pp. 393, 399.

3. Those who are widowed—who are, presumably, older—have much lower rates of work force participation.

parts.[4] An obvious result of these multiple processes is that, over time, an increasing portion—though surely not half—of family income was attributable to wives' earnings.

The relationship of women's increased, but still unequal, earning power to various aspects of family dynamics is less clear. Feminists from various disciplines have questioned the assumption that once we cross the threshold into the private domain of the family, the interests of all family members are identical.[5] Once we admit the possibility that household members, including husbands and wives, have differing as well as similar interests, several questions—none of them resolved by existing research—pose themselves. First, we can query whether income brought in by various family members is equally available to all household members, even if it is pooled. In addition, we can inquire whether bringing in a larger share of the family income confers greater power within the household.[6] We use our Couples Survey to look

---

4. U.S. Bureau of the Census, *Measuring 50 Years of Economic Change Using the March Current Population Survey,* Current Population Reports, P60-203 (Washington, D.C.: U.S. Government Printing Office, 1998), p. 15.

5. On the role of the family in contemporary theories of justice, see Susan Moller Okin, *Justice, Gender, and the Family* (New York: Basic Books, 1989). Heidi Hartmann argues that economists have also neglected to construe the family as a locus for conflict by ignoring the extent to which household members can have different interests at stake. See Hartmann, "The Family as the Locus of Gender, Class, and Political Struggle: The Example of Housework," *Signs* 6 (1981): 366–394.

6. Research on this question provides conflicting answers. Jane Riblett Wilkie cites literature demonstrating that employment outside the home alters power relations within the home, because women who are employed learn bargaining skills and have an enhanced sense of self-esteem and an appreciation of the legitimacy of their own interests. Similarly, Philip Blumstein and Pepper Schwartz use survey results to show that income affects marital power as measured by the response to a question about "who runs the show." See Wilkie, "Marriage, Family Life, and Women's Employment," in *Women Working,* ed. Ann Helton Stromberg and Shirley Harkess, 2nd ed. (Mountain View, Calif.: Mayfield Publishing Co., 1988), pp. 151–152; and Blumstein and Schwartz, "Money and Ideology," in *Gender, Family, and Economy,* ed. Rae Lesser Blumberg (Newbury Park, Calif.: Sage Publications, 1991), p. 273. In "A Theoretical Look at the Gender Balance of Power in the American Couple," *Journal of Family Issues* 10 (1989): 225–250, Rae Lesser Blumberg and Marion Tolbert Coleman argue that gender power within the family depends upon the importance of who brings money into the home, rather than the job per se.

In contrast, Janice Steil argues that it is not income but "rather the husbands' and wives' perceptions of their own careers relative to their spouses' careers" that matter most for marital power. See *Marital Equality* (Thousand Oaks, Calif.: Sage Publications, 1997), xviii.

Table 7.1 Earnings of Husbands and Wives[a]

	Wives		Husbands
Mean Earnings (all)	$9,451	⇔	$30,915
Mean Earnings (full-time workers)	$20,958	⇔	$39,188

Source: Citizen Participation Study—Main Survey.

a. Appendix A contains the valid number of cases for these and other measures used in the tables.

⇔ Difference between women and men is statistically significant at the .05 level.

inside the family and inquire about the implications for husbands and wives of their relative contributions to total family income.

Our data confirm the expectation that, because women are less likely than men to work for pay and, if they work, they earn less, wives contribute less to the household exchequer than do their spouses. Table 7.1 shows that, on average, husbands earn more than wives, even when both husband and wife work full time.[7] Across all couples, on average, husbands bring in twice as much income as wives do.[8] This figure accords with what other scholars have found in surveys.[9] Not unexpectedly, what wives contribute to family income has risen over recent decades, a trend that emerges clearly from the data in Figure 7.2. A survey conducted in Detroit in 1955 showed wives contributing only 13 percent to family income.[10] In short, women seem to be at a disadvantage,

---

7. The data we have on earnings for husbands and wives are, of course, not as accurate as those from other sources, particularly government surveys like the census. We use our own data here because our data set is the only one that has the auxiliary information to which we wish to relate earnings information. The differences we find are consistent with those found in other data sources.

8. The estimate comes from the interviews with the wife and is based on her report of her own earnings as a percentage of her report of the family income. We have similar data for husbands. We can, using the husband's responses, calculate the wife's contribution to family earnings by subtracting his report of his earnings from the family income, and take that as a percentage of family income. There is remarkable agreement between the spouses that the wife brings in about a third of the household income—wives estimate the proportion at 33 percent, husbands at 31 percent.

9. Linda Thompson and Alexis J. Walker, "Gender in Families," *Journal of Marriage and the Family* 51 (1981): 850.

10. Figure calculated from data contained in the Detroit Area Study: The Urban Family,

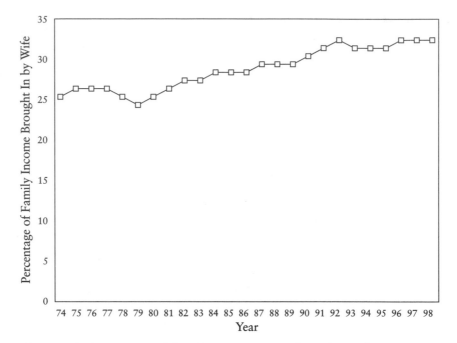

Figure 7.2 Percentage of Family Income Brought In by Wife, 1974–1998. (U.S. Bureau of the Census, Current Population Survey, data from March of each year)

though a diminishing one, when it comes to the generation of family financial resources.

WHO GIVES TIME?

Time is another resource allocated within the family, depending on which spouse has the larger responsibility for time-consuming family obligations. Housework has traditionally devolved to women, and study after study confirms that married couples do not share household and child-rearing chores equally—even when both partners have full-time jobs.[11] It is noteworthy that, even

---

1955, Inter-university Consortium for Political and Social Research (ICPSR) no.7319, Principal Investigator, Robert Blood.

11. Gloria W. Bird, Gerald A. Bird, and Marguerite Scruggs, "Determinants of Family Task Sharing: A Study of Husbands and Wives," *Journal of Marriage and the Family* 46

though technological changes—in particular, the advent of central heating and running water—have transformed housework over the last century, the number of hours spent on housework has not diminished substantially.[12]

Given the emphasis in feminist thought upon the way differential responsibilities for household chores constrain the time women have available for politics, we were particularly interested in how much time members of couples devote to various kinds of tasks. Table 7.2 presents the results obtained when respondents were asked a series of questions about how much time they, and their husbands or wives, spent in an average day on a variety of activities, among them necessary household tasks (including child care), child care, and paid work. We show not only the average amount of time that the respondents claim to devote to a particular activity but also the average amount of time they credit their spouses with giving. In the aggregate, there is a great deal of similarity in the estimates of the husbands and the wives of what they and their partners do. When we linked the estimates made by members of couples, we also found a substantial amount of agree-

---

(1984): 345–355; Blumberg and Coleman, "A Theoretical Look at the Gender Balance of Power"; Martin Browning, "Children and Household Economic Behavior," *Journal of Economic Literature* 30 (1992): 1434–1475; Robin A. Douthitt, "The Division of Labor within the Home: Have Gender Roles Changed?" *Sex Roles* 20 (1989): 693–704; Frances K. Goldscheider and Linda J. Waite, *New Families, No Families?: The Transformation of the American Home* (Berkeley: University of California Press, 1991); Hartmann, "The Family as the Locus of Struggle," p. 383; Arlie Hochschild, *The Second Shift* (New York: Viking, 1989); Ann Oakley, *The Sociology of Housework* (New York: Pantheon, 1974); Scott J. South and Glenna Spitze, "Housework in Marital and Nonmarital Households," *American Sociological Review* 59 (1994): 327–347; and Steil, *Marital Equality*, pp. 50–51. For extensive references, see Francine M. Deutsch, *Halving It All: How Equally Shared Parenting Works* (Cambridge: Harvard University Press, 1999), chap. 1. Deutsch's interviews with couples who have children demonstrate the way that equality—or inequality—between parents in child-rearing responsibilities emerges from the minutiae of day-to-day interactions and decisions.

12. For a fascinating account of the history of housework in America, see Susan Strasser, *Never Done: A History of American Housework* (New York: Pantheon Books, 1982). On the fact that time devoted to housework has not declined appreciably with technological change, see Hartmann, "The Family as the Locus of Struggle," pp. 388–389. There is some evidence that the average amount of time devoted to housework has decreased in very recent years both by women in the work force and by the diminishing proportion of women who are at home full time. See John P. Robinson and Geoffrey Godbey, *Time for Life* (University Park: Pennsylvania State University Press, 1997), pp. 99–106.

Table 7.2 Allocations of Time in the Household Economy

	Time Given by Wife		Time Given by Husband	
	Wife's Report	Husband's Report	Wife's Report	Husband's Report
Mean Hours Housework[a] (all)	5.3	5.4	2.2	3.0
Mean Hours Housework[a] (couples with full-time jobs)	4.1	3.6	1.9	3.0
Mean Hours Child Care (couples with children home)	3.3	3.6	1.5	1.4
Mean Hours Child Care (couples with children home and full-time jobs)	2.4	2.2	1.6	1.5
Mean Hours Housework[a]				
Wife not in work force	6.6	7.9	2.6	2.9
Wife works part time	6.0	6.1	2.1	3.2
Wife works full time	4.1	3.6	2.0	3.1
Mean Hours Paid Work (all)	5.5	5.5	8.5	7.6
Mean Hours Paid Work (couples with full-time jobs)	9.1	9.4	10.5	10.4

Source: Citizen Participation Study Follow-up—Couples Survey.
a. Includes child care.

ment: 59 percent of the couples were in complete agreement or were within an hour of one another when it comes to how many hours the husband devotes to housework, including child care; 47 percent of the couples were in complete agreement or within an hour of one another when it comes to the amount of housework done by the wife. How did members of couples evaluate each other's estimates of their contributions? Members of couples agree, on average, in their estimates of what wives do; however, husbands claim, on average, 48 minutes more housework daily than their wives give them credit for.

Table 7.2 makes clear what others have found: husbands spend more time than wives on paid work, and wives spend more time than husbands on housework and child care. These relationships hold even where both partners in a couple have full-time jobs.

Table 7.3 Contributions to Household

	Wife's Report	Husband's Report
Percentage of housework[a] done by wife[b]		
All	71%	64%
Wife not in work force	72	73
Wife works part time	74	66
Wife works full time	67	54
Percentage of child care done by wife[b]		
Couples with children home	69	72
Couples with children home and full-time jobs	60	59

	Women	Men
Contribution to household income		
All	30%	70%
Full-time workers	35	65

Sources: Citizen Participation Study—Main Survey and Couples Survey.
a. Includes child care.
b. Entry in cell is wife's percentage of the total hours done by husband and wife.

Compared with their wives, husbands in these two-job couples spend somewhat more time on paid work and considerably less time on housework and child care. In fact, while the number of hours wives devote, on average, to home and children declines with growing work force commitment, there is no systematic increase in the hours that husbands put in at home when their wives work full time.

These findings are reflected in Table 7.3, which shows the proportion of housework and child care that wives do. It is interesting to note that the average estimates for contributions of household time and money are mirror images of each other: wives contribute roughly a third of the income and roughly two-thirds of the housework time.[13] Interestingly, when the wife is at home full time, she

13. Although it would have been preferable to base our data about time use on time diaries, we are encouraged that our findings about the proportion of time given to household tasks are consistent with the findings reported in other studies. For example, Juliet Schor (*The Overworked American: The Unexpected Decline of Leisure* [New York: Basic Books,

and her husband exhibit a higher level of agreement about who is taking responsibility for the house and children than when she is in the work force. Earlier we saw that the proportion of family income attributable to the wife's earnings has risen since 1955. When it comes to housework, there has been little change. In the earlier study, wives reported doing, on average, 69 percent of the housework.[14]

It must be noted, however, that despite the fact that they contribute more time to household chores than do men, women, on average, do not appear to have less free time than men. Among married respondents, men and women reported an identical amount of free time per day: six hours.[15] Among those married respondents with full-time jobs and children at home, women have, on average, less free time (3.76 hours) than do similarly situated men (3.99 hours). However, the difference is smaller than might have been expected on the basis of the division of labor at home, because men with full-time jobs and children at home tend to put in longer hours at work.

This point deserves elaboration. Not surprisingly, those who work full time, a group that is disproportionately male, have less free time than those who work part time or are not in the work force, a group that is disproportionately female. We should note, however, that—especially when there are young children in the household—the leisure time of a woman who is at home full time may not be as unencumbered, not as leisurely, as that of her husband. We should also point out that the reduction in leisure deriving from full-time employment is greater for women than for men.

1991], pp. 35–37, 86–87) estimates that women contributed 72 percent of the household time in 1967 and 63 percent in 1987. Using a range of methods of ascertaining relative contributions of household labor, numerous studies arrive at similar results. See Ted L. Huston and Gilbert Geis, "In What Ways Do Gender-Related Attributes and Beliefs Affect Marriage?" *Journal of Social Issues* 49 (1993): 94; Mary-Clare Lennon and Sarah Rosenfield, "Relative Fairness and the Division of Housework: The Importance of Options," *American Journal of Sociology* 100 (1994): 506–531; and South and Spitze, "Housework."

14. Calculated from data in the Detroit Area Study: The Urban Family, 1955, ICPSR no.7319, Principal Investigator, Robert Blood.

15. Gender parity in access to free time has also been noted in the family studies literature. See Thompson and Walker, "Gender in Families," p. 850; and Cathleen D. Zick and Jane L. McCullough, "Trends in Married Couples' Time Use: Evidence from 1977–78 and 1987–88," *Sex Roles* 24 (1991): 471.

This is the result not of greater time spent on the job, but of the fact that, as we have seen, women who work full time continue to assume disproportionate responsibility for caring for home and children; the additional time spent by women on chores at home more than compensates for men's greater time on the job.[16]

In short, women may at one time have been advantaged compared with men with respect to the resource of leisure time, which can be devoted to other pursuits—including voluntary activity. If this advantage ever existed, it has disappeared with women's increasing work force participation. We should, however, recall the comparison with money: when it comes to money, men are unambiguously better off; with respect to time, men and women are, in the aggregate, equally well endowed in terms of leisure.[17]

The data in Table 7.4 amplify these findings about who does what at home. For several common household chores—cleaning, grocery shopping, paying bills, taking care of the car, and caring for the children—we asked each partner whether he or she did all, most, some, little, or none of that task. Table 7.4 shows the distribution of responses for wives and husbands along with roughly parallel reports from wives during the 1950s. Overall, wives and husbands report a similar division of labor, with wives doing more when it comes to cleaning, shopping, caring for the children, and to a lesser extent, paying bills, and men taking primary responsibility for the car. When we compare the husbands' and wives' reports, we find some tendency toward credit claiming: ordinarily each half of the couple makes a more generous assessment of his or her own effort than, by inference, does the spouse. The proportion of couples in which the spouses give contradictory answers—each claiming to do all or most of a particular chore or one spouse claiming to do all while the other claims to do some—varies from

---

16. A regression analysis of how the free time available to women and men relates to family and work circumstances shows that the same life circumstances affect the free time available to women and to men: working (especially full time), having a working spouse, and having children at home. With one exception, there are no gender differences in the coefficients. The exception is that though having preschoolers at home leads to a statistically significant drop in free time for both men and women, women lose twice as much free time from preschoolers as men do.

17. See Goldschieder and Waite, *New Families, No Families,* for similar data.

Table 7.4 Division of Household Chores

A. 1994 Data

	All	Most	Some	Little	None	Percentage of Responses Contradictory[a]
HOUSE CLEANING						
Wives say they do	41%	34	17	3	5 = 100%	20%
Husbands say they do	1%	10	46	31	13 = 101%	
GROCERY SHOPPING						
Wives say they do	47%	34	14	2	4 = 101%	23%
Husbands say they do	9%	13	38	25	15 = 100%	
PAYING BILLS						
Wives say they do	48%	17	13	12	11 = 101%	16%
Husbands say they do	21%	20	14	20	25 = 100%	
CAR REPAIRS						
Wives say they do	7%	13	27	27	27 = 101%	28%
Husbands say they do	67%	24	5	1	3 = 100%	
TAKING CARE OF THE CHILDREN						
Wives say they do	11%	63	22	1	4 = 101%	8%
Husbands say they do	b	7	75	10	9 = 101%	

B. 1955 Data

	Wives' Report						
	She Does It All				He Does It All		
House Cleaning	53%	38	7	2	b	=	100%
Grocery Shopping	37%	20	29	7	8	=	101%
Paying Bills	29%	11	34	7	19	=	100%
Car Repairs	3%	3	7	12	76	=	101%

Sources: 1994–Citizen Participation Study Follow-up—Couples Survey; 1955–Detroit Area Study: The Urban Family (ICPSR no. 7319).

a. Both members of a couple claim to do all or most of the chore, or one claims to do all and the other to do some.

b. Less than 1 percent.

household chore to household chore. Car repair generates the most disagreement: a fourth of the couples give contradictory answers. In contrast, the fewest contradictory responses are found in relation to taking care of the children. Roughly, one couple in ten appears in clear disagreement on this. Most wives—and few husbands—claim to do all or most of the child care. Comparing the 1994 responses with those from 1955, we see that, according to the wives, husbands are doing somewhat more housecleaning now than they did four decades ago, but wives are doing a somewhat larger share of the other tasks than before.

In sum, according to the portrait that emerges from our survey, the contemporary American family is characterized by economic inequality. Wives, who are less likely than husbands to work full time—and less likely to have high-level jobs if they do—bring, on average, about half as much income into the family as do husbands. Couples may be moving in the direction of greater sharing when it comes to housework and child care, but wives still do the predominance of housework. In the last chapter we saw that nine out of ten wives and husbands feel that household chores should be equally shared between spouses. It is striking that what married couples say is not what they do: in direct contradiction to these egalitarian expressions, the actual patterns of behavior within the household demonstrate the continuing hold of traditional patterns of behavior.

The Household as Polity

Just as the household can be construed in terms of economic inequality, it can be construed in terms of political inequality as well. Indeed, it is often taken as axiomatic by feminists that husbands exercise power in the domain of the family. According to Heidi Hartmann, "it is important to remember that within the household as well as outside it, men have more power."[18] Nevertheless, this aspect of domestic hierarchy is more often asserted than substantiated, for the measurement of relative power—a matter about which political scientists have long puzzled—becomes especially complex when decisions are made in the privacy of the home by people who have both convergent and conflicting interests, yet who are intimately connected in many ways.

We focus on this aspect of household relations both for its in-

---

18. Hartmann, "The Family as the Locus of Struggle," p. 376. See also Paula England and George Farkas, *Households, Employment, and Gender* (New York: Aldine, 1986), p. 54, for confirmation and bibliographical references.

trinsic interest in an era when families are changing and for its potential consequences for how the members of a couple take part in political life. Over and above concern about control over whatever resources of money or time are available to the household, the capacity to make independent decisions at home might affect the individual's capacity to take part in politics. Furthermore, individuals may generalize from their experiences with domestic decision making to their roles in the polity. Exercising power at home—either as an equal partner or as the dominant partner in decisions—may enhance feelings of political competence, an expectation supported by work on the family as an agent of socialization.[19] Control over money or time may thus have an impact on both actual political resources and the motivation to use them in politics.

CONTROL OVER MONEY AND TIME

In an attempt to ascertain how household power is allocated, we asked wives and husbands about several aspects of control over family resources. With respect to money, the overwhelming majority of the couples in our sample—including more than eight out of ten couples where both partners are in the work force—pool their resources. This arrangement would seem to indicate widespread equality when it comes to control over finances. However, scholars of family relations argue that a shared bank account may not indicate genuine equality in practice—even though couples believe that joint money belongs equally to both partners.[20] In fact, one analysis of dual-career marriages argues that an individual income is a source of independence in a marriage and that pooled incomes tend to accompany a more traditional view of marriage.[21]

We also asked both husbands and wives about how much responsibility they take for "bigger financial decisions," a question that is similar to one asked in 1955 of wives only. As shown in Table 7.5, according to reports from wives, the past four decades

19. Gabriel A. Almond and Sidney Verba, *The Civic Culture* (Princeton: Princeton University Press, 1963); and Sapiro, *Political Integration*.

20. Carole B. Burgoyne, "Money in Marriage: How Patterns of Allocation Both Reflect and Conceal Power," *Sociological Review* 38 (1990): 634–665.

21. Rosanna Hertz, *More Equal Than Others* (Berkeley: University of California Press, 1986), pp. 101–104.

Table 7.5 Control over Money: Responsibility for Bigger Financial Decisions

A. 1994 Data

	All	Most	Some	Little	None	Percentage of Responses Contradictory[a]
Wives say they have	7%	19	65	7	2 = 100%	24%
Husbands say they have	17%	55	26	1	[b] = 99%	

B. 1955 Data

		Wives' Report			
He Has It All			She Has It All		
7%	58	22	12	1 = 100%	

Sources: 1994–Citizen Participation Study Follow-up—Couples Survey; 1955–Detroit Area Study: The Urban Family (ICPSR no. 7319).
a. Both members of a couple claim to do all or most of the chore, or one claims to do all and the other to do some.
b. Less than 1 percent.

have witnessed a substantial increase in their participation in decisions about family money. In 1955 nearly two-thirds of wives reported having little or no responsibility for major financial matters—in contrast to only 9 percent who made this assessment in the recent survey. Moreover, a quarter of the wives in the latter survey indicated that they took all or most of the responsibility. Nevertheless, this remains a domain in which husbands seem to exercise greater control. Nearly three-quarters of the husbands indicated taking all or most of the responsibility for big financial decisions, compared with about a quarter of the wives.

In addition, we asked wives and husbands about their perceived autonomy in making decisions about using household resources, and what we found does not accord neatly with the results presented in Table 7.5. The survey contained a series of questions about whether they could make decisions regarding the use of time and money on their own or whether their spouse would have "some say in the decision." With respect to finances, we asked about a "substantial" contribution to a charity, a "substantial" contribution to a political candidate or cause, and a "major purchase for [the respondent's] own personal use." In terms of time, we asked about committing "time on a regular basis" to a charity drive, or political cause, or something they enjoy, "a hobby or a sport, for example." As shown by the data in Table 7.6, both husbands and wives report that they would not make a large financial commitment without giving their spouse some say. In nine out of ten couples, both wives and husbands report that they would consult before making a charitable or a political contribution. Only when it comes to a major personal purchase does the proportion who would consult fall below 90 percent—for wives only. Even though, in this case, almost three-quarters of the wives would consult, the notion that wives would feel greater freedom than husbands in withdrawing from the family exchequer contradicts the received wisdom about family dynamics.[22]

With respect to control over time, the pattern is quite different. For one thing, spouses are more willing to spend time than to spend money without consulting. In addition, compared with their husbands, wives were more likely to report being able to give time to voluntary activities—charitable, political, or social—without consultation. We guessed that this unexpected finding might reflect the fact that those who are not in the work force, a group that is disproportionately female, would exercise particular control over their time. When we looked at the data, however, this hypothesis was discredited: women who work full time are as likely as

---

22. Burgoyne, "Money in Marriage," pp. 659–660, makes the point that while women are comfortable spending joint money on the household or family, they are reluctant to spend it on themselves—sometimes to the consternation of their husbands.

The data for parallel questions about small contributions of money and time show that husbands are more likely to consult with wives than vice versa.

	Wife would check with husband	Husband would check with wife
Using Money		
Small charitable contribution	32%	54%
Small political contribution	45	53
Small personal purchase	13	16
Using Time		
A few hours to charitable work	14	33
A few hours to political activity	32	53
A few hours to an enjoyable activity	13	33

Table 7.6 Joint Decision Making: What Couples Say

	Wife Would Check with Husband	Husband Would Check with Wife	Both Would Check
Spend a substantial amount of money			
Charitable contribution	93%	96%	90%
Political contribution	95	96	91
Personal purchase	77	91	71
Commit time on a regular basis			
Charitable work	53	80	45
Political activity	68	88	62
Something enjoyable	44	73	34

Source: Citizen Participation Study Follow-up—Couples Survey.

women at home to make autonomous decisions about the use of large amounts of time.

In short, both partners characterize household decision making as involving a great deal of mutual consultation. Contrary to our expectation and to the earlier finding that husbands take disproportionate responsibility for major financial decisions, husbands report nearly universal consultation with their wives with respect to major expenditures. Again contrary to expectation, when it comes to the allocation of time, wives appear somewhat more independent.

The overall pattern of consultative decision making is reflected in the data in Table 7.7. We asked both members of couples a series of questions about whether they felt they had a chance to express their point of view when discussing serious matters with their spouse, whether their spouse would pay attention if they expressed their point of view, and whether they were generally satisfied with the way in which family decisions are made. The high divorce rate to the contrary, the responses, presented in Table 7.7, indicate both a quite high level of satisfaction with marital decision making and a good deal of symmetry between wives and husbands.[23] Thus couples describe decision-making processes that are

---

23. These data are consistent with other survey data which show high levels of satisfaction with family life. See Angus Campbell, Philip E. Converse, and Willard L. Rogers, *The Quality of American Life* (New York: Russell Sage, 1976), pp. 12, 64, 336–345, 480.

Table 7.7 Family Decision Making

	Wives	Husbands
Can they express their point of view in family discussions?		
Always	79%	86%
Sometimes	21	14
Never	0	0
	100%	100%
How much attention does spouse pay to their point of view?		
A lot	68%	71%
Some	30	29
None	2	a
	100%	100%
How satisfied with how family decisions are made?		
Very satisfied	62%	61%
Somewhat satisfied	37	37
Not too satisfied	1	3
	100%	101%

Source: Citizen Participation Study Follow-up—Couples Survey.
a. Less than 1 percent.

consistent with the data we saw in Chapter 6 that showed very widespread disagreement with the idea that it is best if just the husband is in charge of making family decisions. Nonetheless, the data showing agreement between husbands and wives that husbands take greater responsibility for major financial decisions are an important exception to the overall pattern.

Social Status at Home

A final dimension on which social systems are stratified is the respect or honor accorded to individuals. We can imagine an analogue within the household to this form of stratification within society. Couples differ in terms of both the amount of respect they give to each other and the extent to which that respect is mutual or asymmetrical. Once again, we focus on this form of domestic hierarchy not only for its intrinsic interest but also for its possible consequences for political activity.

Measuring husbands' and wives' respect for each other is extremely difficult. In a series of questions adapted from the General

Social Survey, we asked respondents to choose, in order, three people—for example, their husband or wife, a friend, a member of the clergy, and so on—whose judgment they really trust and with whom they might be likely to discuss important matters. Substantial majorities—73 percent of the wives and 68 percent of the husbands—listed their spouses first, and 86 percent of wives and 87 percent of husbands listed their spouses as either first or second.[24] We can also consider the mutuality of respect within couples by comparing the responses of members of couples to ascertain whether they rank one another at the same place on the list or whether one partner places the other higher on the list than vice versa. This measure indicates considerable symmetry in the rankings of spouses. Sixty percent of the couples put each other at the same point on this list.[25] In 17 percent of couples, he ranks her higher than she ranks him; in 23 percent of couples the situation is reversed. In short, there is a good deal of mutual respect in these couples, and the asymmetries do not appear to be to the systematic detriment of either husbands or wives.

Gender Beliefs and Domestic Equality: A Closer Look

In several ways the data presented in this chapter and the last one do not fit into a neat package. Perhaps the most obvious disjunction is the contrast between the widespread support for gender

---

24. As shown by the data below, there is a fair amount of similarity between wives and husbands in terms of the kinds of people to whom they would turn to for advice.

Sources of Advice Other than Spouse
(percentage who mention a source on a list of three)

	Wives	Husbands
Advisor (e.g., lawyer, clergy)	25%	26%
Friend, neighbor	65	60
Co-worker	18	26
Other close relative	74	53

25. We are concerned with the relative respect accorded by members of the couple. Hence low but equal levels of respect count as equality in this measure: we define the circumstance in which neither partner confides in the other (the case for three couples in our sample) as conferring no relative disadvantage. In fact, the overwhelming share, 88 percent, of the couples who demonstrate mutual respect place one another first on the list.

equality among both husbands and wives as expressed in our survey and the widespread persistence of traditional patterns when it comes to the division of household labor and the management of major financial decisions.

In the last chapter, we categorized our respondents into three groups in terms of their views on issues of gender equality and juxtaposed the social characteristics of the traditionals and the egalitarians. We now ask whether there is any relationship between a husband's views on these issues and the division of housework and child-care responsibilities in their homes. Table 7.8 shows the average number of hours given by both members of the couple to housework and to childcare—according to their own report and the report of their spouses. What comes through clearly in the data is that wives do, on average, considerably more housework and child care than do husbands and that wives with traditional husbands do somewhat more than wives with egalitarian husbands. With respect to how much housework and child care husbands do, it does not seem that husbands' views of gender roles make much difference. Husbands tend to rate their contributions somewhat higher than wives do. However, if we average the husbands' and wives' estimates in order to make no assumptions about who is telling an accurate story, we find that, compared with husbands with traditional views, husbands with egalitarian views do, on av-

Table 7.8 Division of Household Work and Child Care by Husband's Beliefs in Gender Equality

	Time Given by Wife		Time Given by Husband	
	Wife's Report	Husband's Report	Wife's Report	Husband's Report
Mean Hours Housework[a]				
Husband with egalitarian views	4.7	4.7	2.4	3.2
Husband with traditional views	5.7	6.0	2.2	3.0
Mean Hours Child Care[b]				
Husband with egalitarian views	3.3	2.9	1.5	1.9
Husband with traditional views	4.4	4.3	1.6	1.8

Source: Citizen Participation Study Follow-up—Couples Survey.
a. Includes child care.
b. Couples with children at home.

Table 7.9 Responsibility for Major Financial Decisions and Husband's Beliefs in Gender Equality

	All	Most	Some	A Little	None		
Amount of responsibility wife claims							
Husband with egalitarian views	5%	14	73	9	0	=	101%
Husband with traditional views	3%	21	60	14	2	=	100%
Amount of responsibility husband claims							
Husband with egalitarian views	12%	47	39	1	0	=	99%
Husband with traditional views	30%	51	19	a	0	=	100%

Source: Citizen Participation Study Follow-up—Couples Survey.
a. Less than 1 percent.

erage, twelve more minutes of housework and the same amount of child care.

Finally, Table 7.9 presents data about the relationship between responsibility for major financial decisions and husbands' views on gender roles. The overall trend is, as we have seen, for husbands to take more responsibility when major financial decisions are at stake. However, there is some difference between couples in which the husband is a traditionalist and those in which the husband is an egalitarian. Husbands with more traditional views are considerably more likely than their egalitarian counterparts to claim to make all or most of the big financial decisions.

In order to probe further whether beliefs about gender roles have an impact on behavior, we undertook a multivariate analysis of the factors related to the proportion of household work (which encompasses child care as well) done by the wife.[26] As shown in Table 7.10, with other factors taken into account, the single factor that matters is structural, rather than attitudinal: the number of

26. Neither Sarah Fenstermaker Berk, *The Gender Factory* (New York: Plenum Press, 1985), pp. 118–150, nor England and Farkas, *Households, Employment, and Gender,* pp. 94ff., find evidence that attitudes have an independent impact on household division of labor. Other studies, which are not always based on random samples or on multivariate analysis, contain mixed findings. For additional bibliography, see Deutsch, *Halving It All,* p. 4, as well as the review of literature in Beth Anne Shelton and Daphne John, "The Division of Household Labor," *Annual Review of Sociology* 22 (1996): 299–322. They point out the variation among studies and conclude (p. 306) that "attitudes do not account for very much of the variation in the division of household labor."

Table 7.10 Predicting the Percentage of Housework the Wife Does (OLS regression)

WIFE'S CHARACTERISTICS	
Education	−0.05
Hours at Work	−0.26**
Job Level	0.11
HUSBAND'S CHARACTERISTICS	
Education	−0.02
Hours at Work	−0.01
Job Level	−0.00
FAMILY CHARACTERISTICS	
Family Income	−0.02
Percentage of Family Income Wife Brings In	0.11
Preschool Children	0.06
Wife's Age[a]	−0.01
Years of Marriage	−0.03
BELIEF IN EQUALITY	
Her Belief	0.04
His Belief	0.02
Constant	0.62***
Adjusted R-squared	0.02

Source: Citizen Participation Study Follow-up—Couples Survey.

a. Because wives' age and husbands' age are so highly correlated, we include only the wife's age here.

*Coefficient significant at <.05.

**Coefficient significant at <.01.

***Coefficient significant at <.001.

hours the wife devotes to paid work. None of the other factors that we might have expected to affect the division of labor at home has the anticipated impact. The proportion of household tasks done by the wife is related neither to class—as measured by family income and the job and educational levels of both partners—nor to either partner's beliefs about equality at home.

The Family as Social System: A Summary

The data on the family as a social system do not lend themselves to a simple summary, nor do they support either of the competing visions of how households should operate—either old-fashioned patriarchal or feminist. In spite of widespread lip service to equality at home, there is considerable evidence of traditional arrangements. Husbands bring in a disproportionate share of the family income and are more likely to exercise power in managing it. In addition, there is stereotyping in who is responsible for which family chores, with wives assuming a greater share of the household work—even when both spouses are employed full time. Nevertheless, although women spend more time on housework, in the aggregate they do not suffer from a deficit of free time. Moreover, wives seem to exercise greater autonomy than husbands in making decisions about the use of their time. In addition, in spite of high divorce rates, couples report a great deal of mutual respect. Husbands and wives indicate that they trust each other as advisors, that they engage in mutual consultation, and that they are satisfied with the way that decisions are made at home. Finally, we find no strong connection when we view the operations of the household in the context of expressed beliefs about how things ought to work: what makes a difference for the division of housework between husband and wife is not their traditional or egalitarian beliefs but rather how much time the wife spends on the job.

8

∞∞∞

The Workplace Roots
of Political Activity

At this point we move out of the primary group world of the family to the secondary institutions of adult life—voluntary associations, religious institutions, and in this chapter, the workplace. We investigate how these non-political institutions function to shape political involvement and how institutional processes are similar or different for women and men. It is well known that institutional involvement—being in the work force, being a member of a voluntary association, being active in a religious institution—is linked to political activity and to gender differences in political activity. Our enterprise is not only to demonstrate the existence of these linkages but to specify the *mechanisms* that operate within institutions to foster participation. Our conception of the institutional grounding of the process by which individuals become active in politics is derived from the Civic Voluntarism Model.[1] This process entails the accumulation of various factors—resources, location in networks of recruitment, and psychological involvement in politics—that facilitate participation. Our goal is to analyze how institutions work to provide women and men with these participatory factors.

Although we have shifted our focus to secondary institutions, we do not ignore the family. Rather than considering each of these secondary institutions in isolation, we seek to establish the con-

---

1. See Sidney Verba, Kay Lehman Schlozman, and Henry E. Brady, *Voice and Equality: Civic Voluntarism in American Politics* (Cambridge: Harvard University Press, 1995).

nections among them. In particular, we are concerned to understand how what happens at home sets the stage for the institutional involvements that, in turn, shape political activity. This chain of connections contributes to the creation of gender differences in political participation.

Institutions and the Creation of Gender Difference

To understand the institutional roots of gender differences in political activity is a complex enterprise. Those who have jobs—especially jobs that require a high level of educational attainment and on-the-job training—who are involved in voluntary associations or who are active in religious institutions have opportunities to enhance their civic capacity: to acquire resources, to make the connections that lead to requests for political activity, and to cultivate the orientations toward politics that foster participation.

As outlined in Chapter 2, the institutional roots of disparities in participation are potentially the product of one or both of the following: differential *selection* such that people with particular characteristics are recruited into institutions; and differential *treatment* within institutions—that is, experiences at work, in organizations, or in church that have consequences for political activity. We structure our analysis both to allow for the possibility that the processes of selection into institutions and experiences within institutions are different for men and women and to accommodate the heterogeneity among women and among men. Thus we consider separately sub-groups of men and women and use multivariate analysis, discussing the results in the language of probability—for example, "women are more likely than men to . . ." In so doing, we incorporate the understanding that males and females are not undifferentiated categories but rather vary along many dimensions that are relevant for both political participation and political conflict.

An analytic approach that considers, for men and women and for different kinds of men and women, the paths to and experiences within three separate institutions is a complex one indeed. Nevertheless, this complex strategy provides a lens for understanding both the creation of gender differences and the institutional operations of the workplace, voluntary associations, and religious institutions in fostering political participation.

SELECTION INTO INSTITUTIONS

Institutional effects are, obviously, predicated upon institutional affiliation. Interestingly, the proportions in our sample affiliated with these three institutions are nearly identical: about two-thirds of our respondents are employed; about two-thirds are involved with at least one non-political organization; and about two-thirds are affiliated with a religious institution.

We need to rule out the possibility that any participatory distinctiveness on the part of the institutionally affiliated results, not from the consequences of institutional exposure, but from processes of selection such that those who are selected into institutions bring with them characteristics that predispose them to be active. In particular, are those who self-select into the labor force, non-political organizations, and religious activity by nature doers who, on the basis of some unmeasured propensity to be active, would also self-select into political participation? If so we would be unable to distinguish between the participatory effects of institutional exposure and the participatory effects of the unmeasured predisposition to get involved in collective endeavors. In fact, when the results in this chapter and the one that follows are combined with the analysis in Chapter 10, we shall see that participatory outcomes reflect what happens in institutions and not some unmeasured taste for civic involvement.[2]

Let us consider the selection process by which people become affiliated—join the work force, non-political organizations, or religious institutions. Decisions to affiliate represent choices, but these are choices that may be made under circumstances of constraint. An especially constrained choice, we would assume, is the choice to enter the work force. And the range of choices, and the limitations to choice imposed by the constraints, presumably, differ systematically for men and women. Social norms are such that most

---

2. For more discussion of our approach to selection, see Chapter 2, notes 12, 13, and 14.

men really have little choice when it comes to the decision to get a job. Although most women, even married women, who are in the work force need the income, for many women there is an element of choice when it comes to paid work. As we shall see, family constraints operate differently for women and men when decisions about whether and how much to work are being made. In consequence, working women and working men may differ from each other in ways that have implications for political participation.

INSTITUTIONAL PROCESSES AND POLITICAL PARTICIPATION

How do the secondary institutions under discussion function to foster political participation?[3] In our understanding, which uses as a point of departure the Civic Voluntarism Model, participation is related to three sets of factors: resources, recruitment, and psychological involvement in politics. Experiences at work, in organizations, and in church can function to enhance an individual's stockpile of these factors.

Without the essential *resources* of time, money, and civic skills, it would seem impossible to be active in politics. Institutional affiliations would seem to have implications, albeit complicated ones, for all three. Let us consider them in reverse order. Those who command civic skills—who, for example, know how to organize a meeting or to make a public presentation—find it easier to take part politically. In the context of totally non-political activities on the job, in organizations, and at church, individuals have opportunities to develop these organizational and communications skills that can then be transferred to politics. In short, active involvement in all three non-political domains would be expected to cultivate civic skills.

Studies of political participation have been consistent in finding an association between family income and political participation. The relationship is, not unexpectedly, especially strong when it

---

3. As discussed at length in Chapter 2, the boundaries between the political and the non-political are extremely porous. In our discussion of these institutions, we shall explore the ways that essentially non-political institutions get involved in politics. Nevertheless, we should note that when we investigate the consequences of organizational involvement for political activity, we are confining ourselves to involvement with non-political organizations.

comes to making a contribution to a campaign or other political cause. Institutional affiliations have contradictory implications when it comes to money: on one hand, for the majority of households, paid work is the most important source of income; on the other, income devoted to church, charity, and other organizational matters is income not available for politics.

With the exception of making a financial contribution, all forms of political participation require at least some time, and some of them can consume substantial amounts of time. With respect to time, however, the consequences of institutional involvement are just the opposite of what we have been discussing. Presumably, those who are especially active in an organization or church would be more likely to acquire civic skills, and those who work hard earn more. In contrast, the longer the hours devoted to work or to organizational or religious activity, the fewer the hours left over for politics. Hence, in this case, institutional involvements would diminish the resources for political participation.

Often political activity is the consequence of *recruitment,* a request for activity, especially a request from a friend or acquaintance. Those who are embedded in the social networks located at work, in non-political organizations, and in religious institutions are more likely to be targeted by requests for political activity.

In Chapter 4, we discussed several *psychological orientations to politics*—in particular, political interest, information, and efficacy—that are strongly associated with activity in politics. Involvement in secondary institutions outside the home provides the kinds of exposures that draw people into a wider world, including the world of politics. In addition, even institutions that are outside politics may have political objectives: a firm might seek tariff protection for its products or regulatory relief; a non-profit might seek favorable classification under the tax codes; religious groups support an array of policies that range from an end to abortion to assistance to the poor to aid to Israel. Those who are affiliated with institutions often receive messages about these political matters—from the boss, from the officers and staff of an organization, from the pulpit. Moreover, in each of these settings, people chat about politics—providing additional political exposure. Although institutional experiences can affect political attitudes and orientations in a variety of ways, we do not have measures that can link these political predispositions to specific institutional contexts.[4]

The processes by which institutional involvements affect an individual's portfolio of participatory factors are less often the result of intentional institutional design than by-products of ordinary institutional functioning. When union officers admonish the rank and file to get in touch with their congressional representatives to support a pending minimum wage bill, the political effort is clearly self-conscious. In contrast, when a church member who heads the search committee for a new pastor becomes more comfortable chairing meetings and speaking in public, the development of civic skills takes place spontaneously. In addition, these processes may or may not be central to the main functions of these institutions. The wages derived from work—which can be devoted, among many purposes, to political donations—are at the heart of the purpose of the work relationship in a way that conversations among fellow employees about current political happenings simply are not. In short, as many non-political institutions go about their business, they enhance participatory capacity.

This multi-stage model of the impact of non-political institutions on participation encompasses a long causal chain that includes selection into institutions and institutional experiences. In order to understand the direct or indirect consequences of each stage for political participation, we shall proceed systematically. By comparing the experiences of women and men through multiple stages, we incorporate our understanding both that gender dif-

---

4. We should note that the various participatory factors differ in terms of whether we have measures of their being accrued in a specific institutional venue. All of them can be acquired in a variety of contexts: earnings can derive from the factory or the race track; requests for activity can originate in the office or in church; political interest can be cultivated in conversations at work or at the PTA. For a number of these factors—for example, earnings, time use, civic skills, or recruitment attempts—we have measures of the acquisition of factors in a particular setting. For other factors, this information is not available. For example, it would have been possible to ask a question about whether the respondent has had an experience with discrimination on the basis of sex that was related to employment—say in hiring, wages, or promotion. Instead, the question about experiences with discrimination on the basis of sex was asked more generally, and experiences at work were combined with experiences in other domains of life—say, at school or in church. However, for certain participatory factors—in particular, political engagement and gender consciousness—it would be impossible to determine the contribution of particular institutions to their development.

ferences are *contextual* and that there are connections across contexts. The mechanisms that make sex matter are not uniform across social institutions; nonetheless, what happens in one context has implications for what happens elsewhere.

In tracing connections across institutions, we shall look for *cumulative* and *compensatory inequalities*. We consider several stages across several institutions. We seek to ascertain whether the effects are cumulative or whether relative advantages for one group in one setting are balanced by relative deficits elsewhere and, therefore, to assess some kind of net institutional effect for men and women.

Gaining Participatory Factors at Work

We begin our quest for the non-political roots of gender differences in political activity with the workplace. For most of us, work is, along with family, one of the principal commitments of adult life. And just as family relationships have been transformed in the second half of the twentieth century so, too, has the relationship of women and men to the workplace undergone massive change. These developments in the family and the workplace are, of course, related. In each domain much has been altered with respect to gender roles, yet many traditional patterns remain as well.

We saw in Chapter 3 that, contrary to what might be expected, women who are in the work force are more politically active than those who are at home full time.[5] In fact, the relationship of work to participation has long been a subject of concern to scholars interested in gender and politics.[6] Studies of political participation

---

5. Although we ordinarily use the locution "women [or men] who are in the work force," we sometimes abbreviate and refer to "working women [or men]." In so doing, we in no way mean to imply that women (or men) who are at home full time—managing a household and raising children—are not "working."

6. Relevant works include Cornelia B. Flora and Naomi B. Lynn, "Women and Political Socialization: Considerations of the Impact of Motherhood," in *Women in Politics*, ed. Jane S. Jaquette (New York: John Wiley and Sons, 1974), pp. 37–53; Kristi Andersen, "Working Women and Political Participation, 1952–1972," *American Journal of Political Science* 19 (1975): 439–453; Susan Welch, "Women as Political Animals? A Test of Some Explanations for Male-Female Political Participation Differences," *American Journal of Political Science* 21 (1977): 711–730; Eileen McDonagh, "To Work or Not to Work: The Differential Impact of Achieved and Derived Status upon the Political Participation of

propose a number of possible explanations for the higher levels of activity of women who are employed outside the home. In general, the emphasis is on processes of adult socialization, the differing sets of social cues that accompany alternative roles for adult women.[7] For women, the experience of being at home full time is said to reinforce traditional views about appropriate gender roles and to communicate that the rough-and-tumble domain of politics is alien territory for those who would tend the hearth.[8] In addition, some authors emphasize domestic isolation: the extent to which a woman at home is cut off both from the informal political discussions that cultivate interest in politics and from the networks of communication through which requests for activity are mediated.[9] Curiously, academics rarely consider the contrary effect that immediately occurs to non-academic observers: that, because paid employment is the single most time-consuming adult endeavor, women at home, who enjoy more free time than do women in the work force, might actually be more politically active, not less.

While these studies raise important lines of reasoning, they leave many questions unanswered. First, there is no consensus as to actual empirical results. The various studies were conducted at

---

Women, 1956–76," *American Journal of Political Science* 26 (1982): 280–297; Nancy McGlen, "The Impact of Parenthood on Political Participation," *Western Political Quarterly* 33 (1980): 297–313; Virginia Sapiro, *The Political Integration of Women* (Urbana: University of Illinois Press, 1983); Kristi Andersen and Elizabeth A. Cook, "Women, Work, and Political Attitudes," *American Journal of Political Science* 29 (1985): 606–625; Karen Beckwith, *American Women and Political Participation: The Impacts of Work, Generation, and Feminism* (New York: Greenwood Press, 1986); Kent L. Tedin, David W. Brady, and Arnold Vedlitz, "Sex Differences in Political Attitudes and Behavior: The Case for Situational Factors," *Journal of Politics* 39 (1977): 448–456; M. Kent Jennings, "Gender Roles and Inequalities in Political Participation: Results from an Eight-Nation Study," *Western Political Quarterly* 36 (1983): 364, gives a particularly helpful discussion of how women's alternative roles might affect their participation. For an especially useful, though not terribly recent, review of the literature, see Cal Clark and Janet Clark, "Models of Gender and Political Participation in the United States," *Women and Politics* 6 (1986): 5–25.

7. Sapiro, *The Political Integration of Women*, is especially helpful in delineating the nature and impact of adult socialization as it derives from the cues given to those who occupy particular adult roles. Emphasizing the social learning that could be traced to the women's movement, Andersen, "Working Women and Political Participation," makes clear that external events can provide an alternative form of adult socialization.

8. See, in particular, Patricia Gurin, "The Political Implications of Women's Statuses," in *Spouse, Parent, Worker*, ed. F. J. Crosby (New Haven: Yale University Press, 1986), p. 178.

9. See, for example, Gurin, "Political Implications," p. 178, and Sapiro, *The Political Integration of Women*, p. 129.

different points in time with data sets that do not contain the full range of relevant variables. A number show differences in women's political activity associated with differing roles. Others find no association.[10] Moreover, these studies do not establish *why* work is linked to political activity. Because the appropriate variables are often not available, in those studies that demonstrate an association between political activity and paid work, the reason for the linkage is often inferred, not established. Hence even if there were agreement that women at home are less active in politics, the explanation remains a matter of speculation.

Finally, researchers have tended to ignore the possibility that it is processes of selection rather than the impact of alternative roles that are responsible for the association between paid work and political activity among women. Those who remain at home may differ systematically from those who enter the work force in ways that have implications for political activity—in their beliefs about gender relations, in their interest in and knowledge about political subjects, or in other characteristics such as education that are associated with participation. In fact, the only study that explores these issues using panel data—that is, interviews with the same respondents who are interviewed more than once—finds some support for the impact of selection effects.[11]

Selection into the Work Force

We have noted that the proportion of women in the work force has increased dramatically in recent decades. Nevertheless, substantial

---

10. Compare, for example, Andersen, "Working Women and Political Participation" and Welch, "Women as Political Animals?" with Sapiro, *The Political Integration of Women,* and Beckwith, *American Women and Political Participation.* Furthermore, a compelling case is made that the relationship between political activity and work force status need not be invariant across categories of women who differ in ways that are germane for politics. For example, alternative roles for women need not have similar political consequences for the political activity of women who differ in terms of social class. However, once again, there is no agreement among studies when it comes to empirical results. Compare Welch, "Women as Political Animals?"; McGlen, "The Impact of Parenthood"; and McDonagh, "To Work or Not to Work."

11. Andersen and Cook, "Women, Work, and Political Attitudes." See also Sapiro, *Political Integration of Women,* p. 65.

gender differences in work force participation still remain. In our sample, 76 percent of the men are in the work force and 71 percent of the men work full time. In contrast, 58 percent of the women in our sample are in the work force and 43 percent are there full time. In short, men are more likely than women to work for pay and to work full time if they do. If employment enhances political activity, men are better positioned to benefit.

Table 8.1 presents the results of a logistic regression, conducted separately for women and men, in which we predict entry into the work force.[12] Among the explanatory variables, we include two variables associated with education. The first, educational level, is widely known to be a strong predictor of political activity.[13] The other, involvement in student government and other school activities in high school, is also associated with participation, either because high school activity imparts skills that are relevant for adult endeavors or because it serves as an indicator of "activity proneness," a long-standing predisposition to take part.[14] Labor economists demonstrate that family circumstances—marriage and the number and ages of children—are related to decisions about the allocation of time to home, paid employment, and leisure and that family circumstances figure differently in decisions made by women and men.[15] Hence we include variables indicating whether the respondent is married and has children—preschool and/or school age—living at home. In order to test how decisions about

---

12. The dependent variable is a dichotomy distinguishing between those who are and are not in the work force. Our consideration of the process of entry into the work force, though more complete than most such analyses in relation to political activity, does not purport to be a full human capital model. However, our results are consistent with the findings of labor economists.

13. It is widely recognized that women's increased work force participation since 1960 has come disproportionately from the well educated. Compared with those of limited educational attainment, well-educated women are more likely to be in the work force, a gap that has grown in recent decades. See, for example, William H. Chafe, "Looking Back to Look Forward: Women, Work, and Social Values in America," in *Women and the American Economy*, ed. Juanita M. Kreps (Englewood Cliffs, N.J.: Prentice-Hall, 1976); and Daphne G. Spain and Suzanne M. Bianchi, *Balancing Act: Motherhood, Marriage, and Employment among Married Women* (New York: Russell Sage Foundation, 1996), chaps. 3–4.

14. See Verba, Schlozman, and Brady, *Voice and Equality,* chap. 15.

15. See, for example, Francine D. Blau, Marianne A. Ferber, and Anne E. Winkler, *The Economics of Women, Men, and Work,* 3rd ed. (Upper Saddle River, N.J.: Prentice-Hall, 1999), chap. 4.

Table 8.1 Predicting Working (logistic regression)

	Women		Men
EDUCATION AND CHILDHOOD			
Education	2.01***		1.86***
High School Activity	0.28		0.45
FAMILY			
Married	−0.15	⇔	0.63**
Preschool Children	−1.03***	⇔	1.56***
School-age Children	−0.06	⇔	1.97***
Other Family Income	−5.52***	⇔	−8.78***
OTHER VARIABLES			
Age	−1.19***	⇔	−2.67***
Age over 65	−2.81***	⇔	−1.68***
Black	−0.02		−0.14
Latino	−0.66*	⇔	−0.05
Citizen	−0.07	⇔	1.89***
Constant	1.41**	⇔	0.06
Log Likelihood	−675		−381

Source: Citizen Participation Study—Main Survey.
*Coefficient significant at <.05.
**Coefficient significant at <.01.
***Coefficient significant at <.001.
⇔ Difference in the coefficients for men and women is significant at <.05 (by *t*-test) or one coefficient is significant at <.05 and the other is not.

work are affected by the availability of other family resources, we include a measure of family income other than that, if any, produced by the respondent's earnings. Finally, the equation contains measures of age, race and ethnicity, and citizenship. Since they are related both to work force participation and to political activity, these variables function as controls.

The data in Table 8.1 tell a quite striking story about the circumstances under which women and men enter the work force. For both men and women, education is positively related to work force participation, with the effect somewhat, but not significantly, larger for women. Activity in high school—whether a skill builder for the future or an index of a pre-existing inclination to be active—is not, however, a significant predictor of work force participation for either women or men. We had not expected that an "activist-predisposition" would affect the likelihood that men would join the work force, but thought it might have an effect on women, for whom the expectations about paid work are less clear. The data in Table 8.1 suggest that neither women nor men who enter the work force do so because they are, by personal predisposition, doers.[16]

Especially notable in Table 8.1 is the sharp gender difference in the effect of family characteristics. The coefficients on being married, on having preschool children, and on having school-age children are all significant and positive for men. For women these coefficients are negative, with the coefficient for having preschoolers significant. In addition, for each of these family characteristics, the difference between the coefficients for women and men is significant.[17] The data illustrate the way in which gender differences in one institution, the family, have forward links to other institutions—in this case, the workplace—and create additional gender differences.

That family circumstances—differential responsibility for home and child care—reduce work force participation for women and increase it for men suggests that what Judith Lorber found in her study of physicians probably obtains for many other occupations as well: when the male doctors in her study altered their work lives to accommodate the needs of their families, they worked longer hours and sought work commanding higher pay—for example, by giving up an academic position for private practice; when the women doctors made sacrifices at work in the name of the family, they tended to cut back their hours—seeking time rather than money.[18] Francine M. Deutsch's interviews with couples in which responsibility for child rearing is shared equally by some and un-

---

16. We should recall from Chapter 6 that, for wives, there is an association between egalitarian views on gender roles and work force participation. The direction of causality is uncertain, however. That is, we cannot discern whether egalitarian attitudes predispose wives to enter the work force or whether work force experiences inculcate egalitarian attitudes.

17. The statistical significance of the relationship between marriage and work force participation varies with the precise specification of the model. However, it is clear that any impact of marriage on work force participation is opposite in direction for men and women—predisposing men to go to work and women to stay home. The results for the impact of children on work force participation, which are also opposite in direction for women and men, are less specification dependent.

18. Judith Lorber, *Women Physicians: Careers, Status, and Power* (New York: Tavistock, 1984), pp. 93–95.

equally by others suggest that parents' decisions about their commitment to paid work are not necessarily based on sheer economic logic. Even when the wife earns more than her husband, she may be the one to diminish the amount she works—with the result that he will eventually become the partner with the higher earnings.[19]

Although there is a clear distinction between women and men when it comes to the way family and work responsibilities interact, our data do not establish definitively whether demands at home influence women's choices about work or whether career trajectories influence women's choices about marriage and children. Those who have looked closely at women's lives find evidence of both patterns: often women scale back their work commitments in order to spend time at home; yet women also make decisions about children based on their progress at work—opting to quit and have children when their careers are blocked or choosing to postpone or forgo children when their careers are advancing.[20]

Surprisingly, men and women differ relatively little when it comes to the way family economic circumstances shape choices about work. Although, on average, men's earnings constitute a higher proportion of family income, the more family income comes from other sources, the less likely it is for either a woman or a man to be in the work force. It is worth noting that the economic constraints operate so similarly for women and men while family constraints, though important for both women and men, work in opposite directions.

The same patterns obtain when we predict not whether but how much an individual works.[21] As before, family circumstances have

19. Francine M. Deutsch, *Halving It All: How Equally Shared Parenting Works* (Cambridge: Harvard University Press, 1999), chap. 7.

20. See Kathleen Gerson, *Hard Choices: How Women Decide about Work, Career, and Motherhood* (Berkeley: University of California Press, 1985); and Rhona Mahony, *Kidding Ourselves: Breadwinning, Babies, and Bargaining Power* (New York: Basic Books, 1995).

21. The results of regressions predicting the number of hours worked in an average week (conducted separately for men and women) can be found in Appendix C, Table C8.1.1. We undertook several analyses, all of which produced essentially the same results. We used OLS with different dependent variables: the number of hours the respondent spends at work and a trichotomy measuring not in the work force, working part time, and working full time. We also constructed hierarchical models and a model with an unordered categorical dependent variable.

an impact, but the consequences differ for men and women. Marriage and small children make women less likely, and men more likely, to work more hours. In short, the process by which individuals make decisions about whether and how much to work for pay is quite different for women and men. The result is, of course, a much smaller representation of women than of men among full-time workers.

JOB LEVEL

The kinds of jobs that men are more likely to hold also confer participatory advantages. When it comes to the aspects of work that have consequences for participation, what matters is not only being in the work force but having a job that requires education and on-the-job training.[22] Compared with lower-level jobs, professional positions provide more opportunities for participation-enhancing experiences. Among those in the work force, men are more likely than women to be in jobs requiring high levels of education and on-the-job training; indeed, as shown in Table 8.2, they are twice as likely to be in the top category of the job-level scale—a category comprising jobs requiring either a college degree and at least two years of on-the-job training or a graduate degree.[23]

Table 8.3 reports the results of an OLS regression in which we predict, for working respondents, the level of their jobs—that is, the amount of education and on-the-job training needed for the position.[24] Not surprisingly, those with higher levels of education and those who work more hours are more likely to have jobs re-

---

22. Verba, Schlozman, and Brady, *Voice and Equality,* chaps. 10–13.

23. The job-level variable, which is discussed in Chapter 6, note 8, is a five-category variable measuring the respondents' assessments of the amount of education and on-the-job training required to do their jobs.

24. We repeated the analysis including a measure of the extent to which one would "expect" a woman to be in the work force. The measure, which is based on the analysis of what predicts being in the work force presented in Table 8.1, was calculated using the residuals from a probit model predicting whether a person is employed. It is based on the now-standard approach to controlling for processes of self-selection developed by James Heckman, "Sample Selection Bias as a Specification Error," *Econometrica* 47 (1979): 153–161. The variable was not significant, indicating that the "unexpectedness" of work force participation by a woman neither increases nor decreases the job level obtained. For elaboration of our method, see Kay Lehman Schlozman, Nancy E. Burns, and Sidney Verba, "What Happened at Work Today?: A Multi-Stage Model of Gender, Employment, and Political Participation," *Journal of Politics* 61 (1999): 29–54.

Table 8.2 Job Level (among those in the work force)[a,b,c]

	Women	Men
Least training		
1	19%	11%
2	37	24
3	15	32
4	17	11
5	11	23
Most training	99%	101%

Source: Citizen Participation Study—Main Survey.

a. Appendix A contains the valid number of cases for these and other measures used in the tables.

b. Respondent's assessment of the amount of education and on-the-job training needed for the job.

c. Overall distribution of responses is statistically significant with Chi-squared = 195.18444, p <.001.

Table 8.3 Predicting Job Level among Working Women and Men (OLS regression)

	Working Women		Working Men
EDUCATION AND CHILDHOOD			
Education	4.12***	⇔	3.32***
High School Activity	0.05	⇔	0.22*
INSTITUTIONAL COMMITMENT			
Hours at Work	1.31***		1.20***
OTHER VARIABLES			
Age	0.64***		0.93***
Age over 65	−0.23	⇔	0.67**
Black	−0.21	⇔	−0.46***
Latino	−0.21	⇔	−0.32*
Citizen	−0.28		0.07
Constant	0.33		0.44
Adjusted R-squared	0.46		0.45

Source: Citizen Participation Study—Main Survey.

*Coefficient significant at <.05.

**Coefficient significant at <.01.

***Coefficient significant at <.001.

⇔ Difference in the coefficients for men and women is significant at <.05 (by *t*-test) or one coefficient is significant at <.05 and the other is not.

quiring education or training.[25] Since men outpace women on both of these dimensions, we see a process of cumulative disadvantage for women such that small differences having ramifications for participation begin to pile up.[26]

The effects for women and men of differential family constraints on work force participation, part- or full-time work, and job level are thus cumulative. Women are less likely to be employed, to be working full time, and to be in jobs that demand education and training. The result of this chain of selection processes is that men are considerably more likely than women to be in high-level jobs: among all respondents, 17 percent of the men, compared with 6 percent of the women, work full time in a position at the highest rank of the job-level measure. If being in the work force and, beyond that, being in the right kind of job matter for political participation, men are more likely than women to be in the right place. As we shall see, these sorting processes figure importantly in the process by which workplace experiences contribute to the gender gap in activity.

---

25. We should also note that being Black or Latino has a negative impact—significant for men—on job level, a finding that deserves further analysis.

26. The literature on the wage gap between men and women is suggestive in interpreting the gender difference in job levels. Labor economists warn that any wage gap between men and women of similar educational attainment must be interpreted in light of other human capital differences between the sexes. See, for example, Claudia Goldin, *Understanding the Gender Gap* (New York: Oxford University Press, 1990), chaps. 3–5; and Blau, Ferber, and Winkler, *The Economics of Women, Men, and Work,* chap. 6.

Two factors that are relevant here are differences between men and women with respect to college major and the gender disparity with respect to work-based training programs—both of which would give men a relative boost in job level. (Since our dependent variable is not earnings, but the education and on-the-job training needed for a job, one human capital factor that is often cited with respect to the gender gap in wages, men's greater work force attachment, is less germane in this context.) If we had measures of college major and participation in workplace training programs, we would be able to understand more fully women's disadvantage with respect to job level. Women's deficit with respect to workplace training is unmistakable (see Paula England, *Comparable Worth: Theories and Evidence* [New York: Aldine de Gruyter, 1992], chap. 3). However, Barbara Bergmann points out that it is important to recognize that this deficit can reflect discrimination by employers as well as decisions by women not to invest in themselves by getting further training. Furthermore, she notes there are human capital variables for which women are advantaged—for example, rates of alcoholism, vehicle injury–related disabilities, or arrest—that are rarely incorporated into analyses of the wage gap. See *The Economic Emergence of Women* (New York: Basic Books, 1986), p. 80.

What Happens on the Job

The next step is to penetrate the workplace and consider a variety of ways that work might have an impact on participation. In Table 8.4 we report the results of a series of regressions—as usual, conducted separately for men and women—predicting each of the participatory factors. Our main concern is with the effect on the acquisition of these participatory factors of the nature of the job—the job level and the number of hours each week spent working. In all the equations, we include as controls educational attainment, activity in high school, race or ethnicity, and age. In the equations that predict participatory factors that can be acquired only at work and not elsewhere—income earned from work, job skills and job supervision, and recruitment—we consider only those respondents in the work force and investigate how the nature of the job affects the acquisition of those factors. To simplify the presentation, we report the coefficients only for the variables in which we are mainly interested: number of hours worked and job level. Let us give a brief sketch of the results contained in Table 8.4.

Paid work has implications for all three of the *resources* that influence the capacity to take part politically: skills, money, and time. Work experiences operate in various ways to enhance politically relevant skills. First, many activities undertaken on the job—organizing meetings, giving presentations, and the like—develop skills that can be transported to political settings.[27] In addition, supervising others in the workplace might have an analogous effect, developing leadership capacities useful for political action.[28] As for money, the consequences of the workplace in enhancing the stockpile of resources for participation are obvious. Since work consumes time, the effects of employment are precisely the opposite when it comes to time—diminishing rather than augmenting the resources available for activity in politics.

---

27. See Verba, Schlozman, and Brady, *Voice and Equality,* chaps. 11–12; and Paul Freedman and Steven J. Rosenstone, "Workplace and Political Participation" (paper presented at the annual meeting of the Midwest Political Science Association, Chicago, April 1995).

28. Our measure of supervisory experiences in the workplace is the number of workers supervised—either directly or indirectly.

Table 8.4 The Effect of Job Characteristics on Participatory Factors (regression coefficients)[a]

	Women		Men
RESOURCES			
Effect on earnings from job[b,c]			
Hours worked	3.11***		2.34**
Job level	1.33***	⇔	3.04***
Effect on job skills[c]			
Hours worked	1.75***		1.39***
Job level	1.75***	⇔	2.75***
Effect on job supervision[c,e]			
Hours worked	2.28***		2.64***
Job level	1.48***		2.31***
Effect on free time[d]			
Hours worked	−9.27***	⇔	−12.31***
Job level	1.07**		0.85*
RECRUITMENT			
Effect on recruitment on the job[c]			
Hours worked	0.26*	⇔	−0.01
Job level	0.20*	⇔	0.02

Source: Citizen Participation Study—Main Survey.

a. Controlling for education, activity in high school, race or ethnicity, age, and citizenship.

b. Also controlling for "other family income."

c. Among working respondents.

d. Among all respondents.

e. Logistic regression.

*Coefficient significant at <.05.

**Coefficient significant at <.01.

***Coefficient significant at <.001.

⇔ Difference in the coefficients for men and women is significant at <.05 (by *t*-test) or one coefficient is significant at <.05 and the other is not.

The data in Table 8.4 show that, for each resource, those who work longer hours and those who have high-level jobs accrue these resources at a higher rate. However, men seem to have an additional advantage. As they move up job levels, men gain more in terms of earnings and civic skills than women do, thus continuing the cumulative process we noted earlier and compounding men's advantage. The pattern is very different when it comes to time. Working reduces free time, and working long hours, obviously, reduces it more. The effect is greater for men, who work, on average, more hours.[29]

Often political participation takes place, not spontaneously, but as the result of a request for activity. Work-based connections form an important source of this kind of *recruitment*.[30] Not only do fellow employees and professional colleagues sometimes solicit one another, but employers themselves may take the initiative and make requests for participation. Requests for activity raise problems of causal direction: rational recruiters hunt where the ducks are and target their appeals at those who have been active in the past. However, even though recruiters look for likely prospects, there is good reason to believe that their efforts make a difference in actually activating those who are more likely to take part anyway.[31] Besides, when the impetus comes from the employer, there is reason to assume that the request generated the participation rather than vice versa. As shown in Table 8.4, the characteristics of the job have less impact on recruitment than on the development of skills. This pattern will be repeated when we consider the way that participatory factors are acquired in other institutions: our models are better at predicting the development of civic skills than they are in predicting institutional recruitment to participation.

The Results: Participatory Factors for Women and Men

The data we have examined demonstrate that the work-related processes that create gender differences in participation are lo-

---

29. Men's greater loss of free time through work is counterbalanced by women's greater loss of free time if they are married or have small children at home. We included the relevant measures in the equations predicting time in Table 8.4. The coefficients are as follows:

	Women	Men
Married	−.86***	−.32***
Preschool children	−2.29***	−.53***
School-age children	−.88***	−.53***

30. See Verba, Schlozman, and Brady, *Voice and Equality*, chaps. 5 and 13; and Steven J. Rosenstone and John Mark Hansen, *Mobilization, Participation, and Democracy in America* (New York: Macmillan, 1993).

31. Henry E. Brady, Kay Lehman Schlozman, and Sidney Verba, "Prospecting for Participants: Rational Expectations and the Recruitment of Political Activists," *American Political Science Review* 93 (1999): 153–168.

Table 8.5 Participatory Factors by Gender and Work Force Participation

	All Respondents		Working Respondents	
	Women	Men	Women	Men
INCOME				
Mean Earnings from Job (in $10,000s)	$1.05 ⇔	$2.59	$1.78 ⇔	$3.31
Mean Family Income (in $10,000s)	$3.68 ⇔	$4.40	$3.85 ⇔	$4.74
SKILLS				
Practice a Civic Skill on the Job	45% ⇔	62%	75% ⇔	79%
Supervise Others on the Job	26% ⇔	47%	33% ⇔	49%
TIME				
Mean Hours Work	5.0 ⇔	7.7	8.4 ⇔	9.9
Mean Hours Free Time	6.5	6.5	4.2 ⇔	4.6
RECRUITMENT				
Recruited on the Job	12%	14%	19%	18%

Source: Citizen Participation Study—Main Survey.
⇔ Difference between women and men significant at .05 level.

cated both in the selection processes that bring men and women into the work force and in the allocation of participatory factors once there. Workplace experiences clearly have many consequences for the accumulation of participatory factors, and several aspects of these complicated processes operate in such a way as to leave men better off than women.

Table 8.5, which presents data about the bundle of participatory factors for women and men who are in the work force and for all women and men, shows the results of the processes we have been discussing: as expected, the bottom line is an overall advantage to men. Among men and women who are in the work force, men earn substantially more and develop more civic skills. The fact that more men work exacerbates the gender differences in the work-related factors that produce political activity. Thus the outcome shown on the table results from both selection effects and experiences on the job: women are less likely to be in positions where they acquire these factors, and even when similarly located in the work force, they receive a smaller share of these factors than do their male counterparts. Moreover, the male advantage—in terms of resources if not recruitment—is greatest in those jobs nearer to the top of the job-level hierarchy, the very jobs that provide the greatest enhancement of participatory capacity.

Time is the single participatory resource that is diminished, not enhanced, by work. As we see from Table 8.5, men work, on average, more hours than women—both because they are more likely to be employed and because, even among full-time workers, they log longer hours on the job. In this instance, the differential work force involvement of women and men would appear to operate in favor of women's political capacity, since it diminishes the time available to men more than that available to women. However, as we saw in Chapter 7, women's lesser commitment to paid work does not translate into greater free time. Since, on average, women devote more time to household and child care than men do, women are not, in the aggregate, advantaged with respect to free time. In fact, while working men spend, on average, more time on the job per day than do working women, working women's commitments at home leave them with, on average, less free time than working men have.

9

---∞∞∞---

The Realm of Voluntarism:
Non-Political Associations and
Religious Institutions

Civil society in America is characterized by a rich variety of formal and informal institutions located between the private world of home and workplace and the public world of politics. In this chapter we turn to two of the main components of civil society, voluntary associations and religious institutions. Social observers often take pains to differentiate the institutions of civil society from those of the market economy. When it comes to political participation, however, these institutions function similarly to the workplace in fostering participation. In the course of their activity in non-political organizations and religious institutions, individuals develop civic skills and receive requests to take part in politics—just as they do at work.

Voluntary Associations and Political Participation

In Chapter 3, we discussed the special role of voluntary associations in American social and political life. As we indicated, associational life in America is characterized by abundance and diversity, and organizations play a significant and complicated role in relation to politics. On one hand, organizations in America are more likely to be politically autonomous—not sponsored by either the state or the political parties—than elsewhere. On the other, they are deeply embedded in public life. Organizations are themselves important actors in politics: they engage in multiple activities—ranging from funding campaigns to lobbying legislatures to filing suit—designed to influence political outcomes. Furthermore, they undertake many projects—for example, encouraging voter registration, supporting art museums, and staffing soup kitchens—for which governments take responsibility in other democracies. In addition, voluntary associations, even ones that are entirely outside politics, stimulate political participation.

In many ways, non-political organizations and the workplace function analogously in fostering political activity. In both domains individuals develop civic skills, are exposed to political messages and discussion that stimulate interest in politics and enrich political information, and are asked to take part in political life. Even when experiences in organizations or on the job have nothing to do with politics, these activities can have similar effects on political participation.

In other ways that are germane to our concerns, the worlds of work and organizations are very different. Most fundamentally, they differ in the ratio of choice to constraint that governs decisions about whether to take a job or join an organization and, if so, which one and how many to select. The dictates of earning a living imply that, especially for men, the decision to go to work is rarely completely voluntary. Affiliating with an organization ordinarily involves a greater element of choice. The voluntary nature of voluntary associations presents a problem of causal inference that is much less tractable than in relation to work. Several factors that lead to organizational affiliation also lead to political activity—among them, a high level of education and a psychological propensity toward activism. In considering organizational involvements, we thus need to be especially cautious in making causal inferences.

As realms of adult activity, work and non-political organizations differ in other ways as well. Although a small fraction of the work force holds more than one job, most people with jobs have only one. In contrast, multiple organizational memberships are the norm, not the exception. In our sample, among those who are members of or donors to a non-political organization, the mean number of such affiliations is 2.3; and a third of the sample belongs to three or more. Even with these multiple affiliations, however, individuals spend a lot more time on the job than in organizations.

Lastly, the workplace and organizations may differ in how hospitable they are to women. As we saw in Chapter 8, men derive much more from the workplace that would be useful in fostering participation—both because they are more likely to be in the work force and because, among workers, even with education taken into account, men are more likely to have the kinds of jobs that pay well and develop civic skills. In contrast, as we indicated in Chapter 3, historians have documented the long neglected involvement of women in charitable and organizational life. Moreover, although men are, on average, affiliated with more non-political organizations than women are, there is otherwise rough gender parity when it comes to non-political organizations: overall, women and men are equally likely to be affiliated, to attend meetings, and to be active. In addition, on balance, there is more similarity than difference in the kinds of organizations to which they belong. Hence in contrast to what we found for the workplace, we might expect a level playing field for women in non-political organizations and a less gender-structured pattern for the distribution of participatory factors to men and women.

SELECTION INTO ORGANIZATIONS

As we did with work force participation, we begin by asking what brings someone into the institutional setting. To analyze the critical phase of selection into organizations, we use the same strategy we used to understand the differential processes that bring women and men into the work force. The explanatory variables are the same ones that we used in the analysis of work force participation. We include the measures of school experiences, level of education and involvement in student government and other high school activities, both of which have been shown to be related to organizational involvement and to political participation.[1] In

---

1. See Sidney Verba, Kay Lehman Schlozman, and Henry E. Brady, *Voice and Equality: Civic Voluntarism in American Politics* (Cambridge: Harvard University Press, 1995), p. 432. As we mentioned in Chapter 8, we are uncertain whether activity in high school is

addition, we include controls for age, race or ethnicity, and family status—marital status and children. We also add three variables to the original model: work force participation, family income, and job level, none of which, of course, could have been used to explain work force participation. For organizational affiliation, however, these variables represent reasonable explanatory factors.

Table 9.1 reports the results of a logistic regression analysis predicting affiliation with—that is, membership in or contribution to—a non-political organization. As usual, we analyze the data separately for women and men. Not surprisingly, for both sexes, education and high school activity are strong predictors of organizational affiliation. It is interesting to recall that data in the previous chapter showed the measure of high school activity not to be a predictor of work force participation. Since decisions about organizational involvement have a greater voluntary component than do decisions to go to work, it makes sense that activity in high school would be more important for organizational affiliation than for work force participation. Other measures of social class also play a role: family income predicts organizational involvement for women, as does job level for men. Family constraints work very differently for organizational involvement than for work force participation: neither being married nor having children is associated with organizational affiliation for either women or men. In summary, two patterns are notable when it comes to organizational involvement: first, the process is driven largely by socioeconomic factors; second, on the whole, the process is more similar than different for women and men.

ACQUIRING PARTICIPATORY FACTORS IN ORGANIZATIONS

Except for the fact that jobs generate income, work and non-political organizations otherwise function similarly in providing participatory factors. In both settings civic skills are developed and requests for political activity are generated. Hence, as we did for the

---

related to subsequent participation in politics because it is a surrogate for a generalized propensity to take part that is carried throughout life or because it serves as a training ground imparting generalized participatory skills, or both.

Table 9.1 Predicting Organizational Affiliation (logistic regression)[a]

	Women		Men
EDUCATION AND CHILDHOOD			
Education	2.48***		2.27***
High School Activity	0.85***		0.55*
INCOME			
Family Income	2.68**	⇔	1.48
WORKPLACE			
Working	−0.30		0.18
Job Level	0.45	⇔	0.76*
FAMILY			
Married	0.07		0.06
Preschool Children	−0.24		0.31
School-age Children	0.19		−0.06
OTHER VARIABLES			
Age	0.94**	⇔	0.48
Age over 65	0.20	⇔	0.72*
Black	−0.49*	⇔	−0.00
Latino	−1.03***	⇔	−0.55
Citizen	0.38		−0.18
Constant	−1.45**	⇔	−1.17**
Log Likelihood	−692		−658

Source: Citizen Participation Study—Main Survey.

a. Appendix A contains the valid number of cases for these and other measures used in the tables.

*Coefficient significant at <.05.

**Coefficient significant at <.01.

***Coefficient significant at <.001.

⇔ Difference in the coefficients for men and women is significant at <.05 (by *t*-test) or one coefficient is significant at <.05 and the other is not.

workplace, we asked our respondents about opportunities in non-political organizations to make a public presentation, to take part in a meeting where decisions were made, or to plan or chair such a meeting. In addition, we asked about requests, by the organization or its officers or staff, to vote for or against certain candidates in an election or to take some other action on a local or national political issue.

These questions were asked about the respondent's most important organization—which might be political or non-political.[2] Respondents, especially women, were more likely to choose a non-political organization: 67 percent of the women, and 58 percent of the men, designated a non-political organization as their most important.[3] Because we are concerned about the way that institutional experiences outside politics are politically enabling and because we included affiliation with a political organization in the dependent variable as a form of political participation, we focus on skills developed and requests for political activity arising in non-political organizations.

However, we should make clear the consequences of this decision. Many kinds of experiences as a political activist would function powerfully to foster more political activity: like experiences on the job and in non-political organizations, they would be sources of civic skills and recruitment; in addition, they would nurture political interest and political knowledge in a way that experiences outside politics might not. Among the many forms of political participation, activity in political organizations would be expected to have especially strong multiplier effects, effects that we are not including in our analysis. Compared with non-political organizations, organizations that take stands in politics, in fact, provide somewhat greater opportunities for the exercise of civic skills and, not unexpectedly, generate many more requests for political activity. Because men are more likely than women to be affiliated with and active in political organizations, the participatory impact of experiences in organizations that take political stands would be more substantial for men.

---

2. As indicated in Chapter 3, the questionnaire asked, first, a short battery of questions about involvement in twenty kinds of organizations. This organizational census was followed by a longer series of items about a single organization. For respondents who were affiliated with more than one organization, their most important organization was chosen as follows: they were asked to name the organization to which they gave the most time and the organization to which they gave the most money; if these were different organizations, they were asked to choose the one of these two organizations that was most important to them.

3. Because a majority of those who chose a political organization as their most important were also affiliated with a non-political organization, for these respondents, we used independent information about the nature of those non-political organizational involvements to make imputations about the civic skills developed and requests for political activity in non-political organizations. Twenty-one percent of the men, and 17 percent of the women, fall into this category.

In order to assess whether there are gender differences in the acquisition of skills and in requests for political activity in non-political organizations, we conducted two sets of OLS regression analyses for men and women who are affiliated with organizations. In one the dependent variable is the number of civic skills acquired in non-political organizations; in the other, the number of requests for political activity. As in the analysis of the participatory factors acquired on the job, we carry as controls a set of class, family, and other demographic variables. In order to ensure that we are not simply capturing the effect of organizational activity, we also include a control for the amount of time given to the organization.

The results of these analyses, presented in Table 9.2, are inter-

Table 9.2 Predicting Participatory Factors from Non-Political Organizations (OLS regression)[a]

	Civic Skills		Recruitment	
	Women	Men	Women	Men
EDUCATION AND CHILDHOOD				
Education	0.66***	0.95***	0.08** ⇔	0.05
High School Activity	0.29*	0.39**	0.01	0.01
INCOME				
Family Income	0.71*	1.30***	−0.05	0.01
INSTITUTIONAL COMMITMENT				
Hours of Organization Work	5.70***	5.06***	0.26***	0.21*
OTHER VARIABLES				
Age	0.30 ⇔	0.55**	0.01	0.03
Age over 65	0.05	−0.06	−0.00	−0.04
Black	−0.00	0.00	0.01	−0.00
Latino	−0.14	−0.17	−0.04	−0.04
Citizen	0.03 ⇔	−0.48*	−0.06 ⇔	−0.10**
Constant	0.04	0.23	0.08 ⇔	0.13***
Adjusted R-squared	0.23	0.19	0.02	0.01

Source: Citizen Participation Study—Main Survey.
a. Regression includes only those respondents whose main organization is non-political.
*Coefficient significant at <.05.
**Coefficient significant at <.01.
***Coefficient significant at <.001.
⇔ Difference in the coefficients for men and women is significant at <.05 (by t-test) or one coefficient is significant at <.05 and the other is not.

esting. First, as we saw when we considered the workplace in Chapter 8, our models are more successful in explaining the development of civic skills than in explaining recruitment in non-political organizations. In contrast to the workplace, however, there is much more similarity between women and men in how organizational affiliation functions to foster participatory factors than we saw for the work force. Thus we can once again contrast the world of non-political organizations and the world of work. In the former the distribution of participatory factors is much less structured by gender than in the latter.

Among those whose most important organization is non-political, men enjoy a small, and not always statistically significant, advantage with respect to participatory factors. As shown in Table 9.3, men are slightly more likely than women to be an officer or board member, to exercise civic skills, or to be recruited to political activity in conjunction with their involvements with non-political organizations. By and large, then, the domain of non-political organizations—unlike the domain of work—operates more or less the same way for men and women in providing endowments for political participation. Those who benefit most in participatory terms from their organizational affiliations are differentiated more in terms of social class than in terms of gender.[4]

An Organization of One's Own:
Gender Segregation in Organizations

Voluntary associations differ from the other two domains in which participatory factors are cultivated—workplaces and churches—in

---

4. As we mentioned earlier, compared with non-political organizations, political organizations provide somewhat greater opportunities to develop skills and generate more requests for activity. The data for those who are affiliated are as follows:

	Non-Political Organization		Political Organization	
	Women	Men	Women	Men
Average civic skills	.86	1.04	1.29	1.28
Asked by organization to take political action	12%	13%	53%	59%

Table 9.3 Participation Factors Acquired in Most Important Organization (for those whose most important organization is non-political)

	Affiliated		
	Women		Men
Practice a civic skill in organization	37%		41%
Mean number of civic skills	0.86	⇔	1.04
On board or officer of organization	18%		23%
Asked by organization to take political action	12%		13%

Source: Citizen Participation Study—Main Survey.
⇔ Difference between women and men is significant at the .05 level.

that they are frequently segregated by gender. Although the American economy is characterized by a great deal of occupational segregation, many people in gender-segregated occupations work in mixed settings. For example, while nurses and secretaries are overwhelmingly female occupations, hospitals and offices are gender integrated. Moreover, religious congregations bring together women and men—even if women cannot serve in the clergy and even if, as in Orthodox Judaism, men and women are seated separately during worship. In contrast, many organizations—ranging from softball leagues to garden clubs—are composed solely, or largely, of either men or women.[5]

In Chapter 3, we discussed the historical role played by organizations of women: at a time when women were excluded from positions of leadership in many spheres—for example, politics,

---

5. Lynn Smith-Lovin and J. Miller McPherson argue that the network "created by voluntary organization memberships is, if anything, more gender segregated than the world of work" and develop a comparison between the consequences of gender segregation at work and gender segregation in voluntary organizations in "You Are Who You Know: A Network Approach to Gender," in *Theory on Gender/Feminism on Theory*, ed. Paula England (New York: Aldine, 1991), p. 238. An important analysis of the relationship between institutional sex-segregation and women's experiences within those institutions is Rosabeth Moss Kanter, *Men and Women of the Corporation* (New York: Basic Books, 1977). Barbara F. Reskin, Debra B. McBrier, and Julie A. Kmec review literature and discuss the adverse consequences of gender segregation at work in "The Determinants and Consequences of Workplace Sex and Race Composition," *Annual Review of Sociology* 25 (1999): 335.

Table 9.4 Gender Composition of Main Non-Political Organization[a]

Share of Organization That Is of the Respondent's Own Sex	Women	Men
Few	4%	4%
Mixed	62	56
Mostly	15	25
All	19	15
	100%	100%

Source: Citizen Participation Study—Main Survey.
a. The distribution of responses is statistically significant with Chi-squared = 22.2796, $p < .001$.

business, or labor unions—women's organizations offered opportunities to exercise leadership and to develop the motivation and capacity to be active in civic life. Moreover, studies of women political elites have emphasized the importance, at least until recently, of activity in voluntary associations as a route to elected office for women.

We can investigate the relationship between the gender composition of organizations and their role in fostering political activity. In so doing, however, we keep open the possibility that there are consequences for men as well as for women of being in a gender-segregated organization. As shown in Table 9.4, a majority of respondents, both male and female, designated as their most important organization one that is mixed in its gender composition. However, about a fifth of the women and a sixth of the men indicated that their main organization is exclusively female or male. It is worth noting that although the emphasis has traditionally been on the implications of gender-segregated organizations for women, men are actually more likely than women to have indicated that all or most of the members of their main organization are of their sex.[6]

---

6. We were curious to know more about the organizational categories into which the main organizations described as single sex fell. Although there is dispersion across many organizational categories for men, 24 percent of the gender-segregated main organizations are either service/fraternal organizations or veterans' organizations, 31 percent are unions or business/professional associations, and 16 percent are hobby/sports clubs. For women there is even more dispersion among organizational categories for main organizations described

Table 9.5 summarizes data about several aspects of experiences in mixed and gender-segregated non-political organizations.[7] Several of these—including opportunities to serve as an officer or on the board or to develop civic skills and requests for political activity—are by now familiar. The final one is respondents' ability to exercise voice in organizational affairs: feeling at least some control over the purposes and policies of the organization; reporting that, in the past year, their opinion had been asked about issues confronting the organization; and indicating that, in the past year, they had volunteered an opinion about such issues at a meeting.

Several patterns are clear. First, data in the first and third columns show that, compared with men, women are disadvantaged in gender-mixed organizations with respect to each of these aspects of organizational experience.[8] They are less likely than men to serve as officers or board members, to exercise voice within the organization, to have opportunities to develop civic skills, or to receive requests from the organization to become active in politics. Furthermore, both men and women are, in general, more likely to

---

as single sex: 16 percent are service/"fraternal"; 13 percent are organizations associated with the respondent's religion; 10 percent are business/professional associations; and 9 percent are educational institutions or associations, including PTAs.

7. In differentiating mixed from gender-segregated organizations, we consider the circumstance in which the respondents indicated that few organization members are of their sex to be an example of a "mixed" organization. As shown in Table 9.4, however, this circumstance is rare.

The savvy reader might notice that the figures in Table 9.5 are somewhat higher than the analogous figures in Table 9.3. Because completely inactive members were unable to answer questions about the characteristics of organizations, the section containing the question about the gender composition of organizations was preceded by a filter specifying a minimal level of organizational activity (giving more than $25 or spending some time on organization activity). Those who scaled this minimum threshold of activity were considerably more likely than completely inactive members to have had these kinds of opportunities and experiences.

8. This finding is confirmed by scholars who study gender segregation and voluntary organizations. See Smith-Lovin and McPherson, "You Are Who You Know," p. 238; J. Miller McPherson and Lynn Smith-Lovin, "Sex Segregation in Voluntary Associations," *American Sociological Review* 51 (1986): 61–79; J. Miller McPherson and Lynn Smith-Lovin, "Women and Weak Ties: Differences by Sex in the Size of Voluntary Organizations," *American Journal of Sociology* 87 (1982): 883–904; J. Miller McPherson and Lynn Smith-Lovin, "Homophily in Voluntary Organizations: Status Distance and the Composition of Face-to-Face Groups," *American Sociological Review* 52 (1987): 370–379; and Cecilia L. Ridgeway and Lynn Smith-Lovin, "The Gender System and Interaction," *Annual Review of Sociology* 25 (1999): 195.

Table 9.5 Participatory Factors and the Gender Composition of
Non-Political Organizations

	Women		Men	
	Mixed Org.	Women's Org.	Mixed Org.	Men's Org.
Served on board or as officer	24% ⇔	39%	29% ⇔	41%
Exercising voice in organizations				
Feel some control over policy	41% ⇔	54%	45%	49%
Opinion has been asked	39% ⇔	58%	45%	48%
Expressed opinion at meeting	35% ⇔	53%	42%	50%
Civic skills in organizations				
Write a letter	13% ⇔	29%	19% ⇔	28%
Go to decision-making meeting	40% ⇔	71%	48% ⇔	62%
Plan a meeting	19% ⇔	29%	21% ⇔	32%
Make a speech	16% ⇔	31%	28%	32%
Mean organizational skills	.85 ⇔	1.57	1.12 ⇔	1.52
Requests for political action				
Asked to vote	3% ⇔	7%	7%	4%
Asked to take other action	9% ⇔	17%	12%	15%
Asked to vote or take other action	11% ⇔	20%	16%	18%

Source: Citizen Participation Study—Main Survey.

⇔ Difference between mixed organization and single-sex organization is significant at the .05
level.

have these participation-enhancing experiences in gender-segregated than in gender-integrated organizations. Finally, as shown
by the data in the second and fourth columns, for most aspects of
organizational experience, the boost given to women in organizations of women is so substantial as to put them on a level with
or at an advantage when compared with men in organizations
of men.

   In short, in crucial ways, organizations of women provide the
kinds of experiences that have been attributed to them: providing
opportunities for leadership, facilitating the exercise of voice in organizational matters and the development of civic skills, and generating requests for political activity. But this formulation leaves
out half the picture. Organizations dominated by men—which actually constitute a larger share of the organizations that male re-

spondents designated as their most important—have some of the same effects for men. Thus, as has been the case a number of times in our analysis, it turns out to be important to consider both men and women.

Religious Institutions and Participation

Religious institutions are a crucial component of civil society in America. As we discussed in Chapter 3, Americans are more religiously committed and active than are citizens in many other developed democracies. Separation of church and state to the contrary, religious institutions—like voluntary associations—have a complex relationship to politics in the United States. They often play a direct political role—as when they take principled stands on issues as diverse as peace, hunger, and abortion or when they provide the infrastructure for social movements.

When it comes to citizen political participation, however, there might be reason to suspect that religious involvement would dampen activity: after all, Marx's formulation of religion as the "opiate of the masses" is well known, and religious orthodoxies around the world have been known as the foes of democracy. In America, however, religious institutions, like the workplace and voluntary associations, function to bring citizens into political life by nurturing the factors associated with political activity. Religious institutions operate both to incubate civic skills and to recruit congregants to politics through explicit requests for political action from clergy or church officials.[9]

In light of the complex relationship between gender and religion discussed in Chapter 3, we are especially curious to find out how these processes work for women and men. We saw, on one hand,

---

9. On the relationship between religious involvement and political participation, see Verba, Schlozman, and Brady, *Voice and Equality*, chaps. 9, 11, and 13. For a nuanced discussion of these matters based on participant observation, see Anna Greenberg, "The Church and the Revitalization of Politics and Community," *Political Science Quarterly* 115 (2000): 377–394; and, for a survey-based analysis that illumines denominational differences, see Robert Wuthnow, "Mobilizing Civic Engagement: The Changing Impact of Religious Involvement," in *Civic Engagement in American Democracy*, ed. Theda Skocpol and Morris P. Fiorina (Washington, D.C.: Brookings Institution Press, 1999), chap. 9.

that religious doctrine has long been invoked to legitimate traditional sex roles and that religious institutions have historically excluded women from positions of authority. Indeed, a substantial minority of Americans profess faiths in which, even today, women cannot be ordained, and those denominations are among the largest social institutions in America to retain de jure prohibitions on the full inclusion of women. On the other, women have traditionally been more religiously devout and active than men. In the past, when women's participation in public life was narrowly circumscribed, women were permitted, even expected, to attend services and to take on supportive roles in their churches, where their voluntary service often built competence and confidence.

BECOMING RELIGIOUSLY ACTIVE

As usual, we begin our investigation of the roots of political activity in non-political institutions by probing the processes by which individuals come to be institutionally affiliated. We conducted logistic regression analyses predicting the likelihood of being affiliated with a religious institution—that is, belonging to a local church or attending services regularly in the same congregation—for men and women. In our analysis, we considered the same set of factors adduced to account for selection into the work force or into non-political organizations: aspects of social class—including education, family income, and job level; activity in high school; family circumstances; age; and race or ethnicity.

Table 9.6, which presents the results, shows a process of selection that is quite different from what we saw for either the work force or non-political organizations. The relative weakness of association between measures of socioeconomic status and religious affiliation is quite striking. The propensity to be active that is presumably indicated by activity in high school is, however, related to church affiliation. Family circumstances are important—once again, especially for men. Religious affiliation increases appreciably with having school-age children and, for men only, with marriage.[10] In short, it seems that for men, church affiliation is depen-

---

10. Data about attendance at religious services are especially revealing: on average, single men attend church 18 weeks a year and married men with children attend church 33 weeks a year; the average figures for women are 32 weeks and 36 weeks respectively.

Table 9.6 Predicting Church Affiliation (logistic regression)

	Women		Men
EDUCATION AND CHILDHOOD			
Education	0.69		−0.22
High School Activity	0.56**		0.97***
INCOME			
Family Income	−1.15		1.14
WORKPLACE			
Working	−0.23	⇔	0.38*
Job Level	0.07	⇔	−0.61*
FAMILY			
Married	0.01	⇔	0.43**
Preschool Children	−0.01		0.34
School-age Children	0.37***		0.73***
OTHER VARIABLES			
Age	0.15		−0.12
Age over 65	0.79***		0.96***
Black	0.43		0.24
Latino	−0.05		−0.26
Citizen	0.38		0.64
Constant	−0.12	⇔	−1.18**
Log Likelihood	−712		−742

Source: Citizen Participation Study—Main Survey.
*Coefficient significant at <.05.
**Coefficient significant at <.01.
***Coefficient significant at <.001.
⇔ Difference in the coefficients for men and women is significant at <.05 (by t-test) or one coefficient is significant at <.05 and the other is not.

dent upon life circumstances while, for women, it is a more consistent part of life.

We have thus seen that the configuration of factors that predict affiliation is quite different for work, non-political voluntary associations, and church. High school activity matters for religious and organizational affiliation, but not for work force participation. Socioeconomic factors are important for work force participation and, especially, organizational affiliation, but not for religious affiliation. The impact of family circumstances differs for the various domains of activity and for men and women. Family responsibilities—marriage and children, both preschool and school-age—bring men into the work force; preschool children operate just as strongly to keep women at home. Marriage and children draw men to church; for women only school-age children influence religious affiliation. Finally, for organizational affiliation, all else equal, family circumstance make no difference.

That socioeconomic factors play so little a role in religious affiliation is noteworthy. Affiliation with non-political organizations is highly stratified on the basis of socioeconomic class. Furthermore, education is strongly related to work force participation and is even more strongly related to the distribution of those in the work force into particular jobs. In contrast, religious institutions—which are, ironically, often hierarchically governed and congregationally segregated on the basis of class and race—are overall more democratic in their recruitment patterns.[11] Because they draw members almost uniformly across the class hierarchy, they are, in the aggregate, the most egalitarian of the secondary institutions of American civil society.

We should recall that there is also a significant gender gap in affiliation with religious institutions. As we saw in Chapter 3, 74 percent of the women, as opposed to 58 percent of the men, are members of a church. The clue to the disparity between the gender difference in the *level of affiliation* as opposed to the *process of affiliation* is in the statistically significant difference between the constant terms in Table 9.6. That the constant term is lower for men means that, with the other variables taken into account, men are still less likely to be members of a local congregation.

The critical gender difference that explains the disparity in affili-

---

11. For a summary of the literature and discussion of the complicated relationship between social status and religious commitments, see Darren E. Sherkat and Christopher G. Ellison, "Recent Developments and Current Controversies in the Sociology of Religion," *Annual Review of Sociology* 25 (1999): 368. Their summary of findings indicates that higher levels of education are negatively associated with traditional religious beliefs and with religious affiliation and attendance. In contrast, the well educated are more likely to be involved with organizations associated with a religious denomination. In addition, the affluent donate more money, though a lower proportion of their incomes, to religious organizations. According to Wade Clark Roof, *A Generation of Seekers* (San Francisco: HarperCollins, 1993), p. 166, religious activity was positively related to education during the 1950s. The change in the relationship between religious participation and education reflects the fact that well-educated Baby Boomers have not returned to religious activity after the "religious moratorium" characteristic of young adults.

ations with religious institutions is women's deeper religious commitment. Sixty-seven percent of women, as opposed to 49 percent of men, consider religion to be very important in their lives. The belief that religion is important and religious behavior are strongly connected: with other social characteristics taken into account, those for whom religion is not important almost never attend services, and those for whom it is very important attend church almost every week. However, we cannot ascertain whether the belief that religion is important is the cause or the effect of frequent attendance at religious services.

If we replicate the analysis in Table 9.6 and include the respondent's subjective evaluation of the importance of religion, the gender difference in religious affiliation disappears. That is, once the assessment of the importance of religion to one's life is taken into account, the difference in the constant terms fades to insignificance, indicating that we have located the source of women's higher level of affiliation with religious congregations in more intense religious commitment.[12]

RELIGIOUS INVOLVEMENT AND PARTICIPATORY FACTORS

As it was for work force participation and organizational affiliation, the next step is to analyze how participatory factors are acquired in religious institutions. Table 9.7 reports the results of OLS regressions predicting the development of civic skills and the likelihood of exposure to requests for political activity at church for those who are affiliated with a church. In order to ensure that we are not simply measuring the effects of the amount of time given to church work, we add to the usual abbreviated list of predictor variables a measure of the average number of hours each week spent on educational, charitable, or social activity in a religious institution. As we would expect, for both men and, especially, women, the more time devoted to church work, the greater the number of civic skills developed. Furthermore, the number of requests for activity also rises with time given to activity in a religious institution. Once again, the impact, which is less substantial

---

12. The results of the logistic regressions are contained in Appendix C, Table C9.6.1.

Table 9.7 Predicting Participatory Factors from Religious Institutions (OLS regression)[a]

	Civic Skills		Recruitment	
	Women	Men	Women	Men
EDUCATION AND CHILDHOOD				
Education	0.59** ⇔	0.31	0.50***	0.35**
High School Activity	0.45***	0.46**	0.27***	0.31***
INCOME				
Family Income	0.33	−0.19	−0.20	−0.26
INSTITUTIONAL COMMITMENT				
Hours of Church Work	5.39***	5.01***	0.69**	0.47*
OTHER VARIABLES				
Age	0.31 ⇔	0.51**	−0.11	0.14
Age over 65	−0.11	−0.10	−0.17*	−0.28**
Black	0.11	−0.01	0.09	0.09
Latino	−0.01	−0.07	−0.09 ⇔	−0.35**
Citizen	0.11	−0.20	0.16	−0.16
Constant	−0.24	0.17	−0.07 ⇔	0.38*
Adjusted R-squared	0.20	0.24	0.08	0.07

Source: Citizen Participation Study—Main Survey.
a. Regression includes only those affiliated with religious institutions.
*Coefficient significant at <.05.
**Coefficient significant at <.01.
***Coefficient significant at <.001.
⇔ Difference in the coefficients for men and women is significant at <.05 (by *t*-test) or one coefficient is significant at <.05 and the other is not.

than the impact of time spent in church on the number of civic skills exercised, is equal for men and women.

As shown in Table 9.8, these processes of selection into religious institutions and the distribution of participatory factors within them yield a small advantage for women. Women are slightly more likely than men to exercise a civic skill or to be asked to take part politically in connection with religious involvement. However, as indicated by the figures for the religiously affiliated, the small gender disparity is not a function of any affirmative action for women in religious institutions. In fact, among church members, men and women are equally likely to exercise a civic skill and men are

Table 9.8 Participatory Factors Acquired in Church

	All Respondents		Religiously Affiliated	
	Women	Men	Women	Men
Exercise a Civic Skill	22% ⇔	18%	30%	30%
Mainline Protestant	22%	21%	29%	32%
Evangelical Protestant	30%	27%	36%	40%
Catholic	11%	8%	13%	12%
Mean Civic Skills	.48 ⇔	.39	.65	.67
Mainline Protestant	.50	.50	.66	.76
Evangelical Protestant	.59	.62	.73	.92
Catholic	.23	.13	.28	.20
Asked to Take Political Action	24% ⇔	21%	33%	37%
Mainline Protestant	18%	22%	23% ⇔	34%
Evangelical Protestant	33% ⇔	26%	40%	39%
Catholic	25%	25%	30%	37%

Source: Citizen Participation Study—Main Survey.
⇔ Difference between women and men is significant at the .05 level.

slightly more likely to have been recruited politically in the context of religious involvement. Instead, the gender disparity reflects women's higher level of religious involvement. It is their greater religious commitment, rather than any special encouragement from religious institutions, that is responsible for the slightly enhanced level of participatory factors that accompanies their religious activity.

Table 9.8 also presents information about church-based civic skills and political recruitment for three large religious groups: mainline Protestants, evangelical Protestants, and Catholics.[13] The data show some gender differences: among affiliated Catholics, women exercise on average more civic skills in the context of religious activity than do men; among affiliated Protestants the relationship is reversed. However, it is not the gender differences but the denominational differences that emerge most clearly from the table. The data show that a politicizing church is not necessarily a skill-endowing church. Although Catholics are as likely as

---

13. See Chapter 3, note 48, for the definitions of mainline and evangelical Protestants.

Protestants to receive requests for political activity, they are much less likely to develop civic skills in conjunction with church activity—which, presumably, reflects the hierarchical structure of the Catholic Church, the larger size of Catholic parishes, and the more limited role for the laity in the liturgy and in church governance.[14] Evangelical Protestants, a composite of denominations whose members are not especially well educated or affluent, are actually the most likely to acquire church-related participatory factors.

The Role of Women in Religious Institutions: A Closer Look

Underlying our discussion so far is a puzzling disjunction. On one hand, women are more religiously committed and active than men. On the other, religious institutions long excluded women from positions of authority, and many still do. Yet we know that women have not confined their religious activity to denominations in which they now are permitted fully equal roles and rights. On the contrary, they are very active in denominations that exclude them from ordination. For example, among affiliated Catholics, women are more likely than men to give time to educational, social, or charitable activities associated with their parishes.

We were interested to probe further the religious commitments and activities of men and, especially, women in churches that continue to make gender distinctions. Respondents in the third-wave survey who expressed a religious preference were asked whether in their religion women can be full members of the clergy. A substantial minority of respondents—more than a third of both women and men—reported that in their faith women cannot be full members of the clergy.[15] Close analysis of these data suggest that respondents were quite accurate in their assessments.[16]

---

14. For amplification of the theme of denominational differences in the provision of participatory factors and the special character of the Catholic Church in the process, see Verba, Schlozman, and Brady, *Voice and Equality*, pp. 320–330.

15. Sixty-three percent of the men and 55 percent of the women who indicated that their denomination does not ordain women are Catholic.

16. All the Mormons and Eastern Orthodox and virtually all the Catholics reported that

Table 9.9 Approval of Women as Full Members of
Clergy in Religion[a]

	Women	Men
Among Respondents in Denominations in Which		
Women can be members of clergy	91%	95%
Women cannot be members of clergy		
Catholic	60%	68%
Other denominations	15%	46%

Source: Citizen Participation Study Follow-up—Couples Survey.
a. Percentage of respondents who prefer women as full members of clergy in their denomination.

Those who indicated that women cannot be full members of the clergy in their religion were then asked whether they would prefer there to be women clergy or whether they prefer it the way it is now. We also asked those in denominations that do ordain women whether they would prefer there to be no women clergy or whether they prefer it the way it is now.

Table 9.9 presents data about the proportion of women and men who approve of women as clergy. It is striking that men are, overall, somewhat more favorably disposed toward women clergy than women are. In addition, the overwhelming majority—both male and female—of those in denominations that do ordain women approve of the status quo. Of those in denominations in which women cannot be full members of the clergy, a majority of

---

women cannot be full members of the clergy in their religion. In contrast, all the Unitarian-Universalists, Disciples of Christ, Episcopalians, Presbyterians, and virtually all the Methodists said that women can be full members of the clergy in their religion. For good reason, there was much less agreement among the various groups of Baptists. Although congregational autonomy is a bedrock principle for Baptists, Southern Baptist congregations that have ordained women have faced sanctions from local Baptist associations and from the national association, the Southern Baptist Convention, which in 2000—well after our survey—passed a resolution opposing women serving as pastors. (See Nancy Tatom Ammerman, *Baptist Battles* [New Brunswick, N.J.: Rutgers University Press, 1990]; Sarah Frances Anders and Marilyn Metcalf Whittaker, "Women as Lay Leaders and Clergy: A Critical Issue," in *Southern Baptists Observed,* ed. Nancy Tatom Ammerman [Knoxville: University of Tennessee Press, 1993], chap. 11; and "Southern Baptist Convention Passes Resolution Opposing Women as Pastors," *New York Times,* June 15, 2000, p. A-18.) Two-thirds of the Southern Baptists indicated that their church does not permit women to be full members of the clergy.

the Catholics—again, both male and female—would prefer there to be women. In contrast, a majority of those in the mixture of other denominations that do not permit women as clergy are content with the current situation.[17] In this case, however, the gap between women and men is notable: of non-Catholics in denominations that do not ordain women, 54 percent of the men and fully 85 percent of the women approve of that circumstance.

While students of organized religion indicate that there is a great deal of church shopping,[18] some of it across denominational lines, our data do not permit us to understand the extent to which the circumstances described by the data in Table 9.9 reflect effective persuasion by the denominations in question or processes of sorting out such that the disaffected find more congenial denominational homes or leave religious life altogether.

We can, however, shed light on the religious and political commitments of those who approve or disapprove of their denomination's position on the ordination of women. Reading from left to right, the first three columns of Table 9.10 present data about three categories of women: those who approve of the fact that their denominations permit women to be full members of the clergy; those who disagree with their denominations' resistance to ordaining women; those who are content with the refusal to allow women to be rabbis, ministers, or priests. The right-hand three columns present analogous data for men.

Among the women, those who are content with their denomination's exclusion of women from the clergy are both religiously and ideologically distinctive. They are by far the most religiously active and devout: fully 94 percent consider religion to be very important

---

17. These data are consistent with the findings of Wade Clark Roof and William McKinney, *American Mainline Religion* (New Brunswick, N.J.: Rutgers University Press, 1987), who describe post–Vatican II Catholicism as "more pluralistic, more voluntary, more American" (p. 95) and note that Catholics are much more favorable to women's rights than are conservative Protestants (pp. 204–209).

18. See Roof and McKinney, *American Mainline Religion,* chap. 5; and Roof, *A Generation of Seekers.* According to Roof and McKinney, the processes of switching exacerbate differences among denominations, because switchers "are more similar to the groups they switch to than to those they leave behind" (p. 221) in terms of both their political and moral views and their level of religious commitment (p. 178). Because their survey-based data focus on individuals, they are unable to consider the effects of intermarriage on denomination shopping.

Table 9.10 Approval of Denomination's Position on Women Clergy by Political and Religious Commitments

	Women			Men		
Does respondent's denomination allow women clergy?	Yes	No	No	Yes	No	No
Does respondent approve of denomination's position?	Yes	No	Yes	Yes	No	Yes
Attend religious services weekly	41%	32%	73%	24%	29%	36%
Say religion is very important	76%	43%	94%	47%	45%	55%
Give time to religious activity[a]	52%	19%	64%	36%	46%	56%
Support traditional gender roles at home[b]	13%	8%	49%	50%	21%	55%
Conservative political ideology[c]	33%	17%	57%	46%	39%	60%
Republican identifier[d]	30%	5%	39%	41%	31%	46%

Source: Citizen Participation Study Follow-up—Couples Survey.
a. Over the last year.
b. Lower third on scale measuring support for equal gender roles in the household.
c. 1–3 on a seven-point scale measuring self-defined political ideology.
d. 1–3 on a seven-point scale measuring self-defined partisan identity.

in their lives. They are also the most likely to favor traditional gender roles at home, to consider themselves conservative in politics, and to identify as Republicans. At the other extreme are the women in the same denominations who would like to see women ordained. They are the least religiously involved of the groups of women and the most liberal of all groups in terms of their views on gender roles, political ideology, or partisanship. Between these groups of women are those who approve of the fact that their denominations allow women clergy.

By and large, the same patterns obtain for men. However, the differences among groups of men distinguished by their denominational preferences and approval or disapproval of women's taking clerical roles are much more muted. The three groups of men are much more similar to one another than are the three groups of women. The greater polarization among women is striking in light of the extent to which discussion of the "culture wars"—political and social conflicts over such matters as traditional morality, family values, abortion, and multiculturalism—has ordinarily focused on men. Our data show that these themes are being played out among women to an extent not always recognized.

These data attest to an outcome in which a great deal of sorting is taking place. Many women are staying with, or being attracted to, churches that exclude them from clerical and leadership roles. Compared with other women, they are quite distinctive—both more devout and more politically and socially conservative. In contrast, women in the same faiths who disapprove of their denomination's exclusionary policies are dropping out, staying away, or finding more congenial denominational homes. Among them, those who continue to express a denominational preference for a faith that does not allow women clergy are also distinctive—less faithful, less religiously active, and less conservative in political and social terms.

In order to pin down the complicated processes underlying these data we would need panel data collected over a long period of time. Such data would permit us to understand whether it is the denominational position on permitting women full roles as clergy—or some other characteristic that is associated with this particular policy—that is responsible for the outcome we have described. Such data would also allow us to specify the extent to which the status quo reflects switching across denominations or processes of activation and deactivation within denominations. Finally, they would, perhaps, suggest whether what is behind the processes of sorting out is the success or failure of the persuasive efforts of the clergy in denominations that do not ordain women or some other distinctive characteristics of women who approve or disapprove of their denomination's excluding them from full participation.

These data make clear an important difference between religious and political life. The process that is alleged to operate in politics such that the exclusion of women—in the past from citizenship, today from the most powerful positions of presidential and legislative leadership—has led women to internalize the message and to opt out does not seem to obtain for religious life. A common interpretation, which we shall consider in Chapter 13, is that many women conclude from a circumstance in which they are underrepresented among those who exercise political power at the highest levels that politics is a man's world—in which they should, therefore, not be engaged. In the domain of religion, even when women are kept out of the pulpit, they are overrepresented in the pews and as lay activists in the congregation. The women who are the backbone of these very traditional faiths are themselves in many ways traditional. In politics, as we have already seen, the process works differently. Women are less likely than men to adopt roles that are the political equivalent of loyal lay service to the congregation. While the role of church activist has been a traditional one for women in American society, the role of citizen political activist has not—perhaps because women were so long altogether excluded from citizenship and have yet to obtain the most powerful positions in national politics. In any case, the repercussions of traditions of exclusion of women are very different in religious and political life.

Summary

In the last two chapters we have presented a complex set of processes by which individuals acquire the factors that facilitate participation in the context of their involvement in the non-political institutions of adult life. Our argument has been a complicated one, because we are juggling differences among three institutions—the workplace, non-political organizations, and religious institutions; differences between the process of selection into institutions and the acquisition of participatory factors within institutions; differences between two kinds of participatory factors, civic skills and requests for activity; and differences between women and men. Not surprisingly, a number of separate patterns emerged.

While we cannot easily simplify our findings, we have presented them schematically in Table 9.11. Using a combination of pluses and minuses, we summarize the relationship between a series of predictors and each of three outcomes—institutional affiliation, development of civic skills, and recruitment to political activity—for men and women in each of the three institutional domains.

Let us consider portion A of the table, which focuses on distinct processes of institutional affiliation. The factors that drive processes of affiliation vary with the institution in question: for both women and men, education is related to work force participation and to organizational affiliation but plays no role in church membership; high school activity is associated with organizational and

Table 9.11 The Acquisition of Participatory Factors in Institutions: Summary[a]

	Workplace		Non-Political Organizations		Religious Institutions	
	Women	Men	Women	Men	Women	Men
A. Affiliation with Institutions						
Activity in high school	0	0	+	+	+	+
Education	+	+	+	+	0	0
Family income			+	0	0	0
Working			0	0	0	+
Job level			0	+	0	+
Family circumstances						
Married	0	+	0	0	0	+
Preschool children	−	+	0	0	0	0
School-age children	0	+	0	0	+	+
B.1. Acquisition of Participatory Factors (among affiliated): Civic Skills						
Activity in high school	+	+	+	+	+	+
Education	+	+	+	+	+	0
Institutional commitment[b]	+	+	+	+	+	+
B.2. Acquisition of Participatory Factors (among affiliated): Recruitment						
Activity in high school	+	+	0	0	+	+
Education	+	+	+	0	+	+
Institutional commitment[b]	+	0	+	+	+	+

a. + Positive effect.
  0 No significant effect.
  − Negative effect.
 b. Work: number of hours each day; organization or religious institution: number of hours each week.

religious affiliation, but has nothing to do with work force participation.

In contrast, when it comes to the impact of family circumstances, the patterns are not only institutionally specific but gender specific. Family circumstances matter greatly when it comes to decisions about entering the work force and belonging to a church, but do so in opposite ways for men and women. With other factors taken into account, married men and fathers are more likely to be in the work force and in religious institutions. Marriage makes no difference for women in either domain, but mothers of toddlers are much less likely to be in the work force and mothers of school-age children are more likely to be religiously affiliated.

In spite of the common perception that community involvement increases when there are children at home, none of the variables measuring family circumstances—marriage, preschool children, or school-age children—is related to organizational involvement for either women or men. In short, then, the process of affiliation varies across institutions and, in two of the three cases, the process is different for women and men.

The patterns are somewhat less complex with respect to the acquisition of participatory factors among those who are institutionally affiliated. For the exercise of civic skills, summarized in portion B.1, the pattern is actually quite straightforward: in each of the three institutional domains, activity in high school, educational attainment, and the extent of institutional commitment are all associated with the development of civic skills for both men and women.[19] When it comes to requests for political participation, summarized in portion B.2, activity in high school, educational attainment, and, for women, the extent of institutional commitment are all related to recruitment at work and in church. The pattern is much more mixed in non-political organizations. Overall, however, our models were less helpful in explaining requests for political activity than in explaining the development of civic skills.

Having gone to some effort to map out the complicated processes by which participatory factors are acquired in institutions, we now turn to the main task, understanding how these factors foster activity.

---

19. For men, education is positively but not significantly related to the acquisition of civic skills in church.

10

Gender, Institutions,
and Political Participation

We have devoted considerable attention to the building blocks
with which an analysis of gender differences in political participation can be assembled. Now it is time to construct the edifice. In
these final chapters we bring together the separate components we
have presented in order to understand how men and women come
to be politically active and why their rates of activity are somewhat
different.

As we saw in Chapter 3, there is a small disparity in the overall political participation of men and women. For all forms of
participation except for attendance at protests, men are more
active than women. However, the pattern for particular forms of
activity—activity in informal efforts to solve community problems, involvement in political organizations, making campaign
contributions, and so on—does not conform to what is sometimes assumed about the kinds of activity in which women might
be expected to specialize. In fact, the size of the gender difference
varies across political acts in ways that are somewhat surprising.
When the differences are summed across the eight political acts
about which we asked, the resulting difference is about one-third
of a political act—or, to be more precise, .31 of an act. This disparity is roughly equivalent to the difference in average political activity between Blacks and Whites, or between someone who attended
college but did not graduate and someone with a B.A.

The Stockpile of Participatory Factors

We have seen that processes of differential selection into institutions and differential treatment once there result in an allocation of participatory factors that, by and large, gives the advantage to men. Tables 10.1 through 10.4 repeat data presented in previous chapters regarding the stockpile of factors accumulated by women and men through their institutional involvements.

Table 10.1 has information on exposure to politics within the family at age sixteen, educational attainment, and experiences in high school. As we saw before, girls and boys differ little when it comes to their experience at home or in high school, although girls report somewhat more activity in clubs at the high school level. As noted earlier, men have somewhat higher levels of educational attainment, the result of their traditional dominance in higher education. Because education is perhaps the single most important factor in fostering participation, the educational disparity presumably has consequences for the gender gap in participation.

Table 10.1 Participatory Factors Acquired in Family and School[a]

	Women		Men
IN FAMILY AS ADOLESCENT			
Mean on "Family in Politics" scale[b]	1.76		1.76
EDUCATIONAL ATTAINMENT			
No more than high school degree	54%	⇔	47%
College graduates	22%	⇔	29%
Mean number of grades completed	12.9	⇔	13.4
EXPERIENCES IN HIGH SCHOOL			
Very active in high school government	8%		7%
Very active in high school clubs	24%	⇔	16%
Very active in high school sports	20%	⇔	37%
Took a course in civics	78%		79%

Source: Citizen Participation Study—Main Survey.

a. Appendix A contains the valid number of cases for these and other measures used in the tables.

b. Sum of measures of political activity by mother and father and of political discussion at home.

⇔ Difference between women and men is statistically significant at the .05 level.

With respect to the factors produced in adult secondary institutions shown in Table 10.2, the figures indicate the combined effects of differential selection into an institution and different experiences within it. The overall results reflect the complex interaction of by now familiar patterns. As we have noted, compared with men, women are less likely to be in the work force and more likely to be affiliated with a religious institution. The bottom line is that men end up better off with respect to both recruitment and, especially, civic skills, an outcome that is driven, by and large, by gender differences in work force participation and experiences on the job. To the extent that there are gender differences in skill acquisition or requests for activity for the institutionally affiliated, the only consistent pattern is that where there is a gender difference, men gain an advantage.

We should also pause to look across institutions in Table 10.2, especially the contrast between the workplace and religious institutions. With respect to the development of civic skills, a process that is largely a by-product of activities that are divorced from political content, the workplace provides the most opportunities, churches the fewest. When it comes to the much more overtly po-

Table 10.2 Participatory Factors Acquired in Adult Institutions

	All Respondents		
	Women		Men
MEAN CIVIC SKILLS PRACTICED			
On the job	1.10	⇔	1.71
In an organization[a]	.59		.64
In church	.48	⇔	.39
All three institutions	2.17	⇔	2.74
MEAN REQUESTS FOR POLITICAL ACTIVITY			
On the job	.15		.17
In an organization[a]	.09	⇔	.12
In church	.30		.28
All three institutions	.70	⇔	.84

Source: Citizen Participation Study—Main Survey.

a. Means include imputed skills and requests for those whose main organization is political but who are also affiliated with a non-political organization.

⇔ Difference between women and men is statistically significant at the .05 level.

Table 10.3 Time and Income as Participatory Resources

	Women		Men
TIME			
Mean hours working	5.0 hours	⇔	7.7 hours
Mean hours housework	5.2 hours	⇔	2.7 hours
Mean hours free time per day	6.5 hours		6.5 hours
INCOME			
Mean family income	$36,752	⇔	$44,013
Mean earnings from work (all respondents)	$10,500	⇔	$25,896
Mean earnings from work (working only)	$17,799	⇔	$33,127

Source: Citizen Participation Study—Main Survey.
⇔ Difference between women and men is statistically significant at the .05 level.

litical act of making requests for political activity, it is interesting to note that this ranking does not hold. In fact, recruitment requests are most likely in church, least likely on the job.[1]

Every form of political activity requires at least some time or some money. Time is a limited resource that can be devoted to politics or to countless other uses, including other kinds of voluntary engagement. No matter how motivated one is, how many resources one has, how many times one is asked to be politically active, there are only twenty-four hours in a day. As shown in Table 10.3, on average, women and men are equally busy, but they devote their busy hours to different pursuits. Compared with women, men spend more time at work, a relationship that obtains even for women with full-time jobs. In contrast, men—even the husbands of women with full-time jobs—devote less time to housework and child care. The result is what counts: women and men have the same amount of free time—time that could be devoted to political activity.

Women are disadvantaged when it comes to the other major form of participatory input, income. As shown in Table 10.3, women have lower family incomes than men. While married women and men report similar family incomes ($46,700 and

---

1. We should recall that requests for activity are, not surprisingly, most common in political organizations.

$48,800, respectively), there is, not unexpectedly, a significant dif-
ference in the family incomes of unmarried men and women
($36,900 and $28,800). Women also report lower income from
work, a gap that is substantial even when we consider only those
in the work force.[2]

Lastly, our summary of factors that might be relevant to political participation brings us to a matter originally discussed in
Chapter 4: exposure to discrimination based on sex. As we noted,
we consider reports of experiences with gender discrimination to
be neither entirely objective nor entirely subjective. Women and
men presumably vary not only in their exposure to discrimination
but also in their propensity to interpret the same encounter as discriminatory. We had contradictory expectations regarding the consequences for participation of perceived experiences of discrimination. On one hand, experiences of discrimination might depress
political activity—either because discrimination has psychological
repercussions, making victims feel less efficacious, or because victims of discrimination are barred from the kinds of opportunities
that permit the development of civic skills. On the other, the feelings of anger engendered by an experience of perceived discrimination might have a mobilizing effect, thus generating political activity. As Table 10.4 shows, women are twice as likely as men to
report having been exposed to discrimination based on sex. Although we did not distinguish explicitly among settings in asking
about bias, the data in Table 10.4 seem to indicate that those
who stray from the path of traditional gender-role expectations—
women with full-time jobs, women who are not members of a local church, and men with part-time jobs—were somewhat more
likely to have reported experience with discrimination. We have
no way of discerning whether this pattern is evidence that those
who choose less conventional roles are more likely to be the ob-

2. The ratio of women's to men's earnings among those in the work force reflects the fact
that the women in our sample are much more likely to be in the work force part time. At the
time the survey was conducted, the ratio of women's to men's earnings among full-time,
year-round workers was .72. See Daphne Spain and Suzanne M. Bianchi, *Balancing Act:
Motherhood, Marriage, and Employment among American Women* (New York: Russell
Sage, 1996), p. 111.

Table 10.4 Experiences of Gender Discrimination[a]

	Women		Men
All	11%	⇔	6%
Not in the work force	7	⇔	2
Part-time worker	9		16
Full-time worker	15	⇔	6
No organizational affiliation	8		5
Affiliated with a non-political organization	11	⇔	6
Not a member of a local religious institution	17	⇔	5
Member of a local religious institution	8	⇔	6

Source: Citizen Participation Study—Main Survey.
a. Percentage who say they have experienced discrimination.
⇔ Difference between women and men is statistically significant at the .05 level.

jects of discrimination or that they are more sensitive to potentially discriminatory acts—or, probably, both.

The Gender Gap in Participation: An Outcomes Analysis

Having described in some detail the stockpile of participatory factors amassed by women and men, we next assess how these factors affect political participation. The impact of any particular factor on political activity depends on two things: *level,* or how much of the factor is commanded; and *effect,* the extent of the boost given to political activity by an incremental increase in the factor. Both of these matter for our analysis of the disparity between men and women in political activity. For a human attribute that we would expect to have no relationship to political participation—say, physical strength or the ability to sew—a gender difference in the attribute, even if substantial, would have no participatory consequence. For factors known to be strongly associated with political participation—say, educational attainment—a gender difference in the level of the attribute would be crucial.

However, as we have cautioned many times, we must not assume that the effects are uniform across groups. That is, members of different groups may convert a particular factor into political participation at different rates. An extreme example would be the

Table 10.5 Participation Factors and Political Activity: An Outcomes Model[a]

	Level of Factor		Effect of Factor		Overall Outcome		Contribution to Participation Gap
	Women	Men	Women	Men	Women	Men	
	EFFECT OF NON-POLITICAL INSTITUTIONS						
HOME AND EDUCATION							
Home Politics	.24	.24	.98***	.55**	.18	.18	
Education	.38 ⇔	.42	1.73***	1.60***	.63	.70	+.07
Experience in School	.37 ⇔	.34	.63***	.58***	.23	.21	−.02
ADULT INSTITUTIONAL EFFECTS							
Job Factors	.17 ⇔	.26	.98***	.85***	.16	.24	+.08
Organization Factors	.10	.11	.94***	.85***	.10	.10	
Church Factors	.13	.12	1.28***	1.26***	.17	.17	
TIME AND INCOME							
Available Time	.61	.61	.14	−.19	.00	.00	
Family Income	.12 ⇔	.13	2.26***	1.96***	.25	.27	+.02
Own Income	.03 ⇔	.08	−1.54***	−.32	.00	.00	
Total Male Advantage Due to Resources and Recruitment							+.15
	EFFECT OF DISCRIMINATION						
Gender Bias	.11 ⇔	.06	.51***	.30	.06	.00	−.06
Constant	1.00	1.00	−.52*	.10	−.42	.00	
Total Male Advantage Due to Resources, Recruitment, and Discrimination							+.09

Source: Citizen Participation Study—Main Survey.
a. Age and age over 65 in equation as controls.
*Coefficient significant at <.05.
**Coefficient significant at <.01.
***Coefficient significant at <.001.
⇔ Difference is significant at <.05 or one coefficient is significant at <.05 and the other is not.

case of African-Americans in the South under segregation. Because Blacks were prevented from voting or otherwise taking part in politics, the relationship between education and participation in the Jim Crow South must have been very different for Blacks and Whites.

Table 10.5 reports the results of an "outcomes analysis."[3] The outcome with which we are concerned is the overall consequence for political activity of the level and the effect of the various participatory factors. Because it is summarizing an extremely complex process, Table 10.5 contains many numbers; let us explain what they represent. We begin by calculating, for women and men, the average level of each of the participatory factors. These averages, shown in the left-most columns of the table, are derived from the findings presented in Tables 10.1–10.4. In order to facilitate comparisons among variables that use different scales, they have, once again, been rescaled to vary between 0 and 1. As usual, we indicate a significant difference between men and women in the average amount of a factor they hold by the symbol $\Leftrightarrow$.

We then use multiple regression to calculate the effect of each of the participatory factors on political activity—measured by the eight-act summary scale of political activity. As in the past, we conduct the analyses separately for women and men in order to uncover gender differences in the process by which participatory factors are converted to political activity. These effects, presented in the second pair of columns, are measured by the unstandardized regression coefficients from multiple regression equations in which all of the factors have been included. The coefficients measure the maximum effect on activity of the independent variable; that is, the effect on activity moving from the lowest to the highest category of the variable. Where the coefficients are significantly different, we again indicate that with the symbol $\Leftrightarrow$. In the last pair of columns, we enter the product of the first two sets of columns; that is, the product of the amount of any factor and the effect of that factor on activity.[4] This measure indicates, for women and men,

---

3. For a fuller description of our method, see Appendix D.

4. Where there is no significant difference between the coefficients for women and men, we have not used the actual numbers contained in Table 10.5 in calculating the overall effect of a factor. Instead, we used the average of the coefficients for the two groups.

the overall impact on political activity of each of the factors in the analysis.

Finally, we present a single column of numbers which notes, for each of the independent variables, any difference in the outcome for women and men. These numbers capture the contribution—in terms of the number of political acts on the eight-point summary scale—of each variable to the overall gender gap in participation. Positive numbers indicate a masculine advantage and a widening of the disparity in activity. Negative numbers indicate a feminine advantage and a narrowing of the disparity. For example, the +.07 figure for education indicates that men's greater educational attainment gives them a boost in activity of .07 of a political act over women. This differential increment—.07 of an act—does not sound like a difference worth talking about. However, it represents nearly a quarter of the .31 gender gap in activity. Let us consider the various factors contained in Table 10.5.

EARLY EXPERIENCES AT HOME AND IN SCHOOL

Although socialization experiences at home do not contribute to the disparity between men and women in participation, the difference in educational attainment is an important factor.[5] We have noted that men are, on average, better educated than women. While the difference is not enormous, education is so strongly related to participation that the result is a fairly substantial increase in the gender disparity in participation. A small compensatory effect derives from the fact that women were somewhat more likely to report having been active—particularly in clubs—while in high school.

ADULT INSTITUTIONS: WORK, ORGANIZATIONS, CHURCHES

These institutions, which have occupied so much of our attention, play a significant role in the participation gap between women and

---

5. We constructed several scales. One, the sum of measures of mother's political activity, father's political activity, and political discussion at home, measures the respondent's political environment at age sixteen. Another, which combines aspects of activity in high school, is the sum of activity in school clubs and school government.

On the effects of parental activity and school participation on later political activity, see M. Kent Jennings, "Participation as Viewed through the Lens of the Political Socialization Study" (paper presented at the conference on "Political Participation: Building a Research Agenda," Center for the Study of Democratic Politics, Princeton University, October 2000).

men. In order to highlight the differences among institutions in their impact on participation, we have combined the measures of skills and recruitment into a single measure for each of the three institutions: that is, we have added together skills and recruitment on the job, in organizations, and in church to create separate summary measures of the factors acquired in each institution.[6]

The left-hand pair of columns in Table 10.5, which present a transformed version of familiar data, show that men have a substantial edge for participatory factors acquired on the job, an edge that derives from both higher levels of work force participation and a disproportionate share of the kinds of jobs that provide opportunities for the exercise of skills.

The pattern in the data in the next two columns, which show the effects of these factors on participation, is striking. The fact that, within any institutional domain, the coefficients measuring the effects of the participatory factors are not significantly different for women and men indicates that, at any particular level of institutional factors, women and men get the same boost toward political activity. What matters is not the differences between men and women, but the differences among institutional domains. Participatory factors acquired in church have a more substantial payoff for activity. Nevertheless, when we consider the next pair of columns, we see that because the workplace is such a rich venue for the acquisition of participatory factors, especially civic skills, it contributes strongly to participatory outcomes.

In the right-hand column we see how these complex processes work together to widen the gender gap in political participation. Men's advantage in terms of the level of factors acquired in the workplace translates into a substantial widening of the participation gap. We might have expected women's greater religious commitment to have a compensatory effect on the gender gap in activity. However, women's religious activity yields no significant

---

6. This strategy entails the possibly unwarranted assumption that skills and recruitment requests function the same way in fostering participation and, therefore, can be added together.

The summary scales are weighted to take account of the fact that the maximum number of skills exercised in each domain is 4 and the maximum number of institutionally based requests in each domain is 2. To compensate, each request is given twice the weight of each skill in constructing the scale.

advantage in terms of participatory factors. Thus although involvement in religious institutions has a participatory payoff for women, there is a payoff for men as well. The cumulative effect of the three institutions is a fairly substantial boost in activity for both women and men but an even larger one for men than for women.

In Chapter 8 we raised the concern that what we are construing as the result of institutional processes is really the result of selection processes such that those who end up in the work force, in non-political organizations, or in religious institutions are doers, individuals with an innate propensity to become active. Our results put that worry to rest. We have seen that activity in high school is a powerful predictor of organizational and religious affiliation, but is not related to work force participation. If what really matters is not institutional effect, but instead a predisposition to activity, then we would expect participatory factors acquired in organizations or at church to play a larger role in facilitating political participation than those acquired on the job. In fact, factors derived from the three sets of institutions operate in the same way to generate participation—suggesting that it is not simply some unmeasured taste for various kinds of activity that explains political participation.

AVAILABLE TIME

In our earlier research we approached the question of the relationship between leisure and political activity with contradictory expectations. On one hand, given the constraints on available time, we would expect that time already committed to other activities would diminish time devoted to politics and that the busiest people at work and at home would not have time left over for political participation. On the other, there is obvious wisdom in the adage "If you want something done, ask a busy person." In fact, when we undertook systematic analysis of the data, we found that leisure—that is, the time remaining after taking account of the time spent on work, school, and necessary tasks at home—is not related to political participation.[7] Given the differentiated patterns of

---

7. Sidney Verba, Kay Lehman Schlozman, and Henry Brady, *Voice and Equality: Civic*

men's and women's lives, however, we were interested to find out whether this result obtains for both women and men. It does. Not only do men and women command, on average, equal amounts of leisure, but leisure has no systematic impact on political participation for either group. Although we tried many specifications including interactive models, we were unable to find a relationship between available time and political activity.

INCOME

Income differences have only a relatively small impact on the gender gap in participation. Family income has a strong effect on activity, but the difference in average family income for men and women is not large. There is a large and significant gender disparity when it comes to the respondent's own earnings, but this factor has no additional effect on participation over and above family income. What counts for activity is the family income, not what the individual brings in on his or her own.

NON-POLITICAL INSTITUTIONS: THE BOTTOM LINE

The last column of Table 10.5, which records the difference in the extent to which each of these factors augments the participation of men and women, summarizes this analysis. Positive numbers indicate that the factor in question confers a participatory advantage on men and widens the gender gap in activity. Negative numbers indicate the opposite. Together these multiple processes give men a differential boost of .15 of a political act. While this is only a small portion of the eight acts in the additive scale, it represents about half the difference in participation between men and women.

EXPERIENCES WITH DISCRIMINATION

The analysis presented on Table 10.5 contains one other variable that enhances participation, at least for women: experiences with discrimination on the basis of gender. As we have seen, women are much more likely than men to perceive that they have been the objects of bias. And for women, but not for men, this perception is associated with higher levels of political activity. The result is

Voluntarism in American Politics (Cambridge: Harvard University Press, 1995), pp. 350–368.

that experiences with discrimination would seem to narrow the gender gap in political participation almost as much as job factors widen it.

It is ironic that what we can only assume to be negative experiences with discrimination provide women with their largest positive participatory boost compared with men. All of the other participatory factors can reasonably be considered benefits of institutional involvement. One becomes better off in various ways, not just more active in politics, by virtue of being richer, better educated, or more skilled. It is difficult to consider experiencing gender discrimination to be an advantage. Furthermore, although we cannot measure it, gender discrimination also has the contradictory effect of diminishing the stockpile of work- and church-based participatory resources. That is, while the recognition that one has been the object of discrimination may enhance participation, the missed opportunities for occupational advancement or church leadership that are the result of discrimination imply forgone participatory resources. We have no way to assess the net impact.

UNDERSTANDING THE GENDER GAP IN ACTIVITY

We are now in a position to summarize what we have learned from the complex analysis in Table 10.5 about the sources of the gender gap in participation. Before we turn to that task, it is important to recognize that explaining the gender gap in participation is a different enterprise from explaining participation. The data in Table 10.5 also tell us a great deal about the process by which individuals come to be politically active. Scanning the third set of columns in Table 10.5 helps us to understand the relative weight of various factors in generating participation: these data demonstrate the primacy of education among participatory factors; they also show the significance of adult institutions in the participatory process; and they make clear that two factors we had anticipated to be important—leisure time and the respondent's own earnings—do not play a role in fostering activity.

For a factor to contribute to the gender gap in participation, however, not only must it be among the factors that facilitate participation, but there must be a significant gender difference in either the *level* or the *effect*—or both—of that factor. That is, there must be a disparity in the endowments of men and women with respect to that factor or in the extent to which that factor has a participatory payoff or both. If there is no difference in either level or effect, then the factor does not contribute to the gender gap in participation, even if it has substantial consequences for participation. We can illustrate this by considering, once again, political experiences at home during the high school years. Growing up in a household with politically active parents who discussed politics regularly has a significant impact on later political activity. However, since women and men do not differ in their early political experiences (level) and since those experiences give the same boost to men's and women's activity (effect), early political experiences do not contribute to the gender gap in participation—much as they do contribute to participation.

Our central finding—that gender differences in participation are the result of disparities in the stockpile of factors that facilitate participation, not of gender differences in the way participatory factors are converted into activity—amplifies in an important way our understanding of how non-political institutions create gender differences in politics. Table 10.5 shows a number of significant differences between women and men in the level of factors they possess, but only one significant difference in how those factors produce participation. Increments to the reserves of participatory factors—whether more education, income, or the civic skills and requests for activity derived from involvements on the job, in organizations, or in church—foster activity for women and men in essentially the same way. What counts is the size of those reserves.

Men's advantage with respect to institutionally based factors explains about half of the gap in participation. The explained part of the gap results from men's higher levels of income and, especially, education as well as from institutional factors gained at work. Women gain a slight compensatory advantage from their higher levels of activity in high school. Women also reclaim some of the lost ground through the "benefit" of experiencing discrimination on the basis of gender—although we cannot measure the extent to which those experiences simultaneously erode participatory resources. Experiencing discrimination is the only variable for which both level and effect make a difference. Not only are women more likely than men to report having experienced discrimination, but that experience boosts women's activity but not men's.

Of Time and Participation

We have seen that, contrary to expectations, the overall availability of free time does not have implications for political participation. However, given that women and men devote their time to such different pursuits, we were interested to investigate further. We wanted to probe whether different kinds of committed time have an impact on time devoted to politics for women and men. Does time spent at home somehow have different consequences for participation than time spent at work? Moreover, we were curious whether time given to other non-political forms of voluntary activity, whether religious or secular, would enhance or diminish the time contributed to politics, again for women or men.

In Table 10.6, we report the results of a regression analysis designed to investigate these relationships. The dependent variable is the total number of hours per week that our respondents report giving to political matters (to campaigning and community activity). The explanatory variables in which we are interested are measures of rival demands on time: time spent on obligatory activities at work and at home as well as time spent on voluntary activity in non-political organizations and religious institutions. We also include in the analysis a familiar array of other attributes.

The results indicate that neither time devoted to obligatory commitments on the job or at home nor the time given to voluntary activity in organizations or at church diminishes the time given to politics. This finding holds for women and for men. Since we often hear that the combined demands of household chores and working hours make it impossible to find time for voluntary activity, especially for women with families and full-time jobs, the results in Table 10.6 deserve to be underlined.

In short, time given to political activity is constrained neither by obligations to other activities nor by voluntary time given to other activities. Voluntary activity in secular and religious non-political domains is compatible with activity in politics.

Table 10.6 Effect of Obligated Hours and Hours Volunteered for Other Purposes on Hours Given to Politics[a]

	Women	Men
Effect of		
Hours of Housework	0.31	0.23
Hours on Job	0.02	−0.56
Hours to Organization	2.85	1.87
Hours to Church	1.59	0.79

Source: Citizen Participation Study—Main Survey.

a. Unstandardized regression coefficients, with political exposure at home, education, high school activity, family income, own income, working, organizational and church affiliation, sex discrimination, age, and age over 65 in the equation.

*Coefficient significant at <.05.

**Coefficient significant at <.01.

***Coefficient significant at <.001.

⇔ Difference in the coefficients for men and women is significant at <.05 (by t-test) or one coefficient is significant at <.05 and the other is not.

Political Contributions

The continuing outcry over the need to do something about campaign finance reflects the distinctive properties of political contributions as a form of political input: they can vary tremendously in size, and the political significance of a contribution is a function of its size. One of the most striking findings to emerge from Chapter 3 is the gender difference in making political contributions. Women are not only less likely than men to make political donations, but among givers, they write smaller checks than men do. This pattern obtains for contributions to charity and churches as well: for all three domains, when men make donations, they are more generous in the amounts they give. In light of these regularities, we were curious to assess whether the institutional model we applied to overall political activity in Table 10.5 can tell us anything about the process of contributing and the gender gap in donations.

The protestations of sanctimonious political candidates to the contrary, it matters not only whether someone makes a contribution but whether the check is big or small. Because the factors that

Table 10.7 Participation Factors and Amount of Money to Politics: An Outcomes Model (among those who made a contribution)[a]

	Level of Factor		Effect of Factor		Overall Donation		Contribution to Gap in Donations
	Women	Men	Women	Men	Women	Men	
HOME AND EDUCATION							
Home Politics	.24	.24	91	99	0	0	
Education	.38 ⇔	.42	87	10	0	0	
Experience in School	.37 ⇔	.34	118	84	0	0	
ADULT INSTITUTIONAL EFFECTS							
Job Factors	.17 ⇔	.26	−132	22	0	0	
Organization Factors	.10	.11	101	89	0	0	
Church Factors	.13	.12	−81	82	0	0	
TIME AND INCOME							
Available Time	.61	.61	6	720	0	0	0
Family Income	.17 ⇔	.18	1139***	1454***	221	233	+13
Own Income	.05 ⇔	.13	173 ⇔	1107***	0	144	+144
DISCRIMINATION							
Gender Bias	.11 ⇔	.06	77	72	0	0	
Constant	1	1	−187	−536	0	0	
Total Difference Due to the Level and Effects of Participatory Factors							+157

Source: Citizen Participation Study—Main Survey.

a. Age in equation as control.

*Coefficient significant at <.05.

**Coefficient significant at <.01.

***Coefficient significant at <.001.

⇔ Difference is significant at <.05 or one coefficient is significant at <.05 and the other is not.

affect whether to give at all might differ from the factors that predict how much is given, we model the process of contributing as a
two-stage process. First, we consider what has an impact on the
decision to donate. Then, for those who have contributed, we
present an outcomes analysis, indicating the impact of various of
the participatory factors on the size of the contribution and on the
disparity in what women and men give.

With respect to the likelihood of making a political contribution, not only are the factors that foster contributions similar to
those that facilitate overall participation but, by and large, these
factors work similarly for women and men.[8] As we might expect,
when it comes to making a donation, the single most important
factor is family income. Family political background and education also play a role for both men and, especially, women. We do
find a gender difference in the effects of adult institutional factors.
Factors acquired in the three institutional domains increase the
likelihood of contributing for men, but not women. It is noteworthy that exposure to gender bias also raises the likelihood that a
woman will make a political contribution.

Of course, it is not simply giving but the size of the contribution
that counts. Table 10.7 presents the results of an outcomes analysis—parallel to that reported on Table 10.5—in which we predict
the amount given by those who contributed at least some money
to a political campaign or cause. Our purpose, once again, is to ascertain how gender differences in the level and effect of participatory factors work together to produce a gender gap in activity, in
this case the disparity in the magnitude of contributions. In contrast to overall political activity or the decision to make a contribution, for which many factors are relevant, only two factors
make a difference for how much is contributed. As has been
shown elsewhere, family income is the single most important de-
terminant of political contributions.[9] Raising family income from
the lowest to the highest family income category—that is, from under $5,000 to more than $200,000—increases political contribu-

---

8. Full results of the logistical regression are included in Appendix C in Table C10.7.1.
9. See Verba, Schlozman, and Brady, *Voice and Equality*, chap. 11.

tions by more than $1,000 for both women and men.[10] Since women have somewhat smaller family incomes on average than do men, the result from family income is a small advantage, about $13, to men as contributors.[11] In short, it seems that if you want something done in politics, you can ask a busy person; however, if you want a political donation, you should not ask a poor one.

A more substantial portion of the gender gap in contributions can be attributed to the impact of the respondent's own earnings. This case is one of the rare instances in which a participatory factor works differently for men and women. Men not only earn more than women do but, as their earnings rise so, too, do their political contributions. A man in the highest earning category gives, on average, nearly $1,100 more than a man in the lowest earning category.[12] In contrast, women's political contributions do not increase as their earnings rise. The result of this part of the process is to widen the gender gap in political contributions by $144.

The interpretation of the gender difference in the impact of the respondent's own earnings is not obvious. We saw in Chapter 7 that the vast majority of both husbands and wives reported being likely to check with the other before making a major political donation, but that husbands are more likely to control the family finances. The point is sometimes made that, contrary to the dominant economic model, people do not construe all dollars as equivalent and fungible and that, in particular, husbands' and wives' earnings do not figure in the same way in the family exchequer.[13] Furthermore, one study demonstrates that, although wives are quite willing to spend family money on behalf of the household and the children, they feel uncomfortable dipping into the joint

---

10. The coefficients for women and men—the effects measures—on Table 10.6 are different, but the difference is not statistically significant. Thus we consider the average effect of female and male family income on contributions to apply to both women and men.

11. The average income figures in Table 10.3 have been rescaled to vary between 0 and 1. For actual average income figures, see Table 10.3.

12. Those in the lowest category earned less than $1,000 in the year preceding the survey; those in the highest earned more than $200,000.

13. See, for example, Viviana A. Rotman Zelizer, *The Social Meaning of Money* (Princeton: Princeton University Press, 1997), chap. 2.

account for themselves.[14] These findings suggest that men and women have somewhat different orientations to money—with potential implications for making contributions. These issues deserve further study.

Psychological Orientations to Politics

Our analysis has illuminated the process by which women and men come to take part in politics and the way institutions shape the gender gap in activity. Overall, our analysis of the role of nonpolitical institutions, starting in Chapter 8, has elaborated the processes of selection into institutions and treatment within institutions that leave in their wake significant differences between men and women in the size and composition of their respective stockpiles of participatory factors. As substantial as are the gender differences in participatory endowments, however, when it comes to the conversion of these factors into activity, the processes are remarkably similar for the two groups. With the exception of the fact that experiences with discrimination on the basis of gender enhance the participation of women but not of men, the factors that foster participation operate in the same way for men and women.

The process we have delineated is one in which no single factor dominates. Instead, the outcome in question, the gender gap in political activity, is the result of several factors, almost all of which operate to widen the disparity in activity. Together, these cumulative inequalities account for about half the participation disparity between women and men.

However, this analysis omitted a set of factors that cannot be linked directly to institutional experiences but that we would presume to be related to participation: measures of psychological involvement with politics, including political interest, political efficacy, and political information; and the group-specific orientation to politics, women's consciousness. We did not include these psychological factors because they differ in important ways from the resource and recruitment factors that formed the backbone of

14. Carole B. Burgoyne, "Money in Marriage: How Patterns of Allocation Both Reflect and Conceal Power," *Sociological Review* 38 (1990): 660.

the outcomes analysis. For one thing, we cannot link the psychological orientations to specific institutional exposures. Political interest or gender consciousness may derive from experiences in non-political institutions, but they may also be influenced in many other ways—for example, by the media or by informal friendship networks. Moreover, we cannot be fully certain of the order of causality. That is, it is difficult to know whether psychological orientations beget political activity or vice versa.[15]

Nevertheless, because they are so obviously related to political participation, we cannot ignore psychological orientations to politics. Table 10.8, which repeats data from Chapter 4, shows that, compared with men, women are less politically engaged: less politically informed, less interested in politics, and less politically efficacious. However, Table 10.8 also shows that a majority of women demonstrate some kind of gender consciousness: 81 percent of women indicated that women have common problems; of those seeing common problems, 78 percent, or 63 percent of all women, indicated that the government ought to help solve these joint problems. Thus we would expect these two sets of orientations to have contradictory effects on the disparity in activity between men and women. While women's lower levels of psychological involvement with politics would be expected to contribute to the participation gap with men, their sense of solidarity with other women and belief that government should respond to women's shared problems would be expected to help to overcome it.

In fact, these political orientations do not have exactly the effects on participation that we had anticipated. We added measures of political interest, information, and efficacy, as well as a measure of women's consciousness, to our overall model of the factors that foster participation. Table 10.9 presents the coefficients for this analysis.[16] As expected, the measures of psychological involvement in politics—interest, efficacy, and information—are strongly asso-

---

15. For discussion of this issue and data that suggest strongly that political interest, information, and efficacy precede participation, see Verba, Schlozman, and Brady, *Voice and Equality*, chap. 12.

16. The model also includes all the factors included in the analysis presented in Table 10.5.

Table 10.8 Psychological Orientations to Politics

	Women		Men
POLITICAL INTEREST			
Very Interested in Politics (Screener)	24%	⇔	29%
Very Interested in National Politics	29%	⇔	38%
Very Interested in Local Politics	21%		22%
POLITICAL INFORMATION			
Mean Number of Correct Answers (out of 10)	4.5	⇔	5.2
Respondent above Average in Political Information (interviewer's rating)	32%	⇔	42%
POLITICAL EFFICACY			
Mean for Efficacy Scale	5.08	⇔	5.45
WOMEN'S CONSCIOUSNESS			
Believe Women Have Problems They Must Solve Jointly	81%		
Believe Government Should Help Solve Joint Problems[a]	78%		

Source: Citizen Participation Study—Main Survey.
a. Among those who say women have problems.
⇔ Difference between women and men is statistically significant at the .05 level.

ciated with activity for both women and men. Just as the importance of religion to the respondent's life turned out in Chapter 9 to be a critical factor in understanding religious participation, orientations such as political interest turn out to be critical in explaining political participation. Contrary to our expectation, however, group consciousness for women has no significant effect on political activity and thus does not act as a counterbalance to women's lower levels of psychological involvement with politics.

The next step is to ascertain the extent to which disparities in psychological involvement in politics can explain that portion of the participatory difference between women and men not explained by institutional effects. When we add measures of political interest, information, and efficacy to our model, we are able to account fully for the disparity in activity between men and women. Table 10.10 presents the results of a series of regressions intended to highlight the magnitude of the gender difference in activity that remains after taking successive sets of factors into account. Because we found so much similarity between women and men in the coefficients measuring the effects of participatory factors, we use a

Table 10.9 The Effect of Psychological Orientations to Politics on Political Activity[a]

	Women	Men
Effect of		
Political Interest	1.25***	1.60***
Political Information	0.97***	0.96***
Political Efficacy	0.68***	1.09***
Women's Consciousness	0.06	

Source: Citizen Participation Study—Main Survey.

a. Unstandardized regression coefficients with political exposure at home, education, high school activity, family income, own income, job factors, organization factors, church factors, sex discrimination, free time, age, and age over 65 in the equation.

*Coefficient significant at <.05.

**Coefficient significant at <.01.

***Coefficient significant at <.001.

⇔ Difference in the coefficients for men and women is significant at <.05 (by *t*-test) or one coefficient is significant at <.05 and the other is not.

Table 10.10 Explaining the Gap in Political Activity[a,b]

The zero-order difference between men and women	−0.31***
With institutional and socioeconomic factors taken into account	−0.22***
With institutional and socioeconomic factors and political engagement taken into account	−0.10

Source: Citizen Participation Study—Main Survey.

a. Negative coefficients mean women are less active.

b. Unstandardized regression coefficients, with political exposure at home, education, high school activity, family income, own income, job factors, organization factors, church factors, free time, age, and age over 65 in the equation.

*Coefficient significant at <.05.

**Coefficient significant at <.01.

***Coefficient significant at <.001.

single regression equation for men and women and allow the coefficient on gender to indicate the size of the residual gap. The first row of numbers in Table 10.10 shows the relationship between gender and activity with nothing else taken into account; the next row, the relationship after controlling for the various measures of institutional resources and recruitment from the outcomes analysis in Table 10.5; and, finally, the bottom row, the relationship after incorporating the measures of political interest, efficacy, and information. Once we take these political orientations into account, the gender gap in participation is reduced to insignificance. In short, by including all the participatory factors—resources, recruitment, and psychological involvement—we solve the riddle of the disparity between men and women in participation.

Nevertheless, in solving one puzzle, we create another. We understand a great deal about the origins of gender differences when it comes to the other participatory factors. We know why, for example, men acquire more skills at work or have higher family incomes. In contrast, the same kinds of analyses do not account for men's greater political interest, information, and efficacy.[17] The enigma of the gender differences in psychological involvement with politics is one to which we shall return.

The Effect of Women's Consciousness: A Further Probe

The fact that women's consciousness—their belief that women have common problems that the government has a responsibility to help solve—has no significant effect on participation seems counterintuitive.[18] The results of previous studies of the relationship between group consciousness and participation have been mixed—with some showing consciousness to have the expected impact on activity and others showing little or no relationship.[19] Still, we wanted to push the analysis further.

---

17. It has been suggested to us that gender differences in political orientations have their origins in women's religiosity. However, when we included various measures of religious commitment in multivariate analyses of the correlates of political interest, efficacy, and information, we could find no evidence that women's religiosity depresses their political engagement.

18. Roberta S. Sigel encourages scholars to pay attention to the priority that members of a disadvantaged group give to their group membership and argues that this is the missing link, the reason why scholars often fail to find relationships between gender consciousness and a range of outcomes. See *Ambition and Accommodation* (Chicago: University of Chicago Press, 1996), p. 127. Were we designing our survey today, we would take her point into account.

19. Analyses of data from the late 1960s suggests that Black consciousness encourages Black political participation (see Sidney Verba and Norman H. Nie, *Participation in America* [New York: Harper and Row, 1972], and Richard D. Shingles, "Black Consciousness and Political Participation: The Missing Link," *American Political Science Review* 75 [1981]: 76–91, as well as the theoretical discussion in Hanes Walton, Jr., *Invisible Politics* [Albany: State University of New York Press, 1985]). Using the 1984 National Black Elec-

We reasoned that group consciousness might operate, not by generating activity, but by channeling activity. That is, gender-conscious women might not be any more active than would be predicted on the basis of characteristics we have already discussed. However, they might direct their activity toward particular kinds of issues. To explore further, we return to the questions about the issues and problems associated with participatory acts. In Chapter 4 we discussed the bundles of issue concerns brought to political activity by various groups and noted that women's political activity is animated by a number of participatory concerns, among them abortion and a set of policy matters related to women's traditional roles as caregivers: issues involving education and children and issues involving basic human need.[20] We also noted how rarely any of a broad category of "women's issues"—including support for women's rights in the workplace or concern about problems

---

tion Study, Clyde Wilcox, "Racial and Gender Consciousness among African-American Women: Sources and Consequences," *Women and Politics* 17 (1997): 73–94, found that race, but not gender, consciousness among Black women led to higher levels of political participation. In contrast, Ardrey's study of Black women's political participation in Raleigh, North Carolina, found that race consciousness did not encourage participation. See Saundra Ardrey, "The Political Behavior of Black Women: Contextual, Structural, and Psychological Factors," in *Black Politics and Black Political Behavior: A Linkage Analysis,* ed. Hanes Walton (Westport, Conn.: Praeger, 1994).

With respect to the association between gender consciousness and action, the results have been mixed, with stronger results coming from data in the 1970s than from later years. Using data from 1972 and 1976, Arthur Miller, Patricia Gurin, Gerald Gurin, and Oksana Malanchuk found that gender consciousness increased women's turnout and affected somewhat their participation in non-electoral activities. See "Group Consciousness and Political Participation," *American Journal of Political Science* 25 (1981): 494–511. Using data from 1972 and 1976, Ethel Klein found that feminist consciousness predicted support for protest activities in *Gender Politics* (Cambridge: Harvard University Press, 1984), p. 136. In her careful examination of the links between gender identification, egalitarianism, and participation, Sue Tolleson Rinehart finds stronger relationships in the earlier years she studies (1972–1980) than in the later years (1984–1988). See *Gender Consciousness and Politics* (New York: Routledge, 1992), pp. 134–139. For evidence from a bivariate analysis that the association between feminist consciousness and participation has weakened significantly since 1972, see M. Margaret Conway, Gertrude A. Steuernagel, and David W. Ahern, *Women and Political Participation* (Washington, D.C.: CQ Press, 1977), pp. 88–91. For an interesting analysis of the 1992 election, see Virginia Sapiro with Pamela Johnston Conover, "The Variable Gender Basis of Electoral Politics," *British Journal of Political Science* 27 (1997): 497–523. For a helpful review of much of this literature, see Janet Flammang, *Women's Political Voice* (Philadelphia: Temple University Press, 1997), pp. 116–119.

20. See Chapter 4 for definitions of these issues.

such as rape or domestic violence—were raised in connection with activity.

Table 10.11 presents data for women on the association between gender consciousness and participation animated by concern about these issues—with other factors taken into account. Group-conscious women are no more active than we would expect on the basis of their other characteristics when it comes to participation directed at issues involving either children and education or basic human needs. In contrast, although very few women were active on behalf of issues affecting women, gender-conscious women are more likely to participate on these issues. With respect to abortion, the pattern is particularly complicated. When we consider abortion activity in general—that is, on either side of the dispute—we find a pattern similar to that for activity on children, education, and human needs. Consciousness plays no role. However, we can take the analysis one step further. When we separate abortion activity by the position taken on this contentious issue, we find clear evidence of a relationship between women's consciousness and participation with significant, but opposite, effects for pro-choice and pro-life activity. With other factors taken into account, gender-conscious women are significantly more likely to en-

Table 10.11 Effect of Gender Consciousness on Women's Issue-Based Activity[a,b]

Education	−0.04
Children	0.02
Basic Human Needs	0.04
Women's Issues	0.03**
Abortion	0.00
Abortion (pro-choice)	0.08***
Abortion (pro-life)	−0.08**

Source: Citizen Participation Study—Main Survey.

a. Model included women only.

b. Unstandardized regression coefficients, with political exposure at home, education, high school activity, family income, own income, job factors, organization factors, church factors, free time, sex discrimination, political interest, political efficacy, political information, age, and age over 65 in the equation.

*Coefficient significant at <.05.

**Coefficient significant at <.01.

***Coefficient significant at <.001.

gage in pro-choice activity and significantly less likely to engage in pro-life activity. Thus the findings about abortion activity provide even sharper evidence for the specificity of the effects of consciousness in channeling political participation.

These data demonstrate the special character of women's consciousness as a participatory factor. The participatory factors at the heart of our model—for example, civic skills, requests for activity, or political interest—are all issue-neutral and can be harnessed to the pursuit of any policy goal. In contrast to the other participatory factors that figure so importantly in our analysis, gender consciousness for women is linked to particular issue content and, in the case of abortion, to activity on a particular side of a deeply contested issue. If we had many more respondents—and thus many more cases of activity animated by issues that are only infrequently the objects of participatory attention—we could refine this analysis further and elaborate the policy concerns on behalf of which gender-conscious women are active. As it is, our analysis provides strong evidence of the way that women's consciousness directs political activity.

Conclusion

We began this chapter with a seemingly simple question: what explains the difference between women and men in political activity? We have answered the question, but our answer has not been a simple one. Like many outcomes in the social world, the gender gap in participation has no single cause. Instead, it results from women's cumulative deficits with respect to an array of factors that facilitate activity—resources, recruitment, and psychological involvement with politics, all of them contributing in some measure to the disparity in participation between men and women. And the multiple causes that contribute to the creation of the participation gap between men and women have their roots in many aspects of experience that differentiate the lives of males and females in American society. Among them are unequal access to the highest levels of education, traditional gender roles that impel fathers into the workplace and keep mothers at home, discrimination against women on the job, and women's greater involvement in religious life and men's greater involvement in political life.

In another sense, however, our analysis might have been much more complicated. Our method allowed for the possibility that the factors that foster participation might work differently for men and women in producing participatory outcomes. In fact, there are no important gender differences in the process that produces political activity. Instead, the gender gap in activity results from the cumulative advantages that men accrue earlier in the process that leave them with a larger stockpile of participatory assets to bring to political life. It is men's advantage with respect to most of the factors that foster activity, not any distinctive capacity to use those factors, that is responsible for their higher level of political participation.

11

Gender, Race or Ethnicity,
and Participation

Our inquiry into gender differences in civic activity has been informed by our understanding that we must not reify the distinction between men and women. Women differ among themselves—and men differ among themselves—in countless ways that have consequences both for their propensity to be active in politics and for political conflict in America. In fact, the differences among men, or among women, are often more significant either for political participation or for public controversy than are the differences between women and men. So far, we have incorporated into our analysis diversity along many lines—among them, education and income, experiences on the job, religious commitment, and activity in the non-political institutions of adult life. However, we have neglected one of the most enduring and important sources of social and political division in America, race or ethnicity. In this chapter we train our attention on the groups at the intersection of two important axes of cleavage in American politics, on one hand, race or ethnicity and, on the other, gender: African-American women, African-American men, Latinas, Latinos, Anglo-White women, and Anglo-White men.[1]

As we increase the number of groups on which we focus from two to six, we juggle multiple concerns: gender, race or ethnicity,

---

1. As indicated in Chapter 1, we use the term "race or ethnicity" because African-Americans are usually referred to as a racial group and Latinos as an ethnic group. The racial or ethnic groups are defined on the basis of self-identifications. Respondents were asked

and the interaction of these statuses. Our consideration is informed by an understanding that plural minority statuses are not simply additive. As the historian Evelyn Brooks Higginbotham argues, it is impossible to "bifurcate the identity of black women (and indeed of all women) into discrete categories—as if culture, consciousness, and lived experience could at times constitute 'woman' isolated from the contexts of race, class, and sexuality that give form and content to the particular women we are."[2] Similarly, according to the philosopher Elizabeth V. Spelman, scholars have assumed that "the womanness underneath the Black woman's skin is a white woman's and deep down inside the Latina woman is an Anglo woman waiting to burst through."[3] Analogously, we can extend Spelman's insight by noting that we cannot assume that there is a Black male lurking inside every Black female or a Latino inside each Latina.[4]

Although our task in this chapter is more complex, our inquiry

first whether they considered themselves to be Hispanic or Latino. Then all respondents— regardless of their answer to the first question—were asked their race. The small number who identified themselves both as Latino (or Hispanic or Chicano) and as African-American (or Black) were asked which they considered themselves mostly, Hispanic or Black.

2. Evelyn Brooks Higginbotham, "African-American Women's History and the Metalanguage of Race," in *The Second Signs Reader,* ed. Barbara Laslett and Ruth-Ellen Boetcher (Chicago: University of Chicago Press, 1996), p. 25.

3. Elizabeth V. Spelman, *Inessential Woman: Problems of Exclusion in Feminist Thought* (Boston: Beacon, 1988), p. 13.

4. We have been guided in our understanding of the comparative role of race and gender in politics by Don Herzog, *Poisoning the Minds of the Lower Orders* (Princeton: Princeton University Press, 1998); and Mary R. Jackman, *The Velvet Glove: Paternalism and Conflict in Gender, Class, and Race Relations* (Berkeley: University of California Press, 1994). With respect to intersectionality, we have drawn from bell hooks, *Feminist Theory: From Margin to Center* (Boston: South End, 1984); Patricia Hill-Collins, *Black Feminist Thought* (New York: Routledge, 1990); Evelyn Brooks Higginbotham, "African-American Women's History and the Metalanguage of Race," *Signs* 17 (1992): 251–274; Kimberlé Crenshaw, "Whose Story Is It, Anyway? Feminist and Antiracist Appropriations of Anita Hill," in *Race-ing Justice, En-gendering Power,* ed. Toni Morrison (New York: Pantheon Books, 1992), pp. 402–440; Gail Bederman, *Manliness and Civilization: A Cultural History of Gender and Race in the United States, 1880–1917* (Chicago: University of Chicago Press, 1995); and Ann Laura Stoler, "Carnal Knowledge and Imperial Power," in *Feminism and History,* ed. Joan Wallach Scott (Oxford: Oxford University Press, 1996), pp. 209–266.

replicates the analysis so far.[5] We begin by describing in some detail the differences in political activity across the six groups. The next step is to investigate the distribution of the various participatory factors among the six groups, paying particular attention to how processes of selection into and experiences within the nonpolitical institutions of adult life affect opportunities to exercise civic skills and to be recruited to political activity. Then we undertake an outcomes analysis, parallel to that in Chapter 10, in order to ascertain how group differences in the levels of participatory factors and their effects on political activity operate to produce disparities in political activity among the six groups. Finally, we incorporate political orientations—group consciousness and psychological involvement in politics—into our analysis.

Our results fall into no single pattern and reinforce our understanding that the nature and magnitude of group differences vary across social contexts. With respect to time devoted to paid work and home work, gender differences outweigh differences on the basis of race or ethnicity. When it comes to religious preference, race or ethnicity takes precedence over gender. And in terms of educational attainment, both seem to matter—creating striking differences among the six groups. This variation across contexts underlines the social complexity intrinsic to intersecting identities and makes clear that a research strategy based on making comparisons among groups is in no way incompatible with a recognition of group uniqueness.

Who Is Active?

Previous research, including our own work, has shown that men are more politically active than women and that Anglo-Whites are more active than African-Americans and, especially, Latinos.[6]

---

5. Because this chapter relies so heavily on the methodology developed in Chapter 10 for understanding the origins of gender differences in participation, we strongly urge readers not to read this chapter on its own but rather to read it in tandem with the preceding one.

6. On race or ethnicity with respect to political activity, see, for example, Marvin E. Olsen, "Social and Political Participation of Blacks," *American Sociological Review* 35 (1989): 682–697; Sidney Verba and Norman H. Nie, *Participation in America* (New York: Harper and Row, 1972), chap. 10; Carole Uhlaner, Bruce E. Cain, and D. Roderick

Figure 11.1 shows the differences across the six groups with respect to two summary measures: averages on the eight-point scale of overall political activity and on the amount contributed to political campaigns and causes.[7] The data are easy to summarize: both race or ethnicity and gender play a role. In a pattern that will be repeated over and over with respect to the individual acts, Anglo-White men are the most active, Latina women the least. Overall, Anglo-Whites are more active than African-Americans, who are, in turn, more active than Latinos. Within each group defined by race or ethnicity, women are less active than men. However, the size of the gender gap varies across the groups defined by their race or ethnicity and is widest, by far, among Latinos and narrowest among African-Americans.[8] With respect to political giving,

Kiewiet, "Political Participation of Ethnic Minorities in the 1980s," *Political Behavior* 11 (1989): 195–231; Lawrence Bobo and Frank D. Gilliam, "Race, Sociopolitical Participation, and Black Empowerment," *American Political Science Review* 84 (1990): 377–393; Sidney Verba, Kay Lehman Schlozman, Henry E. Brady, and Norman H. Nie, "Race, Ethnicity, and Political Resources: Participation in the United States," *British Journal of Political Science* 23 (1993): 303–319; and Frederick C. Harris, *Something Within: Religion in African-American Political Activism* (New York: Oxford University Press, 1999).

On the intersection of gender and race with respect to participation, see Sandra Baxter and Marjorie Lansing, *Women and Politics: The Visible Majority*, rev. ed. (Ann Arbor: University of Michigan Press, 1983), chap. 6; Susan Welch and Philip Secret, "Sex, Race, and Political Participation," *Western Political Quarterly* 34 (1981): 5–16; Clare Knoche Fulenwider, "Feminist Ideology and the Political Attitudes and Participation of White and Minority Women," *Western Political Quarterly* 34 (1981): 17–30; Carol Hardy-Fanta, *Latina Politics, Latino Politics: Gender, Culture and Political Participation in Boston* (Philadelphia: Temple University Press, 1993); and Sheila F. Harmon-Martin, "Black Women in Politics: A Research Note," and Saundra Ardrey, "The Political Behavior of Black Women: Contextual, Structural, and Psychological Factors," in *Black Politics and Black Political Behavior: A Linkage Analysis*, ed. Hanes Walton, Jr. (Westport, Conn.: Praeger, 1994). On the puzzle of Asian-American women's relatively low levels of participation, see Jane Junn, "Assimilating or Coloring Participation?: Gender, Race, and Democratic Political Participation," in *Women Transforming Politics*, ed. Cathy J. Cohen, Kathleen B. Jones, and Joan C. Tronto (New York: New York University Press, 1997), pp. 387–397.

7. Note that throughout this chapter we have reversed our usual practice of placing columns of numbers for women on the left and columns of numbers for men on the right. Because they are both the most active and the best endowed with participatory resources of the six groups, we often make comparisons between Anglo-White men and each of the other groups. Hence we place them at the far left.

In addition, as we have in previous chapters where we made comparisons among several groups, we have omitted measures of statistical significance. As will become clear, the differences among the six groups form a consistent pattern.

8. Because non-citizens cannot vote and might otherwise have reason not to take part

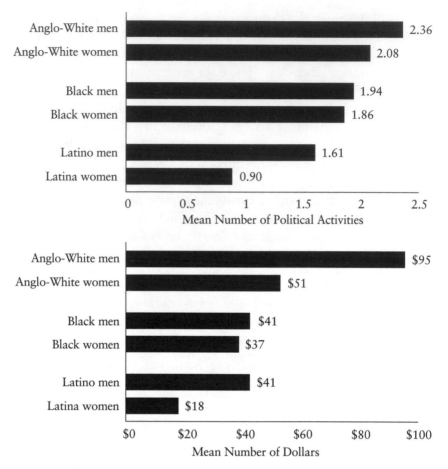

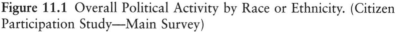

Figure 11.1 Overall Political Activity by Race or Ethnicity. (Citizen Participation Study—Main Survey)

Anglo-White men donate by far the largest amounts, and the gender disparity is widest in absolute dollars among Anglo-Whites, whose levels of contributions are highest, and widest in relative terms among Latinos.

---

politically, it is useful to consider the figures for Latino citizens. Considering only the citizens among Latinos raises their participation, bringing Latino men to an average 1.91 acts, which is very close to Black men, and Latina women to an average of 1.08. Thus the gender gap is even wider among Latino citizens than among all Latinos.

Table 11.1 Political Activity by Gender and Race or Ethnicity[a]

	Anglo-White		Black		Latino	
	Men	Women	Men	Women	Men	Women
Voted in 1988	75%	72%	60%	68%	48%	37%
Worked in a campaign	8%	8%	11%	12%	11%	4%
Made a campaign contribution	28%	22%	21%	22%	19%	5%
Worked informally in the community	19%	16%	19%	18%	14%	10%
Served on a local governing board	5%	4%	3%	3%	5%	3%
Contacted a government official	41%	37%	25%	19%	26%	11%
Attended a protest	5%	6%	11%	8%	5%	4%
Affiliated with a political organization	56%	47%	38%	37%	34%	18%
Mean number of political acts	2.36	2.08	1.96	1.85	1.58	0.89
Participatory deficit[b]		.28	.40	.51	.78	1.47
Mean dollars to politics	$95	$51	$41	$37	$41	$18

Source: Citizen Participation Study—Main Survey.
a. Appendix A contains the valid number of cases for these and other measures used in the tables.
b. Difference between mean activity for group and mean for Anglo-White males.

Table 11.1 breaks the scale for overall activity into its constituent parts. The pattern for several kinds of electoral activity—voting, working in campaigns, and making campaign donations—replicates that for overall activity. Latina women are consistently the least active. Especially noteworthy is the fact that Blacks are, on average, slightly more active than Anglo-Whites in campaigning—a result that may reflect the timing of the survey in the aftermath of the 1988 presidential campaign, during which many Blacks supported Jesse Jackson's bid for the Democratic nomination.

When it comes to various different types of non-electoral activity—getting involved in the local community, contacting a public official, attending a protest, march, or demonstration, and being affiliated with an organization that takes stands in politics—Latina women are, once again, consistently the least active. For contacting and organizational affiliation, the data resemble those for overall activity. In contrast, for informal community activity, neither gender nor race or ethnicity is especially powerful in structuring activity.[9] And Blacks are most likely to report having protested. It is sometimes argued that because women specialize in informal and organizationally based activity, participation data that focus on electoral activity and activity in the context of formal institutions underestimate women's activity. Table 11.1 casts doubt on this contention.

At the bottom of Table 11.1 we repeat the figures for the average activity for each of the six groups and show the participatory deficit for each of the other five groups relative to Anglo-White males. These figures pose the puzzle for the rest of this chapter.[10] In Chapter 10, our goal was to explain the moderate, but not insignificant, gender difference in political activity of about one-third of a political act. When we consider six groups defined by their gender and their race or ethnicity, many of the gaps are substantially wider. Not surprisingly, the difference between Anglo-White women and men in political activity of .28 is about the same as that between all women and all men, .31 of a political act. The disparity in participation between Anglo-White men and each of the other four groups is considerably larger; in fact, for Latinas it is almost five times larger. Our explanation, however, is largely the same as that adduced to account for the overall gender gap in participation: disparities in the factors—most importantly, education, income, and experiences in the non-political institutions of adult life—that foster political activity. It should come as no surprise that there are substantial differences among these six groups with respect to these factors.

---

9. The data about informal community involvement amplify the findings in Hardy-Fanta, *Latina Politics, Latino Politics,* on the extent to which Latinas specialize in this kind of political activity. Our national data corroborate that participation in informal efforts to solve local problems occupies an especially large portion of the total bundle of Latina political activity. However, Latinas are not more likely than the members of the other groups to get involved in this particular way; in fact, they barely reach parity with the other groups when it comes to informal activity in the community.

10. This way of posing the issue for this chapter is not meant to imply that Anglo-White males are, in some way, a standard against which the behavior of other groups is to be judged. However, as we made clear in Chapter 1—where we confronted this issue for women and men irrespective of race or ethnicity—we do believe that those who are less active receive less attention and response from public officials and, thus, that disparities in participation matter.

Non-Political Voluntary Activity

Because experiences in the non-political domains of voluntary activity provide such an important part of the background for political participation, we begin our examination of the roots of political activism by reviewing briefly group differences in non-political involvement. We have noted that feminist scholarship has documented a long and vigorous tradition of women's organizations.[11] While organizations have been crucial to the political successes of women, African-American women and, to a lesser extent, Latinas have historically been excluded from the leadership of both the most visible organizations based on gender and the most visible organizations based on race or ethnicity.

Our own data showed that, in contrast to the political arena, men and women do not differ substantially in their affiliations with non-political organizations; nevertheless, quite similar levels of involvement with non-political organizations go hand in hand with an advantage for men when it comes to organization-based civic skills and, especially, requests for activity. The data in Table 11.2 show that the pattern becomes more complicated when we consider all six groups. We see that the rough gender parity reported earlier for affiliation holds only for Anglo-Whites. Among both Blacks and, especially, Latinos, men are more likely to be affiliated with a non-political organization, with the result that, just as in politics, Latinas are the least active group—lagging behind significantly in their involvement. With respect to other measures of activity in non-political organizations, however, the differences among the groups defined by their race or ethnicity are much more substantial and more consistent than the differences between

11. See, for example, Paula Baker, "The Domestication of Politics: Women and American Political Society, 1780–1920," *American Historical Review* 89 (1984): 620–647; Nancy F. Cott, "Across the Great Divide: Women and Politics before and after 1920," in *Women, Politics, and Change*, ed. Louise A. Tilly and Patricia Gurin (New York: Russell Sage Foundation, 1990); and Ann Firor Scott, *Natural Allies: Women's Associations in American History* (Urbana: University of Illinois Press, 1991). On organizations of Black women, see Paula Giddings, *When and Where I Enter: The Impact of Black Women on Race and Sex in America* (New York: Morrow, 1984); and Angela Y. Davis, *Women, Race and Class* (New York: Vintage Books, 1981).

Table 11.2 Secular Activity outside Politics

	Anglo-Whites		Blacks		Latinos	
	Men	Women	Men	Women	Men	Women
NON-POLITICAL ORGANIZATION						
Affiliated	70%	72%	63%	55%	47%	35%
Attended meeting (past twelve months)	38%	41%	33%	34%	22%	16%
Served on board or as officer (past five years)	16%	15%	11%	14%	7%	4%
Mean number of non-political organization affiliations	1.5	1.6	1.1	1.0	.8	.16
Mean civic skills[a]	.67	.65	.54	.48	.32	.21
Mean requests for activity[a]	.19	.17	.14	.14	.10	.04
CHARITY						
Gave time to charity	35%	41%	35%	34%	35%	21%
Gave money to charity	70%	73%	66%	50%	53%	44%
Mean number of hours given to charity[b]	4.45	4.31	5.93	5.23	4.46	6.92
Mean contribution to charity[c]	$348	$256	$178	$174	$148	$195

Source: Citizen Participation Study—Main Survey.

a. Imputed scores for those whose main organization is political but who are affiliated with a non-political organization.

b. Among those who give time.

c. Among those who give money.

men and women. On all the measures—affiliation, attendance at meetings, service on the board or as an officer, and number of organizational affiliations—Anglo-Whites report higher levels of involvement than do African-Americans or, especially, Latinos.

With respect to the acquisition in non-political organizations of factors that facilitate political activity, there is patterning by both gender and race or ethnicity. Overall, Anglo-Whites are the most likely—and Latinos the least likely—to develop civic skills and to receive requests for political participation. Within groups defined by their race or ethnicity, men tend to garner a larger share of the participatory factors acquired in non-political organizations.

These patterns do not hold when we focus explicitly on charitable activity. Although Anglo-Whites are the most likely to give money to charity and Anglo-White men make the largest contributions, otherwise clear distinctions on the basis either of gender or of race or ethnicity do not emerge. It is interesting to note that, when it comes to the amounts donated by those who give time or money to charity, Latinas are not in their usual position. In fact, among those who give time to charity, Latinas give, on average, the most time.

RELIGIOUS ORIENTATIONS AND ACTIVITY IN
RELIGIOUS INSTITUTIONS

Religious institutions have played an especially crucial but complicated role throughout our analysis. With respect to gender, although religious denominations have traditionally discriminated against women in such matters as ordination and denominational leadership, we have seen that women have long been more active than men in religious institutions. With respect to race or ethnicity, the fact that both religious denominations and religious congregations are structured along ethnic lines has inevitable consequences for the distribution of church-based civic skills and recruitment. Black churches are known as being especially effective as politicizing institutions.[12]

In Table 11.3 we consider differences among the six groups with respect to a variety of aspects of religious preferences, orientations, and activity. Although evidence of women's greater religious commitment pervades the data in Table 11.3, including those that show men to be much more likely to say that they have no religion, with respect to denominational preference, it is race or ethnicity rather than gender that matters. While respondents from all groups are overwhelmingly Christian, African-Americans are

---

12. On the role of politicized Black churches in fostering political participation, see Hanes Walton, Jr., *Invisible Politics: Black Political Behavior* (Albany: State University of New York Press, 1985); Katherine Tate, "Black Political Participation in the 1984 and 1988 Presidential Elections," *American Political Science Review* 85 (1991): 1159–1176; Katherine Tate, *From Protest to Politics: The New Black Voters in American Elections* (Cambridge: Harvard University Press, 1994); Frederick C. Harris, "Something Within: Religion as a Mobilizer of African-American Political Activism," *Journal of Politics* 56 (1994): 42–68; Yvette Alex-Assensoh and Karin Stanford, "Gender, Participation, and the Black Urban Underclass," in *Women Transforming Politics*, ed. Cathy J. Cohen, Kathleen B. Jones, and Joan C. Tronto (New York: New York University Press, 1997), pp. 398–411; Harris, *Something Within*; and Michael Dawson, "Black Visions" (manuscript), n.d.

Table 11.3 Religious Preferences and Activity

	Anglo-Whites		Blacks		Latinos	
	Men	Women	Men	Women	Men	Women
Express a religious preference	90%	96%	89%	96%	89%	95%
Denomination						
Protestant	58%	67%	71%	88%	22%	29%
Mainline	28%	32%	21%	23%	5%	12%
Evangelical	18%	22%	48%	60%	10%	10%
Catholic	27%	26%	12%	4%	64%	66%
Jewish	2%	2%	0%	0%	0%	1%
Other	3%	2%	6%	4%	3%	a
None	10%	4%	11%	4%	10%	5%
	100%	101%	100%	100%	99%	101%
Religious attitudes						
Say religion is very important	46%	65%	70%	81%	60%	58%
Think Bible is God's word	39%	53%	63%	67%	54%	68%
Have had a "born again" experience	30%	36%	47%	61%	26%	34%
Affiliated[b]	58%	74%	64%	81%	52%	69%
Attends religious services						
Never or less than once a year	16%	13%	10%	7%	14%	9%
Weekly or more	28%	40%	32%	44%	29%	35%
Mean weeks per year	23.2	28.1	26.9	33.0	23.6	29.7
Active in a religious institution	21%	29%	23%	38%	18%	20%
Mean number of hours per week given to church work	.90	1.02	1.71	1.72	.88	.67
Served on board or as officer within past five years[c]	26%	20%	33%	33%	15%	12%
Participatory factors						
Mean civic skills	.38	.48	.52	.64	.28	.27
Mean requests for activity	.29	.30	.37	.38	.08	.14

Source: Citizen Participation Study—Main Survey.
a. Less than 1 percent.
b. Among those expressing a preference.
c. Among those affiliated with a religious institution.

overwhelmingly Protestant, Anglo-Whites are majority Protestant, and Latinos are majority Catholic.

When it comes to the distribution of denominational preferences among Protestants, the patterns are especially complex. The recent political visibility of Anglo-White evangelical Protestants may obscure several other important aspects of denominational preference. Because Anglo-Whites are by far the majority group, the modal evangelical Protestant is, indeed, an Anglo-White.[13] In fact, among Protestants, African-Americans and Latinos are much more likely to be evangelicals than are Anglo-Whites. A majority of African-American and Latino Protestants—and a majority of all African-Americans—are evangelical Protestants.[14] Each of these alternative perspectives on the same data tells us something important: that most evangelical Protestants are Anglo-Whites; that most Latinos are not Protestant, but most Latino Protestants are evangelicals; and that most African-Americans are evangelical Protestants.

By and large, the other data in Table 11.3 fall into a consistent pattern, with both gender and race or ethnicity having an impact. With regard to multiple measures, African-Americans show greater religious commitment than do Anglo-Whites or Latinos, and women show greater religious commitment than do men. These patterns hold whether we are focusing upon affiliation with a religious congregation and attendance at services; upon activity in a religious institution—giving time to educational, social, or charitable activities associated with or serving on the board or as an officer of a religious institution; or upon religious attitudes—for example, considering religion to be important in one's life or considering the Bible to be the word of God. Among the religiously active, women are more likely than men to be active within

13. As elsewhere, we consider as mainline all Protestant denominations in the National Council of Churches. For elaboration, see Chapter 3, note 48.

14. The careful reader will note that we were unable to code all Protestants as either mainline or evangelical. Furthermore, in our data, a bare majority of the Latina Protestants who could be coded are actually mainline, not evangelical, Protestants. Because the number of Latina Protestants is quite small, we have chosen not to cite this finding, one that contradicts the widely noted tendency for Latino converts to Protestantism to join evangelical churches.

a religious congregation in each racial or ethnic group. However, among those affiliated with a congregation, men are more likely than women to have served on the board or as officers of the congregation. For this reason, women's advantage when it comes to church-based participatory factors—civic skills and requests for political activity—is less than might have been predicted simply on the basis of their greater religious activity.

The Stockpiles of Participatory Factors

Having reviewed in some detail the voluntary activity of these six groups, we can consider how their non-political experiences are related to group differences in the stockpile of factors that foster political activity.

HOME AND EDUCATION

We begin, as usual, with early experiences at home and school. With respect to exposure to politics—either hearing family discussions about politics or having parents who were politically active—during adolescence, the absence of gender difference that we observed in Chapter 5 obtains only for Anglo-Whites. As shown in Table 11.4, among African-Americans and Latinos, women are less likely to have been exposed to politics as adolescents. Latino men and women were less likely to report politicizing experiences at home, with Latinas substantially less likely than the members of any of the other five groups.

When it comes to an especially powerful predictor of political participation, education, Table 11.4 shows relatively sharp differences among the six groups in terms of the proportions that graduated from high school and from college.[15] Anglo-Whites have higher educational levels than Blacks and, especially, Latinos. Within each of these three groups, men have higher educational

---

15. For a helpful portrait of the changing levels of education among Anglo-White, Black, and Latina women during the 1980s, see Tamara Jones and Alethia Jones, "Women of Color in the Eighties: A Profile Based on Census Data," in *Women Transforming Politics,* ed. Cathy J. Cohen, Kathleen B. Jones, and Joan C. Tronto (New York: New York University Press, 1997), pp. 15–46.

Table 11.4 Participatory Factors Acquired in Family and School

	Anglo-Whites		Blacks		Latinos	
	Men	Women	Men	Women	Men	Women
POLITICAL BACKGROUND						
Mother active in politics[a]	34%	33%	38%	42%	33%	19%
Father active in politics[a]	42%	43%	45%	34%	41%	28%
Frequent political discussions	20%	21%	19%	18%	13%	15%
Mean score family politics	1.77	1.84	1.78	1.61	1.51	1.17
EDUCATION						
No education beyond high school	46%	51%	52%	64%	60%	74%
Graduated from college	30%	24%	16%	14%	12%	6%
"VERY ACTIVE" IN HIGH SCHOOL[b]						
High school government	7%	8%	10%	12%	5%	7%
Clubs and other activities	16%	24%	14%	24%	16%	18%
Sports	35%	19%	51%	28%	46%	22%

Source: Citizen Participation Study—Main Survey.
a. "Very" or "somewhat" active in politics.
b. Among those who attended high school.

levels than women, a gap that is particularly pronounced for Latinos. The familiar pattern does not emerge when it comes to another aspect of educational experiences that is related to subsequent political activity, taking part in student government and other high school clubs and activities. The group differences are quite muted, and African-Americans report relatively high levels of activity.

THE INSTITUTIONAL BASES OF PARTICIPATORY FACTORS
One of our themes has been the consequences for the political participation of men and women of the major adult institutions—the workplace, non-political organizations, and church. In Table 11.5, we present data across all three institutions about group differences in the acquisition of institutionally based participatory factors—both skills and recruitment—including some of the data already reviewed.

The top portion presents data of several kinds about experiences at work. In contrast to religious institutions—for which we

Table 11.5 Institutionally Based Participatory Factors

	Anglo-Whites		Blacks		Latinos	
	Men	Women	Men	Women	Men	Women
WORKPLACE						
Work Force Participation						
Full time	72%	42%	65%	52%	68%	39%
Not employed	24%	42%	28%	40%	22%	51%
Job Level[a]						
Upper (top 2 of 5)	37%	31%	17%	22%	15%	10%
Lower (bottom 2 of 5)	30%	52%	55%	69%	63%	76%
Mean Job Skills	1.8	1.2	1.2	1.0	1.3	0.7
Mean Requests for Activity	.17	.16	.16	.14	.19	.05
NON-POLITICAL ORGANIZATIONS						
Affiliated	70%	72%	63%	55%	47%	35%
Mean Organization Skills	.66	.65	.54	.48	.32	.21
Mean Requests for Activity	.19	.17	.14	.14	.10	.04
RELIGIOUS INSTITUTIONS						
Belong to a Church	58%	74%	64%	81%	52%	69%
Mean Church Skills	.38	.48	.52	.64	.28	.27
Mean Requests for Activity	.29	.30	.37	.38	.08	.14
SUMMARY SCORE: ALL INSTITUTIONS						
Mean Skills	2.82	2.29	2.29	2.16	1.94	1.14
Requests for Activity	.66	.63	.67	.67	.38	.23

Source: Citizen Participation Study—Main Survey.
a. Among those in work force.

saw consistent patterns of greater religious commitment and activity among African-Americans and among women no matter what the particular measure—the relevance of gender or race or ethnicity varies depending upon which aspect of workplace involvement is being considered. With respect to work force participation, the data in Table 11.5 show substantial differences on the basis of gender and limited ones on the basis of race or ethnicity: regardless of race or ethnicity, men are more likely than women to be employed, especially full time. Among women, Latinas are the least likely to be in the work force.[16]

---

16. Historically, Black women have had much higher rates of work force participation than have Anglo-White women. Census data show that recent decades have witnessed con-

Not all jobs are the same. Among workers, there are differences on the basis of both gender and race or ethnicity in the amount of education and on-the-job training required for particular jobs: in general, Latinos and African-Americans are in lower-status jobs than Anglo-Whites, and women are in lower-status jobs than men, with the result that, compared with Latinas, Anglo-White males are nearly four times as likely to have jobs in one of the two highest job-level categories.[17] Note that, among African-Americans, women are more likely than men to be in both the top two and the bottom two job levels.

These processes of differential work force participation and differential assignment to jobs yield group differences in all three workplace-based participatory factors: job-based civic skills, requests for political activity, and as shown in Table 11.6, earnings. When all respondents are considered, both gender and race or ethnicity play a role, with the result that Anglo-White males are decisively advantaged and Latinas decisively disadvantaged when it comes to all these work-based factors.

Table 11.5 also presents information that we have already seen about participatory factors acquired in non-political associations and religious institutions. Although the patterns of gender and racial or ethnic difference are less consistent and less pronounced for organizations than for the workplace, once again the Anglo-White males and Latina females anchor the extremes. As we have seen, the usual patterns do not emerge for involvement in religious institutions. In contrast to organizational affiliation, religious involvement tends not to follow the lines of socioeconomic stratification. However, women tend to be more involved with churches than men, and Blacks somewhat more involved than Anglo-Whites or, especially, Latinos. The result is a very different distribution of in-

---

vergence and the disappearance of the racial gap in female work force participation in the early 1990s. Census data also confirm that Latinas have lower work force participation rates but show a smaller disparity than emerges in our data. See U.S. Bureau of the Census, *Statistical Abstract of the United States: 1996*, 116th ed. (Washington, D.C.: U.S. Government Printing Office, 1996), p. 393.

17. The job-level variable, a five-category variable measuring the respondents' assessments of the amount of education and on-the-job training required to do their jobs, is described in Chapter 6, note 8.

Table 11.6 Mean Time and Income

	Anglo-Whites		Blacks		Latinos	
	Men	Women	Men	Women	Men	Women
TIME						
Hours Working	7.7	5.0	7.3	5.6	7.6	4.4
Hours of Housework	2.6	5.1	3.2	5.1	3.1	6.4
Hours of Free Time	6.6	6.7	6.2	6.3	5.8	5.7
MONEY[a]						
Family Income	$46	$39	$35	$26	$33	$25
Earnings	$27	$11	$18	$11	$20	$7
Earnings (among working)	$35	$18	$24	$18	$24	$13

Source: Citizen Participation Study—Main Survey.
a. In $1000s.

stitutionally based participatory factors: African-Americans, both female and male, are the most likely both to develop civic skills and to be recruited to political activity in church, and the usual predominance of Anglo-White men does not obtain.

At the bottom of Table 11.5, we summarize the results of these complex processes of the acquisition of participatory factors in institutions. Not surprisingly, there are group differences along the lines of both gender and race or ethnicity with respect to the average number of civic skills practiced and requests for activity received on the job, in organizations, and at church. In terms of skills, Anglo-White men report more than twice as many as do Latina women. Blacks and Anglo-Whites are more likely to be recruited than Latinos.[18]

---

18. We also undertook multivariate analyses in order to determine the extent to which the relationships just discussed are explained by group differences in education, age, or for organization- and church-related variables, job level. Among those in the work force, men—especially Anglo-White men—have a significant advantage, beyond what would be expected on the basis of their age and education, in getting the kinds of jobs that require high levels of education and on-the-job training and that provide opportunities for the development of civic skills. Although race or ethnicity and gender figure quite importantly in who gets high-level jobs, once individuals are sorted into particular jobs, group differences matter less for opportunities to acquire skills. In terms of religious institutions, Blacks and women are significantly more likely to belong to religious institutions even when age, education, income, and job level are taken into account. Among those affiliated with a church,

TIME AND MONEY

We have already seen that available time is less relevant to explaining the gender gap in political activity than we might have expected. Nevertheless, we wanted to consider these issues with respect to the six groups as defined by their gender and their race or ethnicity. The data in Table 11.6 indicate that it is gender rather than race or ethnicity that is more strongly related to how time is used. Within each racial or ethnic group, men work longer hours on the job, women longer hours at home.[19] Within each of these three groups, neither women nor men are privileged with respect to free time.

Chapter 10 made clear that income figures importantly in participation—with respect both to overall activity and, especially, to the size of financial contributions. Table 11.6 indicates, not surprisingly, that income is structured both by gender and by race or ethnicity. In terms of family income and, especially, individual earnings, women have, on average, lower incomes than men, and Blacks and Latinos have lower incomes than Anglo-Whites, with Latinas, once again, particularly deprived. Although these findings contain no real surprises, they are fraught with potential implications for political activity.

EXPERIENCES OF BIAS

We mentioned in the previous chapter that, with one exception, all of the factors that foster participation—education, income, skills and the like—are benefits in and of themselves. The single exception is the presumably negative experience of being the object of discrimination, an experience that women are more likely than men to have. We now extend our analysis—considering bias on the basis of not only gender but also race or ethnicity for all six

---

African-Americans are also more likely to acquire participatory factors there—beyond what would be expected on the basis of their other demographic characteristics. Full data are available from the authors.

19. In their studies of time use, John P. Robinson and Geoffrey Godbey, *Time for Life: The Surprising Ways Americans Use Their Time* (University Park: Pennsylvania State University Press, 1997), chap. 15, find that African-Americans have, on average, slightly more free time than do Whites. Unfortunately, however, they do not consider either Latinos or gender differences within groups defined by race.

Table 11.7 Reports of Experiences with Discrimination

	Anglo-Whites		Blacks		Latinos	
	Men	Women	Men	Women	Men	Women
On the Basis of Race or Ethnicity	7%	3%	30%	20%	16%	19%
On the Basis of Sex	6	11	6	10	5	7
On the Basis of Either or Both	9	13	31	23	19	21

Source: Citizen Participation Study—Main Survey.

groups. All respondents were asked whether they had experienced bias or prejudice on the basis of their sex or on the basis of their race or ethnic background. Table 11.7, which repeats data from Chapter 4, shows, not unexpectedly, that Latinos and, especially, African-Americans are more likely than Anglo-Whites to report having experienced bias on the basis of race or ethnicity. In contrast, there are, overall, fewer reports of gender bias than of racial or ethnic bias. Women are much more likely than men to say that they had been subjected to gender discrimination. Among women, Latinas are the least likely to report gender discrimination, and Black and Latina women each report more than twice as much racial or ethnic bias as gender bias.

ORIENTATIONS TO POLITICS

Political activity is fostered not only by resources and recruitment but also by various orientations to politics. Table 11.8 compares the six groups in terms of several familiar measures of psychological involvement with politics—political interest, efficacy, and information—and a summary measure. We see a familiar pattern: those advantaged with respect to resources are more advantaged in terms of psychological involvement as well, and Latinas are consistently the least psychologically engaged with politics. The group differences are especially notable when it comes to political information—a measure that is objective rather than subjective.[20]

---

20. Multivariate analyses demonstrate that, although education is perhaps the most potent predictor of various aspects of psychological involvement with politics, especially political information, a large number of the differences found in Table 11.9 are significant even when education is taken into account. These analyses are available from the authors.

Table 11.8 Political Engagement

	Anglo-Whites		Blacks		Latinos	
	Men	Women	Men	Women	Men	Women
Mean Political Interest	6.5	6.2	6.6	5.8	5.5	4.4
Very interested in national politics	38%	31%	40%	25%	29%	17%
Very interested in local politics	21%	22%	31%	27%	19%	9%
Mean Political Efficacy	5.5	5.2	4.9	4.7	5.2	4.0
Mean Political Information	5.3	4.8	4.1	3.8	4.2	3.0
Mean civic knowledge	3.1	2.8	2.6	2.5	2.8	2.2
Mean knowledge of names	2.3	2.0	1.5	1.2	1.4	0.8
Mean Political Engagement	5.3	4.9	4.7	4.3	4.5	3.3

Source: Citizen Participation Study—Main Survey.

Table 11.9 presents data, some of which we saw in Chapter 4, about a potential mechanism for overcoming group disadvantage with respect to political activity, group consciousness.[21] The table shows the proportion of respondents in the six groups who reported that the government ought to provide special programs to help three different disadvantaged groups: Blacks, Latinos, and women. These data allow us to compare the views of beneficiaries of these programs with the views of other groups and to consider, in particular, the views of the two groups potentially disadvantaged by their gender and their race or ethnicity, African-American and Latina women. The data are quite striking: the driving force appears to be race or ethnicity rather than gender. Blacks and Latinos, whether male or female, are much more supportive of programs to assist the disadvantaged, even disadvantaged groups of which they are not a part. Furthermore, male and female members

---

21. On the consequences for political behavior of group consciousness among Blacks, see, for example, Richard Shingles, "Black Consciousness and Political Participation: The Missing Link," *American Political Science Review* 75 (1981): 76–91; Arthur H. Miller, Patricia Gurin, Gerald Gurin, and Oksana Malanchuk, "Group Consciousness and Political Participation," *American Journal of Political Science* 25 (1981): 494–511; Walton, *Invisible Politics;* Clyde Wilcox, "Race, Gender Role Attitudes, and Support for Feminism," *Western Political Quarterly* 43 (1990): 113–121. For an alternative view with respect to Latinas, see Carol Hardy-Fanta, "Latina Women and Political Consciousness," in *Women Transforming Politics,* ed. Cathy J. Cohen, Kathleen B. Jones, and Joan C. Tronto (New York: New York University Press, 1997), pp. 223–237.

Table 11.9 Group-Based Political Orientations by Gender and Race or Ethnicity

A. Support Government Help to Various Groups[a]

	Anglo-Whites		Blacks		Latinos	
	Men	Women	Men	Women	Men	Women
Government Should Help Blacks	18%	17%	38%	42%	34%	34%
Government Should Help Latinos	16	14	34	37	42	42
Government Should Help Women	21	23	41	43	45	45

B. Expressions of Group Consciousness by Gender and Race or Ethnicity

	Feel Close to Others in the Group	Believe They Have Problems in Common	Government Should Help[b]
Feel about Blacks			
Black women	15%	86%	89%
Black men	17	88	88
Feel about Latinos			
Latina women	14	82	84
Latino men	14	78	78
Feel about Women			
Anglo-White women	10	81	77
Black women	11	84	86
Latina women	13	77	82

Source: Citizen Participation Study—Main Survey.
a. First 3 points in a 7-point scale.
b. Of those who believe they have problems in common.

of both minority groups are substantially more favorably disposed to programs for women than are Anglo-Whites, whether female or male.

Finally, in the lower portion of Table 11.9, we report data on three measures of group consciousness: whether respondents feel close to other group members; whether they think that there are problems of special concern to group members that they need to work together to solve; and, if so, whether the government should be doing more about these problems. These questions were asked only of African-Americans, Latinos, and women; we have no measures of male or Anglo-White consciousness. In general, with respect to group consciousness as measured here, the similarities across groups are more striking than the differences. Only a modest proportion in each group report feeling particularly close to other group members.[22] In light of the domination of the contemporary women's movement by Anglo-White women, it is striking that African-American women are as likely to say that women have joint problems that government has a responsibility to solve as to say that Blacks have shared problems that government should assist in solving.

From Non-Political Institutions to Political Activity

In the previous chapter, we developed an "outcomes" analysis to trace the origins of the gender gap in participation. The process involved discerning how differences between women and men in the levels and effects of various participatory factors translate into disparities in participation. We have seen that the six groups we are comparing in this chapter differ even more sharply than do women and men in their non-political experiences and in the stockpiles of participatory factors they derive from those experiences. The next step is to put the pieces together in order to see how these differences in participatory factors generate differences in political activity. Although the task is much more complicated now that we are dealing with six groups rather than two, the logic is the same.

STOCKPILES OF PARTICIPATORY FACTORS
In Table 11.10, which presents the data on the level of the various participatory factors at the command of each of the six groups, we have rescaled the variables to vary between 0 and 1 and, in some cases, combined them into indices.[23] In order to highlight significant disparities in the level of participatory factors, we place a " + " or " − " beside any figure that is respectively significantly higher or significantly lower than that for Anglo-White men. Thus

22. In retrospect, we wish that we had asked the ethnic identity questions about nationality sub-groups among Latinos (that is, that we had asked, for example, closeness to "Mexican-Americans," rather than about closeness to "Hispanics"). On this issue, see Rodolfo O. de la Garza et al., *Latino Voices: Mexican, Puerto Rican, and Cuban Perspectives on American Politics* (Boulder: Westview Press, 1992); and *Ignored Voices*, ed. Rodolfo O. de la Garza (Austin: University of Texas, 1987).

23. All variable definitions are the same as those used in Table 10.5.

Table 11.10 Level of Participatory Factors

	Anglo-Whites		Blacks		Latinos	
	Men	Women	Men	Women	Men	Women
HOME AND EDUCATION						
Home Politics	.24	.25	.25	.23	.20⁻	.17⁻
Education	.43	.39⁻	.35⁻	.33⁻	.32⁻	.27⁻
Experience in School	.34	.38⁺	.36	.38	.28⁻	.26⁻
INSTITUTIONAL FACTORS						
Job Factors	.26	.18⁻	.19⁻	.16⁻	.22	.10⁻
Organization Factors	.11	.10	.09	.08⁻	.05⁻	.03⁻
Church Factors	.12	.13	.16⁺	.18⁺	.06⁻	.07⁻
TIME AND INCOME						
Available Time	.61	.61	.60	.60	.59	.59
Family Income	.14	.12⁻	.12⁻	.09⁻	.10⁻	.08⁻
Own Income	.09	.03⁻	.06⁻	.04⁻	.06⁻	.02⁻
EXPERIENCE OF BIAS						
Gender Bias	.06	.11⁺	.06	.09	.05	.07
Race/Ethnic Bias	.07	.03⁻	.29⁺	.20⁺	.16⁺	.19⁺

Source: Citizen Participation Study—Main Survey.

⁻ Significant disadvantage to the group, compared with Anglo-White men. Difference significant at <.05, by *t*-test.

⁺ Significant advantage to the group, compared with Anglo-White men. Difference significant at <.05, by *t*-test.

we can see at a glance the overall shape of the distribution of participatory factors. Scanning across any row shows group differences with respect to a particular factor. Scanning down any column indicates whether a particular group is privileged or deprived with respect to participatory factors. The overall pattern is one of association between disadvantage in participatory factors and being female rather than male, a member of a minority group rather than Anglo-White, or, especially, both.

THE EFFECT OF PARTICIPATORY FACTORS
The next step in seeking the origins of group differences in political activity is to determine the effects of the various factors on political activity. In order to determine these effects, we conducted separate regression analyses for each of the six groups. The resulting unstandardized regression coefficients measure the maximum ef-

fect of the independent variables on the eight-point scale of overall political activity. Because there are six groups (some of which have relatively few cases) and a large number of variables, these analyses produced many numbers. However, the overall finding is clear: the same set of institutional factors, in general, predict political activity across all of the groups.[24] The institutional model we have developed seems to function in the same way for the various groups, and the coefficients for the various factors do not differ substantially from group to group. In short, the factors that foster participation for women and men by and large operate in the same way when we consider groups defined not only by gender but also by race or ethnicity.

UNDERSTANDING DISPARITIES IN ACTIVITY: AN OUTCOMES ANALYSIS

Overall, our story has been of substantial differences among groups in access to participatory factors and substantial similarities among groups in the conversion of participatory factors into activity: the six groups have very different endowments of participatory factors but use these factors in quite similar ways.

We must now take a final step in order to bring together the pieces of our analysis in an account of the origins of group differences in political activity. To do so we calculate a series of "outcome" measures—the product of the level of each factor possessed by the various groups and the effect of the factors on activity. Each outcome measure shows, for each of the six groups, the overall impact on political activity of each of the factors in the analysis.[25]

The results of these complex processes for group differences in participation are shown in Table 11.11. Each of the entries in the table indicates how a factor operates for a particular group to create disparities in participation between that group and the group

---

24. Appendix D contains an explanation of our method and justification for the strategic decisions made. Appendix C contains complete results of these regressions. See Table C11.10.1.

25. As mentioned, the initial analysis, which was conducted for each of the groups separately, demonstrated that there were no significant differences in the magnitude of the effects. On the basis of these findings, we replicated the analysis using separate equations for women and men. The analysis produces many numbers. The data, which are contained in Appendix C, Tables C11.10.1 and C11.11.1, make clear that the same factors matter for participation in all six groups.

Table 11.11 The Source of Group Differences in Political Activity

	Deficit in Activity Relative to Anglo-White Males Resulting from Effects of Participatory Factors				
	Anglo-Whites	Blacks		Latinos	
	Women	Men	Women	Men	Women
HOME AND SCHOOL					
Home Politics	.00	−.01	+.01	+.04	+.06
Education	+.06	+.13	+.16	+.18	+.26
Experience in School	−.03	−.01	−.02	+.03	+.04
INSTITUTIONAL FACTORS					
Job Factors	+.07	+.06	+.09	+.02	+.15
Organization Factors	.00	+.01	+.03	+.06	+.07
Church Factors	.00	−.03	−.06	+.09	+.08
TIME AND INCOME					
Free Time	.00	.00	.00	.00	.00
Family Income	+.05	+.05	+.11	+.09	+.13
Own Income	.00	.00	.00	.00	.00
EXPERIENCE OF BIAS					
Gender Bias	−.06	.00	−.04	.00	−.04
Race or Ethnic Bias	.00	.00	.00	.00	.00
NET EFFECT OF FACTORS	+.09	+.20	+.28	+.51	+.75

Source: Citizen Participation Study—Main Survey.

that is both best endowed with participatory factors and most active, Anglo-White men. The figures are presented as differences between Anglo-White males and each of the other groups. As in Table 10.5, where we presented the results of an outcomes analysis for all men and women, positive numbers indicate an advantage for Anglo-White men and a widening of the disparity in activity. Negative numbers indicate a disadvantage for Anglo-White men and a narrowing of the disparity.

Consider, for example, the impact of education. The entries in the cells demonstrate the fact that education widens the participatory gap with Anglo-White men by .06 acts for Anglo-White women; .13 acts for African-American men; .16 acts for African-American women; .18 acts for Latino men; and .26 acts for Latina women. Note that the operation of church-based factors narrows the disparity in activity with Anglo-White men for African-American men and women but widens it even further for Latinos—both female and male.

Because disparities in participation among the six groups have their origins in differences in participatory endowments rather than in differences in the way that participatory factors translate into activity, the results in Table 11.11 confirm what we learned earlier in the chapter when we considered group differences in levels of participatory factors. Without dwelling on the details of each number in the table, we can highlight the following general findings:

- Women and members of minority groups—African-Americans and, especially, Latinos—are disadvantaged vis-à-vis Anglo-White men; those who are both female and minority are particularly disadvantaged, with Latinas lagging far behind all the other groups.
- Both socioeconomic factors—in particular education, but also family income—and experiences in the non-political institutions of adult life widen the participation gap between Anglo-White males and the other groups.
- For Black men and women, church involvement narrows the disparity in activity somewhat; for Latinos and Latinas, both because they are not especially religiously active and because even if they are, they tend to be affiliated with less skill-endowing Catholic churches, religious involvement does not have this outcome.
- Exposure to gender bias provides a small compensatory boost for women. Exposure to racial bias, however, does not have an analogous participatory payoff. Since discrimination can have negative consequences for the acquisition of participatory resources in various social institutions, the net effect of racial or ethnic discrimination would be to depress political activity.

A Note on Political Orientations

As shown in Table 11.11, a model based on resources and recruitment helps to account for the differences among the six groups at the intersection of gender and race or ethnicity. However, that model omitted a set of factors that we found in Chapter 10 to be strongly associated with political participation, orientations to politics. In order to see how incorporating political orientations into the analysis alters the disparities in political activity among the groups, we follow the same strategy used in the previous chapter. We have already seen in Tables 11.8 and 11.9 that there are substantial differences among the six groups when it comes to two kinds of political orientations: psychological involvement in politics—as measured by political interest, efficacy, and information; and group consciousness—gender consciousness for women, race consciousness for Blacks, and ethnic consciousness for Latinos. Table 11.12.A presents the coefficients for the impact on participation of these political orientations. As in Chapter 10, we see that, with resources and recruitment taken into account, all three measures of psychological involvement in politics are strongly related to participation, but consciousness is not. In light of our concerns about the absence of a relationship between gender consciousness and political activity for women, we were interested to note that the results for race or ethnic consciousness parallel those for gender consciousness.

In portion B of the table, we show the results of a three-stage analysis in which we incorporate successive categories of factors into a regression analysis: we consider the original disparity in activity between Anglo-White men and the other five groups with no other factors taken into account; the disparity that remains when institutional resources and recruitment have been taken into account; and the final disparity once psychological involvement in politics—interest, efficacy, and information—and group consciousness have been included.[26] The left-hand columns of data merely reaffirm what we have seen throughout this chapter, disparities of varying magnitudes between Anglo-White men and the other groups, with the largest disparity between Latina women

---

26. In order to highlight the size of the disparities among groups, we follow the strategy used in Chapter 10 and use a single regression equation with dummy variables for each of the groups. The omitted group is Anglo-White men. Thus the coefficients represent the size of the gap between a particular group and Anglo-White males with other factors taken into account. Given the absence of group differences in the size of the effects of participatory factors, we feel justified in using a single equation.

Table 11.12 Psychological Orientations to Politics and Political Activity

A. The Effects of Psychological Engagement on Political Activity

	Women	Men
Political Interest	1.24***	1.59***
Political Efficacy	0.68***	1.09***
Political Knowledge	0.99***	0.95***
Gender Consciousness	0.06	
Black Consciousness	0.22	−0.12
Hispanic Consciousness	−0.07	−0.04

B. The Gap in Political Activity between Anglo-White Males and the Other Five Groups

	Zero-Order Activity Gap	Adding Institutions and Socioeconomic Resources	Adding Psychological Engagement Measures
White Women	−0.28***	−0.23***	−0.11
Black Men	−0.38*	−0.20	−0.08
Black Women	−0.48***	−0.21	+0.04
Latinos	−0.76***	−0.14	−0.02
Latinas	−1.44***	−0.57***	−0.18

Source: Citizen Participation Study—Main Survey.
*Coefficient significant at <.05.
**Coefficient significant at <.01.
***Coefficient significant at <.001.
⇔ Difference in the coefficients for men and women is significant at <.05 (by *t*-test) or one coefficient is significant at <.05 and the other is not.

and Anglo-White males. The middle columns of data—taking into account institutional resource factors—confirm that we explain a large portion of the differences in participation using these resource and recruitment variables. Taking into account the various measures of orientations to politics leaves no significant differences at all. The group disparities have been explained.

GROUP CONSCIOUSNESS AND ISSUE-BASED ACTIVITY
Since neither race consciousness nor ethnic consciousness enhances participation when other factors are taken into account, we were interested to pursue our inquiry one step further by asking

Table 11.13 Effect of Consciousness on Issue-Based Activity[a]

	Women		Men
Activity about Women			
Black consciousness	−0.00		−0.01
Hispanic consciousness	−0.01		−0.01
Gender consciousness	0.03***		
Activity about Blacks or Civil Rights			
Black consciousness	0.11***		0.07***
Hispanic consciousness	0.03	⇔	0.10***
Gender consciousness	0.02		
Activity about Latinos or Civil Rights			
Black consciousness	0.03		0.02
Hispanic consciousness	0.06*	⇔	0.23***
Gender consciousness	0.02		

Source: Citizen Participation Study—Main Survey.

a. Unstandardized regression coefficients, with political exposure at home, education, high school activity, family income, own income, job factors, organization factors, church factors, free time, sex discrimination, racial discrimination, political interest, political efficacy, political information, age, and age over 65 in the equation.

*Coefficient significant at <.05.

**Coefficient significant at <.01.

***Coefficient significant at <.001.

⇔ Difference in the coefficients for men and women is significant at <.05 (by *t*-test) or one coefficient is significant at <.05 and the other is not.

whether group consciousness for African-Americans or Latinos behaves as it does for women—by channeling activity rather than increasing it. The answer, shown in Table 11.13, is unambiguously yes. There we present data, analogous to those in Table 10.12 about the association between group consciousness and activity that is animated by concerns about group-related issues. In the top portion of the table, we see—as we did in Chapter 10—that, with other factors taken into account, there is, for women, an association between women's consciousness and undertaking political activity animated by concerns about women's issues. In contrast, neither race consciousness for Blacks nor ethnic consciousness for Latinos is related to activity on women's issues.

The bottom two sections of the table demonstrate that group consciousness functions in an analogous fashion for African-Americans and Latinos. With other factors taken into account,

Blacks who are race conscious are more likely to be active on behalf of issues involving either civil rights, in general, or Blacks, in particular. Similarly, with other variables controlled, Latinos are more likely to be active on issues involving civil rights or Latinos. Thus the way that group consciousness functions in increasing activity on group-based issues for women, for Blacks, and for Latinos lends credibility to our interpretation that group consciousness does not create activity but, instead, channels activity.

Conclusion: Gender, Race or Ethnicity, and Participatory Agendas

This chapter has gone beyond earlier analyses—our own and others'—that have probed differences in political activity between groups defined by their gender or by their race or ethnicity. Often women and men are treated as uniform categories undifferentiated by other characteristics such as race or ethnicity; analogously, internal diversity—on the basis of, among other attributes, gender—within racial or ethnic groups is ignored. To achieve a fuller picture it is necessary to consider the intersection of these characteristics. What we find is not six different groups, each distinct in its relation to political activity. Rather, when it comes to political activity, what we have found is a mixture of differences and similarities—some on the basis of gender, some on the basis of race or ethnicity, and some on the basis of a combination of the two. In this way we have shed light on what it is about intersectional experiences that makes a difference for levels and content of political action, and we underline the extent to which group differences vary across social contexts.

Our most general finding is that groups differ less in what they do with the participatory factors than in whether they get them in the first place. We have seen that disparities in participation in the United States have their roots in social processes, many of which are based in the non-political institutions of adult life, that structure differently the experiences of groups defined by gender and by race or ethnicity. These processes leave in their wake individual and group differences in the factors that foster activity and a net advantage to Anglo-White men. Once the members of different groups have acquired participatory factors, there is more similarity than difference in their ability to translate these factors into political activity. Our analysis has thus shown what it is about being non-male or non-Anglo-White, or both, that results in disparities among groups in political participation.

We must make clear that, in explaining group differences in participation in terms of variables like education, civic skills, or psychological orientations to politics, we are not rendering group identities irrelevant to this enterprise. First, the disparities in participatory factors that produce group differences in activity are hardly coincidental but are, instead, related to socially structured experiences associated with group membership. Furthermore, disparities in participation mean that public officials are hearing more from some people than from others—in particular, much more from Anglo-White men than from Latina women—about their distinctive needs and preferences with respect to governmental policy. And the six groups we have been considering are not identical in what they want and need from government.

In Chapter 4, we discussed the issue concerns that animate participation and showed that women and men are quite similar—but not identical—in the issues that they bring to their activity. For example, although education figures prominently among the issue concerns of women and men, it weighs even more heavily in the issue-based activity of women than of men. In Table 11.14, we revisit those data about the issues and problems that prompt participation but break them apart on the basis of both gender and race or ethnicity.[27] These data about the bundles of issue concerns for the six groups show certain regularities on the basis of gender. Both education and abortion weigh more importantly in the issue priorities of women than of men, regardless of race.

It is, however, the differences across groups defined by their race or ethnicity that are striking. Abortion occupies more space in the political agendas of Anglo-White activists than in those of African-Americans or Latinos. In contrast, issues of basic human need as well as crime or drugs weigh more heavily among the issue

---

27. For discussion of how we measured participatory agendas and constructed the issue categories, see Chapter 4, note 41.

Table 11.14 Race and the Issues That Animate Political Participation[a]

	Anglo-Whites		Blacks		Latinos	
	Men	Women	Men	Women	Men	Women
Basic Human Needs	8%	9%	21%	19%	13%	20%
Taxes	16	12	8	9	9	5
Economic Issues (except taxes)	12	9	7	5	6	1
Abortion	8	15	3	6	3	6
Social Issues (except abortion)	1	2	2	2	2	1
Education	13	20	14	19	16	24
Children or Youth (except education)	3	4	10	8	2	15
Crime or Drugs	5	7	23	27	18	16
Environment	11	9	2	1	10	6
Foreign Policy	8	6	7	1	8	6
Women	b	1	1	1	0	0
Blacks, Latinos, or Civil Rights[c]	1	1	11	7	12	6
Number of Respondents	1,006	1,068	92	141	56	85
Number of Issue-Based Acts	1,076	1,009	90	103	41	31

Source: Citizen Participation Study—Main Survey.

a. Proportion of issue-based political activity motivated by concern about particular issues.

b. Less than 1 percent.

c. Anglo-Whites: mention Blacks, Latinos, minorities, or civil rights; African-Americans and Latinos: mention their own group, minorities, or civil rights.

concerns of Latinos or African-Americans than among those of Anglo-Whites.[28] When it comes to issues involving civil rights or minorities, there are differences between, on one hand, Anglo-Whites and, on the other, African-Americans or Latinos, for whom these issues figure more importantly in issue-based activity. There is a gender difference as well: issues connected to civil rights or minorities are higher among the issue priorities of African-American and Latino men than of women.

---

28. There are few studies of the policy priorities of men and women of color in the legislatures. Jeanette Jennings suggests that African-American women mayors may pay more attention to issues of basic human need in "Black Women Mayors: Reflections on Race and Gender," in *Gender and Policymaking*, ed. Debra L. Dodson (New Brunswick: Center for the American Woman and Politics, Eagleton Institute of Politics, Rutgers University, 1991). Melanie McCoy finds few gender differences in the political priorities of tribal leaders, "Gender or Ethnicity: What Difference Does It Make?" *Women and Politics* 12 (1992): 57–68.

That issues of crime and basic human need—unemployment, housing, poverty, health care, and the like—figure much more importantly in the political activity of African-Americans and Latinos implies that there is an important link between the origins of participatory disparities and the content of participatory agendas. We have seen that we cannot understand the differences in activity among the six groups without taking class into account as well. Group differences in education, income, and occupational level have significant consequences for the stockpile of participatory factors. The basic processes that allocate social positions—and do so differently for women and men, for Latinos, African-Americans, and Anglo-Whites—influence who becomes a political activist. Our analysis underlines that participatory gaps reflect an aspect of the experience of being female and/or Latino and/or African-American: that, historically, these statuses, especially the intersections among them, bring with them decreased access to educational opportunity, high income, and the most desirable jobs. With socioeconomic disadvantage come, in addition, distinctive needs and preferences with respect to governmental policy. Thus the very processes that lead to different amounts of participation lead also to different participatory agendas.

12

---⊗⊗⊗---

Family Life and
Political Life

The family is society at its most private; the state is society at its most public. Yet despite Americans' strong belief that government should stay out of family matters, the family and the state are connected in multiple ways. Public policies—on subjects that range from taxes to education to food stamps to child abuse—have enormous implications for the family.[1] As family patterns are transformed by variations in the divorce rate, in rates of fertility and births out of wedlock, in the proportion of women in the work force, and in life expectancy, new policy problems emerge. In an era when politicians are only too anxious to wrap themselves in the mantle of "family values," it is hard not to see the family as an institution with serious political significance.

Our quest for the roots of political activity has led us to the family on several occasions. We have looked at the culture of the family: the extent to which married couples share beliefs on various subjects, among them politics and religion. We have also considered the internal social structure of the married couple as a unit, examining inequalities between husbands and wives in command over the economic resources of the household, in author-

---

1. Jacqueline Stevens, *Reproducing the State* (Princeton, N.J.: Princeton University Press, 1999). Some of this chapter is based on material from Nancy E. Burns, Kay L. Schlozman, and Sidney Verba, "The Public Consequences of Private Inequality: Gender, the Family, and Political Participation," *American Political Science Review* 91 (1997): 373–389. We are grateful for permission to draw on this text in revised form.

ity over decisions, and in mutual respect. And we have noted the key role played by marriage and children in shaping decisions about work force participation. When we tied together the various strands of our analysis in Chapter 10, we saw that early experiences in the family and in school influence the propensity to take part in politics.

In this chapter we focus from several perspectives on the association between family life and participation in politics. We ask, first, is political participation a family matter? That is, we ask whether couples undertake political activity as a joint or an individual pursuit and how political activity fits into the family's various voluntary commitments, particularly its religious involvement.

Then we consider—in terms of both family structure and family hierarchy—whether family matters for political participation. With respect to family structure, our concern is whether being married or having children, especially school-age children, has an independent impact on political activity. Other things equal, are married people more likely to take part politically? Are parents? In addition, we return to the issues of domestic inequality from Chapter 7 to inquire how economic, political, and social power at home affects the political participation of husbands and wives. Does a home in which husbands and wives are equal nurture political activity for either partner?

Because the home was at one time the only domain in which women were able to exercise autonomy and because women's responsibilities at home have traditionally been so central to the definition of their appropriate roles, the family has often been deemed the special sphere of women, and family relations have been assumed to have an especially powerful effect on women. However, we entertain the possibility that domestic relations might have an impact on men as well. Thus in contrast to some studies, we consider the participatory consequences of family life for both wives and husbands.

Families and Politics: A Review of the Evidence So Far

When viewed in the context of the other institutions of adult life, the family is, perhaps paradoxically, the institution for which gender distinctions are both the least and the most relevant. In considering the workplace, organizations, and religious institutions, we have consistently distinguished between two stages: selection into institutions and experiences once there. In contrast to the workplace and religious institutions, gender plays no part in access to families. And in contrast to organizations, families are not segregated by gender.[2] Families are gender-blended: they include sons and daughters, wives and husbands, living together.

As we have seen already, however, when it comes to experiences and treatment within families, gender figures mightily, and the family can be characterized as the institution in which gender is most relevant. Division of labor between women and men is a central feature of family life, and the family acts as the first, and probably the most important, school for the inculcation and reinforcement of gender roles. The combination of equality of access and a gender-based division of labor makes the family a potent social force.

Our findings so far have been threaded with reference to the potential implications of family relations for politics. Let us recapitulate them briefly. In Chapter 5, we considered the families into which we are born. In Chapter 10, we found, not unexpectedly, that those who were exposed to political stimuli in the family—who had politically active parents or who heard political discussion at the dinner table—were, as adults, more likely to be active themselves. What was more surprising to us is that the legacy of having been brought up in a politically engaged family seems to be the same for women and men.

When we looked at the beliefs of married couples in Chapter 6, we found remarkable support for equality between the sexes and a fairly high level of concurrence between wives and husbands in their views on gender roles and the division of labor at home. Likewise, we found considerable—but not complete—agreement on political issues. Husbands and wives tend to think alike on pol-

---

2. These are, of course, overstatements. There are families that—through death, divorce, desertion, happenstance of the sex of children, or sexual orientation—consist of males or females only. Moreover, in societies where the selective abortion or infanticide of females takes place, there is selection by sex into families.

icy regarding government assistance programs; they are quite a bit
more likely to be in agreement when it comes to party identification and social issues such as abortion and school prayer. Furthermore, there is a connection between partisanship and views about
gender equality within the family—with Democrats more egalitarian than Republicans among both husbands and wives. In addition, we found that the correspondence between spouses in political views is overshadowed by an even closer association when it
comes to matters of religion, which is clearly more central to a
couple than is politics.

Considering what couples actually do rather than what they believe complicates the picture. In spite of the consensus on support
for equality at home, in Chapter 7 we found substantial evidence
for traditional arrangements when it comes to the domestic division of labor. Husbands earn a disproportionate share of the family income and retain greater power in financial decision making.
Wives, in turn, are responsible for a greater share of household duties and child care—even if they are in the labor force full time.

The division of labor within the household has several possible
implications for political activity. It is frequently argued that, because they shoulder the major responsibility for household chores
and child care, women may simply have too little time for other
matters, including political activity—especially if they are in the labor force. Our analyses cast doubt on this argument. As we saw in
Chapter 7, although women do indeed devote more time to the
household and child care than men do, men spend more time at
work, with the result that, on average, there is no advantage to either husbands or wives when it comes to leisure time. Besides, as
we showed in Chapter 10, there does not seem to be a relationship—for women or for men—between political activity and obligated time devoted to work and household tasks.

Nevertheless, household responsibilities, particularly child care,
have indirect consequences for political activity. In Chapter 8 we
saw that having children has significant consequences—which are
opposite for men and women—for decisions about entering the
work force. Having children at home is associated with higher
work force participation for men and lower work force participa-

tion for women. The workplace is a major source of skills and re-quests for political action. Because men are considerably more likely to be in the work force than women are, a portion of the gender gap in participation can be attributed indirectly to gender differences in family obligations.

Is Politics a Family Matter?

Traditional political philosophy made the assumption that hus-bands act on behalf of their disenfranchised wives in politics. In contrast, survey research makes the assumption that individuals—even those enmeshed in webs of family relations—act on their own for themselves. However, since many participatory resources are family based, since attitudes may be shared within families, and since decisions about when and how to participate may be made by husband and wife together, it is appropriate to consider partici-pation in the context of families. Using our data about married couples, we look at the relation of the family to the polity from this perspective, considering how the family *as a unit* functions in the broader political world. Rather than regarding the individual as the unit of analysis and analyzing his or her political activity, we look at the way couples take part in political life. Just as we asked whether the partners in a marriage agree when it comes to political matters, we now ask whether they take part as a couple in politics.

TALKING POLITICS TOGETHER

Although we have defined the boundary of political participation as encompassing acts that involve doing rather than talking, we begin by considering political discussion in the family. Some theo-rists of democracy regard political talk—informal political discus-sion that allows people to share ideas, formulate political posi-tions, and come to understand alternative points of view—as essential to democracy.[3] Political talk can take place in many set-

---

3. See, for example, Benjamin R. Barber, *Strong Democracy: Participatory Politics for a New Age* (Berkeley: University of California Press, 1984), and William A. Gamson, *Talking Politics* (Cambridge: Cambridge University Press, 1992).

tings—for example, at work or among friends—but much of it takes place at home between spouses. In Table 12.1, portion A, we report the answers to questions about how often respondents engage in political discussion "with others" and with their spouses. The data show considerable similarity between discussion in general and discussion with one's spouse, which suggests that a large portion of day-to-day discussion takes place between spouses, even if there is also discussion with others.[4]

Although we saw in Chapter 7 that respondents feel that they can express their point of view in family discussions and that their spouses listen to what they say, we are also interested in whether husbands and wives give similar reports about the amount of political discussion that takes place between them. Portion B of Table 12.1 shows considerable, but not perfect, agreement.[5] When one spouse says that mutual political discussion occurs every day or nearly every day, the other spouse usually concurs—and rarely reports discussing politics less than once a week.

DOING POLITICS TOGETHER

We also sought to assess the extent to which political activity is a joint endeavor—either undertaken by the couple participating together or undertaken by one spouse in the name of both. Although we focus in this chapter on the family as an actor in politics, we include data on religious and charitable activity in order both to give a more complete picture of the extent to which voluntary activity

---

4. There is an inconsistency in the responses of the wives, who reported somewhat lower levels of political discussion in response to the first question, which asked about discussion "with others," than in response to the second question, which asked about discussion with their husbands.

Interestingly, Robert Huckfeldt and John Sprague also find (p. 111) that among married people, partners in political discussions are usually spouses. They also find that compared with wives, husbands are less likely to name their spouse as a discussion partner and, when they do, husbands are more likely to devalue their wives' political competence than vice versa. See *Citizens, Politics, and Social Communication* (Cambridge: Cambridge University Press, 1995), pp. 197–199, 201.

5. Paul Beck shows that the most frequent partner for political discussion is one's spouse: "Voter Intermediation Environments in the 1988 Presidential Contest," *Public Opinion Quarterly* 55 (1991): 371–395.

Table 12.1 Political Discussion as a Family Activity[a]

A. Political Discussion at Home and Elsewhere

	Wives Report They Discuss Politics with		Husbands Report They Discuss Politics with	
	Others	Husband	Others	Wife
Every Day	11%	15%	17%	16%
Nearly Every Day	21	24	29	23
Once or Twice a Week	39	35	42	42
Less than Once a Week	25	21	9	14
Never	5	5	2	5
	101%	100%	99%	100%

B. Is Anybody Listening?[b]

	Husband Says They Discuss Politics Nearly Every Day or More Often	Wife Says They Discuss Politics Nearly Every Day or More Often
Spouse Says They Discuss Politics		
Nearly Every Day	61%	59%
Once or Twice a Week	28	33
Less than Once a Week	11	7
	100%	99%

Source: Citizen Participation Study Follow-up—Couples Survey.

a. Appendix A contains the valid number of cases for these and other measures used in the tables.

b. The relationship between husband's and wife's perceptions of the frequency of political talk is statistically significant at the .01 level, gamma = .48.

is a family matter and to put the political activities in perspective. Each time a respondent indicated having engaged in a particular activity, we followed up in order to learn whether or not the activity was joint: for church, campaign, and community activity, we asked if the activity "was something you did on your own, or is this something you and your (wife/husband) did together?"; for contacting and for contributing, we asked if the contact or the money came "from both you and your (wife/husband) or did it basically come from you?"

The left-hand columns of Table 12.2 show the proportions of those active in a particular way who reported that the activity was joint: that is, that they engaged in the activity with their spouse or that the activity came from both spouses. The data tell an interesting, and perhaps somewhat surprising, story. Probably because most households have a common purse, giving money is more likely to be considered a joint activity than is giving time.[6] Consistent with data in Chapter 7 showing that both husbands and wives are overwhelmingly likely to consult the other before making a political or a charitable contribution, checks written by one person—as contributions to church, charity, or politics—are generally thought of as coming from the other partner as well. Giving time is less likely to be considered a joint activity. Even so, with the exception of serving on a local board, which is clearly an individual activity, many participatory acts are undertaken by wife and husband together: roughly half the community activists and over a third of the campaign workers reported joint activity. About one-third of those who reported getting in touch with a government official described their contacts as coming from both partners. We interpret this finding as not necessarily implying a joint contact—a letter signed by both husband and wife, a telephone call with both on the line, a visit by the two to a government office. Rather, we presume that these contacts are perceived by the one actually making the contact as delivering a joint message.

Looking across domains of voluntary action, the data make clear that couples are more likely to act as a team when undertaking religious rather than secular activity. Of the various kinds of contributions—to church, charities, and campaigns—the first is the most likely to be joint. When it comes to activities that take time, attendance at church stands out as the activity that is most likely to be joint. The measure for attendance at religious services specifies a particularly demanding threshold: attending every week or more, rather than ever having engaged in an activity over the past twelve months. About two-thirds of the churchgoing wives

---

6. As we noted in Chapter 7, even when both members of the couple are in the work force, nine out of ten respondents indicated that the family pools its money.

Table 12.2 Voluntary Participation as Joint Activity

	Took Part Together[a]		Spouse Shares Concern[b]	
	Wives	Husbands	Wives	Husbands
POLITICAL ACTIVITY				
Campaign work in past 12 months	35%	40%	77%	91%
Gave money in past 12 months	70	59	85	76
Worked informally past 12 months	47	53	85	87
Active on board in past 12 months	1	19	81	81
Contacted in past 12 months	35	28	88	84
CHARITABLE ACTIVITY				
Worked in past 12 months	16	36	66	86
Gave money in past 12 months	76	79	92	94
RELIGIOUS ACTIVITY				
Attend every week or more[d]	66	90		
Worked past 12 months	33	74	76	93
Gave money in past 12 months	85	89	75	81

Source: Citizen Participation Study Follow-up—Couples Survey.

a. Among those who were active.

b. Spouse very or somewhat concerned about the issue or problem—among those whose activity was *not* joint.

c. As the result of a mistake in directions, the data on giving jointly are for only those couples where both time and money were given.

d. The survey did not ask whether spouse shares concern for religious attendance.

and nine-tenths of the churchgoing husbands indicated that, when they go to services, they are always or usually with their spouses.[7]

Even when activity is undertaken, as it usually is, by the husband or wife alone, the active spouse can represent the views of the other. Whenever respondents indicated having engaged in a particular voluntary act on their own, we followed up by asking

---

7. There might seem to be a discrepancy between the responses of husbands and wives. However, 41 percent of the wives, as opposed to 29 percent of the husbands, are regular churchgoers. Thus, when they go to church, husbands are more likely to be accompanied by their wives. The wives, in contrast, are more likely to go alone. In fact, multiplying out the joint probabilities yields virtually identical numbers. Roughly a quarter of all husbands and all wives reported attending services together at least once a week.

whether their spouse shared their concern about that activity—that is, whether their spouse cared about the issue or problem associated with the activity. The right-hand two columns of Table 12.2 show that politics is a joint concern, if not a joint activity. Both husbands and wives overwhelmingly reported that their spouses also believed the activity to be important—even though they were actually participating alone. There is no particular pattern with respect to whether the activity involves time or money, whether it is political, charitable, or religious, or whether it is the wife or the husband who is reporting. Thus the overall finding is that voluntary activity—including political activity—is a family matter.

Does Family Matter for Activity?: The Impact of Marriage and Kids

Our next task is to invert the question and ask how family matters for political activity. We consider two aspects of family life in relation to political participation. We look, first, at family structure—that is, the impact of marriage and children on activity. Then we consider family hierarchy—that is, the participatory consequences of inequalities between husband and wife in money, power, and social status. As usual, we leave open the possibility that—contrary to the received wisdom—what happens in the private domain of the household has potential implications for men as well as for women.

Because marriage and children play such a significant role in shaping lives, it is natural to assume that they would have implications for political activity.[8] We might entertain a variety of hypotheses, some of them conflicting. On one hand, we might imagine that marriage enhances personal stability and concern about the fate of the community and society and would thus be associated with increased participation. On the other, married couples might

---

8. See Virginia Sapiro's helpful discussion of the variety of meanings marriage could have for women in *The Political Integration of Women* (Urbana: University of Illinois Press, 1983), pp. 67–68.

turn inward and be less inclined to take part politically. Analogously, having children might reinforce a sense of social responsibility or create a stake in a broader set of political issues—for example, child care or school funding—and generate political participation, especially among those with school-age children. Alternatively, having children might absorb so much time and attention that political activity would diminish. Because household management and child care have occupied a special place in women's lives, we might imagine that these effects would be more pronounced for women than for men.

Previous studies have had conflicting findings about the consequences of marriage and children for women's and men's political activity.[9] In seeking to establish the participatory impact of family structure, we are able to refine the analysis in several ways. First, as usual, we differentiate the effects of family structure for women and men by using separate equations for the two groups. In addition, we distinguish between the impact of being married and the impact of having children and between the impact of having preschool children and the impact of having school-age children. Furthermore, we do not merely compare married and unmarried respondents.

As shown in Table 12.3, the unmarried are a diverse group. Although a majority of our respondents, both male and female, are married, the circumstance of being unmarried encompasses a variety of statuses. Thus in our analysis we distinguish among those who are single, divorced, separated, and widowed. Moreover, we consider the family within the framework of other institutions. We have already seen in Chapters 8 and 9 that marital status has implications for relations to secondary institutions, in particular the work force and religious institutions. By taking these institutional affiliations into account, we are able to isolate the effects of family patterns. Moreover, by placing the family in the context of other

---

9. See, for example, Susan Welch, "Women as Political Animals?: A Test of Some Explanations for Male-Female Political Participation Differences," *American Journal of Political Science* 21 (1977): 711–730; Nancy E. McGlen, "The Impact of Parenthood on Political Participation," *Western Political Quarterly* 33 (1980): 297–313; Sapiro, *Political Integration of Women*, chap. 6; and Karen Beckwith, *American Women and Political Participation* (New York: Greenwood Press, 1986), chap. 3.

Table 12.3 Marital Status by Gender

	Women	Men
Married	54%	59%
Marriage-like Relationship	3	4
Widowed	12	3
Divorced	13	11
Separated	3	2
Never Married	15	21
	100%	100%

Source: Citizen Participation Study—Main Survey.

institutions, we can differentiate the direct effects of family patterns from indirect effects through secondary institutions.

In order to explore the consequences of family structure for political participation, we add measures of marital status and children to the participation model developed in Chapter 10: for marital status, dummy variables for being married, divorced, widowed, and separated, compared with never having been married;[10] and for children, having preschoolers and having school-age children. Because all of these circumstances are related to position in the life cycle, we control, as usual, for age.

Table 12.4, which presents the results of this analysis, contains the unexpected finding that neither being married nor having children, whether preschool or school-age, has a significant effect on political activity—either for women or for men.[11] While being married does not enhance participation, ending marriage depresses it: for both men and women, being separated, divorced, or widowed lowers political activity—in some cases significantly. These points are worth underlining. Descriptive data in Chapter 3 gave the impression that marriage fostered political participation

---

10. The small number of respondents who are in a marriage-like relationship are included in the omitted category.

11. In contrast to variables such as education, civic skills, or political interest, which invariably have a positive impact on activity, the effect of marriage and children on participation is unstable. By artfully juggling what is included in the model—in particular, by putting in a single category all marital statuses other than married—it is possible to specify models in which marriage or children are significantly related to political participation.

Table 12.4 The Direct Effects of Marital Status and Children on Overall Political Activity

A. Marital Status, Children, and Political Activity (OLS regression)[a]

	Women		Men
MARITAL STATUS			
Married	0.17		−0.18
Separated	−0.29		−0.56
Divorced	−0.31*		−0.30*
Widowed	−0.21	⇔	−0.66*
CHILDREN			
School-age children	0.10		−0.08
Preschool children	0.11		0.07

B. The Indirect Effects of Marital Status and Children on Overall Political Activity and Political Contributions[b]

	Women	Men
POLITICAL PARTICIPATION		
Children	−0.04	+0.08
Marriage	0.00	+0.02
Separation	0.00	−0.05
Divorce	0.02	−0.04
Widow/widowerhood	0.05	0.00
POLITICAL CONTRIBUTIONS		
Children	−$39	+$81
Marriage	+$39	+$48
Separation	0	0
Divorce	−$26	0
Widow/widowerhood	−$26	0

Source: Citizen Participation Study—Main Survey.

a. Ordinary least-squares regression coefficients, with childhood political exposure, high school activity, job factors, organization factors, church factors, income from a job, family income, sex discrimination, education, free time, age, and age over 65 in the equation.

b. For details on this outcomes analysis, see Appendix D.

*Coefficient significant at <.05.

**Coefficient significant at <.01.

***Coefficient significant at <.001.

⇔ Difference in the coefficients for men and women is significant at <.05 (by *t*-test) or one coefficient is significant at <.05 and the other is not.

for both men and women and that children depressed activity for women. Multivariate analysis has demonstrated the error of these conclusions.[12] The trauma associated with ending a marriage does have an impact on political activity. However, any association between participation and either marriage or parenthood results from the fact that those who are married or parents have other characteristics—for example, higher levels of education and income—that predispose them to take part.

INDIRECT EFFECTS OF FAMILY STRUCTURE

Our analysis so far tells only part of the story of the impact of family structure on political activity. Although we find no direct effect, on the basis of what we learned earlier, we would expect some indirect effects. As we saw in Chapters 8 and 9, being married and having children influence involvement with secondary institutions—bringing men into the work force and into religious institutions and keeping women out of the work force.[13] It is striking that these effects are stronger for men than for women.

We undertook an analysis to estimate the indirect effects of family circumstances on political activity, with noteworthy results.[14]

---

12. These findings are echoed by M. Kent Jennings and Richard G. Niemi, who found ("The Division of Political Labor between Mothers and Fathers," *American Political Science Review* 65 [1971]: 69–82) that neither the presence of children at home nor the age of the children affects the relative political activity of husbands and wives.

13. See, in particular, Table 9.11.

14. To estimate the indirect effects of family circumstances on political activity, we added variables measuring marital status and children to versions of the selection and treatment models in Chapters 8 and 9. We focus on the effects of marriage and children on work force and church involvement, since these are the domains for which the analysis in Chapters 8 and 9 indicated significant effects.

These analyses provided estimates of the impact of marital status and children on the levels of factors to which women and men have access. We combine these estimates with the coefficients from the outcomes analysis we reported in Chapter 10. The numbers we report in portion B in Table 12.4 are the indirect effect of having a particular marital status or of having children. Calculating the total effect for women or men would require one more step than we take here and take into account the proportion of women and men in the sample who are married and have preschool and school-age children, by simply multiplying the numbers in portion B of Table 13.4 by the proper proportions.

The indirect effects we report come from the role marriage and children play in shaping work force participation and church affiliation, and, in turn, from the effect of participatory factors that derive from work and church on political activity. We report the full outcomes analysis for the indirect effects of marriage and family in Appendix C, Tables C12.4.1–C12.4.3.

With other factors taken into account, not only does being married have no direct impact on participation for women, but it has no indirect impact either. In contrast, being married increases men's activity by .02 of an act—largely by increasing the involvement of men in the work force and, to a lesser extent, religious institutions. Having children is associated with an increase of .08 of an act for men—again through enhanced work force and church involvement. However, having children diminishes political activity by .04 of an act for women.[15] With respect to political contributions, the indirect impact of family circumstances is larger for men than for women. For men, both marriage and children increase political donations. For women, being married rather than single raises donations; being divorced or widowed, rather than never having been married, lowers donations.

In short, marriage and children do affect activity—but not as we might have expected. Although the end of a marriage seems to depress rates of participation, neither being married nor having children has significant direct consequences for activity. Instead, family structure affects participation indirectly by channeling individuals into secondary institutions. Ironically, although we ordinarily assume that family life shapes women's destinies much more than men's, the participatory implications of marriage and children are much more substantial for men than for women.

Mothers at Home and Mothers at Work: A Brief Note

One often hears that, now that the housewives who once functioned as the foot soldiers in voluntary endeavors have marched

---

15. Earlier we noted that the statistical significance of the relationship between marriage and work force participation varies with the precise specification of the model. We also indicated that any impact of marriage on work force participation is opposite in direction for men and women—predisposing men to go to work and women to stay home—and that the results for the impact of children on work force participation, which are also opposite in direction for women and men, are less specification dependent. The analysis reported here makes clear that the indirect effects on political participation of children in the household are much stronger than the indirect effects of marriage.

M. Kent Jennings and Richard G. Niemi's 1971 findings are similar, though not identical. They find that a wife's work force participation lowers her husband's participatory advantage somewhat, but not substantially. See "The Division of Political Labor between Mothers and Fathers."

off to work, the relatively small number of women who remain at home are left with all the responsibility for volunteer efforts. This circumstance, part of a larger social conflict that has sometimes been dubbed the "Mommy Wars," has received a great deal of attention in the media.[16]

Yet descriptive data in Chapter 3 show that mothers with full-time jobs are more politically active than are mothers at home full time. Hence we were interested to probe further in order to learn whether there is any truth to the widely held perception that women who work full time have abandoned the voluntary sphere.[17] Because media accounts of the resentment expressed by at-home mothers are so often associated with voluntary activities in the community or in the schools, we expand our focus. We include not only overall participation but also community political activity and two forms of non-political voluntarism—giving time to charitable activities and getting involved in organizations that focus on the young, either school-related organizations like PTAs or organizations like the Boy Scouts or Campfire Girls.[18] Moreover, because community-related activity often centers around youth issues, we confine our consideration to women with school-age children.

In addition, we revert to the use of categorical rather than multivariate analysis. Throughout this inquiry we have used multivariate analyses to demonstrate that participatory differences between groups of people are the result not of the apparent statuses but of other attributes that accompany those statuses. However, observers note the obvious. For example, they will see differences in race rather than the disparities in education, income, and the

---

16. See, for example, Caryl Rivers, "Are We in for a Replay of the Mommy Wars?" *Boston Globe*, August 6, 2000, p. E7.

17. In *Bowling Alone: The Collapse and Revival of American Community* (New York: Simon and Schuster, 2000), pp. 194–203, Robert D. Putnam considers whether the movement of women into the work force has depressed civic engagement construed more generally. He finds that full-time employment does contribute somewhat to the erosion of social connectedness and community involvement. However, as we do, he finds that being in the work force enhances more public forms of civic activities for women.

18. Some of those who are affiliated with PTAs or other organizations concerned about the young characterize those organizations, presumably correctly, as having taken stands on political issues.

like that explain participatory differences between Blacks and Whites. In this case, what would be apparent is the work force status of the mothers whose voluntary service is needed to get this year's Pumpkinfest off the ground and not the differences in civic skills or activity while in high school that are relevant for political activity.

The data in the top rows of Table 12.5 do not change our earlier descriptive findings: among mothers of school-age children, those with full-time jobs are considerably more active in politics, more likely to have gotten involved in community activity, to have given time to charitable activity, and to be affiliated with a PTA or other kid-centered organization. Nevertheless, it is possible that this result is driven by the alarmingly low rates of political activity among unmarried mothers at home. Numbers not on the table underline the extremely low levels of activity of these single mothers: only 4 percent of the at-home single mothers of school-age children are involved in such an organization. Nevertheless, when we focus solely upon married mothers in the next two rows of Table 12.5, we still find gaps.

The figures in the bottom rows of the table, in which we confine our purview to married college graduates, provide a clue as to the origin of the perception that stay-at-home mothers are shouldering the burden for voluntary activity. College-educated, married mothers of school-age children have high levels of political participation—regardless of work force status.[19] Still, compared with those at home, those in the work force are substantially higher in overall political activity and more likely to have gotten involved in community politics and to have given time to charity. However, when it comes to affiliation with a PTA or other organization focusing on the young, we see for the first time the pattern predicted by the stereotype.[20] For this single type of activity, at-home married, college-educated mothers are more active. This result is based

---

19. We build here on Sapiro's analysis in *Political Integration of Women*, pp. 137–138.

20. We should also note that among college-educated, married mothers of school-age children, those who are at home full time are more likely than those who are in the work force full time to attend religious services regularly. However, there is no significant difference between the two groups in the proportion who give time to charitable, educational, or social activities associated with a religious institution or who are active in their churches.

Table 12.5 Mothers at Work and Mothers at Home[a]

	Overall Activity	Community Activity	Time to Charity[b]	Youth Organization[c]
ALL				
Full-time Work	2.35	24%	48%	44%
At Home	1.56	15%	39%	33%
MARRIED				
Full-time Work	2.51	27%	47%	48%
At Home	1.84	17%	42%	42%
MARRIED COLLEGE GRADUATES				
Full-time Work	4.19	46%	80%	46%
At Home	2.77	38%	58%	52%

Source: Citizen Participation Study—Main Survey.
a. Analysis is conducted for women with school-age children.
b. The measure for time to charity comes from the Citizen Participation Study Screener Survey.
c. PTA or youth-oriented organization such as Boy Scouts or Campfire Girls.

on a small number of cases and thus must be interpreted with some caution.

Still, this finding provides a basis for understanding why mothers with full-time jobs are thought not to be doing their share of the volunteer work. Someone who wishes to drum up participation in a gubernatorial campaign or to find volunteers to staff a soup kitchen can cast a wide net in a pool that has no clearly defined boundaries. In contrast, the set of available people for leadership of the school PTA or the local Brownie troop has much more limited membership and more readily recognized boundaries. Thus it is easier to make assessments about who is avoiding responsibility and who is carrying the load. The correct perception that, among the well-educated women who have traditionally provided leadership in these endeavors, those who are at home full time take a disproportionate share of the responsibility leads to an incorrect inference that they are otherwise more active as volunteers. In short, our data demonstrate the fallacy of generalizing from the PTA and the Scouts to political or charitable participation. However, these findings make more comprehensible the source of the characterization of at-home mothers as the backbone of volunteer efforts.

Equality at Home and Equality in the Polity

Over the course of our analysis we have seen complicated effects of family life on political participation in adulthood. On one hand, growing up in a home that is politically involved exercises a significant effect on future political participation. On the other, although the structure of family relationships in adulthood—marriage and children—has an indirect impact on activity through work and church activity, it has no direct consequences for participation. We now examine what goes on at home from another perspective, asking whether egalitarian relations between husband and wife have implications for the political activity of either partner.

One theme of recent political theory is that until women are equal at home, they cannot be equal in the polity. In her pathbreaking study, Susan Okin argues that, although theorists of justice have either neglected the family or exempted the family from the principles by which the polity must be evaluated, patriarchal domestic relationships have consequences for women's ability to participate fully as citizens: "In a just society, the structure and practices of families must give women the same opportunities as men to develop their capacities, to participate in political power and influence social choices, and to be economically secure."[21]

An especially important variant of this line of reasoning emphasizes the way that an unequal division of labor at home—with women assuming a disproportionate share of the domestic responsibilities—deprives women of the essential political resource of time and thus compromises their ability to be active in politics. Anne Phillips offers a particularly articulate statement of this point of view:

> [W]omen are prevented from participating in public life because of the way their private lives are run. The division of labour between women and men constitutes for most women a double burden of work . . . The mere pressures of time will keep most women out of

---

21. Susan Moller Okin, *Justice, Gender, and the Family* (New York: Basic Books, 1989), p. 22.

any of the processes of decision-making . . . the way our private lives are organized promotes male involvement and reduces female participation. Who collects the children and who makes the tea is [*sic*] a vital political concern . . . Whether at the simplest level of having no free time, or as a more complex consequence of always being told what to do, women's experiences in the home continually undercut the possibilities for democracy.[22]

While this theoretical formulation is extremely suggestive, by the theorists' own admission, the empirical evidence on which this theory is predicated is slender. Phillips—who asserts, "I consider the argument won almost as soon as it [is] stated"[23]—seems to find the connection between inequality at home and inequality in politics to be so obvious that the absence of empirical confirmation is hardly a liability. To us, as should be clear by now, the lack of evidence is more problematic.

Furthermore, the theorists who characterize the family as an incubator of citizen inequality consider the implications of family patterns for women's participation in politics but ignore the impact of domestic inequalities on men's participation. As usual, we allow for the possibility that domestic hierarchy of various kinds might have an impact on men's as well as women's comportment in politics.

THE FAMILY AS A MINIATURE SOCIAL SYSTEM

In Chapters 6 and 7, we considered the family as a miniature social system and described the multiple hierarchies within it. We conceptualized the family as a micro-economy in which resources are generated and deployed and in which tasks are allocated according to a division of labor; a micro-polity in which authority is exercised and decisions are made; a micro-society in which status and respect are distributed; and a micro-culture in which beliefs about equality—in particular, equality between wives and husbands—are shaped and shared. We might expect any of these aspects of

---

22. Anne Phillips, *Engendering Democracy* (University Park: Pennsylvania State University Press, 1991), pp. 96–97, 100.

23. Phillips, *Engendering Democracy,* p. 99.

family hierarchy to have consequences for civic participation—and to do so differentially for wives and for husbands. We now ask whether various kinds of domestic inequality have implications for the capacity to take part politically. Our analysis, which uses the data on married couples, contains two kinds of measures: *absolute* measures that capture the amount of a particular household resource—for example, decision-making authority—that the respondent commands; and *relative* measures capturing the amount of that resource compared with his or her spouse.

We begin with economic power at home. Our analysis in Chapter 10 made clear that family income is a major resource for political activity for both wives and husbands.[24] We also considered the impact of the respondent's own earnings on overall political activity and found no effect for either husband or wife beyond that of family income, which can include earnings from the respondent's spouse as well as from other sources, such as interest. However, it may be that what matters for participation is not only the absolute amount of money that is available to the family but the relative earning power of the spouses. Thus our analysis includes—in addition to the usual measure of family income—a measure of the respondent's contribution to family income as measured by the percentage of the family income he or she earns.

We have already seen data casting doubt on the widely held notion that the burden of running a household so diminishes the time that women have available for voluntary pursuits as to explain the gender gap in political participation. Although women do, on average, spend more time on housework than men do, they do not have less leisure than men, because men, on average, spend more time on the job. Moreover, neither the amount of leisure time nor the amount of time spent doing household tasks has an impact on overall political participation. Nevertheless, in order to ensure that we are not missing the effects of the division of labor in the household, we include in the analysis both the number of hours that the respondent devotes to household tasks, including child care, and

---

24. However, when we considered the *size* of political contributions, we found an association between the husband's—though not the wife's—own earnings and the amount given. In this section, we focus on political activity in general.

the respondent's proportion of the total hours that a couple devote to these tasks.

We also consider political power in the household. It seems plausible to expect that an equal voice—or even a dominant voice—at home would foster a sense of competence in politics. Our discussion in Chapter 7 of authority over family decision making yielded a somewhat mixed picture. On one hand, both partners—but especially husbands—indicated that they consult with the other before making major commitments of time or money. Husbands and wives also expressed satisfaction with family decision-making processes and with their ability to express their point of view and to gain a hearing in family discussions. On the other hand, according to both partners, in most couples the husband takes most of the responsibility for making financial decisions. Our analysis includes measures of several aspects of authority in household decision making: control over major financial decisions; ability to express points of view in family discussions; and autonomy in making decisions without consulting. In each case we include both an absolute and a relative measure: that is, the respondents' reports about themselves and respondents' reports in comparison with their spouses' reports.

We consider as well a final aspect of stratification within the household, social status. Enjoying status or respect at home might have consequences for political participation by enhancing the confidence with which an individual confronts the wider world. Evidence in Chapter 7 indicated that marital partners show a good deal of mutual respect for one another: when asked to list three people whose judgment they really trust and with whom they might be likely to discuss important matters, almost all the respondents in the couples study put their spouses on the list, and substantial majorities placed their spouses at the top. Our analysis includes a measure of where respondents' spouses put them on the list of trusted advisors along with a relative measure indicating differences between spouses in placement on the list.[25] We include, in addition, a second measure of relative social status: the relative job

---

25. To create a measure of relative status, we subtract the wife's ranking of the husband from the husband's ranking of the wife.

level of the two partners—with respondents who are not in the work force classified at the lowest job level.

Our analysis incorporates, in addition, consideration of an aspect of household culture: the role of beliefs about gender equality. As mentioned earlier, there is remarkable support, among both husbands and wives, for equality between the sexes and a fairly high level of concurrence between marital partners in views on gender roles and the division of labor at home. We might expect beliefs about appropriate gender roles to have a greater impact on participation for wives but, as always, keep open the possibility that there are consequences for husbands as well. We include both the scale introduced in Chapter 6 that measures the respondent's support for egalitarian gender roles—such matters as whether a mother of young children should be in the work force and whether household chores and decision making should be shared by husbands and wives—and a measure of the difference between wife and husband on the scale.

DOES INEQUALITY AT HOME AFFECT ACTIVITY?
Table 12.6 presents the results—which are surprising—of this analysis. We present these findings cautiously. The case base in our third-wave couples study is smaller than we would prefer, and we are concerned that respondents who could be located for the third wave of a study may not be typical of those who cannot be located a third time. Furthermore, the survey contains multiple measures of a number of concepts, and different specifications of the model do not always yield the same results.[26] We have taken a conservative approach by choosing a model that includes typical results. Nevertheless, we urge prudence in the interpretation of our findings.

As mentioned, the analysis includes, in addition to many familiar variables, indicators of the respondent's position within the social system of the household as well as measures of the relative po-

---

26. Although, in their broad outlines, the findings in Table 12.6 are completely in accord with results published earlier (Burns, Schlozman, and Verba, "The Public Consequences of Private Inequality: Family Life and Citizen Participation") using a somewhat different model, there are divergences with respect to a few details.

Table 12.6 Family Hierarchy and Citizen Participation[a]

	Women		Men
THE FAMILY ECONOMY: CONTROL OVER MONEY			
Control over family finances	0.32	⇔	1.15*
Percentage of the family income the respondent brings in	0.64	⇔	0.91*
THE FAMILY ECONOMY: CONTROL OVER TIME			
Percentage of housework hours done by wife	−0.10		0.02
Preschool children	0.12		0.22
THE FAMILY POLITY: DECISIONAL AUTONOMY			
Respondent's autonomy	1.22*		1.71**
Relative difference in spouses' autonomy	1.01*	⇔	−0.24
THE FAMILY POLITY: DECISIONAL HIERARCHY			
Respondent believes she or he gets a say in family discussions	1.10*	⇔	−0.20
Relative difference in whether the partners get a say	−0.01		−0.20
THE FAMILY SOCIETY: EQUALITY OF RESPECT			
Respondent is a trusted advisor for spouse	−0.40		0.41
Relative difference in whether the respondents turn to each other for advice	−0.21		−0.30
Relative difference between spouses' job levels	−0.12		0.47
THE FAMILY CULTURE: BELIEFS ABOUT GENDER ROLES			
Respondent's belief in equal roles	−0.80		0.29
Relative difference between spouses in views about gender roles	−0.87		−0.42

Source: Citizen Participation Study Follow-up—Couples Survey.

a. Ordinary least-squares coefficients; model also controls for childhood politicization, education, family income, job level, religious attendance, age, and years of marriage.

*Coefficient significant at <.05.

**Coefficient significant at <.01.

***Coefficient significant at <.001.

⇔ Difference in coefficients for men and women is significant at <.05 (by *t*-test) or one coefficient is significant at <.05 and the other is not.

sition of the spouses—variables that are coded so that a positive coefficient implies an association between political participation and an advantageous position with respect to a particular variable relative to one's spouse. Consistent with our expectations, domestic hierarchy has consequences for political participation. Contrary to our expectations, however, there are consequences for both husbands and wives. For both spouses, feeling autonomous in making decisions is associated with political activity. For wives, there is a relationship between political activity and being able to express themselves in family discussions.[27] For husbands, financial power is politically enabling: husbands who bring in a larger share of the family income or who exercise greater control over financial decisions are, all else equal, more politically active.[28]

Strikingly, other aspects of family hierarchy that we might have expected to have consequences for political participation have no effect. The respondent's share of the total hours devoted by both partners to household tasks does not influence political participation for either husbands or, more surprisingly, wives. These data lend further confirmation to what we have found before: time constraints imposed by responsibility for children and household chores do not explain differences in political activity. Moreover, neither beliefs about gender equality in the family nor the hierarchy of respect at home is related to political activity.

In short, incorporating concern with several aspects of inequality at home into our understanding of political participation yields results that are, from the standpoint of the common wisdom, both expected and unexpected. The usual suspects behave as expected: for example, education and church attendance—which proxies for variables not included in the analysis, skills developed and requests for political participation received in religious institutions—are significant predictors of activity. What is surprising is that time devoted to household tasks and child care, beliefs about gender roles, and various aspects of inequality at home have no

---

27. We should note that the direction of causality is not clear. It might be argued that experience in politics would increase a wife's capacity within the household. However, since fully 79 percent of wives indicated that they can always express themselves in a family discussion, it seems more plausible that agency at home breeds the ability to take part politically. Nevertheless, it is possible that some omitted variable—a personality trait or characteristic of family background—might influence a sense of capacity both within the family and in civic life.

28. Bringing in the family income and having a larger say over financial decisions are, as one might expect, closely related to each other. The more the husband brings in, the more he is dominant over family financial decisions—the increase in his dominance over such decisions being almost proportional to his increased contribution to family income. In couples where he brings in more than two-thirds of the family income, two-thirds of the couples report that he makes most major financial decisions; where he brings in less than one-third of the income, only one-third of the couples report that he makes major financial decisions.

consequences for political participation. What is even more unexpected is that, to the extent that domestic hierarchy has an impact on political activity, it does so at least as substantially for husbands as for wives. While we must reiterate that we urge caution in interpreting these results, we are certain that they do not provide unambiguous support for commonly held views about the roots of political inequality in traditional family arrangements. Thus Phillips and Okin are on the right track when they point to the family as a source of political inequality. However, we have shown that the process does not work through the impact of family life on women's leisure time, and it affects men's participation as well as women's.[29]

We should note that our analysis in essence tests whether the *dominance* of either partner with respect to any aspect of domestic hierarchy affects participation—that is, whether being in control at home constitutes training for politics. We were interested to test the alternative possibility—that a circumstance of domestic *equality* facilitates activity. That is, does an egalitarian arrangement at home act as a school for democracy? We experimented with various versions of the model with no change in the results. To repeat, discussions of the links between family and political life often focus exclusively on the effects for wives. Our results remind us to consider both men and women when it comes to the study of gender issues.

The Family and Political Activity

This chapter has attempted an unusual undertaking: to use systematic survey data to subject to empirical test the widely held view that what happens in the private domain of the home has consequences for participation in politics. What we have found confirms that household arrangements affect political activity. However,

---

29. Our findings support both Okin's suggestion that political theory must notice realms outside of politics in order to fully attend to the implications of gender for political equality and her assertion that "[o]nce we admit the idea that significant differences between women and men are *created by* the existing division of labour within the family, we begin to see the depth and the extent of the social construction of gender." Susan Moller Okin, "Gender, the Public, and the Private," in *Feminism and Politics*, ed. Anne Phillips (Oxford: Oxford University Press, 1998), p. 127.

in most respects we have disconfirmed the usual interpretation of how family life operates to place women at a disadvantage in politics.

First, the effect of marriage and children on the differential activity of women and men is very different from what we had expected. Family structure—being married or having children—has no direct impact on political participation. Moreover, contrary to our expectations, there is no indirect effect of marriage or children through the time that women devote to the care of home and children. Try as we might, we could find no evidence that an absence of free time handicaps women as citizens. Not only are women, on average, not disadvantaged when it comes to leisure, but neither the amount of free time nor the number of hours devoted to household tasks and child care has an independent impact on political activity. Being married and having children do have an effect—an indirect effect through access to secondary institutions. By bringing men into the work force and into churches, marriage and children increase the stockpile of participatory factors held by men.

Second, when we cross the threshold of the household and look at the relations between husbands and wives, we again find that domestic hierarchy has consequences for political activity—but not the ones we might have predicted. Construing domestic inequalities very broadly, we find that, overall, domestic inequality has as much, or more, influence on husbands' participation as on wives' participation. Contrary to those who argue that family authority patterns affect the political participation of women, we find that the nature of authority at home affects both spouses—with the effect, in fact, somewhat less clear for wives. For husbands, control over family finances increases activity. Wives who feel they have a voice in family discussions are also more active, but the direction of causality is uncertain.

In one final respect our conclusions depart from the common wisdom. Because family life and family responsibilities are so central to women's lives, it is ordinarily assumed that family patterns exert their influence exclusively on women. Instead, as we have seen several times in this chapter, family life has more substantial consequences for men's activity than for women's.

13

∽∞∽

What If Politics Weren't
a Man's Game?

Early in the spring of 2000, it looked as if, once again, the American electorate would not have the option of voting for a woman for president. Then suddenly into the breach came a female presidential candidate wearing a tailored blue suit, high heels, pearl earrings, and a perpetual smile—Barbie. Mattell's famous toy brought formidable political assets to a presidential bid. She has enviable name recognition. She is unparalleled as a fund-raiser, bringing in more than $1 billion each year. She has traveled to more than 150 countries. Her résumé includes stints as an astronaut, a surgeon, and an airline pilot.[1] And only a grammarian could object to her platform: "If elected, Barbie will institute more opportunities for every kid to develop their talents and be the best they can be."[2]

Although reaction to the presidential candidacy of the doll with the big blond hairdo and the anatomically impossible body was mixed, Geraldine Ferraro, former Democratic representative from New York and, at this writing, the only woman ever to run for vice president on a major party ticket, made a guardedly optimistic assessment: "If girls learn at a young age that they can be president,

---

1. Information about Barbie's background and presidential bid is taken from Marjorie Williams, "Fully Qualified—and Accessorized," *Washington Post,* April 21, 2000, p. A27; Wendy Koch, "Gore vs. Bush—vs. Barbie?" *USA Today,* April 21, 2000, p. 2A; and Ellen Goodman, "She's Got It All," *Boston Globe,* May 1, 2000, p. A19.

2. "What Barbie Believes," July 3, 2000 <http://www.barbie. com>. At some point before the November 2000 election, Barbie seems to have dropped out of the race, and information about her candidacy disappeared from her Web site.

maybe they will grow up believing they will be."[3] While we have no inkling as to whether Barbie's presidential bid made American girls feel less shut out of politics, the logic behind her presidential run reflects our understanding that there are implicit cues communicated by an absence of visible women in the political environment.

We have discovered that the disparity between women and men in citizen political participation has multiple sources. Among the most important is the fact that women are less likely to be psychologically involved with politics—to be politically interested, informed, or efficacious.[4] Although we made substantial headway in uncovering the origins of gender differences with respect to other participatory factors, we have made much less progress when it comes to the psychological orientations to politics that predict activity. In Chapter 5 we glanced backward at early experiences at home and at school and found no unambiguous answers about the pre-adult roots of political involvement. Nor did we learn anything definitive when we turned our attention to adult institutions. Although the thrust of our analysis has been to underline the significance for citizen political participation of adult experiences, what we have learned about the legacy of childhood or experiences in non-political institutions does not illumine why men are more psychologically involved with politics than women are.

What if politics were less a man's game? That is, if the world of politics were more fully gender integrated, would women feel more psychologically engaged with the political process? In order to search further for the source of the gender difference in psychological orientations to politics, we turn our attention in this chapter to the major institution of adult life that we have thus far ig-

3. Letter to the Editor, *New York Times*, May 4, 2000, p. A26. Another controversy erupted over Barbie's candidacy. Although Mattel manufactured Caucasian, African-American, and Latina versions of the "Barbie for President 2000" doll, a planned Asian-American type did not materialize, a situation that Patsy Mink, Democratic representative from Hawaii, called an "outrage." See Patricia Wen, "Barbie's Missing Face," *Boston Globe*, May 24, 2000, pp. A1, A15.

4. See Chapter 4, notes 1 and 2, and Chapter 5, notes 2 and 3, for extensive bibliographical references.

nored, politics itself. In so doing, we turn on its head the concern with representation that animates our concern with participatory inequality. An important justification for our focus on the participation gap between men and women is its potential consequences for unequal influence on public outcomes. We now consider how one kind of public outcome—the wide disparity in the representation of men and women among visible political elites—might have implications for political participation.[5]

Learning about Politics from Politics

From one perspective, women's lesser interest in and knowledge about politics is surprising. Since the late 1960s, traditional gender roles have come under scrutiny in many domains of life. As we saw in Chapter 6, among husbands and wives there is nearly universal support for equality at home in terms of sharing household chores and making important decisions. Moreover, attitudinal support for equality between women and men has been accompanied by measurable change in behaviors. The most pronounced change has been the entry of women—especially married women with children—into the work force. However, there have been many other notable departures. As we have seen, among younger cohorts, women's educational attainment matches or exceeds men's except when it comes to the most prestigious advanced degrees. In addition, the gender gap with respect to wages has eroded considerably. Furthermore, women are increasingly inhabiting domains ranging from the executive suite to the construction site that had been more or less exclusively male. Progress has even been made in that especially masculine preserve, competitive athletics: a substantial portion of girls engage in inter-scholastic sports; women athletes have distinguished themselves in the Olympics; and women's sports ranging from figure skating to college basketball

---

5. We are grateful to Laura Stoker, not only for the specific suggestion that, in considering how the composition of political elites affects participation, we are inverting the usual representation question but also for her very helpful comments on an earlier version of this chapter.

to professional soccer have generated large audiences and media attention.

The political arena has witnessed change as well. As shown in Figure 13.1, there has been erosion in the expressed opposition to women in politics. In 1972, a substantial majority of both women and men indicated a willingness to vote for a woman for president if their party nominated a qualified candidate, but a noticeable minority did not. By the mid-1990s, support for a qualified woman candidate—at least as expressed in surveys—was overwhelming. Furthermore, in 1974, the public, both men and women, was divided almost equally over the question of whether most men are better suited emotionally for politics than most women. Twenty years later, opinion among both women and men was divided roughly three to one against this proposition.

Moreover, the changes were noticeable not only in what citizens say in surveys but also in the composition of political elites. In 1968 there were eleven women in the House and a lone woman in the Senate. Three decades later, after the election of 2000, the number of women in Congress had risen to sixty-one in the House and thirteen in the Senate.[6] Over the same period, the proportion of women in the state legislatures increased from 4 percent to 22 percent.[7] While the Supreme Court was an exclusively male preserve for nearly the first two hundred years of our nation's life, now two women sit on the Court. The maps in Figure 13.2— which show, by decade, which states have had a woman as governor, senator, or member of the U.S. House—make clear the increasing representation of women in elected office.

Nevertheless, it is easy to overestimate the magnitude of the changes on the political front. The maps in Figure 13.2 also make clear that increasing female representation has not meant universal female representation. The law of averages would suggest that states having a large number of members in the House would be

---

6. The figure for the House includes two non-voting members, one from Washington, D.C., and one from Puerto Rico. See "Incremental Progress for Women in Politics," *New York Times,* November 12, 2000, p. 22, and the Web site of the Center for American Women and Politics <www.rci.rutgers.edu/~cawp/facts/summary2000.html>.

7. Center for American Women and Politics, "CAWP Fact Sheet: Women in Elective Office 2000," Eagleton Institute, New Brunswick, N.J., 2000.

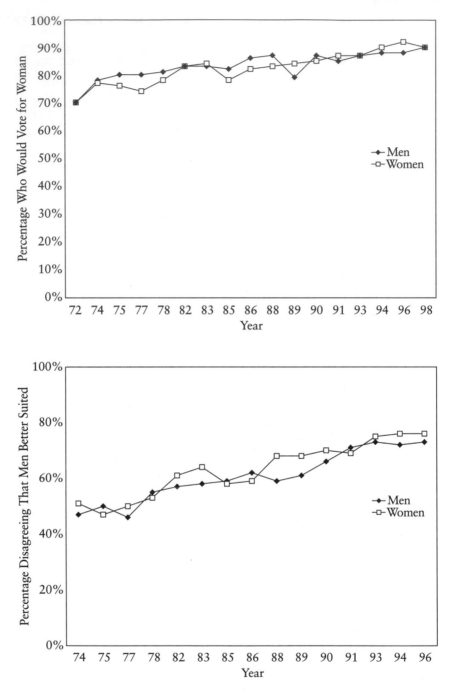

Figure 13.1 Is Politics for Women? Percentage Willing to Vote for a Woman for President *(top)* and Percentage Disagreeing That Men Are Better Suited for Politics *(bottom).* (General Social Survey, National Opinion Research Center, University of Chicago)

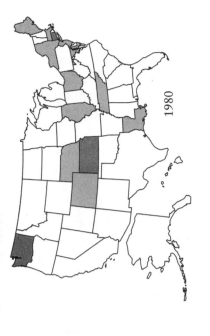

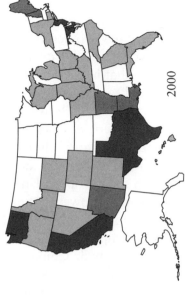

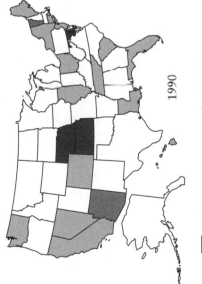

■ At least one woman in the U.S. House

■ Woman senator or governor

■ At least one woman in the U.S. House and a woman senator or governor

Figure 13.2 Where the Women Are

likely to include at least one female representative in their delegations. Yet there are large states—most notably, Pennsylvania—that have elected very few women to Congress. And there are historically progressive states—for example, Massachusetts, Minnesota, and Wisconsin—that have elected very few women to visible public offices. Indeed, a few states have never sent a woman to the governor's mansion, U.S. House, or Senate.[8]

In comparative terms, when it comes to the proportion of women in managerial and administrative positions outside government, the United States is at the top of the list—ahead of all fifteen countries in the European Union and just about all of the nations of the world. However, figures about the proportion of women in the national legislature tell a different story. The United States is behind a majority of the EU nations as well as countries as diverse as Eritrea, Chad, China, and Argentina.[9] Moreover, the American record is less impressive with respect to the more visible and more powerful offices. Very few women have served as governors, and no woman has served in the leadership of either party in Congress. In addition, the United States is not on the list of nations that have elected a woman as president or prime minister—a list that encompasses a varied group of countries including India, Israel, Norway, the Philippines, and Sri Lanka.[10]

Thus it is reasonable to posit that the aggregate gender difference in preferences—that is, in the taste for politics—is related to the implicit message transmitted to women by the dearth of women in the most visible and powerful political positions in the United States: "Politics is not my world." Since tastes clearly have social as well as individual roots, we are curious about the processes of social learning that leave as a residue gender differences

8. Information in this paragraph is taken from the Web site of the Center for American Women and Politics <http:/www.rci.rutgers.edu/~cawp/facts/Stbyst>.

9. Information in this paragraph is taken from United Nations, *The World's Women 1995* (New York: United Nations, 1995), table 14, pp. 171–175. Figures for the national legislature refer to the lower house if the legislature is not unicameral. The EU nations with a lower proportion of women legislators are Belgium (9 percent), France (6 percent), Greece (6 percent), Portugal (9 percent), and the United Kingdom (9 percent). At the time the United Nations data were assembled, the figure for the United States was 11 percent.

10. United Nations, *The World's Women*, p. 152.

in political involvement. It is hardly novel to point out that American democracy was nearly a century and a half old before women were admitted to full citizenship and that the exclusion of women was supported by centuries of engrained custom. Women have been enfranchised, and social mores have changed, but the implicit lesson that politics is a male domain is still taught in various ways—among them, in the fact that the overwhelming majority of political figures, especially powerful ones, are male.

To use a sports analogy, football fans are not just born but made. Any natural inclination that boys may have for rough sports and aggressive play is reinforced by the cues from family, peers, and school: American boys are expected to be interested in football. And that expectation is reinforced throughout life by the observation that, in fact, football *is* a man's game, played exclusively by men. We are led to ask whether, just as they see who plays and appreciates football, women learn that the sport of politics is played by men and appreciated by men. Is the gender difference in the taste for politics rooted in the fact that men have a basis for identifying with the vast majority of the key players in politics?

Other studies offer tantalizing bits of evidence. A study of Americans' knowledge of world leaders showed women to be less likely than men to identify any of the long list of leaders on the list. However, the gender gap in information was substantially smaller for Margaret Thatcher, the only female on the list, than for any other name.[11] In addition, Canadian men were more likely to be able to identify Jean Chrétien, who is male, than Kim Campbell, who is female. The result was reversed for women.[12]

---

11. American National Election Study: 1989 Pilot Study.

12. Analysis of data from the Canadian National Election Study. We are grateful to Henry Brady for providing this information. Evidence that women's political knowledge approaches or surpasses men's when the subject is a woman is also contained in Howard Schuman, Robert F. Belli, and Katherine Bischoping, "The Generational Basis of Historical Knowledge," in *Collective Memory of Political Events: Social Psychological Perspectives,* ed. James W. Pennebaker, Dario Paez, and Bernard Rimé (Mahwah, N.J.: Lawrence Erlbaum Associates, 1997), pp. 47–77; and Howard Schuman and Amy D. Corning, "Collective Knowledge of Public Events: The Soviet Era from the Great Purge to Glasnost," *American Journal of Sociology* 105 (2000): 913–956.

Using NES data, Susan B. Hansen, "Talking about Politics: Gender and Contextual Effects in Political Proselytizing," *Journal of Politics* 59 (1997): 73–103, finds the presence of

What If Politics Were Gender Integrated?

To ask about the effects of a political circumstance in which women were equally represented among political elites is, of course, to entertain a counterfactual. However, we have been able to assemble data that permit us to get some purchase on this line of inquiry. The Citizen Participation Study allows us to consider whether the presence of women in politics has an effect on women's knowledge in a context in which the politicians in question are visible—the Senate. In the spring of 1990 when the survey was conducted, there were only two women in the Senate, Barbara Mikulski of Maryland and Nancy Kassebaum of Kansas; in addition, in the election immediately preceding the survey in 1988, the losing senatorial candidate in Wisconsin, Susan Engeleiter, was female.[13] As shown in Figure 13.3, in states with two male senators, 51 percent of women, compared with 65 percent of men, could name one senator from their state. In the three states with a female Senate incumbent or candidate, the percentage of women who could name a senator rises to 79 percent. Men in states with female Senate incumbents or candidates were also more likely to name a senator correctly—75 percent do so—but the increase is more modest.[14] In short, where there is a woman candidate or incumbent for Senate, women are more likely than men to know a senator's name.

There is, of course, a possibility that respondents from Mary-

---

a female Senate candidate on the ballot to be associated with a significant increase in women's attempts to persuade others how to vote in 1992, but not in other years. Virginia Sapiro and Pamela Johnston Conover also find an impact in "The Variable Gender Basis of Electoral Politics: Gender and Context in the 1992 U.S. Election," *British Journal of Political Science* 27 (1997): 497–523. Kim Fridkin Kahn and Patrick J. Kenney use the NES Senate Election Study to examine the impact of candidate gender on a range of outcomes for a pooled sample of women and men; in their pooled analysis, the presence of female candidates affected recall of the candidates' names, likelihood of mentioning campaign issues, and likelihood of correctly identifying campaign themes. See *The Spectacle of U.S. Senate Campaigns* (Princeton: Princeton University Press, 1999), pp. 187–197.

13. In addition, Hawaii's senator Spark Matsunaga was challenged by a woman candidate, Maria M. Hustace, in the 1988 election. However, the sample includes no respondents from Hawaii.

14. The difference is statistically significant for women (at the .001 level) but is not for men. The sample includes 155 respondents from these three states.

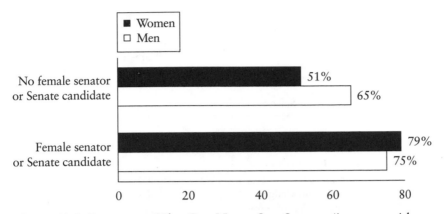

Figure 13.3 Percentage Who Can Name One Senator (in states with and states without a female senator or candidate). (Citizen Participation Study—Main Survey)

land, Kansas, and Wisconsin differ systematically from other Americans in ways that might have implications for political knowledge.[15] Therefore, we extended this analysis in several ways with the findings reported in Table 13.1. Portion A of the table presents the results of a regression analysis predicting respondents' knowledge of the names of the U.S. senators from the states in which they live. As independent variables we include various factors associated with participation along with a dummy variable for living in a state with a female senator or Senate candidate.[16] We report only the coefficients (unstandardized) for the variable measuring the existence of a Senate candidate or incumbent. The results show that for women, but not for men, living in a state with a female Senate candidate or incumbent is associated with a significant increase in the ability to name a senator.

On the basis of this logic we also investigated whether exposure

---

15. For one thing, the male senators from these states, Robert Dole of Kansas and Paul Sarbanes of Maryland, as well as the victor in Wisconsin's 1988 open-seat senatorial contest, department store owner Herbert Kohl, may have been especially well known.

16. The dependent variable is a trichotomy ranging from none correct to two correct. Besides the dummy variable for living in a state with a female senator or Senate candidate, the other independent variables are the same ones we have used throughout to predict political participation. See Table 10.5.

Table 13.1 Women as Candidates and Elected Officials: Impact on Orientations to Politics[a,b]

	Women		Men
A. Effect of a Woman Senator or Candidate on			
Knowledge of Senators' Names	.32**	⇔	.08

B. Effect of a Woman State-wide Incumbent or Candidate on			
Political Information			
Overall scale	.04*	⇔	.00
Civic knowledge	.02		−.15
Knowledge of names	.40**	⇔	.19
Political Interest	.05*	⇔	−.01
Political Efficacy	.04*	⇔	−.02

Source: Citizen Participation Study—Main Survey.

a. Appendix A contains the valid number of cases for these and other measures used in the tables.

b. Ordinary least-squares coefficients; model also controls for childhood politicization, education, family income, job level, religious attendance, age, and years of marriage.

*Coefficient significant at <.05.

**Coefficient significant at <.01.

***Coefficient significant at <.001.

⇔ Difference in the coefficients for men and women is significant at <.05 (by *t*-test) or one coefficient is significant at <.05 and the other is not.

to female politicians has consequences more generally for women's engagement with politics. In our spring 1990 survey, several states had female incumbents or, in the preceding election in 1988, major-party candidates for state-wide office: senator, governor, or lieutenant governor. Using a number of different dependent variables, we undertook parallel analyses, substituting a measure of the number of state-wide female political figures in the respondent's state.[17] Portion B of Table 13.1, which contains unstandard-

---

17. The measure gives the respondent a half-point for each female incumbent or candidate for lieutenant governor; and one point for each female senatorial or gubernatorial incumbent or candidate. A score of 0 indicates that there were no women running as state-wide candidates for or incumbents in visible public office. Because only nine states had both a senatorial and a gubernatorial election in 1988, and fifteen states had neither, the maximum possible score on this scale varies from 3.5 to 8.5. The average *possible* maximum on

ized regression coefficients, shows that, for women, living in a state with a state-wide female politician has a significant impact on each of the components of psychological engagement with politics: political information, interest, and efficacy. When we break political information into its components, we see that it is associated with a significant increase in knowledge of the names of public officials, but not in more general knowledge of principles of government. The difference in the results for the two types of knowledge, in fact, makes sense. We would expect knowledge of principles of government, which is presumably related more directly to schooling, to be less likely to be influenced by the short-term effect of a woman political figure. For men the results are very different. With other factors taken into account, living in a state with a state-wide female politician does not have a significant impact on their psychological orientations to politics.[18]

We took advantage of the capacities of the biennial National Election Studies—a larger number of cases and greater variance in the density of women in the respondents' political environment—to check these suggestive findings about the effects of exposure to

---

the scale is not 8.5, but 5.48. In fact, the highest *actual* value that any state takes on the scale is 1.

18. We were curious as to whether there is an analogous process for African-Americans. In fact, the evidence in the literature on Black empowerment is mixed. In urban settings, Black officeholding does appear to increase the political engagement of African-Americans. As Franklin D. Gilliam, Jr., and Karen M. Kaufmann put it, "[B]lacks living in empowered cities [that is, cities where they hold positions of authority] exhibit greater political knowledge, more political efficacy, and higher levels of trust in government." See Gilliam and Kaufmann, "Is There an Empowerment Life Cycle?: Long-term Black Empowerment and Its Influence on Voter Participation," *Urban Affairs Review* 33 (1998): 741–766, 742. See also Lawrence Bobo and Franklin D. Gilliam, "Race, Sociopolitical Participation, and Black Empowerment," *American Political Science Review* 84 (1990): 377–393; and Gilliam, "Exploring Minority Empowerment: Symbolic Politics, Governing Coalitions, and Traces of Political Style in Los Angeles," *American Journal of Political Science* 40 (1996): 56–81. In contrast, Claudine Gay ("Taking Charge: Black Electoral Success and the Redefinition of American Politics" [Ph.D. dissertation, Harvard University, 1998]) finds that the presence of Black congressional representatives does not appear to have a decisive influence on either Black political engagement or turnout among Blacks, but seems to decrease turnout among Whites. Finally, Katherine Tate finds that Jesse Jackson's candidacy increased Black turnout in the primaries in 1984, but not in 1988, and that in neither case was it associated with higher Black turnout in the presidential election. See "Black Political Participation in the 1984 and 1988 Presidential Elections," *American Political Science Review* 85 (1991): 1159–1176.

visible female politicians. We added data about gubernatorial, senatorial, and congressional races from 1984 through 1996 to the National Election Study (NES) and undertook analyses parallel to those reported in Table 13.1.[19] We constructed a scale measuring the density of women in visible positions in the respondent's political environment: using information about the congressional district and state of residence at the time of the interview, we counted the number of female major-party candidates in elections for governor, House, and Senate on the respondent's ballot; and we awarded an additional point for each victorious female candidate and each current incumbent in one of these offices, yielding a score that could, theoretically, vary between 0 and 12. In fact, while 60 percent of respondents were in a political environment having no women as major-party candidates or incumbents, no respondent was in the opposite circumstance. Indeed, no American has ever been in an environment devoid of men as major-party incumbents or candidates for governor, House, or Senate.

Table 13.2 presents the results of multivariate analyses and shows a strong association—for women, but not for men—between the density of female politicians in a respondent's political environment and several measures of psychological involvement with politics.[20] The more women who vie for or hold important

---

19. We are grateful to Danny Schlozman, who devoted a significant portion of his Christmas vacation to coding information about the large number of races between 1984 and 1996 that involved female candidates for Senate, U.S. House, or governor.

The NES has limitations as a tool for our larger project, understanding the roots of political participation: the regular battery of participatory items is confined to electoral activity, and it does not include a number of the variables—for example, civic skills—that play a central role in our analysis. But because the survey contains a variety of measures of psychological orientations to politics and a large number of cases over a long time span, it is much better suited to our purposes in this chapter.

In previously reported research, we used three years of the NES and found more mixed results than those reported here. At that point we characterized the results of our tests of the effects of women in politics as candidates and incumbents on the political interest of female citizens as a "definite maybe." On the basis of the results in Table 13.2, we would now be much less conservative in interpreting our findings. For the earlier results, see Sidney Verba, Nancy Burns, and Kay Lehman Schlozman, "Knowing and Caring about Politics: Gender and Political Engagement," *Journal of Politics* 59 (1997): 1051–1072.

20. The dependent variables are as follows: followed what's going on in government and public affairs; paid attention to campaign; followed campaign on television, on radio, in

Table 13.2 Women as Candidates and Elected Officials:[a] Impact on Orientations to Politics (NES)[b]

	Women		Men
Effect on			
Political Interest	.52*	⇔	−.13
Campaign Interest	1.02***	⇔	.26
Follow Campaign in Media	.30*	⇔	−.09
Salience of House Candidates	1.30***	⇔	.47

Source: American National Election Studies (1984–1996).

a. The explanatory variable for which the coefficients are presented is the sum, for the respondent's congressional district, of the number of female candidates for office, female winners, and female incumbents for the following offices: governor, senator, and members of Congress. The variable, which can theoretically take on values from 0 to 12, has been re-scaled to vary between 0 and 1.

b. The analysis also controls for education, income, age, age over 65, religious attendance, working, and the specific years.

*Coefficient significant at <.05.

**Coefficient significant at <.01.

***Coefficient significant at <.001.

⇔ Difference in the coefficients for men and women is significant at <.05 (by *t*-test) or one coefficient is significant at <.05 and the other is not.

political offices in the respondent's congressional district or state, the more likely female respondents are to be interested in politics, to be interested in the campaign, to follow the campaign in the media, and to be able to express likes and dislikes about the major-party candidates for the House of Representatives.[21] For men, the presence of women on the ballot or in office has no such effect. In short, the more it looks as if politics is not simply a man's game, the more psychologically involved with politics women are.[22]

---

magazines, and in newspapers; number of likes and dislikes registered in open-ended questions about major-party candidates for House.

21. The measure has no impact on political efficacy for either women or men.

22. Using data taken from the Web site of the Center for American Women and Politics at Rutgers <http:/www.rci.rutgers.edu/~cawp/facts/Stbyst> about the proportion of women among members of the two houses of the state legislature taken together, we also considered the impact of the proportion of women in the state legislature and found small effects that were not consistent across various measures of political engagement. Because different kinds of circumstances produce a relatively high proportion of women in the state legislature, to ensure that characteristics of the states and their legislatures were not masking the impact of female state legislators on women's political engagement, we also esti-

Table 13.3 Do Female Senate Candidates Affect the Gender Gap in Involvement? (states with victorious women candidates in 1992)[a]

	Women		Men	
	1988–1990	1992	1988–1990	1992
Know Senator or Candidate	29% ⇔	47%	43%	45%
Very Interested in Campaign	35 ⇔	53	45	58

Source: American National Election Studies—Pooled Senate Study.
a. California, Illinois, and Washington.
⇔ Difference in political knowledge or political interest is statistically significant at the .01 level.

We were able to conduct still another test of our hypothesis. We used the distinctive design of the NES Pooled Senate Study to reconceptualize the question. Because the Senate Study was conducted on a state-by-state basis over three elections, we were able to consider each state as a mini-laboratory and assess what happened to the gender gap in engagement when an eventually victorious female Senate candidate was on the ballot. Over the period covered by the Senate Study (1988–1992), three states—California, Illinois, and Washington—witnessed Senate elections in which a female candidate was the eventual winner. As shown in Table 13.3, in these three states women were significantly more likely to be able to name a senator or Senate candidate and to be interested in the campaign during the election that yielded a victorious woman—with the result that the gender gap with respect to knowledge closed completely and the gender gap with respect to campaign interest nearly closed.[23] Once again, we have evidence of

---

mated models that controlled for the political culture of the state and the size and professionalism of its legislature. Even in the face of these controls, we could see no systematic impact of women state legislators. We are grateful to Julie Schlozman who gave up her late-summer days of leisure to code these data and who cheerfully volunteered to undertake many other research tasks as we prepared the manuscript for publication.

23. We performed a parallel analysis for states with losing female candidates on the ballot. When the female candidate was not "serious"—that is, when she eventually lost by a large margin—there was no effect upon the gender gap in engagement. The data are more ambiguous for states in which the female candidate lost narrowly.

the impact of the absence of women among salient political elites upon women's psychological involvement with politics.[24]

How Does the Process Work?: Some Data and More Speculation

Our data point unambiguously to the influence of the gender composition of the political environment on women's psychological engagement with politics, but they do not specify the mechanism that operates to produce the effect. *Why* does the appearance of women seeking or holding visible political office have an impact on the political engagement of women, and why is this impact not shared by men? There are a number of possible explanations for this phenomenon.

Some of these posit that elections involving women are in some way distinctive. A number of systematic studies of elections do find that elections are different when there is a woman on the ballot, but taken together, these studies come to somewhat conflicting conclusions and, more importantly, they do not provide a basis for drawing connections between the distinguishing characteristics of elections involving women and the enhanced political engagement of women in the electorate.[25] One suggestion is that just having a woman vying for visible public office is itself a sufficient novelty to

24. We were also curious to see whether these processes operate cross-nationally. Using Eurobarometer data (Studies no. 2443 ["Employment, Unemployment, and Gender Equality," February–April 1996] and no. 6748 ["Policies and Practices in Building Europe and the European Union," January–March 1996], available from the Inter-university Consortium for Political and Social Research) for a number of European countries, we investigated whether there is an association between the proportion of women in a nation's parliament and women's psychological engagement with politics. Although we probed several orientations to politics and conceptualized them in terms of both the absolute levels of women's and men's engagement with politics and the size of the gender disparity in engagement, we could not substantiate any relationship between the gender composition of parliaments and various orientations to politics. Because we undertook only simple bivariate analyses, others may wish to probe this question further. We are grateful to George Rabinowitz for this suggestion.

25. For an interesting comparison of the television spots of men and women candidates, as well as a summary of the conflicting findings contained in other studies, see Leonard Williams, "Gender, Political Advertising, and the 'Air Wars,' " in *Women and Elective Office,* ed. Sue Thomas and Clyde Wilcox (New York: Oxford University Press, 1998), chap. 3.

generate greater interest in the election. However, explanations that focus on the novelty factor of having a female candidate on the ballot cannot account for the fact that women, but not men, respond to the novelty. Another common suggestion is that when women run for office, the media pay more attention. However, in her study of senatorial races between 1983 and 1988, Kim Fridkin Kahn finds that, even with the competitiveness of the race taken into account, races with female candidates attracted less, not more, newspaper coverage than did all-male races. Moreover, newspaper reporting on women candidates was more likely to concentrate on horse race issues.[26]

Still another suggestion focuses on processes of mobilization— which are known to have a powerful independent impact on interest in campaigns and in politics more generally—and the supposition that women voters are more likely to be contacted when a woman is running for office. Using several different measures of voter mobilization contained in the NES cumulative file, we were unable to find an association between the presence of a woman candidate on the ballot and either significantly higher aggregate voter mobilization or disproportionate mobilization of women. In short, if elections in which women contend are distinctive beyond the fact that the ballot is not all male, we are unable to connect their particular characteristics to their politicizing effects for women.

The other point of entry to understanding the consequences of the gender composition of the political environment for women is to focus, not on the special qualities of elections involving women candidates, but on the reactions and characteristics of voters. We considered—but could find no confirmation for—the suggestion that there is an association between a gender-integrated political environment and, among women citizens, egalitarian attitudes toward gender roles.

In addition, NES data contain information useful for assessing whether the gender composition of the political environment changes the considerations that voters bring to the appraisal of

---

26. Kim Fridkin Kahn, *The Political Consequences of Being a Woman* (New York: Columbia University Press, 1996), chap. 4.

candidates. We categorized the answers to open-ended questions about what respondents liked and disliked about the candidates for the House in their districts and created, among others, a measure indicating whether, among the twenty possible bases for evaluating House candidates, the respondent mentioned either candidate's sex.[27]

Although we might have expected that the presence of women as candidates and incumbents for visible office influenced the political discourse surrounding House elections, we found no evidence that gender-integrated environments encourage voters to emphasize particular human qualities such as compassion or trustworthiness or to focus upon particular kinds of domestic policies with which women have traditionally been associated. Nevertheless, as shown in Table 13.4, for women, the density of women in the respondent's political environment is associated with spontaneous reference to a House candidate's sex. For men, the association shows up only once—in 1992, when women candidates and attendant issues figured importantly. Thus the presence of a woman running for the House does not lead to an overall transformation of the way that the election is construed by voters. Rather, when a woman is on the ballot, women—and, under certain circumstances, men—take note.

What psychological processes operate to produce a circumstance such that, when women contest and hold visible public office, women notice and consequently become more interested in and knowledgeable about politics? We can suggest, but cannot assess, two possible mechanisms. On one hand, visible women in politics might function as role models and carry a kind of symbolic significance—sending the message to women citizens that politics is an inclusive domain, open to them. On the other, the process might involve a self-interested assessment. The presence of women contesting or occupying public office politics might in-

---

27. We use data from the NES for 1990, 1992, 1994, and 1996—a period that begins with the year in which the Citizen Participation Study was conducted and brackets 1992, the Year of the Woman. Because women who live in relatively gender-integrated political environments are more likely to have something to say about House candidates, we restrict our focus to those who mentioned something they liked or disliked about the House candidates in their districts.

Table 13.4 Women as Candidates and Elected Officials: Impact[a] on Salience of House Candidate's Sex[b]

	Women		Men
1990	0.07*	⇔	0.01
1992	0.22***	⇔	0.06*
1994	0.07*	⇔	0.01
1996	0.25***	⇔	0.03

Source: American National Election Studies 1990, 1992, 1994, 1996.

a. Ordinary least-squares analysis with education included.

b. The explanatory variable for which the coefficients are presented is the sum, for the respondent's congressional district, of the number of female candidates for office, female winners, and female incumbents for the following offices: governor, senator, and members of Congress. The variable, which can theoretically take on values from 0 to 12, has been re-scaled to vary between 0 and 1. The dependent variable measures respondents' mention of their House candidate's sex as a reason to like or dislike the candidate.

*Coefficient significant at $<.05$.

**Coefficient significant at $<.01$.

***Coefficient significant at $<.001$.

⇔ Difference in the coefficients for men and women is significant at $<.05$ (by t-test) or one coefficient is significant at $<.05$ and the other is not.

crease psychological engagement with politics by suggesting to women citizens that, as public officials, women will produce "woman friendly" public policies. There is nothing mutually exclusive about these processes. Our data do not permit us to evaluate these hypothetical mechanisms or establish the circumstances under which they operate in tandem, singly, or not at all. Hence we invite future researchers to elaborate the symbolic, self-interested, or other processes that operate to link the gender composition of the political environment with women's political engagement.

Can We Close the Participation Gap?

These results are germane to the puzzle generated by our attempt to explain the gender gap in political participation. The disparity in activity between men and women derives from many sources, many of them rooted in the non-political institutions of adult life. We have made much greater progress in locating the sources of differences in participatory factors in processes of selection into and experiences within schools, jobs, non-political organizations, and religious institutions than in understanding the sources of the gender difference with respect to a final, crucial participatory factor, psychological involvement with politics.

Our concern with the puzzle of women's deficit in political involvement has brought us in this chapter to the one institution that we had so far neglected, politics itself. The disparity between women and men in the taste for politics turns out, at least in part, to have political roots. The legacy of centuries of de jure and decades of de facto exclusion from politics is a residual difference in the extent to which women and men know and care about politics. As shown in our data, when women appear on the political scene in visible and powerful positions, the political involvement of women citizens increases significantly.

The final step in our analysis is to assess the impact of those gains on the gap in participation between women and men. To make a bottom-line evaluation of the consequences for women's participation of the gender composition of the political environment requires a two-stage process: we ask, first, about the increment to women's political interest and knowledge that results from an increase in the number of women who contest or occupy state-wide office and, second, about the participatory payoff that would, in turn, result from this enhancement in political engagement.[28] We conduct the analysis for women only because, as shown in Table 13.1, the extent of gender integration of the political environment does not have a significant effect on men's psychological orientations toward politics.

We can use the results presented in portion B of Table 13.1 to ask what would happen if everyone lived in a state having just one female within the group comprising its gubernatorial and senatorial incumbents and candidates. This was a circumstance that represents the maximum gender integration of the political environ-

---

28. Although the coefficient presented in Table 13.1 indicates that the gender composition of the political environment also has an impact on political efficacy for women, we confine our discussion to political information and interest because the result for efficacy is unstable in the Citizen Participation Study data and does not appear in the NES data.

ments of the respondents to the Citizen Participation survey at the time it was conducted in 1990.[29] It was enjoyed by only 10 percent of the public—in contrast to the 81 percent of the American public that then lived in states having no women among those contending for or holding the office of lieutenant governor, governor, or senator.[30] Although it would represent a situation quite different from that which obtained in 1990 or obtains now, a single female among the state-wide political elites constitutes a relatively modest proposal. Even if achieved, state-wide political elites would remain overwhelmingly male.

However, even such a limited change in the gender composition of the political environment would have the effect of diminishing by more than half the disparity between men and women in political interest and information. Since political interest and information have a strong impact on political participation, the increase in political engagement would produce, on average, .09 additional political acts.[31] While less than one-tenth of a political act might sound minuscule, we can recall that it represents about half of the residual gender difference in activity that remained after accounting for institutionally based resources and requests for activity. (See Table 10.5.)

What if, instead, we posit a much more ambitious change—equal representation of men and women among state-wide political elites? To extrapolate from our earlier analysis the implications for women's political activity of a fully gender-integrated political environment entails making an utterly unrealistic assumption—that a world in which women had achieved parity among state-wide political elites would otherwise be no different and, thus, that the relationships underlying our analysis of the sources of the

---

29. Vermont's governor, Madeleine Kunin, had been re-elected in 1988, which makes Vermont the only state to score above 1 on the scale measuring the density of women in the political environment. However, no Vermonters appear in the national probability sample used for the Citizen Participation Study. A score of 1 on the scale could also represent an incumbent female lieutenant governor who had been elected or re-elected in 1988. However, none of the 1990 female lieutenant governors had been elected or re-elected in 1988.

30. Figures in this paragraph are calculated from data contained in U.S. Bureau of the Census, *Statistical Abstract of the United States: 1996*, 116th ed. (Washington, D.C.: U.S. Government Printing Office, 1996), p. 28.

31. See Appendix D for a discussion of the technique we used to arrive at these figures.

gender disparity in participation would remain unchanged. Presumably men, whose psychological orientations to politics are not affected by what are essentially marginal changes in the gender composition of the political environment when those changes occur in a context of massive overrepresentation of men among political elites, might respond differently in a circumstance of gender equality.

Still, it is notable that, if women were represented equally in the political environment, the resultant gains in political interest and knowledge would boost them sufficiently that they would surpass men by a margin roughly equal to men's initial advantage with respect to these measures of political engagement. These enhanced levels of political interest and information would yield, in turn, an average increase in political activity for women of .29 of an act.[32] In short, for women, achieving parity among state-wide political elites would produce concomitant gains in their political participation that would, on their own, almost wipe out the gender disparity in political activity—even without any amelioration of the deficits in participatory factors that result from differences in education and work force experiences. That is, if other current conditions were to persist but women were to achieve equality among state-wide political elites, they would also achieve near equality in political activity even in the absence of other changes in the relative balance of educational and work-based participatory resources.

We subjected these simulated findings to a final reality check. National data from the 1996 NES show the expected deficit for women with respect to campaign interest and general political interest.[33] However, when we consider just the respondents from California—which was then the only state to have two female senatorial incumbents—there is no significant gender difference when it comes to these two measures of political engagement.[34] Because

---

32. See Appendix D for discussion of how we arrived at this figure.

33. Using all the cases in the sample ($N = 1,392$) in a single equation with controls for education, income, age, age over 65, religious attendance, and work force participation yields significant coefficients on gender of $-.50$ (.19) for campaign interest and -1.10 (.16) for political interest indicating a deficit for women.

34. We follow the same strategy and use a single equation ($N = 112$) with controls for

these respondents are not a random sample of Californians, we must interpret this finding with caution. Nevertheless, these data confirm the results of our extrapolation.

Conclusion

By turning to the world of politics itself, we have solved the puzzle created by the unexplained gender difference in psychological orientations to politics. The fact that politics is a man's world has sufficient consequences for women's psychological engagement with politics to account for gender differences in the orientations to politics that facilitate participation.

In this chapter we have inverted our usual concern with representation. Ordinarily we justify a focus on gender inequalities in citizen participation in terms of their implications for inequalities in the responsiveness of political leaders. This analysis has probed the consequences of the deficit of women in political leadership for the political engagement of women citizens. Our findings are relevant to the debate about the nature of representation in a democracy. Political scientists tend not to be very enthusiastic about descriptive representation of demographic groups. That is, they tend to argue that what matters is what elected officials do and whether they reflect the preferences and opinions of constituents, not what they look like and whether they resemble constituents in their gender, race, religion, or other ascriptive characteristics. Without weighing into the contentious debate over descriptive representation, we would suggest that our findings bring an additional consideration to the discussion.[35] The gender composition of the political environment—whether it is balanced between men and women or remains exclusively male—has consequences for women's engagement with politics.

---

education, income, age, age over 65, religious attendance, and work force participation. The resulting coefficients on gender of −.24 (.64) for campaign interest and −.12 (.63) for political interest are not statistically significant. A reduced model containing only a control for education does not change this result.

35. For an argument about the ways descriptive representation can improve communication between representatives and their constituents, see Jane J. Mansbridge, "Should Blacks Represent Blacks and Women Represent Women?" *Journal of Politics* 61 (1999): 628–657.

14

⸎

Conclusion:
The Private Roots of
Public Action

Decades have passed since the Nineteenth Amendment enfranchised women, and the era when women were denied the right to vote exists as a living memory for only a very small, and diminishing, number of Americans. In fact, only 9 percent of the women in the 1990 sample of the American public that forms the basis for most of the analysis in this book were even alive when women won the vote in 1920. Only one-tenth of 1 percent of the women in that sample were of voting age when the amendment was passed. And, of that group, no one was old enough to have lived through an election when she was prevented from going to the polls solely by virtue of being a woman. Thus today the essential citizenship right of casting a ballot has been part of the lives of women and men in America since birth.[1]

Nevertheless, in spite of substantial changes in the opportunities, roles, and responsibilities of men and women, the intervening decades have not witnessed full gender equality in citizen participation. While not large, the disparity between women and men across various forms of political activity is both consistent in direction and surprising in its contours. Although women are somewhat more likely than men to go to the polls, they lag when it comes to other forms of activity. Compared with men, women are less likely to get involved in electoral campaigns either as campaign workers or as financial contributors. The gender inequality

---

1. Of course, many Americans alive today—among them, older southern Blacks and immigrants—have experienced disenfranchisement as adults.

357

is especially pronounced when it comes to political money: women are not only less likely to make campaign donations, but they write smaller checks when they give. Moreover, women are less likely than men to take part in various forms of non-electoral activity—including membership in political organizations and involvement in efforts to solve community problems—that have sometimes been assumed to be their specialty.

The puzzle of unequal participation has constituted the central question of our inquiry. As we warned at the outset, however, the path to a solution to this riddle has not been a straight or simple one. In the search for the multiple sources of the disparity between women and men in political activity, we have sought clues in many places: the home, school, workplace, non-political organizations, and churches. In the process of seeking the roots of the participatory gap between men and women in the important institutions of everyday life, we have learned a great deal about how these institutions—individually and jointly—shape our lives in ways that leave gender differences in their wake. In short, our hedgehog's quest to understand one big thing has entailed confronting enough additional questions and producing enough additional answers to satisfy any fox.

Understanding Gender Differences in Participation

Those who worry about important social problems often seize upon a particular remedy, usually one that is politically congenial and expected to act as a magic bullet. Thus some would deal with lagging educational achievement by enacting school vouchers; others by raising teachers' pay. Some would confront high rates of violent crime by mandating longer prison terms; others by making it harder to acquire handguns. And some would treat the problem of high rates of welfare dependency by limiting welfare eligibility to a finite, brief period; others by providing job training and day care so that public assistance recipients could get and keep jobs. Such solutions are usually, if not wrong, at least incomplete. Significant social phenomena rarely have a single cause.

Our explanation of the gender difference in political participation underlines that we, too, are dealing with a single outcome with multiple causes. In Chapter 1, we listed several common-sense explanations for the gender gap in political participation that had been suggested by the friends, students, and colleagues with whom we discussed this study. Using data from several surveys, we subjected each one to empirical test and learned that no single explanation suffices to account for the gender difference in activity. Some of them turned out to be just plain wrong. Others were confirmed as partial explanations for the disparity in activity—though not always in quite the expected manner. And factors emerged as important in understanding the participatory gap that did not even weigh in the initial guesswork.

Let us review these initial hunches and see how they fared:

- The notion that women, especially women with children at home and full-time jobs, do not have the *time* to take part in politics received no confirmation. Try as we might we simply could not find a relationship between the resource of leisure time and political activity.
- Similarly, we could not substantiate the hypothesis that raising children so absorbs available mental energy that mothers, especially those with toddlers underfoot, do not have the *psychic space* to pay attention to politics.
- We devoted considerable energy to investigating the role of the *patriarchal family* as a school for democratic citizenship. When we opened the door to look inside at the contemporary American family, we found a complicated situation with respect to domestic hierarchy. While we did find some support for the suggestion that domestic inequality has implications for the gender gap in activity, the relationship does not function in quite the hypothesized manner, and the consequences for husbands' political participation are at least as great as for wives'.
- The emphasis upon *socioeconomic resources* turned out, not surprisingly, to be well placed. Women are, on average, disadvantaged with respect to education, income, and occupational status, attributes long known to be associated with political ac-

tivity. These deficits are important in accounting for the participation gap. In particular, the disparity in educational attainment is significant in accounting for gender differences in participation.

- With respect to processes of *discrimination* that erect barriers to the acquisition of the resources that facilitate political activity, our results are contradictory. Although our data cannot be used to measure the results of discrimination, we have seen that, when other relevant attributes are taken into account, men are more likely than women to get the kinds of jobs that develop civic skills and to gain positions of lay leadership in their churches—with potential consequences for their portfolio of participatory resources. However, the perception of having been the object of discrimination actually operates as an independent factor in enhancing women's participation.

- We also investigated the processes of childhood and adult *socialization* that might lead men and women to draw different conclusions about the relevance of politics to their lives. We saw that women are less likely than men to be psychologically engaged with politics: less likely to be politically interested, informed, or efficacious. This attitudinal deficit contributes substantially to the gender gap in activity. However, when there are women candidates on the ballot and incumbents in visible public offices, women, but not men, are more politically interested and informed, thus diminishing significantly gender differences in the psychological orientations to politics.

A set of factors that accounts for a significant portion of the gender disparity in activity did not even appear on the original list. The non-political institutions of adult life—the workplace, non-political voluntary associations, and religious institutions—function in various ways to enhance political participation. In particular, they provide opportunities for the exercise of civic skills, and they place individuals into the networks through which requests for political activity are mediated. The workplace is especially rich in opportunities to acquire participatory factors. Because women are less likely than men to be in the work force and because, even if employed full time, women are less likely to hold jobs that develop civic skills, gender differences in work force experiences figure significantly in explaining gender differences in political activity.

We found only one factor that operates unambiguously to narrow, rather than to widen, the participatory gap between men and women. Women are somewhat more likely than men to have been involved in high school government and other high school clubs and activities. Whether activity in high school acts as a training ground for future voluntarism or whether it indicates a pre-existing propensity to take part, it is unambiguously associated with adult activity. However, compared with the boost given to men's political activity by virtue of their aggregate educational advantage, women's greater activity in high school contributes much less substantially to their political participation.

Thus we explain the gender disparity in participation as the result of the incremental contributions of a number of factors, and our approach is genuinely multifaceted. In contrast to some analysts, who focus on a single source of the origins of politically relevant gender differences, we bring a variety of institutions into our purview—the family, school, workplace, non-political organizations, religious institutions, and politics itself. Furthermore, although our emphasis upon the institutions of everyday life renders our analysis deeply social structural, attitudes and beliefs play a crucial role. Part of the explanation of why men are somewhat more politically active than women is that they are more likely to be politically interested, knowledgeable, and efficacious.

Individuals in Institutional Context

Social science analysis based on surveys is legitimately criticized for treating individuals as self-contained units apart from the social contexts in which they live, learn, work, play, and pray. We have endeavored always to place individuals in context, considering the implications for participation of a variety of non-political institutions. Moreover, we have sought not to treat institutions in isolation. Rather we have attempted to demonstrate the links between institutions, showing the consequences of what happens in one place, for example, at home or in school, for what happens elsewhere, for example, on the job or in church. As we have said, although these institutions are central in generating political participation, they are not themselves political. Their role in providing factors that foster participation is a by-product of institutional functions that are explicitly apolitical.

Furthermore, their role in shaping participatory outcomes can be either direct or indirect. Consider what we have learned about the family. In no institution we discuss is differentiation on the basis of gender more pronounced than in the family. Wives and husbands, mothers and fathers, have traditionally had different roles and responsibilities with respect to breadwinning, child rearing, household management, and overall family authority. In spite of decades of change in both family structures and gender roles, the traditional division of labor at home has proved remarkably resilient. The direct effects of gender-based patterns in the household turned out to be very different from what is usually assumed. Although divorce seems to lower political participation, the expected positive impact on activity of being married rather than single did not materialize. In addition, we were surprised to find that the constraints on time imposed—disproportionately on women—by responsibility for care of home and children do not, with other factors taken into account, reduce political activity. Nor, all things being equal, does lack of decision-making authority at home seem to depress women's political participation. Interestingly, the direct effects of domestic inequality, while relatively modest, are manifest in the husband's political participation: when the husband is boss at home, he is more active in politics.

The indirect impact of family life is much more substantial than any direct effect. While marriage and children draw men into the work force, preschool children have the opposite effect for women—keeping them at home. These gender-differentiated processes have obvious consequences for the relative stockpiles of civic skills and requests for activity derived from the workplace. Thus family responsibilities operate indirectly through the differential impact on work force participation to yield an advantage to men in work-based participatory factors and, in turn, a differential boost to men's political activity. A similar pattern of institutional linkages obtains for processes of affiliation with religious institutions. Family circumstances weigh only very marginally in women's decisions to join a religious congregation. In contrast, for men, marriage and children are strongly associated with church membership and attendance at services. Once again, there are the implications for the acquisition of participatory factors. Family commitments have an indirect effect on the participatory factors that men acquire in church and, thus, on their political activity.

In order to understand the institutional roots of political activity, it is, therefore, also essential to differentiate between processes of institutional selection and institutional treatment: that is, we pay attention both to how individuals end up in institutions and to the experiences they have once affiliated. Processes of institutional selection and treatment do not work the same way from one institution to another—or even within a single institution. As we have seen, for the workplace, these processes reinforce one another. First, men are more likely to be in the work force. Second, even when educational attainment and work force attachment are taken into account, they are more likely to have the kind of jobs that provide opportunities to exercise civic skills and exposure to requests for political activity. Thus differential selection and differential treatment work together to produce a substantial advantage for men in work-based participatory factors.

When it comes to religious institutions, the configuration is quite different. Processes of selection confer an advantage on women, who are more likely to consider religion to be important in their lives, to attend services, and to be active in a congregation. However, among those affiliated with a church, men are more likely to exercise congregational leadership and thus are slightly more likely to acquire church-based participatory factors. The net result of these contradictory forces is that women's advantage with respect to church-based participatory factors—a function of differential selection—is not statistically significant. In short, religious factors, although very important as predictors of political activity, have no impact on the participatory difference between men and women.

UNDERSTANDING PARTICIPATION/UNDERSTANDING THE PARTICIPATION GAP

This discussion of church-based participatory factors reminds us that explaining participation is a different enterprise from explaining the gender gap in political activity. A number of factors that are significant in understanding participation do not contribute to the disparity in activity between men and women.

Only if there is a difference between women and men either in the level of a participatory factor or in the effect of that factor on activity does it have an impact on the gender gap in participation. For example, having parents who were politically active is associated with adult political participation. However, since men and women are equally likely to have been blessed with politically active parents, and since the participatory payoff of coming from a politically active household is the same for women and men, family political background—which functions in the explanation of political participation—does not help to explain why men are somewhat more politically active than women.

Non-political organizations play a similar role in our analysis. All work on citizen participation places great emphasis on non-political organizations, and our analysis shows why they are strongly associated with political participation: they provide opportunities to develop politically relevant civic skills and connections to channels of political recruitment. Feminist historians have uncovered a rich tradition of women's organizational involvement in the era before women were granted the suffrage. Nevertheless, there is no gender difference either in the likelihood of being involved in a non-political organization or in the consequences of organizational involvement for participation.[2] Hence affiliations with non-political organizations, while central to the explanation of political participation, do not contribute to our understanding of the participatory disparity between men and women.

It is striking that the explanation of the gender gap in politi-

---

2. We repeat that we are referring to organizations that do not take stands in politics. Men are more likely than women to be involved in explicitly political organizations. These affiliations with political organizations, which we consider a form of political activity itself, are especially likely to generate requests for other kinds of political activity and thus to lead to enhanced activity in campaigns, contacts with public officials, and the like.

cal activity rests almost entirely on gender differences in level rather than in effect. That is, the cumulative result of experiences in everyday life is that women lag somewhat in participation because their stockpiles of participatory factors—education, family income, institutionally based civic skills, and recruitment—are smaller than men's, rather than because these participatory factors are differentially useful to men and women in fostering political activity.

A Richer Account of Participation

Although our central focus has been on the gender gap in political activity, the model we have developed provides a richer understanding of political participation construed more generally. In 1972 Verba and Norman Nie introduced the "SES model," in which income and education were the principal predictors of activity.[3] Their analysis clarified the nature and extent of stratification in American political participation. However, their model was as much an accounting model as an explanatory model, demonstrating the strong association between socioeconomic status and political activity without explaining how and why higher status fosters activity.

The Civic Voluntarism Model, developed in the early 1990s by Verba, Schlozman, and Henry Brady, filled the explanatory gap by specifying the causal links between a number of participatory factors—resources, motivations, and recruitment networks—and political activity. By demonstrating how these participatory factors, in turn, derive from socioeconomic status, they were able to explain *why* socioeconomic status and participation are connected. In particular, they explained the primacy of educational attainment by showing that education has not only a direct impact on political activity but more important indirect effects by enhancing nearly every other participatory factor: the well educated are more affluent, more likely to exercise civic skills and to receive requests

---

3. Sidney Verba and Norman H. Nie, *Participation in America* (New York: Harper and Row, 1972).

for political activity, and more politically interested and knowledgeable.[4]

The present analysis takes us one step further by specifying the processes by which participatory factors are created in non-political institutions. By distinguishing between processes of selection into institutions and the treatment within institutions and by demonstrating the connections between institutions, we spell out more fully how institutional processes work, thus deepening our understanding of the links between non-political and political life.

In particular, this approach allows us to specify further the institutional underpinnings of the continuing participatory payoff from educational attainment. Those who are born to parents of limited educational attainment begin life with a participatory disadvantage that is difficult to overcome; and any educational deficit upon entering adulthood will be magnified thereafter by the institutions of everyday life. As shown in Table 14.1, the non-political institutions of adult life grant a significant advantage to the well educated with respect both to institutional access and to the acquisition of participatory factors within institutions. Educational attainment plays a particularly powerful role with respect to the workplace, a domain that is a rich lode of participatory factors. For both men and women, education affects who goes to work, what kinds of jobs individuals get once in the work force, and whether they develop civic skills and receive requests for political activity once in a particular job category. A significant exception to the pattern of association between educational attainment and institutional selection is that membership in religious institutions is not related to educational attainment—either for women or for men. Once affiliated with a religious institution, however, well-educated women are more likely both to develop civic skills and to receive requests to take part, and well-educated men are more likely to be recruited to political activity. Thus the non-political institutions of adult life reinforce the educational stratification of the participatory process.

---

4. Sidney Verba, Kay Lehman Schlozman, and Henry E. Brady, *Voice and Equality: Civic Voluntarism in American Politics* (Cambridge: Harvard University Press, 1995), p. 420.

Table 14.1 Does Education Predict the Acquisition of Participatory Factors?

	Women	Men
WORK FORCE		
Selection	X	X
Treatment		
Job level	X	X
Skills	X	X
Recruitment	X	X
NON-POLITICAL ORGANIZATIONS		
Selection	X	X
Treatment		
Skills	X	X
Recruitment	X	
RELIGIOUS INSTITUTIONS		
Selection		
Treatment		
Skills	X	
Recruitment	X	X

THE POLITICAL SOURCES OF POLITICAL ACTIVITY

Because we have been concerned to understand the roots of political activity in everyday life, we have paid less attention to the multiplier effects of political involvement. That is, political participation begets political participation. All things being equal, those who care deeply about some policy issue are more likely to be politically active.[5] Moreover, taking part in politics generates the political skills and requests for political activity that foster future activity. In fact, those who seek to get others involved use direct or indirect evidence of past participation in locating likely prospects.[6]

Nevertheless, the process we have outlined does not neglect en-

5. Verba, Schlozman, and Brady, *Voice and Equality,* chap. 14.

6. See Steven J. Rosenstone and John Mark Hansen, *Mobilization, Participation, and Democracy in America* (New York: Macmillan, 1993); and Henry E. Brady, Kay Lehman Schlozman, and Sidney Verba, "Prospecting for Participants: Rational Expectations and the Recruitment of Political Activists," *American Political Science Review* 93 (1999): 153–168.

tirely the political roots of participation. We have seen that orientations to politics are central to the participatory process. Those who know and care about politics, who feel that they could make a difference politically, and who identify with one of the two major parties are more politically active. Moreover, while group consciousness—the perception that group members have shared problems that the government has a responsibility to confront—does not generate political activity, it does channel participation in the direction of issues that have a special impact on group members, a finding that holds for race or ethnicity as well as for gender.

Most importantly, women's, but not men's, psychological engagement with politics is influenced by the gender composition of the political environment. The indirect consequences on participation of a less gender-segregated political environment are substantial.

A GENERAL APPROACH

Although we have trained our attention fixedly on the understanding of gender differences in participation, the utility of our approach is confined neither to gender nor to political participation. To repeat yet once more, our analytical strategy has been to use separate equations to determine whether the factors that foster political activity operate similarly for women and men and an outcomes analysis to determine how gender differences in the levels and effects of those factors work together to explain gender differences in participation. However, as demonstrated by the analysis in Chapter 11, this approach is applicable to groups defined by characteristics other than gender. As long as the specified groups have reasonably clearly defined boundaries, our approach is appropriate. Thus it provides a template for understanding participatory differences among African-Americans, Latinos, and Anglo-Whites; residents of big cities, suburbs, and small towns; members of the World War II generation, Baby Boomers, and Gen X'ers; Protestants, Catholics, Jews, Muslims, and atheists; and so on. Furthermore, as we saw in Chapter 11, if the data base contains sufficient cases for analysis, groups can be proliferated so as to take into account the inevitable heterogeneity within any social group. Thus one might wish to differentiate between evangelical and mainline Protestants, or between male and female Boomers, or between Black and White urbanites.

Although it would surely be beyond our substantive expertise, this approach would also seem appropriate for understanding group differences in many other domains—wages, reading scores, divorce rates, or the incidence of heart attacks, to name a few. The logic of the analysis would be the same as that outlined here. Only the names of the variables under investigation would be changed to reflect the substantive problem under consideration.

Understanding Gender

The contentious debates about the meaning of political participation and the forces that shape it seem almost tame compared with the discussions surrounding issues involving gender. We hope that our approach illuminates how to think about and to study gender differences in domains beyond our particular concern with gender and political participation. Nevertheless, we make no pretense of being able to offer a definitive account of the origins and meaning of gender differences. Indeed, as should be apparent by now, we do not believe a definitive account to be possible.

In fact, two of the most important principles guiding our analytic strategy militate strongly against the formulation of a Unified Field Theory of Gender—a single, integrated account of gender differences. First, as we have stated repeatedly, women and men are heterogeneous groups, divided along multiple axes of social cleavage—including race, class, generation, religion, and ideology. Any analysis focusing on gender differences must incorporate recognition of this diversity and the ways in which these social dimensions interact with gender differences.

Second, the contextual variation in the expression of gender differences similarly militates against the formulation of a single theory of gender difference. Across disciplines scholars have been probing the extent, nature, and roots of differences between women and men. What is clear, however, is that we can make greater headway in this intellectual project if, instead of asking flatly whether men and women differ, we recognize that the extent and nature of gender differences will vary across domains of endeavor. There is no reason to expect that we can generalize from the committee hearing room to the board room, schoolroom, locker room, operating room, and living room. Gender differences in moral reasoning or the rates of violent crime do not necessarily tell us anything about the realm of politics. What is more, even within a particular realm of activity, there may be no uniformity across different aspects of behavior.[7] For example, patterns of gender similarity or difference characteristic of congressional roll-call voting may not be relevant when it comes to paths of political recruitment or styles of campaigning for the House. The arena of human action on which we have concentrated our attention, citizen political participation, is one in which gender differences are relatively muted. However, what happens in that domain is affected by what happens in two institutions in which gender distinctions matter profoundly, the home and the workplace.

STUDYING GENDER DIFFERENCES EMPIRICALLY
Our approach has been unambiguously empirical. We have grounded our hypotheses in social theories of various kinds, including feminist theory, and we have developed a general model of the origins of gender disparities in participation. Still, the fundamental test for any conclusion we reach is always: what do the data say? The data have not always behaved as we expected—or wished. We were surprised to find that the expected gender disparity in campaign work and contributions also obtains for forms of political participation supposedly more congenial to women—cooperative community activity and involvement in political organizations. Similarly, we had anticipated—incorrectly, it turns out—that constraints on the free time of women who shoulder the twin responsibilities of household management and full-time paid work would figure importantly in the explanation of the gender gap in participation.

When the data confounded our expectations, we pushed further. For example, we had anticipated that, for women, gender con-

---

7. For a similar perspective on the way that the process by which gender differences are socially constructed varies with the nature of the domain of experience, see Candace West and Don H. Zimmerman, "Doing Gender," *Gender and Society* 1 (1987): 125–151.

sciousness—the belief that women have shared problems that the government should provide assistance in solving—would be a significant predictor of political activity. When none of countless specifications confirmed this hunch, we reformulated the question and learned that, while gender consciousness does not, on its own, generate participation, it channels participation in the direction of activity on issues involving women's interests. That is, all things being equal, gender-conscious women are not more politically active; however, when they are active, their participation is more likely to be animated by concern about issues involving equality between men and women or by a pro-choice position on abortion. It is gratifying that this conceptualization holds for race or ethnicity as well as for gender: African-Americans and Latinos who demonstrate group consciousness are more likely to direct their political activity toward issues involving their racial or ethnic group or civil rights more generally.

Similarly, in the case of the gender disparity in the psychological orientations to politics, these redoubled analytical efforts paid off. Men scored higher on a variety of measures of psychological engagement with the political world—from subjective indications of interest or efficacy in political matters to more objective measures of political information. When we introduced measures of the gender composition of the political environment, we learned how strongly the fact that women are underrepresented among political elites influences women's political orientations.

We have no illusions that our empirical conclusions constitute the last word. We fully expect to be challenged by researchers armed with better data, more refined analytical techniques, and cleverer hypotheses. In fact, we welcome the ongoing conversation. Still, we urge those whose interests are primarily theoretical, from whom we have learned so much, to endeavor to inform their work by the results of systematic empirical analyses.

GENDER: MEN AND WOMEN, NOT JUST WOMEN

As we have stressed, studying gender means studying both men and women. Works of feminist scholarship, from which we draw, have highlighted many neglected aspects of women's experiences, sometimes without reference to men's lives. In many ways this approach is understandable. Social cleavages are almost inevitably more germane to those who are disadvantaged by a particular social distinction. In certain respects, the data from our surveys are consistent with an approach suggesting that gender equality is a women's issue. For example, women's, but not men's, political interest and information are influenced by changes in the gender composition in the political environment. Furthermore, with respect to issues involving equality between men and women, women's attitudes are more coherent than men's are: compared with men's views, women's attitudes are more closely related one to another, to other social and political attitudes, and to other social characteristics. In addition, women and men share the view that women have more problems requiring common solution than do men—even though many of the "women's problems" mentioned cannot be solved without men's cooperation. However, with the exception of abortion, public policy issues having special relevance to women's lives were rarely mentioned in association with political activity. Matters such as equal opportunity in the workplace, sexual harassment, or domestic violence register barely a blip on participatory agendas of activists—even though people think that women should work on them together.

There is an additional justification for studying both men and women. On several occasions we have seen that social processes presumed to operate for women turn out to pertain to men as well as to women—or just to men. We have already mentioned that inequality at home has its impact on political participation, not by depressing women's activity, but by enhancing men's. From the perspective of the size of the gender gap in participation, the distinction might be irrelevant. However, from the perspective of understanding how gender differences are created and reinforced, it matters that domestic hierarchy operates—not, as hypothesized, by inhibiting women politically—but instead by empowering men.

In addition, we investigated how gender-segregated organizations operate in providing participatory factors. Advocates for disadvantaged publics have long debated the tradeoff between integrated and segregated institutions. While enforced segregation implies second-class citizenship and denial of opportunity, segregated institutions provide opportunities for the development of distinctive culture, the enhancement of group pride, and the exercise of leadership. These lessons have been applied to discussions of women's experiences in voluntary associations. As expected, in mixed-gender organizations, women are at a disadvantage when it comes to the chance to express their opinions and to exercise leadership—with the result that women acquire fewer participatory factors in mixed-gender organizations than men do. The situation is quite different within organizations of women, which provide greater opportunities for leadership, the exercise of voice in organizational matters, and the development of civic skills and more exposure to requests for political activity.

What we had not anticipated is that organizations dominated by men—which actually constitute a larger share of the organizations that male respondents designated as their most important—have some of the same effects. For example, when it comes to being an officer or board member, the opportunities for men in organizations where they predominate are equivalent to the parallel opportunities for women in organizations of women. In short, while it is reasonable to draw hypotheses from studies that focus solely on women or solely on men, understanding the dynamics of gender issues requires studying the two groups in tandem.

Notes on American Society and Politics

We live in an era of massive social and economic change—including, but not confined to, the opportunities, expectations, and roles of women. As they have periodically in the past, conflicts over morality, culture, and religion have spilled over into politics. The intense feelings generated by a variety of hot-button issues—ranging from the posting of the Ten Commandments in public places to school uniforms to civil commitment ceremonies for gays and lesbians—are often interpreted as symbolic reactions to the breakdown of traditional social arrangements and accepted moral understandings. In fact, analyses of the controversies over abortion and the Equal Rights Amendment emphasize that these issues create political heat because they engage concerns about a larger set of social changes—in particular, changes in women's roles.[8] As we have sought the roots of the gender difference in political participation, we have encountered various kinds of evidence that shed light on the nature of these changes and their implications for political conflict in America.

A PERSPECTIVE ON THE "MOMMY WARS"

The media have focused attention on what they have called the "Mommy Wars"—the perceived hostility between mothers who are at home full time and those who are in the work force full time and the resentment felt by the former, who consider the latter to be so absorbed in their careers that they have abandoned the sphere of voluntary activity and all responsibility for civic participation. Presumably, what is at stake is another manifestation of ambivalence and confusion about changing women's roles and the desire of those who have devoted their lives to the care of home and children to defend the dignity of the lives they have led.

Our evidence neither explains the origins of the "Mommy Wars" nor illumines the extent to which they represent genuine antagonism or constitute a creation of the media. Using systematic data, we do, however, make clear the extent to which there is misperception on the battlefront and give clues as to the sources of the erroneous stereotypes. Systematic evidence shows that, compared with their counterparts who are at home full time, mothers of school-age children who are in the work force full time are *more* active in politics and *more* likely to take part in community political activity, to give time to charity, and to be affiliated with the PTA or another youth-oriented organization.

When we refined our analysis further we discovered a possible explanation for the propagation of the inaccurate view that mothers at home have been left to shoulder all responsibility for voluntary efforts. Within a group of women that has always been very involved in civic activity—married college graduates who are mothers of school-age children—those who are at home full time

---

8. See Kristin Luker, *Abortion and the Politics of Motherhood* (Berkeley: University of California Press, 1984); and Jane J. Mansbridge, *Why We Lost the ERA* (Chicago: University of Chicago Press, 1986).

are more likely than those who are in the work force full time to be involved in one particular kind of activity: they are more likely to be affiliated with the PTA or other youth-oriented organization. Since this is an activity that has a recruitment pool with clearly defined boundaries, it is understandable that those at home full time draw from their experiences with school bake sales the incorrect inference that they are in all ways more participant than those in the work force. Nevertheless, the burden of voluntary activity does not fall exclusively, or even disproportionately, to mothers who are at home full time.

GENDER INEQUALITY AND THE FAMILY

Social learning begins in the family, an institution in which gender distinctions are deeply engrained. It is at home that girls learn to be girls and boys to be boys; women to be wives and mothers, men to be husbands and fathers. It is often assumed that childhood family influences train boys to be politically active and girls to be less politically engaged. Although our data do confirm that having been raised by politically active parents leads, both for men and for women, to political participation in adulthood, we do not have evidence that would allow us to relate gender differences in political involvement to early, gender-based socialization at home.

However, in seeking to establish whether domestic hierarchy creates inequality in the polity, we have been able to probe in some detail the relationships between husbands and wives and to assess the extent of inequality at home. What we found in Chapters 6, 7, and 12 is complicated and ambiguous. For one thing, there is a great deal of variation among couples—with respect to both what they say and what they actually do. Sometimes there is even disagreement within couples about what should be—or is—the case in their own families. On balance, however, married couples tend to express considerable agreement, and quite egalitarian views, when it comes to a number of aspects of household management. Both husbands and wives express support—indeed, more support than we might have expected—for sharing responsibility for the major aspects of keeping a household going: bringing in income, caring for the house, and making decisions.

When it comes to behavior rather than beliefs, the picture is more mixed. On one hand, couples indicate a great deal of mutual respect and satisfaction with the way that decisions are made at home. In addition, both members of the couple, but especially wives, express autonomy in the use of leisure time. On the other hand, there is considerable evidence that traditional habits die hard. Even in couples where both partners work full time, wives continue to do a disproportionate share of the housework while husbands put in more time on the job, bring home a greater share of the income, and are more likely to exercise authority over the family exchequer. In short, we hesitate to characterize couples in unambiguous terms as either traditional or egalitarian.

THE RELIGIOUS CONNECTION

Religion has played a particularly complex part in our story. It is common to note the multiple ways in which men and women have been treated differently in most religious denominations. Orthodox religious doctrine has functioned broadly as a foundation for inequality between the sexes not only within religious institutions but in many spheres of life. Furthermore, in all denominations the ranks of the clergy were traditionally staffed exclusively by men; while the de jure barriers to gender equality are falling in many domains, many religious denominations have explicitly chosen to retain—or, in the case of the Southern Baptists, to increase—prohibitions on what women may seek to attain. Especially germane to our own concerns is a pattern that has attracted much less attention from students of organized religion, the fact that women in the laity were long barred from equal roles in congregational and denominational governance. Even now, among those who are active within a religious institution men are more likely than women to exercise lay leadership within a congregation. At the same time that they have been denied equal roles in clerical and lay leadership, women have been the most faithful members of the flock: more religiously committed than men are, more likely to consider religion to be important in their lives, to attend services, and to be active in their churches. This religiosity, in turn, yields participatory factors. The result is that, if women were not active in what are, in many cases, male-dominated religious institutions, their overall rates of political participation would be lower and the gender gap in participation would be wider.

We have remarked upon the difference between the political and religious domains with respect to the way that women deal with male-dominated institutions. The impact on women's political engagement of a gender-integrated political environment suggests that women conclude from the absence of female political leaders that politics is a game for men. Obviously, they draw a different lesson about their religious participation. In spite of their historical exclusion from lay or clerical leadership, they do not withdraw from religious engagement. If observing the exclusively male domains of football and politics leads women to conclude "Not my world," their response has been very different in church.

By way of explanation, we can observe that piety has traditionally been defined as a feminine virtue and women have long been welcomed in supporting roles in the pews in a way not replicated in politics. Nonetheless, it bears underlining how different the response has been to a circumstance of female exclusion in church than to a circumstance of female exclusion in other domains, including politics.

Our analysis has called attention to another distinction between politics and religion: the latter is simply much more central to the lives of Americans than is the former. In particular, religion is much more deeply embedded in family life than is politics. We noted several indications that married couples share religious commitments much more than they share political ones. Those who attend religious services are more likely to do so as a couple than are political activists to undertake political activity as a joint project. Moreover, couples' assessments of the importance of religion in their lives are more likely to be in harmony than their expressions of levels of political interest. In addition, when it comes to positions on policy issues, couples are more likely to be in agreement on issues like abortion or school prayer that have a religious or moral dimension than on economic issues like government assistance to the needy.

GENDER, RELIGION, AND POLITICAL CONFLICT IN AMERICA

It is noteworthy that husbands and wives tend to be more in accord in their opinions on political issues having religious underpinnings than on the economic issues that once formed the basis for the New Deal political alignment. Our data confirm the trend in contemporary American politics in which attributes that were at one time not connected to one another—religiosity, Republican partisanship, traditional views on family matters and gender roles, and conservative views in politics—now tend to cluster together. This combustible mix of religion, politics, and attitudes toward private social arrangements goes to the heart of what are sometimes called the "culture wars" and undergirds political controversies on a variety of social issues ranging from gays in the military to the teaching of evolution in the schools to abortion.[9]

Although conflicting attitudes toward women's roles are an important piece of this interrelated set of commitments, we were not surprised to find that the fault line of the culture wars does not divide men from women. However, we had not expected to find that the syndrome of religious, political, and ideological commitments holds together more tightly for women than for men. With the exception of one of the first battles fought over this set of concerns, the struggle over the Equal Rights Amendment, where the leaders on both sides of the controversy, Phyllis Schlafly and Eleanor Smeal, were female, the most visible political and religious antagonists in the culture wars have been men. For this reason, we were surprised at the extent to which the tighter bundling of these commitments suggests that they would have greater salience for women.

Although the breakdown of the nuclear family and changing women's roles are surely among the factors that have elicited the emergence of a politics of conflict over cultural issues, nothing in our data suggests that conflict between women and men over women's issues will be at the center of these political struggles. First, with the very important exception of abortion, we found no evidence that what might be considered women's issues—for example, sexual harassment, equal pay, or domestic violence—are at the forefront of the participatory concerns of citizen activists, either male or female. In addition, our data confirm what survey researchers have long noted—that opinions on political issues, even

---

9. See, among others, James Davison Hunter, *Culture Wars: The Struggle to Define America* (New York: Basic Books, 1991).

issues that touch differently on women's and men's interests, rarely divide along gender lines.

The indications of the way that issues with a moral and religious dimension have been built into contemporary American politics contrast with the complex but important role of social class in our analysis. On one hand, class issues seem to have faded from American politics over the last generation. As a result of trends as diverse as the erosion in the power of labor unions, the decline in the appeal of Marxist analysis as an intellectual tool, and the success of the Republican Party in defining itself as the party of common folk, the rhetoric of class has ebbed in American political discourse in recent decades. On the other, if class has become attenuated as a basis for conflict in American politics, it remains profoundly important for shaping the contours of participatory process. As we have seen, at every step of the way, those who are well heeled and well educated accumulate participatory factors, with the result that the social class stratification in participation remains robust and far outweighs that on the basis of race or gender.

The Future of the Gender Gap in Participation

In the heady days of the revival of the women's movement during the late 1960s and early 1970s—when all things seemed possible—advocates for women's rights assumed that the disparity between men and women in political participation would disappear along with gender differences in who scrubs the bathroom floor, sits on corporate boards, performs open heart surgery, teaches kindergarten, or celebrates Mass. To the chagrin of some social observers and the relief of others, the changes have proceeded more slowly than originally anticipated. When it comes to political activity, data presented in Chapter 3 showed surprisingly little diminution of the gap since that time. What can we expect for the future?[10]

---

10. The literature, of course, offers strikingly different views on the future of gender inequality. On one extreme, Robert Max Jackson argues that "[g]ender inequality has been fated for extinction since the emergence of modern economic and political organization," in *Destined for Equality* (Cambridge: Harvard University Press, 1998), p. 241. At the other,

Among the multiple sources of gender differences in political participation, three stand out: men's aggregate advantage in educational attainment; gender differences in work force participation and experiences; and women's deficit with respect to psychological engagement with politics—political interest, knowledge, and efficacy—which is rooted in men's overrepresentation in the ranks of political elites. Let us consider briefly what we might project to be the future scenario with respect to each of these.

APPROACHING EDUCATIONAL EQUALITY

We have seen the fundamental importance of education for political participation and the way that the influence of educational attainment ramifies through the institutions of adult life. Disparities in educational attainment are often at the root of group differences in political participation. Unlike African-Americans and Latinos, however, females do not start out with a potential educational disadvantage bequeathed at birth by virtue of being born to parents of limited educational attainment. Nonetheless, on average, adult women are less well educated than adult men. Recent trends have reduced the gender inequality in education. At present, while men still dominate in programs leading to the most prestigious graduate degrees, women are more likely than men to enter and to finish college and to get master's degrees. If this trend continues, men's aggregate educational advantage—which reflects the accretion of decades of educational difference—will slowly erode. The process of educational equalization will be slowed slightly by the fact that women outnumber men substantially among the elderly, a group for which the gender difference is especially wide. The bottom line, however, is that we can expect attenuation of that portion of the gender gap in participation that is attributable to the gender disparity in educational attainment.

Deborah L. Rhode views gender-based inequality as so complicated, multifaceted, and differently articulated within major social institutions that it is not likely to disappear anytime soon. See *Speaking of Sex* (Cambridge: Harvard University Press, 1997), pp. 141–176, 240–241.

A CLOUDY PICTURE ON THE JOB FRONT

When it comes to work force participation and experiences on the job, the situation is more complicated. In our discussions of this project many people expressed the expectation that, because of the demands on their time, women with jobs and families would be less politically active than women at home full time. Our results confound that expectation. Women in the work force are, in fact, more politically participant than are full-time homemakers. Part of the reason for the disparity is that the workplace is a particularly fruitful source of factors that foster participation: earnings, civic skills, and requests for activity. However, women are less likely to be in the work force and, even if in the work force full time, less likely to have the kinds of jobs that generate high earnings, opportunities to exercise civic skills, and recruitment attempts.

It is difficult to predict how these workplace inequalities will sort themselves out in the future. One of the most substantial changes in the second half of the twentieth century was the entry of large numbers of women into the work force. There is controversy over whether or not that trend has now abated. Even if the movement toward women's greater work force participation were to continue, given women's traditional responsibilities for home and children, there is reason to expect that, at the equilibrium point, women will still be less likely than men to be in the work force full time. Any deficit for women in work force participation has inevitable consequences for political activity: those who are not in the work force at all obviously cannot acquire work-based participatory factors; those whose work force attachment has been uneven will find themselves in jobs that deliver less in the way of earnings and civic skills.

Gender differences in participatory factors acquired at work reflect not only differences in selection into the work force but also differences in experiences on the job. Women and men do different work in our society, and men's work is well known to be better paid and seems to be more likely to provide opportunities for the exercise of civic skills. We cannot predict with certainty whether, and how quickly, job segregation by sex—the result not only of choices made by individual workers but also of treatment by employers—will decline. Similarly, we cannot predict whether, and how quickly, employment discrimination against women will decline. If women and men were more likely to share job titles and if equal job opportunity were to become a reality, then we would expect convergence between women and men in the participatory factors acquired on the job.

At the same time, the net impact on women's participation of an end to gender discrimination in the workplace is not clear. With other factors taken into account, women who perceive themselves as having been the victims of gender bias are more politically active. Our questions on this subject did not specify a particular locus—school, college, church, and so on—for an experience with discrimination. Nevertheless, we surmise that a disproportionate share of these perceived experiences of discrimination derive from the workplace. If progress were made toward equal opportunity on the job and women became less likely to feel themselves the objects of discrimination, we cannot assess the relative balance of the gain in participatory factors and the loss of the mobilizing effect that currently accompanies the experiences of discrimination.

Matters of work force participation and experiences on the job have weighed importantly in our explanation of the sources of continuing gender differences in political participation. In concluding, we wish to make clear our understanding that decisions about whether to enter the work force and how much time to devote to paid work have ramifications for personal well-being and family life that dwarf their consequences for the accumulation of the resources that facilitate political activity. In emphasizing the importance of work for political activity and the disparity between women and men in job-based participatory factors, we are not making even an implicit recommendation as to how women—or men—should conduct their lives.

Toward Equality in Politics and Society

We began this chapter by noting that not a single woman in the sample that forms our principal data base had lived through a presidential election in which she was disenfranchised solely on the basis of her sex. We conclude by pointing out that not a single woman in that sample has lived through a presidential election in which a woman topped the ballot of a major party.

A powerful factor in explaining the disparity between men and women in participation is the gender difference in psychological orientations to politics—political interest, information, and efficacy. And a powerful factor in explaining the gender difference in these orientations is the gender composition of the political environment. We have demonstrated that women are more likely to know and care about politics when they live in a political environment in which women seek and hold visible public offices.

The past decade has witnessed a steady, but very slow, increase in the number of women who seek and capture visible government offices. In spring of 1990, when the survey on which most of our analysis rests was conducted, 81 percent of the public lived in states that had no female incumbents or, in the preceding election in 1988, major-party candidates for state-wide office: senator, governor, or lieutenant governor.[11] When we replicated this analysis as we completed this book soon after the election of 2000, the proportion of the public living in states with no women candidates or incumbents for these visible, state-wide offices had shrunk to 34 percent. Even so, we are far from parity. Moreover, unlike many countries—even nations with a much weaker commitment to equality of opportunity among individuals than the United States—we have never had a woman serve as party leader in either branch of the national legislature or as president.

Our investigation of the private roots of public action has taken us into the major social institutions of American life—the family, school, workplace, voluntary association, church, and politics—domains with which advocates of gender equality have been concerned since before the Civil War. The norm of equal opportunity among individuals, which is so deeply ingrained in the American political tradition, penetrates these institutions very unevenly. In some arenas, equal treatment of boys and girls or women and men

---

11. Figures in this paragraph are calculated from data contained in U.S. Bureau of the Census, *Statistical Abstract of the United States: 1996*, 116th ed. (Washington, D.C.: U.S. Government Printing Office, 1996), p. 28; and "Which States Gained, Which Lost," *New York Times*, December 29, 2000, p. A18.

is a matter of government policy—legislated, if not always implemented, for the workplace by Title VII of the Civil Rights Act of 1964 and for the schoolyard by Title IX of the Educational Amendments of 1972. In others—most notably, political parties, non-political organizations, and religious institutions—the liberties guaranteed by the First Amendment preclude public efforts to mandate equal treatment irrespective of sex. And the promises of liberal individualism have traditionally stopped at the front door, placing domestic arrangements beyond the reach of public commitment to equality.

In 1848 the Seneca Falls Declaration held it a truth "self-evident: that all men and women are created equal" and listed among the "repeated injuries and usurpations of man toward woman": that "He has compelled her to submit to laws, in the formation of which she had no voice"; that "He has monopolized nearly all the profitable employments"; that "He has denied her the facilities for obtaining a thorough education"; and that "He allows her in Church, as well as State, but a subordinate position."[12] Nearly a half century later, in 1892, Elizabeth Cady Stanton testified before the House Judiciary Committee and explained why women need "all the opportunities for higher education, for the full development of her faculties, forces of mind and body . . . the most enlarged freedom of thought and action; a complete emancipation from all forms of bondage, of custom, dependence, superstition . . . a voice in the government under which she lives; in the religion she is asked to believe; equality in social life, where she is the chief factor; a place in the trades and professions, where she may earn her bread."[13] At its first organizing conference in 1966, in the early years of the revival of the women's movement, the National Organization for Women adopted a Statement of Purpose that envisioned "bring[ing] women into full participation in the mainstream of American society now, exercising all the privileges and

---

12. Document 3 in Anne Firor Scott and Andrew MacKay Scott, *One Half the People* (Urbana: University of Illinois Press, 1982), pp. 56–57.

13. Elizabeth Cady Stanton, "Solitude of Self," in *Feminism: The Essential Historical Writings,* ed. Miriam Schneir (New York: Vintage Books, 1972), p. 158.

responsibilities thereof in truly equal partnership with men."[14] The next year NOW adopted a Bill of Rights listing an array of demands, among them: "That equal employment opportunity be guaranteed to all women, as well as men; That women be . . . paid maternity leave; That child care facilities be established by law on the same basis as parks, libraries and public schools; [and] That the right of women to be educated to their full potential equally with men be secured."[15]

If these visions were realized, then it would follow as the day the night: gender differences in political participation would disappear.

---

14. National Organization for Women, "Statement of Purpose," in *Feminism in Our Time,* ed. Miriam Schneir (New York: Vintage Books, 1994), p. 96.

15. "NOW (National Organization for Women) Bill of Rights," in *Sisterhood Is Powerful,* ed. Robin Morgan (New York: Vintage Books, 1970), p. 513.

APPENDIXES

INDEX

Note: Different statistical packages and different versions of the same statistical package implement weights in somewhat different ways. The results we report here were estimated with SPSS 6.1. Were we to have used a different statistical package or a different version of SPSS, the results would be slightly, though not substantively, different. The code file for all the regressions and descriptive statistics in this book is available from the authors.

Numbers of Cases

Table A1 Valid Number of Cases for the Citizen Participation Study[a]

	Women	Men
DEMOGRAPHIC MEASURES		
Gender	1,327	1,191
Married	716	704
Never married	202	246
Have preschool-age children	239	165
Have school-age children	438	324
Have both preschool- and school-age children	122	74
Not working	563	283
Working part-time	197	59
Working full-time	567	848
Education		
Grammar school or less	64	58
Some high school	152	97
High school graduate/GED	498	405
Some college	324	291
College graduate	161	166
Some post-graduate work	48	45
Master's degree	66	81
Ph.D./professional	14	48
Age		
18–24	126	111
25–29	144	154
30–39	343	372
40–49	265	208
50–59	151	130
60–69	155	125
70+	139	88

Table A1 *(continued)*

	Women	Men
Race		
White (weighted)	1,068	1,006
White (unweighted)	803	805
Black (weighted)	142	91
Black (unweighted)	290	188
Hispanic (weighted)	85	57
Hispanic (unweighted)	214	156
POLITICAL ACTIVITY MEASURES		
Contributed time to political cause/campaign	297	305
Contributed money to political cause/campaign	279	340
NON-POLITICAL ACTIVITY MEASURES		
Affiliated with a non-political organization (member or contributor)	896	808
Affiliated with a church	980	692
Attend church 2–3 times a month or more	727	515

a. Weighted.

Table A2 Valid Number of Cases for the Citizen Participation Study Follow-up—Couples Survey

Demographic Measures	Women	Men
Gender	382	382
Working part time	68	17
Working full time	182	276
Homemaker	69	1
Have children at home	236	228
Full-time worker with children at home	129	210

Table A9.9 Valid Number of Cases for Table 9.9

	Women	Men
Among respondents in denominations in which:		
Women can be members of clergy	165	133
Women cannot be members of clergy		
Catholic	57	54
Other denominations	53	34

Table A13.3 Valid Number of Cases for Table 13.3

	State		Washington
Year	California	Illinois	Washington
1988	55	41	64
1990	80	50	52
1992	47	45	44

APPENDIX B

Ranges of Variables

This appendix includes the original ranges for variables that were re-scaled 0–1 for the regression analyses.

Citizen Participation Study—Main Survey

EDUCATION

1 Grammar or less
2 Some high school
3 High school graduate/GED
4 Some college
5 College graduate
6 Some graduate work
7 Master's degree
8 Ph.D. or professional degree

FAMILY INCOME

In tens of thousands of dollars
0.37 to 30

WORKING

0 Not working
1 Part time
2 Full time

JOB LEVEL

0   Haven't had a job recently
1–5   Lowest to highest amount of education and on-the-job training
      needed for the job

MARRIED

0–1

PRESCHOOL CHILDREN

0–1

SCHOOL-AGE CHILDREN

0–1

AGE

1 Less than 25
2 25–34
3 35–44
4 45–54
5 55–64
6 65 and older

AGE OVER 65

0–1

BLACK

0–1

CITIZEN

0–1

LATINO

0–1

HOME POLITICS

Sum of mother's activity (1 = not at all; 2 = somewhat; 3 = very),
father's activity (1 = not at all; 2 = somewhat; 3 = very), and discussion
at home (1 = almost never; 2 = sometimes; 3 = frequently).

EXPERIENCE IN SCHOOL

Sum of activity in high school government (1 = not at all; 2 = not very; 3 = somewhat; 4 = very) and activity in high school clubs (1 = not at all; 2 = not very; 3 = somewhat; 4 = very).

JOB FACTORS

Combination of skills (0–4) and mobilization (0–2), weighted to give skills and mobilization equal weight in the variable.

ORGANIZATION FACTORS

Combination of skills (0–4) and mobilization (0–2), weighted to give skills and mobilization equal weight in the variable.

CHURCH FACTORS

Combination of skills (0–4) and mobilization (0–2), weighted to give skills and mobilization equal weight in the variable.

AVAILABLE TIME

Number of hours available each day

HOURS ON THE JOB

0–16

HOURS OF ORGANIZATIONAL WORK

0–40

HOURS OF CHURCH WORK

0–40

OWN INCOME

In tens of thousands of dollars
0–30

OTHER FAMILY INCOME

In tens of thousands of dollars
0–30

IMPORTANCE OF RELIGION

1 Not important
2 Somewhat important
3 Very important

GENDER DISCRIMINATION

0–1

RACIAL DISCRIMINATION

0–1

GENDER CONSCIOUSNESS

0–1

BLACK CONSCIOUSNESS

0–1

HISPANIC CONSCIOUSNESS

0–1

POLITICAL INTEREST

0–6

POLITICAL EFFICACY

0–12

POLITICAL INFORMATION

0–10

_____ DIVORCED

0–1

_____ WIDOWED

0–1

_____ SEPARATED

0–1

Citizen Participation Study—Couples Survey

_____ EDUCATION

1–6
1 Grammar and less
2 Some high school
3 High school graduate/GED
4 Some college
5 College graduate
6 Some graduate work or graduate degree

_____ HOURS AT WORK

0–16

_____ JOB LEVEL

0   Not recently employed
1–5   Education and on-the-job training needed for the job

_____ FAMILY INCOME

In tens of thousands of dollars
0–30

_____ PERCENTAGE OF THE FAMILY INCOME THE WIFE BRINGS IN

0–100%

PRESCHOOL CHILDREN

0–1

WIFE'S AGE

Age, in years

YEARS OF MARRIAGE

0   1–10 years
1   11–20 years
2   21–30 years
3   31–56 years

BELIEF IN EQUALITY

For women: 0–1.69
For men: 0–1.74

DEMOCRAT

1–7   Strong Republican to Strong Democrat

IMPORTANCE OF RELIGION

0–2

CONTROL OVER FAMILY FINANCES

0–1.52

PERCENTAGE OF HOUSEWORK HOURS DONE BY THE WIFE

0–100%

RESPONDENT'S AUTONOMY

0–12, number of types of decisions about money and time the
respondent would make without consulting

RESPONDENT BELIEVES SHE OR HE GETS A SAY IN FAMILY DISCUSSIONS

1 Never
2 Sometimes
3 Always

IS THE RESPONDENT A TRUSTED ADVISOR FOR HIS OR HER PARTNER?

0–1

APPENDIX C

Supplementary Tables

Table C6.4 Predicting Attitudes on Gender Equality for Wives and Husbands (OLS regression)

	Wife		Husband
EDUCATION AND WORK STATUS			
Education	0.16		0.03
	(0.12)		(0.10)
Hours of Work	0.22*	⇔	−0.04
	(0.11)		(0.10)
Job Level	0.21*		0.22*
	(0.09)		(0.10)
FAMILY INCOME			
Family Income	0.17		−0.02
	(0.16)		(0.13)
Percentage of Family Income Respondent	−0.06		−0.16
Brings In	(0.08)		(0.09)
POLITICS AND RELIGION			
Party Identification[a]	0.17**		0.12*
	(0.06)		(0.05)
Importance of Religion	−0.15*	⇔	0.08
	(0.07)		(0.06)
OTHER VARIABLES			
Age	−0.41*	⇔	−0.26
	(0.18)		(0.18)
Preschool Children	0.02	⇔	0.10*
	(0.06)		(0.05)
Years of Marriage	0.25**	⇔	0.15
	(0.09)		(0.08)
Constant	2.21***		2.36***
	(0.12)		(0.12)
Adjusted R-squared	0.15		0.05
Valid N	299		296

Source: Citizen Participation Study Follow-up—Couples Survey.

a. Party identification is measured by a seven-point scale ranging from strong Republican to strong Democrat.

*Coefficient significant at <.05.

**Coefficient significant at <.01.

***Coefficient significant at <.001.

⇔ Difference in the coefficients for men and women is significant at <.05 (by t-test) or one coefficient is significant at <.05 and the other is not.

Table C6.5 Predicting Couples' Views on Gender Equality in the Family (OLS regression)

WIFE'S CHARACTERISTICS	
Education and Work Status	
Wife's education	2.13***
	(0.59)
Wife's hours at work	1.37**
	(0.49)
Wife's job level	0.54
	(0.42)
Politics and Religion	
Wife is Democrat[a]	0.40
	(0.32)
Importance of religion to wife	−1.60***
	(0.35)
HUSBAND'S CHARACTERISTICS	
Education and Work Status	
Husband's education	−0.23
	(0.54)
Husband's hours at work	0.52
	(0.50)
Husband's job level	0.05
	(0.51)
Politics and Religion	
Husband is Democrat[a]	0.26
	(0.31)
Importance of religion to husband	0.46
	(0.31)
FAMILY CHARACTERISTICS	
Family Income	−0.15
	(0.70)
Percentage of Income Wife Brings In	−0.16
	(0.55)
Preschool children	0.49*
	(0.24)
Years of Marriage	0.67
	(0.42)
Age of Wife[b]	−0.63
	(0.97)
Constant	4.26***
	(0.61)
Adjusted R-squared	0.27
Valid N	242

Source: Citizen Participation Study Follow-up—Couples Survey.

a. Party identification is measured by a seven-point scale ranging from strong Republican to strong Democrat.

b. Because of the high correlation between wives' and husbands' age, we include only the wife's age here.

*Coefficient significant at <.05.

**Coefficient significant at <.01.

***Coefficient significant at <.001.

Table C7.10 Predicting the Percentage of Housework the Wife Does (OLS regression)

WIFE'S CHARACTERISTICS	
Education	−0.05
	(0.10)
Hours at Work	−0.26**
	(0.08)
Job Level	0.11
	(0.07)
HUSBAND'S CHARACTERISTICS	
Education	−0.02
	(0.08)
Hours at Work	−0.01
	(0.09)
Job Level	−0.00
	(0.08)
FAMILY CHARACTERISTICS	
Family Income	−0.02
	(0.12)
Percentage of the Family Income the Wife Brings In	0.11
	(0.09)
Preschool Children	0.06
	(0.04)
Wife's Age[a]	−0.01
	(0.17)
Years of Marriage	−0.03
	(0.07)
BELIEF IN EQUALITY	
Her Belief	0.04
	(0.07)
His Belief	0.02
	(0.09)
Constant	0.62***
	(0.10)
Adjusted R-squared	0.02
Valid N	237

Source: Citizen Participation Study Follow-up—Couples Survey.

a. Because wives' ages and husbands' ages are so highly correlated, we include only the wife's age here.

*Coefficient significant at <.05.

**Coefficient significant at <.01.

***Coefficient significant at <.001.

Table C8.1 Predicting Working (logistic regression)

	Women		Men
EDUCATION AND CHILDHOOD			
Education	2.01***		1.86***
	(0.40)		(0.48)
High School Activity	0.28		0.45
	(0.23)		(0.34)
FAMILY			
Married	−0.15	⇔	0.63**
	(0.16)		(0.22)
Preschool Children	−1.03***	⇔	1.56***
	(0.20)		(0.43)
School-age Children	−0.06	⇔	1.97***
	(0.18)		(0.36)
Other Family Income	−5.52***	⇔	−8.78***
	(0.79)		(1.27)
OTHER VARIABLES			
Age	−1.19***	⇔	−2.67***
	(0.34)		(0.43)
Age over 65	−2.81***	⇔	−1.68***
	(0.33)		(0.35)
Black	−0.02		−0.14
	(0.22)		(0.34)
Latino	−0.66*	⇔	−0.05
	(0.27)		(0.47)
Citizen	−0.07	⇔	1.89***
	(0.44)		(0.45)
Constant	1.41**	⇔	0.06
	(0.50)		(0.51)
Log Likelihood	−675		−381
Valid N	1,300		1,166

Source: Citizen Participation Study—Main Survey.

*Coefficient significant at <.05.

**Coefficient significant at <.01.

***Coefficient significant at <.001.

⇔ Difference in the coefficients for men and women is significant at <.05 (by *t*-test) or one coefficient is significant at <.05 and the other is not.

Table C8.1.1 Predicting Hours Working (OLS regression)

	Women		Men
EDUCATION AND CHILDHOOD			
Education	4.26***	⇔	1.92***
	(0.60)		(0.47)
High School Activity	0.85*		0.75*
	(0.38)		(0.36)
FAMILY			
Married	−0.53*	⇔	1.17***
	(0.25)		(0.24)
Preschool Children	−2.25***	⇔	1.54***
	(0.33)		(0.32)
School-age Children	−0.14	⇔	1.65***
	(0.29)		(0.28)
Other Family Income	−10.79***		−9.15***
	(1.23)		(1.23)
OTHER VARIABLES			
Age	−1.14***	⇔	−2.76***
	(0.55)		(0.50)
Age over 65	−5.19***		−4.89***
	(0.44)		(0.44)
Black	0.44		−0.14
	(0.36)		(0.38)
Citizen	−0.83	⇔	1.75**
	(0.77)		(0.56)
Latino	−0.55		−0.25
	(0.47)		(0.49)
Constant	5.48***		6.16***
	(0.85)		(0.63)
Adjusted R-squared	0.30		0.44
Valid N	1,288		1,177

Source: Citizen Participation Study—Main Survey.
*Coefficient significant at <.05.
**Coefficient significant at <.01.
***Coefficient significant at <.001.
 ⇔ Difference in the coefficients for men and women is significant at <.05 (by t-test) or one coefficient is significant at <.05 and the other is not.

Table C8.3 Predicting Job Level among Working Women and Men (OLS regression)

	Working Women		Working Men
EDUCATION AND CHILDHOOD			
Education	4.12***	⇔	3.32***
	(0.19)		(0.15)
High School Activity	0.05	⇔	0.22*
	(0.12)		(0.11)
INSTITUTIONAL COMMITMENT			
Hours at Work	1.31***		1.20***
	(0.21)		(0.24)
OTHER VARIABLES			
Age	0.64***		0.93***
	(0.16)		(0.16)
Age over 65	−0.23	⇔	0.67**
	(0.25)		(0.25)
Black	−0.21	⇔	−0.46***
	(0.11)		(0.12)
Latino	−0.21	⇔	−0.32*
	(0.16)		(0.16)
Citizen	−0.28		0.07
	(0.24)		(0.21)
Constant	0.33		0.44
	(0.27)		(0.27)
Adjusted R-squared	0.46		0.45
Valid N	752		897

Source: Citizen Participation Study—Main Survey.

*Coefficient significant at <.05.

**Coefficient significant at <.01.

***Coefficient significant at <.001.

⇔ Difference in the coefficients for men and women is significant at <.05 (by t-test) or one coefficient is significant at <.05 and the other is not.

Table C8.4 The Effect of Job Characteristics on Participatory Factors: Regression Coefficients (standard errors in parentheses)[a]

	Women		Men
RESOURCES			
Effect on Earnings from Job[b] (working respondents)			
Hours worked	3.11 (.26)***		2.34 (.74)**
Job level	1.33 (.21)***	⇔	3.04 (.51)***
Effect on Job Skills (working respondents)			
Hours worked	1.75 (.25)***		1.39 (.30)***
Job level	1.75 (.21)***	⇔	2.75 (.20)***
Effect on Job Supervision (working respondents, logit)			
Hours worked	2.28 (.56)***		2.64 (.58)***
Job level	1.48 (.43)***		2.31 (.39)***
Effect on Free Time (all respondents)			
Hours worked	−9.27 (.41)***	⇔	−12.31 (.31)***
Job level	1.07 (.41)**		0.85 (.33)*
RECRUITMENT			
Effect on Recruitment on the Job (working respondents)			
Hours worked	.26 (.12)*	⇔	−.01 (.13)
Job level	.20 (.10)*	⇔	.02 (.09)

Source: Citizen Participation Study—Main Survey.
a. Controlling for education, activity in high school, race or ethnicity, age, and citizenship.
b. Also controlling for "other family income."
*Coefficient significant at <.05.
**Coefficient significant at <.01.
***Coefficient significant at <.001.
⇔ Difference in the coefficients for men and women is significant at <.05 (by *t*-test) or one coefficient is significant at <.05 and the other is not.

Table C9.1 Predicting Organizational Affiliation (logistic regression)

	Women		Men
EDUCATION AND CHILDHOOD			
Education	2.48***		2.27***
	(0.50)		(0.44)
High School Activity	0.85***		0.55*
	(0.24)		(0.25)
INCOME			
Family Income	2.68**	⇔	1.48
	(0.95)		(0.81)
WORKPLACE			
Working	−0.30		0.18
	(0.19)		(0.20)
Job Level	0.45	⇔	0.76*
	(0.32)		(0.31)
FAMILY			
Married	0.07		0.06
	(0.15)		(0.16)
Preschool Children	−0.24		0.31
	(0.18)		(0.20)
School-age Children	0.19		−0.06
	(0.14)		(0.19)
OTHER VARIABLES			
Age	0.94**	⇔	0.48
	(0.33)		(0.35)
Age over 65	0.20	⇔	0.72*
	(0.29)		(0.32)
Black	−0.49*	⇔	−0.00
	(0.20)		(0.25)
Latino	−1.03***	⇔	−0.55
	(0.27)		(0.31)
Citizen	0.38		−0.18
	(0.45)		(0.40)
Constant	−1.45**	⇔	−1.17**
	(0.52)		(0.45)
Log Likelihood	−692		−658
Valid N	1,289		1,151

Source: Citizen Participation Study—Main Survey.
*Coefficient significant at <.05.
**Coefficient significant at <.01.
***Coefficient significant at <.001.
⇔ Difference in the coefficients for men and women is significant at <.05 (by *t*-test) or one coefficient is significant at <.05 and the other is not.

Table C9.2.1 Predicting Acquisition of Civic Skills in Organizations (OLS regression)

	Affiliated Women		Affiliated Men
EDUCATION AND CHILDHOOD			
Education	0.66***		0.95***
	(0.18)		(0.17)
High School Activity	0.29*		0.39**
	(0.11)		(0.13)
INCOME			
Family Income	0.71*		1.30***
	(0.35)		(0.36)
INSTITUTIONAL COMMITMENT			
Hours of Organization Work	5.70***		5.06***
	(0.41)		(0.54)
OTHER VARIABLES			
Age	0.30	⇔	0.55**
	(0.16)		(0.18)
Age over 65	0.05		−0.06
	(0.13)		(0.16)
Black	−0.00		0.00
	(0.12)		(0.15)
Latino	−0.14		−0.17
	(0.19)		(0.21)
Citizen	0.03	⇔	−0.48*
	(0.31)		(0.22)
Constant	0.04		0.23
	(0.32)		(0.24)
Adjusted R-squared	0.23		0.19
Valid N	875		803

Source: Citizen Participation Study—Main Survey.
*Coefficient significant at <.05.
**Coefficient significant at <.01.
***Coefficient significant at <.001.
⇔ Difference in the coefficients for men and women is significant at <.05 (by *t*-test) or one coefficient is significant at <.05 and the other is not.

Table C9.2.2 Predicting Recruitment in Organizations (OLS regression)

	Affiliated Women		Affiliated Men
EDUCATION AND CHILDHOOD			
Education	0.08**	⇔	0.05
	(0.03)		(0.03)
High School Activity	0.01		0.01
	(0.02)		(0.02)
INCOME			
Family Income	−0.05		0.01
	(0.06)		(0.06)
INSTITUTIONAL COMMITMENT			
Hours of Organization Work	0.26***		0.21*
	(0.07)		(0.09)
OTHER VARIABLES			
Age	0.01		0.03
	(0.03)		(0.03)
Age over 65	−0.00		−0.04
	(0.02)		(0.03)
Black	0.01		−0.00
	(0.02)		(0.02)
Latino	−0.04		−0.04
	(0.03)		(0.04)
Citizen	−0.06	⇔	−0.10**
	(0.05)		(0.04)
Constant	0.08	⇔	0.13***
	(0.05)		(0.04)
Adjusted R-squared	0.02		0.01
Valid N	877		813

Source: Citizen Participation Study—Main Survey.
*Coefficient significant at <.05.
**Coefficient significant at <.01.
***Coefficient significant at <.001.
⇔ Difference in the coefficients for men and women is significant at <.05 (by *t*-test) or one coefficient is significant at <.05 and the other is not.

Table C9.6 Predicting Church Affiliation (logistic regression)

	Women		Men
EDUCATION AND CHILDHOOD			
Education	0.69		−0.22
	(0.44)		(0.36)
High School Activity	0.56**		0.97***
	(0.23)		(0.23)
INCOME			
Family Income	−1.15		1.14
	(0.70)		(0.68)
WORKPLACE			
Working	−0.23	⇔	0.38*
	(0.18)		(0.19)
Job Level	0.07	⇔	−0.61*
	(0.30)		(0.30)
FAMILY			
Married	0.01	⇔	0.43**
	(0.15)		(0.15)
Preschool Children	−0.01		0.34
	(0.18)		(0.19)
School-age Children	0.37***		0.73***
	(0.14)		(0.16)
OTHER VARIABLES			
Age	0.15		−0.12
	(0.32)		(0.32)
Age over 65	0.79***		0.96***
	(0.30)		(0.29)
Black	0.43		0.24
	(0.24)		(0.24)
Latino	−0.05		−0.26
	(0.27)		(0.30)
Citizen	0.38		0.64
	(0.42)		(0.37)
Constant	0.12	⇔	−1.18**
	(0.48)		(0.42)
Log Likelihood	−712		−742
Valid *N*	1,288		1,150

Source: Citizen Participation Study—Main Survey.
*Coefficient significant at <.05.
**Coefficient significant at <.01.
***Coefficient significant at <.001.
⇔ Difference in the coefficients for men and women is significant at <.05 (by *t*-test) or one coefficient is significant at <.05 and the other is not.

Table C9.6.1 Predicting Church Affiliation with Religious Importance in the Equation (logistic regression)

	Women		Men
EDUCATION AND CHILDHOOD			
Education	1.08*	⇔	−0.11
	(0.47)		(0.40)
High School Activity	0.44	⇔	0.60*
	(0.24)		(0.25)
INCOME			
Family Income	0.69	⇔	2.70***
	(0.79)		(0.77)
WORKPLACE			
Working	0.05		0.30
	(0.19)		(0.21)
Job Level	−0.01		−0.39
	(0.31)		(0.32)
RELIGIOUS IMPORTANCE	2.55***		2.43***
	(0.20)		(0.19)
FAMILY			
Married	−0.20	⇔	0.34*
	(0.16)		(0.16)
Preschool Children	0.22	⇔	0.57*
	(0.21)		(0.21)
School-age Children	0.32	⇔	0.51**
	(0.19)		(0.20)
OTHER VARIABLES			
Age	−0.35		0.17
	(0.34)		(0.35)
Age over 65	1.42***	⇔	0.59
	(0.31)		(0.31)
Black	0.14		−0.09
	(0.24)		(0.26)
Citizen	0.71	⇔	1.13*
	(0.44)		(0.41)
Latino	0.04		−0.46
	(0.28)		(0.32)
Constant	−2.35***		−3.41***
	(0.53)		(0.49)
Log Likelihood	−667		−658
Valid *N*	1,288		1,150

Source: Citizen Participation Study—Main Survey.

*Coefficient significant at <.05.

**Coefficient significant at <.01.

***Coefficient significant at <.001.

⇔ Difference in the coefficients for men and women is significant at <.05 (by *t*-test) or one coefficient is significant at <.05 and the other is not.

Table C9.7.1 Predicting Acquisition of Civic Skills in Religious Institutions (OLS regression)

	Affiliated Women		Affiliated Men
EDUCATION AND CHILDHOOD			
Education	0.59**	⇔	0.31
	(0.20)		(0.20)
High School Activity	0.45***		0.46**
	(0.12)		(0.15)
INCOME			
Family Income	0.33		−0.19
	(0.39)		(0.41)
INSTITUTIONAL COMMITMENT			
Hours of Church Work	5.39***		5.01***
	(0.40)		(0.37)
OTHER VARIABLES			
Age	0.31	⇔	0.51**
	(0.15)		(0.20)
Age over 65	−0.11		−0.10
	(0.13)		(0.17)
Black	0.11		−0.01
	(0.11)		(0.15)
Latino	−0.01		−0.07
	(0.15)		(0.22)
Citizen	0.11		−0.20
	(0.26)		(0.30)
Constant	−0.24		0.17
	(0.28)		(0.30)
Adjusted R-squared	0.20		0.24
Valid N	887		619

Source: Citizen Participation Study—Main Survey.
*Coefficient significant at <.05.
**Coefficient significant at <.01.
***Coefficient significant at <.001.
⇔ Difference in the coefficients for men and women is significant at <.05 (by *t*-test) or one coefficient is significant at <.05 and the other is not.

Table C9.7.2 Predicting Recruitment in Religious Institutions

	Affiliated Women		Affiliated Men
EDUCATION AND CHILDHOOD			
Education	0.50***		0.35**
	(0.12)		(0.13)
High School Activity	0.27***		0.31***
	(0.07)		(0.09)
INCOME			
Family Income	−0.20		−0.26
	(0.23)		(0.26)
INSTITUTIONAL COMMITMENT			
Hours of Church Work	0.69**		0.47*
	(0.24)		(0.23)
OTHER VARIABLES			
Age	−0.11		0.14
	(0.09)		(0.13)
Age over 65	−0.17*		−0.28**
	(0.08)		(0.11)
Black	0.09		0.09
	(0.06)		(0.09)
Latino	−0.09	⇔	−0.35**
	(0.09)		(0.14)
Citizen	0.16		−0.16
	(0.15)		(0.19)
Constant	−0.07	⇔	0.38*
	(0.16)		(0.19)
Adjusted R-squared	0.08		0.07
Valid N	887		619

Source: Citizen Participation Study—Main Survey.
*Coefficient significant at <.05.
**Coefficient significant at <.01.
***Coefficient significant at <.001.
⇔ Difference in the coefficients for men and women is significant at <.05 (by t-test) or one coefficient is significant at <.05 and the other is not.

Table C10.5 Participation Factors and Political Activity: An Outcomes Model[a]

	Level of Factor		Effect of Factor		Overall Outcome		Contribution to Participation Gap
	Women	Men	Women	Men	Women	Men	
	EFFECT OF NON-POLITICAL INSTITUTIONS						
HOME AND EDUCATION							
Home Politics	.24	.24	.98*** (.19)	.55** (.20)	.18	.18	
Education	.38 ⇔	.42	1.73*** (.22)	1.60*** (.21)	.63	.70	+.07
Experience in School	.37 ⇔	.34	.63*** (.13)	.58*** (.15)	.23	.21	−.02
ADULT INSTITUTIONAL EFFECTS							
Job Factors	.17 ⇔	.26	.98*** (.21)	.85*** (.21)	.16	.24	+.08
Organization Factors	.10	.11	.94*** (.23)	.85*** (.25)	.10	.10	
Church Factors	.13	.12	1.28*** (.17)	1.26*** (.19)	.17	.17	

TIME AND INCOME

Available Time	.61	.61	.14 (.35)	−.19 (.44)	.00	.00	
Family Income	.12 ⇔	.13	2.26*** (.40)	1.96*** (.48)	.25	.27	+.02
Own Income	.03 ⇔	.08	−1.54 (1.05)	−.32 (.50)	.00	.00	
Total Male Advantage Due to Resources and Recruitment							+.15

EFFECT OF DISCRIMINATION

Gender Bias	.11 ⇔	.06	.51*** (.12) ⇔	.30 (.18)	.06	.06	−.06
Constant	1.00	1.00	−.52* (.22) ⇔	.10 (.27)	−.42	.00	
Total Male Advantage Due to Resources, Recruitment, and Discrimination							+.09

Source: Citizen Participation Study—Main Survey.

a. Age and age over 65 in equation as controls.

*Coefficient significant at <.05.

**Coefficient significant at <.01.

***Coefficient significant at <.001.

⇔ Difference is significant at <.05 (by *t*-test) or one coefficient is significant at <.05 and the other is not.

Table C10.6 Effect of Obligated Hours and Hours Volunteered for Other Purposes on Hours Given to Politics[a]

	Women	Men
Effect of		
Hours of Housework	0.31	0.23
	(0.53)	(0.86)
Hours on Job	0.02	−0.56
	(0.88)	(0.75)
Hours to Organization	2.85	1.87
	(1.59)	(1.82)
Hours to Church	1.59	0.79
	(1.49)	(1.21)

Source: Citizen Participation Study—Main Survey.

a. Unstandardized regression coefficients, with political exposure at home, education, high school activity, family income, own income, working, organization and church affiliation, sex discrimination, age, and age over 65 in the equation. The dependent variable is the amount of time given to politics.

*Coefficient significant at $<.05$.

**Coefficient significant at $<.01$.

***Coefficient significant at $<.001$.

⇔ Difference in the coefficients for men and women is significant at $<.05$ (by *t*-test) or one coefficient is significant at $<.05$ and the other is not.

For Table C10.7, see pages 418–419.

Table C10.7 Participation Factors and Amount of Money to Politics: An Outcomes Model (among those who made a contribution)[a]

	Level of Factor		Effect of Factor		Overall Outcome		Contribution to Participation Gap
	Women	Men	Women	Men	Women	Men	
HOME AND EDUCATION							
Home Politics	.24	.24	91 (115)	99 (146)	0	0	
Education	.38 ⇔	.42	87 (127)	10 (139)	0	0	
Experience in School	.37 ⇔	.34	118 (89)	84 (102)	0	0	
ADULT INSTITUTIONAL EFFECTS							
Job Factors	.17 ⇔	.26	−132 (121)	22 (132)	0	0	
Organization Factors	.10	.11	101 (143)	89 (145)	0	0	
Church Factors	.13	.12	−81 (106)	82 (109)	0	0	

TIME AND INCOME

Available Time	.61		.61	6 (291)	720 (379)	0	0	0
Family Income	.17	⇔	.18	1139*** (224)	1454*** (288)	221	233	+13
Own Income	.05	⇔	.13	173 (596)	1107*** (245)	0	144	+144
DISCRIMINATION								
Gender Bias	.11	⇔	.06	77 (71)	72 (115)	0	0	0
Constant	1		1	−187 (185)	−536 (242)	0	0	
Total Difference Due to the Level and Effects of Participatory Factors								+157

Source: Citizen Participation Study—Main Survey.

a. Age and age over 65 are included in the equation as a control. The values in parentheses represent standard errors for the estimated coefficients listed in the "effect of factor" columns.

*Coefficient significant at <.05.

**Coefficient significant at <.01.

***Coefficient significant at <.001.

⇔ Difference is significant at <.05 or one coefficient is significant at <.05 and the other is not.

Table C10.7.1 Participation Factors and Making a Political
Contribution (logistic regression)[a]

	Women		Men
HOME AND EDUCATION			
Home Politics	2.26***		1.25***
	(0.40)		(0.37)
Education	2.71***	⇔	1.43***
	(0.44)		(0.37)
Experience in School	0.51		0.20
	(0.28)		(0.26)
ADULT INSTITUTIONAL EFFECTS			
Job Factors	0.76	⇔	1.14**
	(0.42)		(0.37)
Organization Factors	0.23	⇔	1.41***
	(0.46)		(0.42)
Church Factors	0.70*		0.97**
	(0.35)		(0.32)
TIME AND INCOME			
Available Time	0.27		0.31
	(0.82)		(0.85)
Family Income	3.52***		3.74***
	(0.77)		(0.84)
Own Income	−0.66		1.27
	(2.15)		(1.02)
DISCRIMINATION			
Gender Bias	0.72**	⇔	0.46
	(0.23)		(0.30)
Constant	−4.89***		−4.05***
	(0.55)		(0.56)
Log Likelihood	−508		−566
Valid N	1,257		1,136

Source: Citizen Participation Study—Main Survey.
a. Age and age over 65 included in equation as control.
*Coefficient significant at <.05.
**Coefficient significant at <.01.
***Coefficient significant at <.001.
⇔ Difference in the coefficients for men and women is significant at <.05 (by *t*-test)
or one coefficient is significant at <.05 and the other is not.

Table C10.9 The Effect of Psychological Orientations to Politics on Political Activity[a]

	Women	Men
Effect of		
Political Interest	1.25***	1.60***
	(0.15)	(0.17)
Political Information	0.97***	0.96***
	(0.19)	(0.21)
Political Efficacy	0.68***	1.09***
	(0.15)	(0.18)
Women's Consciousness	0.06	
	(0.09)	

Source: Citizen Participation Study—Main Survey.

a. Unstandardized regression coefficients, with political exposure at home, education, high school activity, family income, own income, job factors, organization factors, church factors, sex discrimination, free time, age, and age over 65 in the equation.

*Coefficient significant at <.05.

**Coefficient significant at <.01.

***Coefficient significant at <.001.

⇔ Difference in the coefficients for men and women is significant at <.05 (by *t*-test) or one coefficient is significant at <.05 and the other is not.

Table C10.10 Explaining the Gap in Political Activity[a,b]

The zero-order difference between men and women	−0.31***
	(0.06)
With institutional and socioeconomic factors taken into account	−0.22***
	(0.06)
With institutional and socioeconomic factors and political engagement taken into account	−0.10
	(0.06)

Source: Citizen Participation Study—Main Survey.

a. Negative coefficients mean women are less active.

b. Unstandardized regression coefficients, with political exposure at home, education, high school activity, family income, own income, job factors, organization factors, church factors, free time, age, and age over 65 in the equation.

*Coefficient significant at <.05.

**Coefficient significant at <.01.

***Coefficient significant at <.001.

Table C10.11 Effect of Gender Consciousness on Women's Issue-Based Activity[a,b]

Education	−0.04
	(0.04)
Children	0.02
	(0.02)
Basic Human Needs	0.04
	(0.05)
Women's Issues	0.03**
	(0.01)
Abortion	0.00
	(0.03)
Abortion (pro-choice)	0.08***
	(0.02)
Abortion (pro-life)	−0.08**
	(0.03)

Source: Citizen Participation Study—Main Survey.

a. Model included women only.

b. Unstandardized regression coefficients, with political exposure at home, education, high school activity, family income, own income, job factors, organization factors, church factors, free time, sex discrimination, political interest, political efficacy, political information, age, and age over 65 in the equation.

*Coefficient significant at <.05.

**Coefficient significant at <.01.

***Coefficient significant at <.001.

Table C11.10.1 The Effects of Participatory Factors on Activity (OLS regression)[a]

| | Anglo-Whites | | | | Blacks | | | | Latinos | | | |
| | Men | | Women | | Men | | Women | | Men | | Women | |
Variable	coeff.	s.e.	coeff.	s.e.	coeff.	s.e.	coeff.	s.e.	coeff.	s.e.	coeff.	s.e.
Home	.61	.24	1.04	.24	-.13	.61	.69	.38	.06	.69	.19	.39
Education	1.55	.25	1.74	.28	1.74	.64	1.94	.54	1.31	.79	1.51	.50
School	.61	.18	.66	.17	.62	.42	.45	.28	-.04	.49	.01	.27
Work Factors	.74	.25	.86	.27	1.64	.55	1.52	.44	1.28	.56	1.44	.50
Org. Factors	.77	.30	.95	.29	1.49	.72	.24	.55	2.31	1.22	1.93	.83
Rel. Factors	1.26	.23	1.18	.22	1.06	.48	2.05	.35	1.56	.88	.66	.51
Fam. Income	1.86	.57	2.32	.50	3.86	1.41	.66	1.08	3.07	2.22	2.05	1.11
Own Income	-.26	.59	-1.25	1.38	-2.41	2.34	-2.10	1.83	1.17	2.23	-2.74	2.96
Free Time	-.39	.54	.13	.45	.30	1.10	.06	.67	1.33	1.06	.11	.68
Sex Discr.	.19	.25	.53	.15	.49	.50	.65	.29	.12	.55	.34	.32
Race Discr.	.14	.22	-.07	.28	.37	.25	-.33	.20	.82	.36	-.19	.21
Age	1.42	.24	1.29	.21	1.40	.57	1.29	.36	-.14	.63	.98	.31
Age 65+	-.23	.22	-.19	.18	-.57	.53	-.63	.33	.69	.66	.02	.39
Constant	.25	.35	-.53	.29	-.67	.70	-.23	.45	-.60	.70	-.27	.44

Source: Citizen Participation Study—Main Survey.

a. Italicized coefficients and standard errors indicate that the group's coefficient is strictly different from that of Anglo-White men, $p < .05$, by a *t*-test. We rely on this test here so that sample size will play a smaller role in creating differences than it otherwise would. s.e. = standard error.

Table C11.11.1 Overall Outcome from Participatory Factors

	Anglo-Whites		Blacks		Latinos	
	Men	Women	Men	Women	Men	Women
HOME AND SCHOOL						
Home Politics	.19	.19	.19	.18	.15	.13
Education	.71	.65	.58	.55	.53	.45
Experience in School	.20	.23	.21	.22	.17	.16
INSTITUTIONAL FACTORS						
Job Factors	.24	.17	.18	.15	.22	.09
Organization Factors	.10	.10	.09	.07	.04	.03
Church Factors	.17	.17	.20	.23	.08	.09
TIME AND INCOME						
Free Time	.00	.00	.00	.00	.00	.00
Family Income	.30	.25	.25	.19	.21	.17
Own Income	.00	.00	.00	.00	.00	.00
EXPERIENCE OF BIAS						
Gender Bias	.00	.06	.00	.04	.00	.04
Race Bias	.00	.00	.00	.00	.00	.00

Source: Citizen Participation Study—Main Survey.

Table C11.12 Psychological Orientations to Politics and Political Activity

A. The Effects of Psychological Engagement on Political Activity

	Women	Men
Political Interest	1.24***	1.59***
	(0.15)	(0.17)
Political Efficacy	0.68***	1.09***
	(0.16)	(0.19)
Political Knowledge	0.99***	0.95***
	(0.19)	(0.21)
Gender Consciousness	0.06	
	(0.09)	
Black Consciousness	0.22	−0.12
	(0.13)	(.18)
Hispanic Consciousness	−0.07	−0.04
	(0.19)	(0.24)

B. The Gap in Political Activity between Anglo-White Males and the Other Five Groups

	Zero-Order Activity Gap	Adding Institutions and Socioeconomic Resources	Adding Psychological Engagement Measures
White Women	−0.28***	−0.23***	−0.11
	(0.07)	(0.06)	(0.06)
Black Men	−0.38*	−0.20	−0.08
	(0.18)	(0.15)	(0.14)
Black Women	−0.48***	−0.21	+0.04
	(0.14)	(0.12)	(0.11)
Latinos	−0.76***	−0.14	−0.02
	(0.22)	(0.18)	(0.17)
Latinas	−1.44***	−0.57***	−0.18
	(0.18)	(0.15)	(0.15)

Source: Citizen Participation Study—Main Survey.
*Coefficient significant at <.05.
**Coefficient significant at <.01.
***Coefficient significant at <.001.

Table C11.13 Effect of Consciousness on Issue-Based Activity[a]

	Women		Men
Activity about Women			
Black consciousness	−0.00		−0.01
	(0.02)		(0.01)
Hispanic consciousness	−0.01		−0.01
	(0.03)		(0.02)
Gender consciousness	0.03***		
	(0.01)		
Activity about Blacks or Civil Rights			
Black consciousness	0.11***		0.07***
	(0.02)		(0.02)
Hispanic consciousness	0.03	⇔	0.10***
	(0.03)		(0.03)
Gender consciousness	0.02		
	(0.02)		
Activity about Latinos or Civil Rights			
Black consciousness	0.03		0.02
	(0.02)		(0.02)
Hispanic consciousness	0.06*	⇔	0.23***
	(0.03)		(0.03)
Gender consciousness	0.02		
	(0.01)		

Source: Citizen Participation Study—Main Survey.

a. Unstandardized regression coefficients, with political exposure at home, education, high school activity, family income, own income, job factors, organization factors, church factors, free time, sex discrimination, racial discrimination, political interest, political efficacy, political information, age, and age over 65 in the equation.

*Coefficient significant at <.05.

**Coefficient significant at <.01.

***Coefficient significant at <.001.

⇔ Difference in the coefficients for men and women is significant at <.05 (by *t*-test) or one coefficient is significant at <.05 and the other is not.

Table C12.4.1 Family Circumstances and Political Activity: Marital Status, Children, and Political Activity (OLS regression)[a]

	Women		Men
MARITAL STATUS			
Married	0.17		−0.18
	(0.11)		(0.12)
Separated	−0.29		−0.56
	(0.23)		(0.29)
Divorced	−0.31*		−0.30*
	(0.14)		(0.16)
Widowed	−0.21	⟺	−0.66*
	(0.17)		(0.28)
CHILDREN			
School-age children	0.10		−0.08
	(0.08)		(0.10)
Preschool children	0.11		0.07
	(0.10)		(0.12)

Source: Citizen Participation Study—Main Survey.

a. Controlling for childhood political exposure, high school activity, job factors, organization factors, church factors, income from a job, family income, sex discrimination, education, free time, age, and age over 65 in the equation.

*Coefficient significant at <.05.

**Coefficient significant at <.01.

***Coefficient significant at <.001.

⟺ Difference in the coefficients for men and women is significant at <.05 (by *t*-test) or one coefficient is significant at <.05 and the other is not.

Table C12.4.2 Chapter 12 Indirect Effects Analysis: Predicting Employment, with Marital Status and Children in the Model

Variable	Women		Men
MARITAL STATUS			
Married	−0.01	⇔	0.10***
	(0.04)		(0.03)
Divorced	0.10*	⇔	0.06
	(0.05)		(0.04)
Widowed	−0.07		0.03
	(0.08)		(0.06)
Separated	−0.08		0.05
	(0.08)		(0.07)
CHILDREN			
School-age Children	−0.01	⇔	(0.13)***
	(0.03)		(0.02)
Preschool Children	−0.20***	⇔	0.05
	(0.03)		(0.03)

Source: Citizen Participation Study—Main Survey.

a. Ordinary least-squares regression coefficients, with childhood political exposure, education, other family income, age, age over 65, citizenship, race, and ethnicity in the equation.

*Coefficient significant at <.05.

**Coefficient significant at <.01.

***Coefficient significant at <.001.

⇔ Difference in the coefficients for men and women is significant at <.05 (by *t*-test) or one coefficient is significant at <.05 and the other is not.

Table C12.4.3 Chapter 12 Indirect Effects Analysis: Predicting Religious Affiliation, with Marital Status and Children in the Model[a]

Variable	Women		Men
MARITAL STATUS			
Married	0.05		0.01
	(0.04)		(0.04)
Divorced	0.03	⇔	−0.19***
	(0.05)		(0.05)
Widowed	0.20***	⇔	0.02
	(0.06)		(0.10)
Separated	−0.01	⇔	−0.22*
	(0.08)		(0.10)
CHILDREN			
School-age Children	0.06*	⇔	0.17***
	(0.03)		(0.03)
Preschool Children	−0.01	⇔	0.10*
	(0.04)		(0.04)

Source: Citizen Participation Study—Main Survey.

a. Ordinary least-squares regression coefficients, with childhood political exposure, education, working part time or full time, job level, other family income, age, age over 65, citizenship, race, and ethnicity in the equation.

*Coefficient significant at <.05.

**Coefficient significant at <.01.

***Coefficient significant at <.001.

⇔ Difference in the coefficients for men and women is significant at <.05 (by *t*-test) or one coefficient is significant at <.05 and the other is not.

Table C12.4.4 Chapter 12 Indirect Effects Analysis

Variable	Women	Men
A. Predicting Job Factors, Controlling for Affiliation[a]		
In Work Force	0.24***	0.25***
	(0.01)	(0.02)
B. Predicting Church Factors, Controlling for Affiliation[a]		
Affiliated with a Religious Institution	0.17***	0.20***
	(0.01)	(0.01)

Source: Citizen Participation Study—Main Survey.

a. Ordinary least-squares regression coefficients, with childhood political exposure, education, age, age over 65, citizenship, race, and ethnicity in the equation.

*Coefficient significant at <.05.

**Coefficient significant at <.01.

***Coefficient significant at <.001.

⇔ Difference in the coefficients for men and women is significant at <.05 (by *t*-test) or one coefficient is significant at <.05 and the other is not.

Table C12.6 Family Hierarchy and Citizen Participation[a]

	Women		Men
THE FAMILY ECONOMY: CONTROL OVER MONEY			
Control over family finances	0.32	⇔	1.15*
	(0.47)		(0.49)
Percentage of the family income the respondent brings in	0.64	⇔	0.91*
	(0.41)		(0.41)
THE FAMILY ECONOMY: CONTROL OVER TIME			
Percentage of housework hours done by the wife	−0.10		0.02
	(0.37)		(0.38)
Preschool children	0.12		0.22
	(0.24)		(0.26)
THE FAMILY POLITY: DECISIONAL AUTONOMY			
Respondent's autonomy	1.22*		1.71**
	(0.56)		(0.58)
Relative difference in spouses' autonomy	1.01*	⇔	−0.24
	(0.44)		(0.48)
THE FAMILY POLITY: DECISIONAL HIERARCHY			
Respondent believes she or he gets a say in family discussions	1.10*	⇔	−0.20
	(0.48)		(0.49)
Relative difference in whether the partners get a say	−0.01		−0.20
	(0.25)		(0.46)
THE FAMILY SOCIETY: EQUALITY OF RESPECT			
Respondent is a trusted advisor for spouse	−0.40		0.41
	(0.27)		(0.28)
Relative difference in whether the respondents turn to each other for advice	−0.21		−0.30
	(0.37)		(0.42)
Relative difference between the spouses' job levels	−0.12		0.47
	(0.78)		(0.65)
THE FAMILY CULTURE: BELIEFS ABOUT GENDER ROLES			
Respondent's belief in equal roles	−0.80		0.29
	(0.59)		(0.62)
Relative difference between spouses in views about gender roles	−0.87		−0.42
	(0.72)		(0.69)

Source: Citizen Participation Study Follow-up—Couples Survey.

a. Ordinary least-squares coefficients; model also controls for childhood politicization, education, family income, job level, religious attendance, age, and years of marriage.

*Coefficient significant at <.05.

**Coefficient significant at <.01.

***Coefficient significant at <.001.

⇔ Difference in the coefficients for men and women is significant at <.05 (by *t*-test) or one coefficient is significant at <.05 and the other is not.

Table C13.1 Women as Candidates and Elected Officials: Impact on
Orientations to Politics[a]

	Women		Men
A. Effect of a Woman Senator or Candidate on			
Knowledge of Senators' Names	.32**	⇔	.08
	(.13)		(.11)

	Women		Men
B. Effect of a Woman State-wide Incumbent or Candidate on			
Political Information			
Overall scale	.04*	⇔	.00
	(.02)		(.02)
Civic knowledge	.02		−.15
	(.09)		(.08)
Knowledge of names	.40**	⇔	.19
	(.13)		(.13)
Political Interest	.05*	⇔	−.01
	(.02)		(.02)
Political Efficacy	.04*	⇔	−.02
	(.02)		(.02)

Source: Citizen Participation Study—Main Survey.

a. Ordinary least-squares coefficients; model also controls for childhood politicization, education, family income, job level, religious attendance, age, and years of marriage.

*Coefficient significant at <.05.

**Coefficient significant at <.01.

***Coefficient significant at <.001.

⇔ Difference in the coefficients for men and women is significant at <.05 (by *t*-test) or one coefficient is significant at <.05 and the other is not.

Table C13.2 Women as Candidates and Elected Officials:[a] Impact on
Orientations to Politics (NES)[b]

	Women		Men
Effect on			
Political Interest	.52*	⇔	−.13
	(.27)		(.26)
Campaign Interest	1.02***	⇔	.26
	(.29)		(.30)
Follow Campaign in Media	.30*	⇔	−.09
	(.14)		(.14)
Salience of House Candidates	1.30***	⇔	.47
	(.28)		(.28)

Source: American National Election Studies (1984–1996).

a. The explanatory variable for which the coefficients are presented is the sum, for the respondent's congressional district, of the number of female candidates for office, female winners, and female incumbents for the following offices: governor, senator, and members of Congress. The variable, which can theoretically take on values from 0 to 12, has been re-scaled to vary between 0 and 1.

b. The analysis also controls for education, income, age, age over 65, religious attendance, working, and the specific years.

*Coefficient significant at <.05.

**Coefficient significant at <.01.

***Coefficient significant at <.001.

⇔ Difference in the coefficients for men and women is significant at <.05 (by *t*-test) or one coefficient is significant at <.05 and the other is not.

Table C13.4 Women as Candidates and Elected Officials: Impact[a] on Salience of House Candidate's Sex[b]

	Women		Men
1990	0.07*	⇔	0.01
	(0.03)		(0.02)
1992	0.22***	⇔	0.06*
	(0.04)		(0.03)
1994	0.07*	⇔	0.01
	(0.03)		(0.01)
1996	0.25***	⇔	0.03
	(0.05)		(0.02)

Source: American National Election Studies, 1990, 1992, 1994, 1996.

a. Ordinary least-squares analysis with education included.

b. The explanatory variable for which the coefficients are presented is the sum, for the respondent's congressional district, of the number of female candidates for office, female winners, and female incumbents for the following offices: governor, senator, and members of Congress. The variable, which can theoretically take on values from 0 to 12, has been re-scaled to vary between 0 and 1. The dependent variable measures respondents' mention of their House candidate's sex as a reason to like or dislike the candidate.

*Coefficient significant at <.05.

**Coefficient significant at <.01.

***Coefficient significant at <.001.

⇔ Difference in the coefficients for women and men is significant at <.05 (by *t*-test) or one coefficient is significant at <.05 and the other is not.

APPENDIX D

Explanation of Outcomes Analysis

Direct Effects

In outcomes analyses, we take account of both the level of the factor with which the group is endowed and the effect of the factor (the coefficient on the factor in the regression analysis predicting political participation). For some time, gender-based analyses have been concerned with accounting for the consequences of inequality in life spaces other than politics. Our method addresses that concern directly.

Our outcomes analyses, such as the one in Table 10.5, present the level of the factors with which the group is endowed; we present the average amount of the factor that members of the group have. In addition, the tables present a test to tell whether one group comes to the regression with an endowment that is statistically different from the endowment of the other groups in the analysis. This part of the analysis asks whether members of groups come to our regression analyses with inequality created in other life spaces.

Then the table both presents the coefficients on these factors for the groups in the analysis and tests to tell whether the coefficients are statistically different from one another. This part of the analysis asks, first, whether the factors make a difference, and, second, whether the process is different for members of different groups.

The third part of the analysis multiplies the level of the factor with the coefficient on the factor (and if the levels or the coefficients are statistically indistinguishable, this part of the analysis uses an average of the two groups' levels or coefficients). The goal here is to take account of the consequences of both level and effect, taken together, for participation. The numbers in the outcomes columns, then, are the average contribution of the factor to the group's political participation, and the numbers are in units of political participation.

The final part of the analysis calculates the difference in outcomes for each factor for the two groups, to indicate how much each factor contributes to the participatory gap between the two groups.

Indirect Effects

Table 12.4 shows the indirect effects of marital status and children on political activity. We calculated these numbers by estimating the models of institutional affiliation in Chapters 8 and 9 as OLS regressions; we added the measures of the range of different marital statuses to these regressions. Our goal in this part of the analysis was to estimate the effect of marital statuses and children on the probability of being in the institution, controlling for the respondent's other relevant characteristics. We needed to be able to untangle the effects of marital status from variables like education to make sure that the effects we attributed to marital status *were* the effects of marital status. We did this via OLS to calculate clear estimates of the probability effects; the probability of affiliation with any of these institutions is sensibly estimated by OLS, because affiliation is neither rare nor universal. Once we calculated the difference the status made to the probability of affiliation, we estimated the effects of affiliation on the level of factors—skills, mobilization, and personal income—respondents received from affiliation. We then multiplied the probability of affiliation resulting from the first equation with the levels of factors that come from affiliation in the second series of equations. These first two stages yielded the effects of marital status and children on levels of factors; all of these effects were the result of the impact of marital status and children on affiliation with institutions.

Once we had these levels in hand, we multiplied them by the coefficients on these factors in the outcomes model in Table 10.5 to get the ultimate, indirect effects of these statuses on political activity. The indirect effects we report in Table 12.4 are the sums of the indirect effects via skills, mobilization, and personal income. In this way, we calculated the outcomes that resulted from the way marital status and children shape institutional affiliation.

Outcomes Analysis for Chapter 13

We use the following technique in Chapter 13 to arrive at an estimate of the change in women's political participation that would result from greater gender integration of the political environment. We posit, first, a scenario in which everyone lives in a state having just one female within the group composed of its gubernatorial, lieutenant gubernatorial, and senatorial incumbents and candidates. On a scale measured from 0 to 1, the gender disparity in political interest is .07, and the gender disparity in political information is .05. The maximum actual score on the 8.5-point scale measuring the density of women in the political environment is 1. The average score on the scale is .16. Bringing everyone to the circumstance of having a female senatorial or gubernatorial incumbent or candidate thus represents an average gain of .84 (1.00 − .16 = .84) on the scale. Applying the coefficients from portion B of Table 13.1, this change yields a gain of .04 (.84 × .05 = .04) in political interest and a gain of .03 (.84 × .04 = .03) in political information, increments that are more than half the initial deficits.

We use the coefficients for the effects on participation of political interest (1.25) and information (.97) from Table 10.9 to calculate the participatory payoff of these increases in psychological engagement with politics. The gain in political interest yields an additional .05 act (.04 × 1.25 = .05). The gain in political information yields an additional .03 act (.03 × .97), for a total of .08. Ordinarily, when the coefficients for men and women are not statistically different, we use their average in calculating outcomes. In this case, the calculations change slightly. The gain in political interest yields an additional .06 act (.04 × 1.425 = .06). The gain in political information yields an additional .03 act (.03 × .965), for a total of .09.

The second scenario posits a circumstance of gender parity in the visible political environment. Because relatively few states had both a senatorial and a gubernatorial election in 1988, the average maximum possible score on the scale is 5.48, and gender parity would be represented by half this average maximum, or 2.74. The average actual score on the scale is, once again, .16. Bringing everyone to a circumstance of gender parity thus represents an average gain of 2.58 (2.74 − .16 = 2.58) on the scale. Applying the coefficients from portion B of Table 13.1 yields a gain of .13 in political interest (2.58 × .05 = .13) and a gain of .10 in political information (2.58 × .04 = .10). Using the coefficients for the effects on participation of political interest (1.25) and information (.97) from Table 10.9 yields a gain in political activity from the added political interest of .16 act (.13 × 1.25 = .16). The increase in political information yields an additional .10 act (.10 × .97 = .10) for a total of .26. Averaging the coefficients for women and men boosts slightly the gain in women's participation to .29 act, the sum of .19 act for political interest (.13 × 1.425) and .10 act for political information (.10 × .965).

Index

abortion: as an Anglo issue, 304; education and, 122–124; family structure and, 309; gender differences on, 30; gender roles and, 373–374; married couples' attitudes, 169; political orientation and, 32, 163–166; religious institutions and, 378; socioeconomic advantage and, 125; as women's issue, 129–131, 133, 271–272, 372

Abramson, Paul R., 100

Adams, Abigail, 10

Adams, John, 10

adult institutions. *See specific institutions*

African-Americans: African Methodist Episcopalians, 85; gender *vs.* racial differences, 31; group consciousness of, 108, 274, 294, 303, 395; issues important to, 306; political interest and, 300; racial discrimination and, 108–110, 283–285, 292; religion and, 88; women in the work force, 288–289

age: as control variable, 208, 214, 222, 318; measuring, 397; party affiliation and, 160; political activity and, 93–95

agenda, political participation and, 118–119, 120–125, 304–306

Ahern, David W., 30, 166, 270

Alex-Assensoh, Yvette, 283

Almond, Gabriel A., 188

Alvarez, R. Michael, 30

American Association of Retired People (AARP), 81

Ammerman, Nancy Tatom, 18, 85, 239

Anders, Sarah Frances, 18, 85, 96, 239

Andersen, Kristi, 12, 30, 34, 51, 63, 111, 204, 205, 206

Apollonio, Dorie, 69

Aquilino, William S., 56

Ardrey, Saundra, 270, 277

athletics, 336–337, 341

attitudes and beliefs: abortion, 163–166; American norms, 155, 373–379; conservatism, 241–242, 378; day care, 163; economic status and, 163; egalitarians, 157–161, 195–197, 397; government assistance, 163–169, 293, 310; household culture and, 162–169; importance of, 361; of married couples, 154–157, 162–169; morality, 167; party identification and, 163, 164–166; religious attitudes and orientations, 105–107, 168–169; school prayer, 163–166; social issues, 164–166; socialization and, 340–341; social status, 163

autonomy, measuring, 397

Baby Boomers, 177, 234

Bachrach, Peter, 23

Baker, Paula, 4, 73, 281

Baptists, ordination of women, 239. *See also* Southern Baptists

Barber, Benjamin, 311

Barbie (doll), 334

Bauer, Raymond, 115

Baxter, Sandra, 100, 277

Beck, Paul, 312

Beckwith, Karen, 34, 63, 100, 205, 317

Bendroth, Margaret Lamberts, 87
Bendyna, Mary E., 111
Bennett, Linda, 100
Bennett, Stephen Earl, 100
Berk, Sarah Fenstermaker, 195
Berliner, David C., 139
Berman, Sheri, 23
Bianchi, Suzanne M., 250
Bird, Gerald A., 180
Bird, Gloria W., 180
birth rates, 17
Bischoping, Katherine, 341
Blevins, Carolyn DeArmond, 18, 86–87
Blood, Robert, 180
Blumberg, Rae Lesser, 178, 181
Blumstein, Philip, 56, 178
Boals, Kay, 4
Bobo, Lawrence, 277, 345
Bock, Gisela, 25
Boetcher, Ruth-Ellen, 275
Boles, Janet K., 112
Bourque, Susan, 62
Bowers, Jake, 138
Bowman, Karlyn H., 30
Boylan, Anne M., 88
Brady, David W., 205
Brady, Henry E., 4, 22, 33, 35, 45, 54,
    68, 69, 75, 83, 90, 94, 114, 118,
    142, 158, 198, 211, 214, 216, 221,
    231, 238, 263, 266, 277, 341, 365,
    367
Brehm, John, 22, 43
Brereton, Virginia Lieson, 87
Brines, Julie, 155
Brownstone, David, 13
Burgoyne, Carole B., 188, 190, 265
Burns, Nancy Elizabeth, 23, 52, 100,
    112, 307, 329, 346
Bush, George H. W., 124, 128

Cain, Bruce E., 276
Calfee, Robert C., 139
California, women politicians in, 348,
    355–356
campaigns, political: contributions, 67–
    68, 261–265; gender differences in
    participation, 358; married couples'
    involvement in, 314; participation in,
    64; women candidates, 349–350

Campbell, Andrea, 68
Campbell, Angus, 61, 100, 191
Campbell, Kim, 341
Carroll, Jackson W., 17, 89
Carroll, Susan J., 63, 86, 112
Castelli, Jim, 88
Catholic Church: compared with
    Protestants, 90; gender roles in, 101;
    ordination of women, 238–240;
    participatory factors and, 299;
    political recruitment and, 237–238;
    racial and ethnic makeup of, 285
causality: egalitarian attitudes and, 209;
    family life and political participation,
    331; gender and, 26; group
    differences and, 97–98; regression
    analysis and, 46–47, 170;
    volunteerism and, 220, 365
Chaney, Carole K., 30
charitable activities and organizations:
    family circumstances and, 312–316;
    gender differences in, 78–79; neglect
    of women in, 221; political
    contributions and, 261–265; racial
    and ethnic differences in, 282–283;
    volunteerism and, 81–82
Chaves, Mark, 17
children and child care: child care
    responsibilities, 180–187, 194;
    childhood experience, 139; as control
    measure, 222; couples' attitudes,
    186–187; day care, 163; effect on
    participation, 97, 310–311, 316–321;
    employment and, 209–210, 321–324;
    family hierarchy and, 331–332;
    indirect effects of, 436–437;
    "Mommy Wars," 374–375; preschool
    children, 397; single motherhood,
    126–127; women's issues and, 131.
    See also family issues and structure;
    households; marriage and married
    couples
Chong, Dennis, 114
Chowdhury, Najma, 1, 84
Chrétien, Jean, 341
Christianity. See religious activity and
    institutions
Christian Right, 84
Christy, Carol A., 20

Church of God, 87
Church of the Nazarene, 86–87
Citizen Participation Study, 54–57, 100, 107, 113–114, 342, 354
citizenship and civic engagement: civic gratification, 115–116; civil society, 22, 219; as control measure, 208; employment and, 199; enfranchisement of women, 1, 10–12, 104, 341, 357, 382–383; family structure and, 57; gender differences in, 9–12, 73, 357–358; importance of, 22; volunteerism and, 4. See also civic skills
civic skills: development of, 203, 245; effect on participation, 201; factors affecting, 243–245; gender differences, 224–225; male's advantages in, 248; non-political organizations and, 282–283; political participation and, 214, 222–226, 255; race and ethnicity, 290; regression analysis of, 53; religious institutions and, 236–238; workplace-related, 217–218, 289
Civic Voluntarism Model, 198–199, 201–204, 365
civil rights: Civil Rights Act (1964), 86, 384; civil rights legislation, 32, 124, 129–131; civil rights movement, 303; issue-based activities and, 305
Clark, Cal, 34, 205
Clark, Janet, 34, 205
class issues, 379. See also equality issues
clergy, women in, 85–86, 232, 238–243, 376–379
Clinchy, Blythe McVicker, 37
Clinton, Bill, 128
Cohen, Cathy J., 277, 283, 286, 293
Cohen, Roberta S., 138
Coleman, James S., 22, 178, 181
collective action, 114
college education, political involvement and, 142–143, 149–150, 151. See also education
community activity, 65, 314, 322
compensatory inequalities, 204
Congregationalists, 85

Congress, women in, 337, 340
Conley, M. Margaret, 30
Conover, Pamela Johnston, 111, 270, 342
conservatism, 241–242, 378
constants in regression analysis, 172
consultation, 191–192, 197. See also decision making in households
contact issues, 64–65, 134–136
contextual gender differences, 203–204
Converse, Philip E., 61, 100, 103, 191
Conway, M. Margaret, 45, 166, 270
Cook, Elizabeth Adell, 34, 51, 63, 96, 107, 111, 112, 205, 206
Corning, Amy D., 341
Cott, Nancy F., 12, 73, 88, 281
Couples Survey, 56–57, 168, 178–179, 194
coverture, 6–7, 9–12
Craig, Barbara Hinkson, 30
credit claiming, 185
Crenshaw, Kimberlé, 275
crime issues, 125–126, 306
Crosby, Faye, 108
Crotty, William, 74
cultural issues, 378. See also race and ethnicity

Daniel, Clifton, 12, 13
Danvers Statement, 87
data gathering, 40–43
Davis, Angela Y., 281
Davis, Belinda Creel, 103
Dawson, Michael, 283
Day, Neil, 22
day care, political attitudes toward, 163
Deaux, Kay, 107, 155
decision making in households, 188, 191–192, 327–330, 362, 375–376
Declaration of Independence, 11
Declaration of Principles, 11
de la Garza, Rodolfo, 295
Delli Carpini, Michael X., 100, 101, 103
Democratic Party, 32, 111
Democrats, 163–169, 310, 397
dependent variables, 46, 169–170
Deutsch, Francine M., 181, 195, 209–210

Dexter, Lewis Anthony, 115
Dietz, Mary G., 110
differences among sexes *vs.* between sexes, 274
differential selection and treatment, 199
Disciples of Christ, 239
discretionary agendas, 118–119
discrimination: effect on participation, 272–273; ethnic or racial, 107–110, 291–292, 299; gender, 107–110, 250–251, 299; gender gap and, 8; political activity and, 257–260; political participation and, 360; in religious institutions, 283–286; sexual harassment, 41–42, 122, 128, 131–132; workplace, 129, 381–382
discussion, political, 102, 104, 140–141, 311–316, 398
division of labor: domestic, 310–311; in family environment, 362–363; family structure and, 95–97; within households, 175–180; leisure time and, 327–328; political resources and, 325; traditional *vs.* egalitarian views, 195–196
divorce, 17, 191–192, 197, 362
Dodson, Debra, 112, 305
domestic issues: domestic hierarchy, 192–193, 329–332, 372–373, 375–376; domestic isolation, 205; gender beliefs and, 193–196; political participation and, 308; political resources and, 325–332
Donahue, Jesse, 100, 110
donations, 261–265. *See also* campaigns, political; charitable activities and organizations
Douthitt, Robin A., 181
drug issues, 125–126
Duverger, Maurice, 62
Dziech, Billie Wright, 42

Eagly, Alice, 37
early experiences, 254
Eastern Orthodox Church, 85, 238–239
Eccles, Jacquelynne S., 139
economic issues: economic inequality, 187; economic status, 163; effect on participation, 127; family income, 177–178; gender gap in economic status, 15–16; household economy, 175–180, 188–192; policy issues, 167–169. *See also* income and finances
education: as control measure, 214; effect on participation, 253, 272; ethnic gaps in, 276; as explanatory variable, 365; extracurricular activities, 151; gender differences in, 133; gender gaps in, 8–9, 14–15, 19–20, 125–127, 276; high school activities, 214, 243–245, 361; high school education, 142; impact on participation, 298; job level and, 211–213; measuring, 396; participatory factors and, 247, 259, 286–287, 366–367; political activity and, 35, 47, 92, 93–94, 141–147, 151, 207–208, 243, 245, 258; political orientation and, 122–123; political participation and, 380; political training and, 147–150; religious affiliation and, 234; "SES model," 365; volunteerism and, 221–222; women's issues and, 127
Educational Amendments (1972), 384
Edwards, Bob, 22, 23
Edwards, Rebecca, 12
efficacy, political, 102, 105, 266–269, 383, 395
egalitarians: gender roles and, 157–160; in household labor, 195–197; measuring, 397; Republicans and, 160–161
elected office, women in: outcomes analysis and, 437–438; in political parties, 114–115; psychological orientations to politics and, 334–336, 342–349, 349–352, 360; traditional routes to, 63; women legislators, 112–113
elections, 104, 111, 349–352, 357
Ellison, Christopher G., 82, 89, 234
Elms, Laurel, 69, 94
Elshtain, Jean Bethke, 110
employment: civic capacity and, 200; full-time, 184–187; gender differences in, 276; "glass ceiling," 16, 129; job

factors, 394; job level, 211–213, 222, 396; participatory factors and, 199–200; political participation and, 47; racial and ethnic differences in, 276, 288–289; selection into work force, 206–213

enfranchisement of women, 1, 10–12, 104, 341, 357, 382–383

Engeleiter, Susan, 342

England, Paula, 195, 227

Episcopalians, 85, 239

Epstein, Cynthia Fuchs, 26

equality issues: compensatory and cumulative inequalities, 204; equal opportunity, 129–131, 383–384; Equal Rights Amendment (ERA), 32, 112, 124–125, 373–374, 378; gender equality scores, 158; in household, 153–157; religion and, 84; in workplace, 129. See also gender gap

Erkulwater, Jennifer, 94

Ester, Peter, 82

ethnicity. See race and ethnicity

Eurobarometer, 349

European Union, 340

evangelical Protestants, 237–238

extracurricular activities, 151

factor analysis, 167–168

Falk, Nancy Auer, 88

family issues and structure: childhood studies and, 140; civic engagement and, 57; contrasted with political environment, 307, 325–332; as control measure, 222; decision making in households, 188–192, 327–330, 362, 375–376; effects of, 320; family as social system, 326–329; family discussions, 312–316, 398; family finances, 177–180, 201–202, 210, 222, 263–264, 331, 395–397; gender roles and, 95–97, 119–120, 308–311, 372–373, 375–376; hierarchical family, 326–329, 329–332; inequality in, 329–332; participatory factors and, 247, 286–287; patriarchal family, 7, 84–85, 325, 359; political activity and, 34–35, 37, 207, 244–245, 307–308,

312–316, 329–333, 362–363; political interest and, 152; religious affiliations and, 233–234, 376–379; trends, 17; work force participation and, 209–211, 211–213. See also domestic issues; households; marriage and married couples

Farah, Barbara, 34

Farkas, George, 187, 195

feminism, 7, 25–29, 84, 115, 181

Ferejohn, John A., 103

Ferraro, Geraldine, 334

finances. See income and finances

Finn, Virginia Sullivan, 88

Fiorina, Morris P., 231

First Amendment, 384

Fiske, Susan T., 107, 155

Flexner, Eleanor, 11, 104, 115

Flora, Cornelia B., 204

Foley, Michael W., 22, 23

Follow-Up Study, 2, 55, 153

Forman, Tyrone A., 108

Fortune, Jim, 104

Fowler, Robert Booth, 86, 88

Franck, Irene, 13

Frankovic, Kathleen, 30, 111

Freedman, Deborah, 156

Freedman, Paul, 214

Freeman, Jo, 10, 12, 32

free time: charity and, 190–192; control over, 188–192; employment and, 218; in family setting, 180–187, 325–326, 327–328, 330, 376; gender differences in, 290–291, 370–371; in household economy, 180–187; as limited resource, 249; measuring, 394; participatory factors and, 260–261; political participation and, 7, 67–68, 202, 207–208, 214, 255–257, 258, 359; volunteerism, 314

Frieze, Irene Hanson, 155

Fulenwider, Clare Knoche, 277

Gamson, William, 311

Gay, Claudine, 110, 345

Geis, Gilbert, 155, 184

Gelb, Joyce, 31

gender gap: causality and, 97–98; consequences of, 24–25; early

gender gap (*continued*)
    findings, 61–63; education, 8–9, 14–
    15, 19–20, 125–127, 151, 276;
    household, 16–17; importance of
    studying, 6–7; income and finances,
    125–127, 177–178, 185; inter-gender
    variation and, 95; in Latino culture,
    95, 98; model of study and, 36–38;
    participatory factors, 251–260;
    political participation, 1–3, 352–356;
    political parties, 31–32; public policy
    and, 24–25; religion and religious
    activity, 89–91; trends in, 18–19; in
    work force, 15–16
gender issues: creation of gender
    differences, 199–204; domestic
    equality and, 193–196; as focus of
    childhood studies, 140; gender
    consciousness, 107–110, 266, 270–
    272, 370–371, 395; gender
    discrimination, 107–110, 250–251,
    299, 381–382, 395; gender
    integration in political environment,
    437–438; gender-mixed
    organizations, 229; gender parity in
    non-political organizations, 221;
    gender segregation, 73, 226–231;
    gender variations, 370; gender *vs.*
    sex, 25–29, 45–48, 60; in household,
    328–329, 372, 375–376; as political
    category, 29–32; political
    participation and, 368; racial
    differences and, 31, 274–276, 298;
    studying, 369–373. *See also* gender
    gap; gender roles
gender roles: couples' views on, 157–
    160; in family setting, 153–162, 330,
    362–363; political participation and,
    152; traditional, 336, 378;
    understanding beliefs about, 160–162
General Social Survey, 192–193
generations, political views transmitted
    across, 152
Gerson, Kathleen, 210
Gerth, H. H., 5, 174
Gertzog, Irwin N., 63
G.I. Bill, 142
Giddings, Paula, 73, 281
Gilbert, Daniel T., 107, 155

Gilliam, Franklin D., 277, 345
Githens, Marianne, 100, 138
"glass ceiling," 16, 129
Godbey, Geoffrey, 181, 291
Goel, M. L., 45, 100
Goffman, Erving, 25
Goldin, Claudia, 213
Goldscheider, Frances K., 181, 185
Goodman, Ellen, 334
Goot, Murray, 62
government assistance, attitudes
    toward, 163–169, 293, 310
government policy, influencing, 118
Grassmuck, Sherri, 138
gratification, 115–118
Greeley, Andrew, 82
Green, John C., 74
Greenberg, Anna, 159, 231
Greenstein, Fred, 62, 138
Gremillion, Joseph, 88
Grindal, Gracia, 87
Gross, Rita M., 88
Grossholtz, Jean, 62
group consciousness and orientation:
    effects on participation, 270–271;
    gender consciousness, 107–110; in
    Latino culture, 294, 295, 303, 395;
    measuring, 395; political interest and,
    300, 301–303; political participation
    and, 368; by race or ethnicity, 293–
    294
gubernatorial candidates, 346
Gurin, Gerald, 107, 270, 293
Gurin, Patricia, 12, 73, 107, 205, 270,
    281, 293

Hansen, John Mark, 45, 69, 117, 216,
    367
Hansen, Susan B., 341
Hardy-Fanta, Carol, 280, 293
Hargrove, Barbara, 17, 86
Harkess, Shirley, 178
Harmon-Martin, Sheila F., 277
Harold, Rena D., 139
Harris, Frederick, 86, 277, 283
Harrison, Cynthia, 32
Hartmann, Heidi, 178, 181, 187
Harvey, Anna L., 12
Heckman, James, 53, 211

Hertz, Rosanna, 188
Hertzke, Allen D., 86, 88
Hess, Robert D., 62, 138
heterogeneity, 50–51, 369
Hiatt, Suzanne Radley, 87
Higginbotham, Evelyn Brooks, 12, 275
higher education, political involvement and, 142–143, 149–150, 151
high school. See education
Hill, Anita, 128
Hill-Collins, Patricia, 275
Hochschild, Arlie, 181
hooks, bell, 275
Horn, Jody D., 112
households: decision making in, 188–192, 327–330, 362, 375–376; domestic labor, 155–156, 180–187, 194, 276, 310–311, 327, 331–332, 397; household culture, 162–169, 328–329; household economy, 175–180; leisure time in, 327; as political unit, 187–192; social stratification and, 174. See also family issues and structure; marriage and married couples
House Judiciary Committee, 384
House of Representatives, 14, 337, 346–347, 351–352
Huckfeldt, Robert, 167, 312
Hunter, James Davison, 378
Hustace, Maria M., 342
Huston, Ted, 55, 155, 184

Iglitzin, Lynne B., 138
Illinois, 348
income and finances: family hierarchy and, 188–192, 327, 330; financial decisions, 331; gender gap in, 86, 125–127, 177–180, 185, 250, 290–291; measuring, 394–396; participatory factors and, 249–250, 259; political contributions, 263–265; political participation and, 47, 201–202, 214, 257, 258, 289; "SES model," 365; traditional vs. egalitarian views, 195; variations in, 291; volunteerism and, 222; work force participation and, 210
indirect effects, 320, 436–437

inequality. See equality issues
informal organizations, 280
information, political, 266–269, 383, 395
Inglehart, Margaret L., 101, 104
institutions: factors affecting institutional affiliation, 243–245; gender differences in, 199–200; institutional context, 361–363; institutional involvement, 202–203; institutional model, 297; institutional resources, 300; links between, 52–53, 361–362; participation gap in, 254–256; participatory factors of, 51–52, 247–251, 287–290; political participation and, 201–204, 363; role of, 34–36; selection into, 200–201
interest, political, 266–269
Islam, 84
issues, political: issue-based activities, 301–303; participation and, 119–120, 120–125; women-specific issues, 128–131
Iyengar, Shanto, 103, 104

Jackman, Mary R., 25, 275
Jackson, James S., 108
Jackson, Jesse, 279, 345
Jackson, Robert Max, 379
Jacob, Herbert, 31
Jacobs, Janis E., 139
Jacobsen, Joyce P., 20
James, Susan, 25
Jaquette, Jane S., 138, 204
Jaros, Dean, 62, 138
Jennings, Jeanette, 305
Jennings, M. Kent, 34, 122, 138, 139, 166, 167, 205, 254, 320–321
John, Daphne, 195
Jones, Alethia, 286
Jones, Kathleen B., 277, 283, 286, 293
Jones, Tamara, 286
Judaism, 84
Junn, Jane, 15, 142

Kahn, Kim Fridkin, 342, 350
Kanter, Rosabeth Moss, 227
Kassebaum, Nancy, 342
Kathlene, Lyn, 112

Katosh, John P., 66, 101
Katzenstein, Mary Fainsod, 32, 86
Kaufmann, Karen M., 30, 111, 345
Keeter, Scott, 100, 101, 103
Kelly, Rita Mae, 112
Kennedy, Edward M., 5
Kenney, Patrick J., 342
Kenski, Henry C., 111
Kerber, Linda K., 9, 10
Kessler, Ronald C., 108
Keyssar, Alexander, 12
Kiewiet, D. Roderick, 276–277
Kim, Jae-On, 20
Kinder, Donald, 23
Kirkpatrick, Jeanne J., 63, 114–115
Klein, Christa Ressmeyer, 87
Klein, Ethel, 107, 111, 270
Kmec, Julie A., 227
Knoke, David, 117
Koch, Wendy, 334
Kraditor, Aileen S., 11, 115
Kuklinski, James H., 103
Kunin, Madeleine, 354

Ladd, Everett Carll, 22, 30, 83
LaFrance, Marianne, 107, 155
Lake, Celinda C., 111
Lane, Robert, 62
Lansing, Marjorie, 100, 277
Laslett, Barbara, 275
Latino culture: discrimination against, 292; as ethnic group, 274–275; gender gap in, 95, 98; group consciousness, 294, 295, 303, 395; group orientations of, 108; issues of, 306; political inactivity of Latina women, 279, 299; political interest and, 300; religion and, 298–299
Lebsock, Suzanne, 12
Lehman, Edward C., 86
leisure time, 184–187, 359
Lennon, Mary-Clare, 184
Lerner, Gerda, 73
level of participatory factors, 53–54, 258–259
level of significance, 171–172
Levine, Ann D., 20
Lewis, Sinclair, 13
Lewontin, Richard, 28
liberal tradition, 9–12

Lindzey, Gardner, 107, 155
local government participation, 65, 66–67
Lohmann, Suzanne, 114
Lorber, Judith, 209
Luker, Kristin, 374
Lummis, Adair, 17, 86
Lutherans, 85, 87
Lynn, Naomi B., 204

Mahajan, Hapreet, 111
Mahony, Rhona, 210
Main Street (Lewis), 13
Main Survey, 54
Malanchuk, Oksana, 107, 270, 293
Mandel, Ruth B., 112
Mansbridge, Jane J., 22, 55, 356, 374
Mansfield, Edward, 10
marriage and married couples: as control measure, 222; equality and, 309–311, 326–329; gender roles, 152, 157–160; household chores and, 180–187; household structure and, 174; indirect effects of, 436–437; legal status and, 9–12; measuring, 397; political attitudes and, 162–169; political participation and, 10, 97, 244, 316–321, 332–333; religious affiliation and, 234; single mothers, 323; spousal abuse, 131–132; studying, 153, 156; variation among, 375–376; work force participation and, 209
Martin, William, 84, 88
Marx, Karl, 153, 231
material benefits, 115
maternity leave, U.S. and New Zealand compared, 20
Matsunaga, Spark, 342
McBrier, Debra B., 227
McCoy, Melanie, 305
McCullough, Jane L., 184
McDonagh, Eileen, 34, 204, 206
McGlen, Nancy E., 152, 205, 206, 317
McGrath, Wilma E., 100
McHugh, Maureen C., 155
McKay, David, 138
McKinney, William, 240
McPherson, J. Miller, 227, 229
measurement issues: credit-claiming,

185; measuring childhood experiences, 138–140; random sampling, 42–45, 59; selecting independent variables, 170; self-identification, 274–275; self-selection, 43, 200; surveys, 2–3, 41–43, 43–45, 51

media, exposure to, 102, 105

men's issues, 128–131

Mezey, Susan Gluck, 112

Mickelson, Kristin D., 108

Mikulski, Barbara, 342

Milbrath, Lester W., 45, 100

Miller, Arthur H., 107, 111, 270, 293

Miller, Warren E., 61, 100

Mills, C. Wright, 5, 174

Minkoff, Debra C., 73

mobilization, measuring, 394

"Mommy Wars," 322, 374–375

Mondak, Jeffrey J., 103

monetary constraints on participation, 67–68. See also income and finances

Monitoring the Future Study, 148, 149

morality, measuring attitudes toward, 167

Morgan, Robin, 384

Mormons, 85, 238–239

Morrison, Toni, 275

motherhood. See children and child care

motivations for political participation, 115–118

Moyser, George, 22

Mueller, Carol McClurg, 32, 111

multiple affiliations, 220–221

multivariate analysis: described, 39–41, 45–48, 169–173; effects of institutions and, 59; heterogeneity, 50–51; household issues and, 195–196; ordinary least-squares (OLS) regression, 436–437; purpose of, 160; reading regression tables, 169–173; separate analyses by sex, 48–50, 59–60; subgroups and, 50. See also regression analysis

Myrdal, Gunnar, 10

Nagler, Jonathan, 30

National Election Studies (NES), 345–348, 355

National Organization of Women, 384–385

Nauta, Rein, 82

Neft, Naomi, 20

Nelson, Barbara J., 1, 84

New Deal, 32, 377–378

Newton, Kenneth, 22

New Zealand, 20

Nie, Norman H., 15, 20, 142, 269, 276, 277, 365

Niemi, Richard, 111, 122, 167, 320–321

Nineteenth Amendment, 1, 12, 357

non-political organizations and activity: civic skills and, 224–225; education and, 366–367; employment and, 200; fostering participation, 6; gender gap in, 254–256; group differences in, 281; non-electoral activity, 358; participatory factors from, 57–58, 289–290, 303–304; political activity compared with, 224; political participation and, 9, 57–58, 203, 257, 295–299, 360–361, 364; racial and ethnic groups in, 281–286, 303–306; secular activities, 81–82; selection, 221–222, 224; volunteerism and, 36, 219–226, 281–286; women's participation in, 72–74

non-profit organizations, 5. See also charitable activities and organizations

Norem, Julie K., 37

Norrander, Barbara, 30, 111

Norris, Pippa, 111

O'Brien, David M., 30

occupational segregation, 227

O'Connor, Karen, 152

Okin, Susan Moller, 178, 325, 332

Olsen, Marvin E., 276

O'Neill, William L., 11

ordinary least-squares (OLS) regression, 436–437

ordination of women, 85–86, 232, 238–243, 376–379

organizations, 72–79, 222–226, 394. See also non-political organizations and activity

orientations to politics. See psychological orientations to politics

Orthodox religions, 85–86, 376–379
Ortner, Sherry, 6
Orum, Amy, 138
Orum, Anthony M., 138
outcomes analysis, 53–54, 251–260,
    261–265, 295–299, 435–438
over-reporting, 66
oversampling, 113

Paez, Dario, 341
Palley, Marian Lief, 31
panel data, 206, 242
parenthood: political activity and, 244,
    316–321, 332–333, 364; religious
    affiliation and, 234; single
    motherhood, 126–127. See also
    children and child care
Parry, Geraint, 22, 23
participation and participatory
    factors: acquiring, 203, 222–226;
    benefits of, 6; Civic Voluntarism
    Model, 198–199, 201–204, 365;
    defining, 55; explanations for gaps
    in, 33–34, 306; factors affecting,
    243–245; forms of, 20–21; free time
    and, 260–261; gender gap in, 7–9,
    36–38, 226, 247–251, 251–260;
    gender, race, and ethnicity, 286–295,
    295–296, 303–306; gender
    segregation and, 226–231; in
    household decisions, 188–189;
    institutional bases of, 259, 287–290;
    level and effect of, 53–54, 251–260,
    296–297, 297–299; measuring, 394–
    398; non-political institutions and,
    57–58, 303–304; participatory
    agendas, 125–127; participatory
    assets, 273; political activity and, 4,
    251–260; political contributions
    and, 261–265; psychological
    orientations and, 265–269; religious
    institutions and, 231–238; rewards
    of, 113–118; strategies for studying,
    39–41; women's consciousness and,
    271–272; workplace participation
    and, 204–206, 214–216, 216–218,
    381–382
party affiliation: in couples, 169;
    egalitarians vs. traditionals, 159;
    gender differences in, 111; measuring,

170–171; political attitudes and, 163,
    164–166
Pateman, Carole, 23, 25
patriarchal family, 7, 84–85, 325, 359
pay gap, 16
Pear, Robert, 49
Pennebaker, James W., 341
Pennsylvania, 340
Petrocik, John R., 30, 111
Phillips, Anne, 325–326, 332
Pintrich, Paul R., 139
Planned Parenthood v. Casey (1992),
    122
plural minorities, 275
policy issues, 6, 29, 167–169, 305
political contributions. See campaigns,
    political
political environment: gender
    composition of, 349–352, 352–356,
    372; integration of, 437–438;
    political attitudes, 155–157, 162–
    169, 293; political cues, 102, 105,
    138–141; political information, 101–
    107, 342–344, 354, 395; political
    interest, 101–102, 353–354, 383,
    395; political orientation, 33, 132–
    133, 299–301; political parties, 12,
    31–32; women among political elite,
    63, 112, 334–341, 342–349, 355,
    360, 383
political involvement and activity, 4;
    conflict in, 29; consequences of
    gender gap, 24–25; defining, 20–21,
    57–58, 64–66; education on, 141–
    147; enfranchisement and, 14; as a
    family matter, 307–308, 311–316;
    gender differences in, 2, 61–63, 110–
    113, 246, 383; gender integration in,
    334–336, 342–349; in household
    setting, 187–192; measuring political
    efficacy, 395; membership in political
    organizations, 79–81, 358;
    motivations for, 115–118; political
    activity and, 367–368; political acts,
    64–66, 132; political attitudes, 111;
    political discussion, 102, 104, 140–
    141, 311–316, 398; political
    donations, 277–278; political
    socialization, 138–141; positive
    effects of, 22–24; racial and ethnic

disparities in, 276–280, 293, 297–
299, 300; religion and, 150–151,
231–238; in school setting, 147–150;
time constraints on, 7; voluntary, 3–
5; women as candidates, 342–349.
See also campaigns, political
Pool, Ithiel de Sola, 115
Pooled Senate Study, 348
poverty, 17, 306
pre-adult experience, 137
Presbyterians, 85, 239
presidency, 14, 334, 337–339
Prestage, Jewel L., 100, 138
process of affiliation, 234
professional positions, 211–213
protest, 65–66, 280
Protestants, 88, 89–90, 237–238, 285
psychic space, 7, 359
psychological orientations to politics:
Civic Voluntarism Model, 198, 201–
204; described, 99–107; effect of
women in office, 334–336, 344–345,
349–352, 352–356; gender
differences in, 9, 132, 265–269, 272,
371; outcomes analysis and, 437–
438; political participation and, 292–
295, 360, 383; political sources of,
367–368; race or ethnicity, 300;
women's issues and, 380
public officials, contact with, 119–120
public policy, 24–25, 307, 372
Purvis, Sally, 86
Putnam, Robert D., 22, 23, 68, 69, 322

Rabinowitz, George, 349
race and ethnicity: as control measure,
208, 214, 222; ethnic consciousness,
300; ethnic *vs.* racial groups, 274–
275; gender differences and, 50; non-
political organizations, 281–286;
political participation and, 93–94,
368–369; racial bias, 107–110, 395;
racial differences *vs.* gender
differences, 31, 274–276, 297;
socioeconomic advantage and, 133.
See also discrimination; segregation
Rahn, Wendy, 22–23
Randall, Vicky, 62, 63
random sampling, 42–43, 43–45, 59
rape, 131–132

Rapoport, Ronald B., 100
Reagan, Ronald, 111
recruitment to political activity: civic
skills and, 255; Civic Voluntarism
Model, 198, 201–204; factors
affecting, 243–245; gender differences
in, 248–249, 272; political
participation and, 33; by race or
ethnicity, 300; religious affiliation
and, 234, 236–238; requests for
political activity, 290; workplace and,
216, 222–226, 289
Reform Judaism, 85
reform movement, 73–74
regression analysis: described, 39–41,
169–173; *level* and *effect* in, 53–54;
linked, 51–54; multiple regression,
59; ordinary least squares (OLS)
regression, 436–437; outcomes
analysis and, 435–438; purpose of,
160; regression coefficients, 46, 170–
171, 435; separate analyses by
gender, 48–50; Statistical Package for
the Social Sciences (SPSS), 388;
statistical significance and, 172; on
variables relating to free time, 185.
See also multivariate analysis
Reid, Elizabeth, 62
Reingold, Beth, 112
Reiter, Rayna R., 6
religious activity and institutions:
attitudes and orientations, 105–107;
Baby Boomers, 235; church activism,
106–107; civil society and, 82–91;
compared with secular activities,
314–316; educational attainment
and, 366–367; family circumstances
and, 312–316; gender gap in, 82–91,
285–286, 376–379; institutional
affiliation and, 200; measuring, 394,
395; as non-political institution, 198;
ordination of women, 17–18, 85–86,
232, 238–243, 376–379;
participatory factors of, 231–238,
255–256, 289–290, 298–299;
political issues and, 202–203;
political orientation and, 269;
political participation and, 37, 58,
150–151, 254–256, 273, 299, 360–
361, 363; predicting church

religious activity and institutions
(*continued*)
affiliations, 233; racial and ethnic
differences in, 276, 283–286;
religious commitment, 132, 168–169;
religious participation, 57;
volunteerism and, 36
representation, gender disparity in, 336,
337–340, 354
Republicans: egalitarianism and, 160–
161; family issues and, 310; gender
preferences, 111; issue orientation of,
163–169; religious affiliations and,
159–160, 241, 376–379;
traditionalism and, 32
Reskin, Barbara F., 227
resources: Civic Voluntarism Model,
198, 201; institutional, 300; political
participation and, 33, 272; resource
allocation, 175; workplace-related,
214–216, 217–218
respect, 192–193, 197, 328–329, 330,
375–376
retirement, 177
Rhode, Deborah L., 25, 380
Ridgeway, Cecilia L., 229
Ries, Paula, 112
Rimé, Bernard, 341
Rinehart, Sue Tolleson, 63, 100, 107,
138, 155, 270
Rivers, Caryl, 322
Robinson, John P., 181, 291
Rockefeller, Jay, 5
Rogers, Willard L., 191
role models, women leaders as, 351.
See also elected office, women in
roll-call votes, 118
Roman Catholicism, 85, 88
Roof, Wade Clark, 89, 234, 240
Roper Trends in American Political
Participation, 68–71
Rosenfield, Sarah, 184
Rosenstone, Stephen J., 45, 69, 214,
216, 367
Ruddick, Sara, 110
Ruth, Babe, 13
Ryan, Mary P., 84

Saint-Germain, Michelle A., 112
Saline, Carol, 60

Sapiro, Virginia, 8, 24, 27, 29, 47, 49,
96, 100, 110, 138, 155, 205, 206,
270, 316–317, 323, 342
Sattel, Jack W., 37
Schlafly, Phyllis, 378
Schlozman, Kay Lehman, 3, 22, 31, 33,
35, 42, 45, 52, 54, 69, 74, 75, 83,
90, 94, 100, 114, 118, 142, 158,
198, 211, 214, 216, 221, 231, 238,
263, 266, 277, 307, 329, 346, 348,
365, 367
Schneir, Miriam, 384–385
school environment: activities and
organizations, 148, 254, 322, 394;
early development in, 35; gender
differences in, 148; measuring school
experiences, 394; political
participation and, 104, 141–147,
147–150, 247; religious affiliation
and, 233; school prayer, 106, 163–
166, 169
Schor, Juliet, 183
Schumaker, Paul, 112
Schuman, Howard, 341
Schwartz, Mildred A., 74
Schwartz, Pepper, 56, 178
Scott, Andrew MacKay, 10, 11, 384
Scott, Anne Firor, 1, 10, 11, 73, 74,
281, 384
Scott, Joan Wallach, 275
Screener Survey, 54, 56, 146–147
Scruggs, Marguerite, 180
Secret, Philip, 277
secular activity, 282
segregation: gender, 16, 226–231; South
Africa, 253; workplace, 16, 227,
381–382
selection: differential selection and
treatment, 199; into institutions,
51–52; non-political organizations,
221–222, 224; religious institutions, 232; selecting independent
variables, 170; selection effects, 206;
selection issues in families, 309; self-
selection, 43, 200–201; work force,
206–213
self-identification, 274–275
Senate, women in, 14, 337, 342–344,
346, 348, 355–356
Seneca Falls Declaration, 11, 384

separate analyses by gender, 52–53, 59–60
separation of church and state, 83
"SES model," 365
sexual harassment, 41–42, 122, 128, 131–132
sex *vs.* gender, 25–29, 45–48, 60
Shapiro, Robert Y., 111
Sharma, Arvind, 84
Shelton, Beth Anne, 195
Sherkat, Darren, 82, 89, 234
Shingles, Richard D., 269, 293
Sigel, Roberta S., 25, 37, 45, 129, 269
Sigelman, Lee, 108, 111
significance in regression analysis, 171–172
single motherhood, 126–127
skills for participation, 73–74, 83, 394
Skocpol, Theda, 22, 231
Smeal, Eleanor, 378
Smith, Rogers M., 10
Smith-Lovin, Lynn, 227, 229
social context, linked regressions and, 51–52
social issues: attitudes toward, 164–166; basic needs issues, 126–127, 305, 306; married couples' attitudes, 168–169; social cleavages, 372; social gratification, 115–116; social institutions, 49, 137; social learning, 340–341; social organizing principles, 6; social processes, 27, 49–50. See *also* socialization; social status
socialization: gender differences in, 8, 27, 205, 375–376; political, 138–141, 340–341, 360
social reform movements, 12
social service organizations, 78–79
social status: within family, 192–193, 328–329; political attitudes and, 163; political participation and, 47–48; social cleavages, 372; social domains, 27; stratification, 174, 379; volunteerism and, 222
socioeconomic status: participatory agendas and, 125–127; political participation and, 47, 299, 306; racial differences in, 133; religious affiliation and, 233; resources, 7–8, 359–360; "SES model," 365
Soule, John W., 100
South, Scott J., 181, 184
Southern Baptists, 18, 85, 87, 239, 376
Spain, Daphne, 250
Spelman, Elizabeth V., 275
Spitze, Glenna, 181, 184
spousal abuse, 131–132
Sprague, John, 167, 312
Stämpfli, Regula, 1
standard error, 171
Stanford, Karin, 283
Stanley, Harold W., 111
Stanley, Susie C., 87
Stanton, Elizabeth Cady, 384
Statistical Package for the Social Sciences (SPSS), 388
statistical significance, 171–172. See *also* measurement issues
Stehlik-Barry, Kenneth, 15, 142
Steil, Janice, 178, 181
stereotypes, political, 66–67
Steuernagel, Gertrude A., 30, 166, 270
Stevens, Jacqueline, 307
Stoker, Laura, 55, 138, 166, 336
Stokes, Donald E., 61, 100
Stoler, Ann Laura, 275
Stone, Anne J., 112
Stromberg, Ann Helton, 178
student government, 149–150, 207–209. See *also* education
supervisory experience, 214–215
surveys, 2–3, 41–43, 43–45, 51
Swers, Michelle, 119

Tamerius, Karin L., 119
Tate, Katherine, 110, 283, 345
Tedin, Kent L., 205
telephone interviews, 55, 77
Thatcher, Margaret, 341
Thomas, Clarence, 122, 128
Thomas, Sue, 104, 111, 112, 113, 119
Thompson, Linda, 179, 184
Thornton, Arland, 156
Tilly, Charles, 40, 281
Tilly, Louise A., 12, 73
Title VII, 86, 384
Title IX, 142, 384

Tocqueville, Alexis de, 72, 76–77
Torney, Judith V., 62, 138
traditionalism: gender roles and, 157–160, 272, 336, 376; in household labor, 195–197; ordination of women and, 238–243; religious institutions and, 84, 119–120, 232, 378; traditional societies, 19
Traugott, Michael W., 66, 101
trends in gender gaps, 18–19
Tronto, Joan C., 110, 277, 283, 286, 293
trust, 192–193, 328–329, 398
t-statistic, 171–172

Uhlaner, Carole, 276
Underwood, Kenneth E., 104
unequal participation, 7–9
unions, political participation and, 58
Unitarians, 85, 239
United States, compared with New Zealand, 20
Universalists, 85, 239
unmarried mothers, 323

variables, measuring, 392–398. *See also* measurement issues
variation between and among sexes, 28–29, 30–31
varimax rotation, 167–168
Vedlitz, Arnold, 205
Verba, Sidney, 3, 20, 22, 33, 35, 45, 52, 54, 69, 75, 83, 90, 94, 100, 114, 118, 142, 158, 188, 198, 211, 214, 216, 221, 231, 238, 263, 266, 269, 276, 277, 307, 329, 346, 365, 367
verbatim issues, 133–136
Verweij, Johan, 82
violence toward women, 131–132
volunteerism and voluntary organizations: causality and, 220, 365; Civic Voluntarism Model, 198–199, 201–204, 365; education and, 149–150; free time and, 314; gender segregation in, 226–231; married couples' involvement with, 314; motherhood and, 321–324, 374–375; as non-political institution, 57, 81–82, 198; participation and, 3–5, 58–

59, 64, 72–74, 219–226; in religious institutions, 88–89; settings for, 36
voting: gender differences in, 111, 357–358; participation by, 64; voter mobilization, 350; voter turnout, 13, 66

wages. *See* income and finances
Waite, Linda J., 181, 185
Walker, Alexis J., 155, 179, 184
Walton, Hanes, Jr., 269, 270, 277, 283
Warren, Mark E., 22
Watts, Franklin, 84
Weber, Max, 4, 5, 153, 174
Webster v. *Reproductive Health Services* (1989), 122
Weiner, Linda, 42
Weisenburger, William, 104
Welch, Susan, 8, 34, 47, 48, 62, 63, 108, 111, 112, 204, 206, 277, 317
welfare policy issues, 167–169. *See also* government assistance, attitudes toward
Wen, Patricia, 335
Wessinger, Catherine, 17, 18, 85
West, Candace, 25, 155, 370
Whittaker, Marilyn Metcalf, 18, 85, 239
Wigfield, Allan, 139
Wilcox, Clyde, 30, 111, 112, 270, 293
Wilkie, Jane Riblett, 178
Williams, David R., 108
Williams, Marjorie, 334
Wilson, James Q., 117
Wingrove, Elizabeth, 7
Wirls, Daniel, 30, 111
Wolbrecht, Christina, 32
women's issues and organizations: abortion, 30, 32, 122–124, 125, 129–131, 133, 163–166, 169, 271–272, 304, 309, 372, 373–374, 378; economic status of women, 15–16; effects on participation, 270–271; enfranchisement of women, 1, 10–12, 104, 341, 357, 382–383; group consciousness of women, 294; ordination of women, 85–86, 232, 238–243; promoting participation, 364; representation of women, 14;

women-exclusive issues, 128–131; women in elected office, 63, 112–115, 175–180, 334–336, 342–349, 349–352, 360, 437–438; women's movements and groups, 75, 79–80, 230, 281, 373, 379–380; women's rights movement, 11, 79–80. *See also* specific issues and topics

work force participation: African-American women, 288–289; discrimination, 227, 273; educational attainment and, 366–367; factors affecting, 206–213; gender gap in, 15–16, 254–256; gender roles and, 95–97; household responsibilities and, 184; male advantage in, 248; motherhood and, 321–324, 374–375; as non-political institution, 198; participatory factors and, 35–36, 204–206, 287–290, 381–382; political participation and, 37, 47, 214–216, 243, 360–361, 363; regression analyses, 53; selection into, 206–213; supervisory experience in, 214–215; volunteerism and, 222; women and, 321–324, 336, 340, 374–375; work hours, 394, 396

Wuthnow, Robert, 72, 231

Young, Iris Marion, 107
Young, Katherine K., 84

Zaller, John, 101
Zick, Cathleen, 184
Zikmund, Barbara Brown, 88
Zimmerman, Don H., 25, 155, 370